❧ CATO ❧
SUPREME COURT
REVIEW
2004 — 2005

WITHDRAWN

⤜ CATO ⤝
SUPREME COURT
REVIEW
2004 — 2005

ROGER PILON
Publisher

MARK K. MOLLER
Editor in Chief

ROBERT A. LEVY
Associate Editor

TIMOTHY LYNCH
Associate Editor

CENTER FOR CONSTITUTIONAL STUDIES

INSTITUTE
Washington, D.C.

THE CATO SUPREME COURT REVIEW
(ISBN 1-930865-80-5) is published annually at the close
of each Supreme Court term by the Cato Institute, 1000
Massachusetts Ave., N.W., Washington, D.C. 20001-5403.

CORRESPONDENCE. Correspondence regarding subscriptions,
changes of address, procurement of back issues, advertising and
marketing matters, and so forth, should be addressed to:

Publications Department
The Cato Institute
1000 Massachusetts Ave., N.W.
Washington, D.C. 20001

All other correspondence, including requests to quote or
reproduce material, should be addressed to the editor.

CITATIONS. Citation to this volume of the *Review* should
conform to the following style: 2004-2005 Cato Sup. Ct. Rev. (2005).

DISCLAIMER. The views expressed by the authors of the articles
are their own and are not attributable to the editor, the editorial
board, or the Cato Institute.

INTERNET ADDRESS. Articles from past editions are available to
the general public, free of charge, at www.cato.org/pubs/scr.

Contents

CONTENTS

Foreword

Politics and Law

*Roger Pilon**

The Cato Institute's Center for Constitutional Studies is pleased to publish this fourth volume of the *Cato Supreme Court Review*, an annual critique of the Court's most important decisions from the term just ended, plus a look at the cases ahead—all from a classical Madisonian perspective, grounded in the nation's first principles, liberty and limited government.

We release this volume each year at Cato's annual Constitution Day conference—held on September 14th this year since Constitution Day falls on a Saturday. That is far from the only thing that is out of the ordinary this year, however. At this writing we are less than a fortnight away from the start of Senate confirmation hearings concerning the nomination of Judge John G. Roberts Jr. for a seat on the Supreme Court. More than a decade has passed since the nation last witnessed such hearings, and it was almost fifteen years ago that we saw hearings as politically charged as those upcoming may be.

Quite apart from the salvos Democrats have been hurling at Judge Roberts, even in the president's own party the gauntlet has been thrown down. Two weeks ago and again today, for example, Senator Arlen Specter, who will be chairing the Senate Judiciary Committee hearings, has written to Roberts to give him "advance notice" that he will be pressing the nominee for his views on the Rehnquist Court's "judicial activism" of recent years—in particular, its decisions finding that there are limits on Congress' regulatory power, which Specter sees as the Court's "usurping Congressional authority."

*Vice President for Legal Affairs; Director, Center for Constitutional Studies, Cato Institute.

The hearings may yet go smoothly, of course, as did those for then-Judges Ruth Bader Ginsburg in 1993 and Stephen Breyer in 1994, both of whom declined to answer a wide range of questions posed by members of the committee. The question remains, however: Why have confirmation hearings—not only for Supreme Court but for appellate court nominees as well—become so political of late? The answers are several, but in this brief foreword I will focus on only two, drawing on the Court's recent term to illustrate the second.

The first answer begins innocently enough: Confirmation hearings for Supreme Court nominees are "political" because, under our Constitution, those are occasions on which politics and law come naturally together. Although the Constitution belongs to all of us, and judges are expected to adjudicate impartially under it, not legislate, the president's selection of a nominee for the Court is a political, not a legal act, as is the Senate's decision whether or not to confirm the nominee. That means that the president and members of the Senate are free to decide on any ground they wish—including "politics," in its many senses—not simply on such neutral criteria as the nominee's competence and integrity, as Alexander Hamilton recommended.

The problem with going down that political road, however, is its potential for undermining the rule of law, for turning everything into politics. At the extreme, for example, both the president and the Senate might demand that a nominee pass a so-called ideological litmus test as a condition for being nominated or confirmed—the idea being to try to bind him to deciding future cases in accordance with his answers on the test. Were that approach to prevail—and we are already part way there—the independence of the judiciary would be seriously compromised as judging would no longer be a function of dispassionate and apolitical reason but of nomination and confirmation politics. That political process would determine the legal process, in effect, rendering the latter a sham.

To more fully explore those issues, let me begin by outlining the connection between politics and law that the Constitution contemplates. (This is drawn from my Cato study of a few years ago on the emergence of ideological litmus tests.) In a limited constitutional republic like ours, the relation between politics and law is set, for the most part, by law—by the law of the Constitution. Drawing upon reason and interest, the Framers drafted a constitution that became law through ratification, a political act that reflected, in large measure, the will of the founding generation. As amended by subsequent acts of political will, the Constitution authorizes the political branches to act pursuant only to their enumerated powers or to enumerated ends. It further limits the exercise of those powers and the powers of the states either explicitly or by recognizing, with varying degrees of specificity, rights retained by the people. And, by fairly clear implication, made explicit in the *Federalist* and shortly thereafter in *Marbury v. Madison*, the Constitution authorizes the judiciary to declare and enforce that law of authorizations and restraints consistent with the document itself.

Thus, the scope for "politics"—understood as will or the pursuit of individual or group interests through public or political institutions—is limited. Consistent with constitutional rules and limits, the people may act politically to fill elective offices. And those officers may in turn act politically to fill nonelective offices. But once elected or appointed, those officials may act politically only within the scope and limits set by the Constitution. In particular, not everything in life was meant to be subject to political or governmental determination. In fact, the founding generation wanted most of life to be beyond the reach of politics, yet under the rule of law. In a word, our Constitution does not say, "After periodic elections, those elected may do what they wish or pursue any end they wish or any end the people want." On the contrary, it strictly limits, by law, the scope of politics. And it falls to the judiciary, the nonpolitical branch, to declare what the Constitution says that law and those limits are, thereby securing the rule of law.

The aim in all of this, then, is to constrain the rule of man—and politics—by the rule of law. The Framers understood that legitimacy begins with politics, with the people. Thus, "We the people . . . do ordain and establish this Constitution." But once ratification—the initial political act—establishes the rule of law, that law constrains politics thereafter, at least in principle. And it is the nonpolitical judiciary that declares and enforces that law. It is essential, therefore, that the judiciary act nonpolitically—not from will or interest but from reason, according to law, consistent with the first principles of the system. If it does not, then to that extent the rule of law is undermined and politics trumps law.

Competence and integrity in a nominee go together, therefore. A competent and principled nominee will understand the subtle relationships between law and politics in our system and, if confirmed, will let politics reign where it is authorized to do so while enforcing law where the Constitution calls for that. Unfortunately, especially over the twentieth century, we have strayed very far from the ideal Hamilton and the other Framers envisioned. Today, so much is politics, so little is law, that even the judiciary is involved, ineluctably, in making "political" decisions. Thus the second and far more searching reason why judicial confirmation hearings have become so political: Given that judges are so often called upon today to "make" law, we want to know not simply whether the nominee is competent and principled but what his "politics" are as well.

I will develop that point more fully in a moment, but let me note first that I alluded to the problem in this space a year ago when I addressed the question, can law this uncertain be called law? Citing a number of cases the Court had recently decided—concerning campaign finance, affirmative action, property rights, and more—I argued that the Court's opinions too often reflected politics more than law, all of which has led to a sorry state of law. I am hardly alone in reaching that assessment, of course. In fact, a related, if sometimes wandering, thesis was recently set forth in some detail by one of the nation's most prominent students of constitutional law, Harvard's Laurence Tribe.

Writing in the spring 2005 issue of the eclectic legal periodical, *The Green Bag*, Tribe explains, first in a letter to Justice Breyer, then in a much longer "Open Letter to Interested Readers of *American Constitutional Law*," why he has decided not to complete and publish the projected second volume of the third edition of his treatise by that name. Published originally in 1978, with a second edition in 1988 and a third, at least in one volume, in 2000, the treatise was envisioned from the outset to be more than a hornbook. It was to bring together a large body of judicial decisions, thereby to call attention to the organizing themes that become apparent—all by way of attempting "a synthesis of some enduring value." But Tribe has come to have profound doubts, he says, "whether any new synthesis having such enduring value is possible at present." Thus, he has set the project aside.

The reasons underlying Tribe's doubts are several. In essence, in area after area, he writes, we find ourselves at a fork in the road: things could go in several directions "because conflict over basic constitutional premises is today at a fever pitch . . . with little common ground from which to build agreement." Thus, no treatise of the kind he has been writing can be true to this moment in our constitutional history, he says, for "profound fault lines have become apparent at the very foundations of the enterprise." And he does not have, he claims, nor has he seen "a vision capacious and convincing enough to propound as an organizing principle for the next phase in the law of our nation."

When Tribe began his enterprise, however, things were different. Unlike in the late 1940s, when "conflict and irresolution organized the elaboration of constitutional law" following the New Deal constitutional revolution of the late 1930s, the mid-1970s amounted to a time when the Burger Court was in important respects simply extending the groundbreaking work of the Warren Court. Thus, it was a period, Tribe writes, when a considerable body of judicial work had accumulated that needed to be pictured as a whole "in order to be properly appreciated, extended, or reconsidered." A treatise was possible at that time since even critics of controversial decisions like *Roe v. Wade* were "in an important sense reading from the same page as the majority." Then-Justice William Rehnquist, for example, one of two dissents in that case, did not disagree "that the Constitution imposes *some* substantive constraints on government in such matters."

Today, however, Tribe sees fissures looming large, reflecting fundamental and seemingly irreconcilable divisions. Fastening on the Court's work "over the past decade or so," he writes that "a period of reassessment in several doctrinal contexts" appears to be largely over, "but plainly we see no new constitutional law emergent and ready for synthesis." In all of this, he continues, "justices write as though self-consciously in the midst of unresolved, ongoing struggle, sometimes choosing to present their views in exaggerated, polemical forms, and sometimes too conspicuously trying to restrict the reach of their ideas as though in this way to give them space to survive."

What are we to say? Tribe is largely right. For too long, as many of us have long said, the Court has been without a compass. At the same time, Tribe's main concern—to explain why "ours is a particularly bad time to be going out on a limb to propound a Grand Unifying Theory"—seems to disable him from articulating—

perhaps even from seeing—the deeper implications of his thesis. For it is not simply the Court's decisions of the past decade that have brought the current state of uncertainty upon us; that state and those decisions, however much they may help to explain the judicial confirmation battles that go back even further, are but the latest manifestations of a much deeper problem.

In his wide-ranging canvass of the elements that constitute our "constitutional culture," as he calls it, Tribe touches on several important sources of today's conflicting worldviews. All of that is instructive and illuminating. But the world has been beset with conflicting worldviews for a long time. In fact, it was to enable people with conflicting worldviews to coexist, peacefully, that the Constitution was written in the first place. That peaceful coexistence could be achieved, however, only if the constitutional regime allowed each of us to go his separate way—in fact, protected us in our right to do so. And that, I submit, is the main source of our problem today. For as long as we are forced, by law, to abide by and live under one worldview—today, that of the public planner, in all of its manifestations—we will continue to see "profound fault lines" that go, as Tribe puts it, to issues "as fundamental as whose truths are to count and, sadly, whose truths must be denied."

The source of this deeper problem is well known, of course, even if today it is largely ignored. It is the Progressive mindset, institutionalized by the New Deal's constitutional revolution, before which time Tribe's essay barely goes. It was then that we were all thrown into the common pot, so to speak. Modern Progressives talk often about freedom, of course, and to their credit they have often served that end far better than conservatives, modern or ancient. But to take license with Justice Hugo Black's memorable expression: What is there about the word "free" that they don't understand? Where is the freedom in taxing us to establish a failing retirement system and then forcing us into it? Where is the freedom in taxing us to establish a mediocre public education system and then forcing us to place our children in it—unless we want to pay yet again to get them out of that system? Where is the freedom in the government's telling us how to run our businesses in a thousand and more ways? I could go on *ad infinitum*, of course, but the point should be clear. In those and so many other ways today, we live under "law" that arises not from principle but from politics. And we do because the

New Deal Court opened the constitutional barriers to ubiquitous government—in a word, the Court replaced law, the law of liberty, with politics.

Although the seeds of the New Deal revolution were sown somewhat earlier, as Richard Epstein's B. Kenneth Simon Lecture below brings out, the 1937 Court, following on the heels of President Roosevelt's infamous Court-packing scheme, eviscerated the centerpiece of the Constitution, the doctrine of enumerated powers, thus opening the floodgates for the modern regulatory and redistributive state. Then a year later the Court bifurcated the Bill of Rights and invented a bifurcated theory of judicial review, effectively instituting political adjudication, the practical result of which was to unleash state legislative juggernauts. Often mistaken for restraint, the activism of the New Deal Court—ignoring constitutional limits that had largely stood for 150 years—would soon rise again in the form of interstitial lawmaking once the surfeit of legislation worked its way back to the Court, as inevitably happened. But yet a third wave of activism set in once the planners, unable to win every legislative battle, realized that the courts might sanction their plans. Not all of that last form of activism was unwarranted, of course. Some, in fact, was long overdue, like that which abolished Jim Crow, not a moment too soon. But enough was written from whole cloth to have led to a conservative backlash.

Regrettably, that backlash, when it came, made its peace, for the most part, with the political premises of the New Deal's constitutional revolution, attacking mainly that third form of "judicial activism"—and calling into question in the process the Court's good work, such as there was, in recognizing the unenumerated rights the Ninth and Fourteenth Amendments were written to secure. In its own way, therefore, the conservative backlash misconceived the constitutional design as fully as the Progressive juggernaut that gave rise to it. Both camps, that is, conceived of the Constitution as essentially democratic, not libertarian. Both saw scope for public and hence political power in wide areas of life. They differed simply over the ends to be served by that power, grounded as they were in their different worldviews.

Over the past decade that Tribe demarcates, however, the Rehnquist Court has begun to rediscover a few pre-New Deal principles. Thus, in 1995 the Court resurrected the doctrine of enumerated powers, which had lain dormant for nearly sixty years. And over a series of decisions it began to put teeth in the Fifth Amendment's Takings Clause, thus better protecting property rights, which the 1938 Court had reduced to "poor relations" in the Bill of Rights, as James Ely documents below. After the term just ended, however, it is hard to know where that "Rehnquist revolution" stands. The *Raich* decision, upholding Congress' power under the Commerce Clause to regulate medicinal marijuana that never enters even intrastate commerce, makes a mockery of the doctrine of enumerated powers, as Douglas Kmiec illustrates below. And the Court's three property rights decisions, as Professor Ely shows, reflect little but abject judicial deference to political power.

Yet even at its best, when it has grasped for first principles, the Rehnquist Court's reach has fallen far short, barely scratching the surface of the problem. That problem was well stated by our board member, Gary Lawson, in the 1994 *Harvard Law Review*: "The post-New Deal administrative state is unconstitutional," he wrote, "and its validation by the legal system amounts to nothing less than a bloodless constitutional revolution." The problem, then, goes far deeper than our inability at the moment to discern the Court's organizing principle. The Court has no such principle because it has abandoned its roots in the law of the Constitution. That mistake is simply playing itself out, for what is left when law withers is mere politics. And that is why the judicial confirmation battles today are about politics, and only seemingly about law.

Introduction

Mark K. Moller*

The fourth volume of the *Cato Supreme Court Review* arrives at the end of an era: As this edition of the *Review* goes to press, Justice O'Connor has announced her retirement, signaling that the Court's current five member conservative majority will soon be no more. Her announcement is no surprise: Change has been anticipated since President Bush's election in 2000. But what it augurs remains anyone's guess.

There is a temptation to predict more of the same: The Court's changes tend to come in increments rather than in revolutions. But, some have suggested that deeper change in the direction of constitutional law may be silently under way.[1] One scenario—a pessimistic one from the *Cato Supreme Court Review*'s Madisonian standpoint—has been sketched in a provocative 2003 article on the Rehnquist Court by law professor Thomas Merrill.[2] His analysis of voting behavior on the current Court suggests that the first casualty of a change in the conservative majority may be the Court's halting efforts to reinvigorate constitutional federalism.[3]

---

*Editor in Chief, Cato Supreme Court Review.

[1] Laurence H. Tribe, The Treatise Power, 8 Green Bag 2d 291, 292 (2005) ("in area after area, we find ourselves at a fork in the road—a point at which it's fair to say things could go in any of several directions").

[2] Thomas Merrill, The Making of the Second Rehnquist Court: A Preliminary Analysis, 47 St. Louis U. L.J. 569 (2003). I am indebted to Jonathan Adler for bringing this article to my attention.

[3] Merrill does not speculate on the effect of changes on the future course of the Court, but his analysis of the voting dynamics on the current Court, if correct, nonetheless suggests that the Court's federalism revolution is one area that may be a casualty of personnel changes.

Merrill tells the story, which centers around Antonin Scalia, this way: Justice Scalia came to the Court uninterested in federalism.[4] Instead, in his early years on the Court, he yearned to achieve different goals: (1) scaling back judicial "interference" with democratic decisionmaking in morally contentious areas like abortion and religion; (2) promoting executive power; and (3) replacing the Court's multi-factored balancing tests with hard-and-fast rules.[5] By 1993, however, it was clear that he was doomed to failure on each those fronts, as he could not enlist the other four conservative justices in his efforts.[6]

Accordingly, suggests Merrill, Scalia decided to engage in "strategic voting."[7] Observing that the chief justice, and Justices O'Connor, Kennedy, and Thomas, shared a commitment to federalism, he saw an opportunity. By joining the federalism bandwagon, and forging a five to four majority that decided *New York v. United States, United States v. Lopez, Printz v. United States,* and *United States v. Morrison,* he became, for the first time, part of an influential governing voting bloc and, in return, gained token collegial support from other conservatives for his idiosyncratic pet projects—such as the promotion of executive power and the use of rules rather than standards to decide cases.[8] If Merrill is right, the story of the Rehnquist Court is a story of the chaining and channeling of Scalia's ambition.

The 2004–2005 term is, in all likelihood, if not the end, then at least the twilight of the Rehnquist era—and, with two great architects of the Court's federalism "revolution" (O'Connor and, eventually,

---

[4]*Id.* at 609–11. Scalia, during the heady days of the first Reagan administration, chastised conservatives for failing to realize that "the federal government is not bad but good." "The trick," he said, "is to use it wisely." See, e.g., Antonin Scalia, The Two Faces of Federalism, 6 Harv. J.L. & Pub. Pol'y 19, 22 (1982), quoted in Merrill, *supra* note 2, at 610 n.152.

[5]Merrill, *supra* note 2, at 604–05.

[6]*Id.* at 580–84, 604–06.

[7]*Id.* at 606–09 (describing the Scalia "strategic voting" thesis).

[8]*Id.* at 607. For example, in exchange for his support for federalism, the chief has given Scalia more opportunity to write key majority opinions, an opportunity that Scalia, in turn, has exploited (in cases like *Printz v. United States*) to smuggle in dicta favoring distinctive positions (in *Printz,* his support for the "unitary executive") that previously had been rejected by other conservatives. See Jay S. Bybee, Printz, the Unitary Executive, and the Fire in the Trash Can: Has Justice Scalia Picked the Court's Pocket?, 77 Notre Dame L. Rev. 269 (2001).

Rehnquist) on the way out, Scalia is poised to be the incoming dean of the conservative majority. If the stars are aligned properly—if Bush appoints justices who share Scalia's distinctive disinterest in federalism, his zest for democratic decisionmaking, his wariness of unelected judges, and his frustrated ambition to revisit hot-button issues like abortion rights and the separation of church-and-state— Scalia's star may at last be in ascendance, emboldening him to once again press his long-silenced agenda. If so, we may see a significant shift in the priorities of this conservative Court.

Of course, we can only speculate whether this change will materialize. But this uncertainty makes this term all the more instructive, since it provides a snapshot of the state-of-the-Court—highlighting not only aspects of its legacy worth defending but also its unrealized potential.

Professor Richard Epstein frames analysis of the 2004–2005 term by looking at the Court in another time of transition—the Progressive Era. As Epstein details, the Progressives, led by Justices Louis Brandeis and Felix Frankfurter, overthrew nearly a century-and-a-half of constitutional learning in the service of a single dubious economic theory: that economic "progress" required the creation of state-run monopolies to remedy the supposedly weak bargaining position of consumers and laborers. To facilitate the implementation of that theory, the Progressive Court dismantled well-established learning rooted in constitutional text, history, and precedent—including a liberty-oriented understanding of state police power, correspondingly robust protections for private property, and rigorous judicial enforcement of the limits, textual and implied, on the scope of federal regulatory power. Progressive economic theory now lies on the ashheap of history, but, says Epstein, the Progressives' radical transformation of the Constitution—including their evisceration of the Constitution's protections for freedom of property, contract, and association—remains with us, rendering all of our liberties, economic and personal alike, less secure.

Professor James W. Ely Jr. begins review of the term by focusing on the Court's treatment of constitutional protections for private property. He concludes that *Lingle v. Chevron*, *Kelo v. City of New London*, and *San Remo Hotel v. City and County of San Francisco* together have rendered the Takings Clause virtually toothless, leaving owners' possession of private property at the mercy of state and

3

municipal legislatures. That outcome is very far from the intent of the Founders, who, says Ely, intended the Takings Clause, and private property rights generally, as a potent curb on majoritarian excess. Indeed, notes Ely, the facts of *Kelo*—in which a municipality transferred property of middle-class homeowners to a rich, politically well-connected developer at the behest of a powerful corporation—underscore the wisdom of the Framers' conviction that property rights are an essential safeguard for the vulnerable and politically marginalized. While Ely notes that these cases contain some underreported bright spots, they illustrate, nonetheless, that a majority of the Court remains firmly in thrall to the worst legacy of the Progressive Era: the New Deal Court's demotion of the property clauses of the Bill of Rights to second class legal status.

Property rights were not the only front on which the Progressive vision of the Constitution emerged victorious this term. In *Gonzales v. Raich*, notes Professor Douglas W. Kmiec, the Court not only appeared to abandon its halting effort to limit the reach of Congress' regulatory power under the Commerce Clause, but may have displaced the New Deal-era precedent *Wickard v. Filburn* as the broadest articulation of federal commerce power to date. As Kmiec notes, the Court's reasoning in *Raich* is deeply at odds with the original understanding of the Commerce Clause, which was intended, he argues, to reach only those interests that states are demonstrably incompetent to regulate or that inhere in the nation as a whole. As Kmiec discusses, *Raich* is not only a startling defeat for the Rehnquist Court's efforts to redress the New Deal Court's radical expansion of the commerce power, but it marks Justice Scalia's bolt from the Court's federalism coalition in its twilight hours. Professor Kmiec criticizes Scalia for abdicating his judicial duty to respect the Commerce Clause for what it is—one of a set of powers that were enumerated so that states and individuals would otherwise be left free.

As Roger Pilon argues, *Town of Castle Rock v. Gonalzes* is the latest in a long line of cases that have misread the Fourteenth Amendment. In *Castle Rock*, the Court was asked to decide whether a Colorado municipality, the Town of Castle Rock, should be held liable to a Colorado mother under section 1983 of the Civil Rights Act of 1871 after its police officers, exhibiting gross negligence, failed repeatedly to enforce a temporary restraining order (TRO) against her estranged husband, who kidnapped their three children in broad daylight. As

Pilon explains, Justice Scalia's strained opinion for the Court bent over backwards to deny the plaintiff any recovery, despite the clear intent of the Colorado legislature to make enforcement of such restraining orders mandatory, not discretionary. Employing the first principles of the Fourteenth Amendment, Pilon explains how the confusions that surround the Amendment today could lead to so counterintuitive a result as the Court produced in *Castle Rock* when it reversed the en banc court below.

Completing the term's quartet of exceptionally ill-reasoned cases, *Johanns v. Livestock Marketing Association* continues the Court's long-standing under-enforcement of the Free Speech Clause. In that case, the Court, in an opinion written by Justice Scalia, implicitly refused to accord commercial speech First Amendment protection comparable to that afforded political speech. *Johanns* involved a First Amendment challenge to a federal program that compels beef producers to underwrite financially the content of state-mandated advertising on their behalf. As Supreme Court litigator Daniel Troy explains, the Court's willingness to uphold this coercion demonstrates its continuing belief that commercial speech is less constitutionally important than other speech—a myopia that, he argues, defies the Founders' understanding of the Free Speech Clause. Nonetheless, Troy argues that *Johanns* has a little-noticed silver lining: The majority's reasoning departs from past precedents by refusing to *expressly* acknowledge that commercial speech is accorded lesser First Amendment protection. Accordingly, Troy argues that, in the right circumstances, savvy litigators may use *Johanns* as a wedge to nudge First Amendment protection for commercial speech closer to the protections accorded political speech by non-commercial actors.

Fortunately, the Court's 2004–2005 case list does have a few bright spots. Among them, says noted religious liberty scholar Marci Hamilton, number the term's Establishment Clause cases, *Cutter v. Wilkinson*, *VanOrden v. Perry*, and *McCreary County v. ACLU*. In this trilogy, religious pressure groups asked the Court to expand the scope of permitted government favoritism toward religious organizations. As Hamilton notes, the Court held its ground. In *Cutter*, it dealt the religious pressure groups an under-reported blow by clear-sightedly recognizing that Congress' efforts to "accommodate" religion— here, by enacting the Religious Land Use and Institutionalized Persons Act (RLUIPA)—must be interpreted in the same manner as any other interest-group driven legislation. More fundamentally, in *Van Orden* and *McCreary County* (the so-called Ten Commandments cases), the Court refused to overrule *Lemon v. Kurtzman*. Professor Hamilton suggests that religious groups should celebrate, not criticize, the Ten Commandments cases since the First Amendment's insulation of religious practice from government meddling has contributed greatly to the richness and diversity of religious speech in our public square. Unfortunately, she notes that a cohesive minority on the Court, lead by Justice Scalia, would open the door to far more government entanglement with religious speech, jeopardizing the vitality of our distinctively American religious traditions.

Professor John Hasnas argues that *Arthur Andersen LLP v. United States*, a case related to the Enron scandal, is another bright spot in the 2004–2005 term. In *Andersen*, the Court rejected federal prosecutors' creatively expansive reading of the federal "witness tampering" statute. Prosecutors asked the Supreme Court to find that Arthur Andersen violated the statute when it executed a longstanding, and otherwise legal, corporate document retention policy. While the decision will have little direct effect on Arthur Andersen—which has ceased to exist due to this litigation—the case, says Hasnas, may indicate the Court's recognition that the federal law of "white collar crime" has come dangerously close to granting federal prosecutors unlimited power over corporate defendants. If so, argues Hasnas, the case is a welcome development for all concerned about excessive federal prosecutorial discretion and federal overcriminalization of corporate conduct.

In his article on *United States v. Booker*, Cato's Timothy Lynch suggests that celebration of the Court's revolutionary decision to upend the federal sentencing guidelines may be premature. To be sure, *Booker* demonstrates that a majority of the current Court recognizes that the Sixth Amendment constitutionalizes key features of the common law adversarial criminal system, including jury determination of facts essential to the imposition of punishment. However, he warns that the *Booker* majority—led by Justice Scalia—is insufficiently committed to the common law adversarial model, failing as it does to recognize that other aspects of the Court's criminal procedure cases have fatally truncated the right to jury trial. For example, *Booker*'s holding may be more form than substance, he says, if the Court does not revisit its permissive attitude toward coercive plea bargaining, which prosecutors have used to harshly penalize defendants who insist on their jury trial rights. He concludes by surveying, and criticizing from a policy standpoint, likely legislative responses to *Booker*.

Turning to the Court's regulatory cases, co-authors David G. Post, Annemarie Bridy, and Timothy Sandefur explore the implications of *MGM Studios Inc. v. Grokster, Ltd.*, concluding that the Court's decision leaves for another day key questions regarding the legality of Internet file-sharing technology. Post et al. argue that record companies, much like movie studios in the days of the VCR, have simultaneously overreacted to the commercial threat posed by an innovative new technology and underestimated the possibility that this technology may be harnessed in ways that will promote both consumer and record industry welfare. After carefully unpacking *Grokster*'s contribution to the evolving test for third party copyright infringement, the authors conclude that we will have to wait for later cases to learn whether file-sharing software programs, considered apart from their distributors' culpable acts of inducement, come within the protective limits of previously recognized safe harbors.

Legal historian Stuart Banner examines a different case involving the intersection of law and Internet technology: *Granholm v. Heald*, in which the Court held the Twenty-first Amendment does not authorize state discrimination against out-of-state Internet wine shippers. A coalition of wine distributors and wholesalers, who benefit from state protection against Internet competition, urged the Court to hold otherwise. Focusing on the history of the Twenty-first Amendment, Professor Banner concludes that *Granholm* reached the right result, correctly interpreting the original understanding of the Amendment's Framers. As he demonstrates, the Amendment's Framers were committed to preserving the protection of the so-called dormant Commerce Clause—the term for the Commerce Clause's implicit ban on state discrimination against interstate commerce—as a background constraint on state regulatory power in the area of liquor commerce. His article provides an illuminating illustration of the Court's and Congress' understanding of the dormant Commerce Clause before, during, and immediately after the Prohibition Era, underscoring, in the process, the importance of the Constitution's protections for open markets in an age in which technology has rapidly expanded the scope of interstate competition.

While the legal issues implicated by the war on terror have not yet percolated back to the Supreme Court, the Court did have an occasion to consider the legality of yet another sweeping assertion of executive foreign affairs power, this time in *Medellin v. Dretke*, a case arising out of the death penalty conviction of a Mexican national in a Texas state court. In *Medellin*, the petitioner challenged his death penalty conviction by relying on a judgment of the International Court of Justice (ICJ), which ruled that an international treaty required Texas courts to re-consider his sentence. Although the president rejected the ICJ's ruling as a blatant misinterpretation of the treaty, the president has nonetheless "directed" state courts to follow the ICJ, arguing that he has inherent power to command state courts to alter the structure of criminal justice proceedings when doing so furthers American interests overseas. As noted international law scholar Mark Weisburd meticulously demonstrates, the president's assertion of power in this case is unfounded, both as a matter of treaty and of constitutional structure.

Professor Jonathan Adler rounds out this volume of the *Review* by looking forward to the Court's next term. As he underscores, the 2005–2006 term will provide strong preliminary signals about the future direction of the changing Court. It will, for example, include another significant federalism decision, *Gonzales v. Oregon*, which may offer Justice O'Connor's replacement an early test of his fidelity to the Court's federalism jurisprudence. The next term will also include opportunities to revisit the abortion debate in a case involving parental notification rights and, perhaps, in a case in which a certiorari petition is now pending, involving partial birth abortion. Together, the federalism and abortion appeals may serve as early bellwethers for Scalia's changing influence over the new conservative majority. Professor Adler outlines the issues at stake in these and many other cases, venturing some predictions.

I thank our contributors for their generous participation. I thank, too, my colleagues at the Cato Institute's Center for Constitutional Studies, Roger Pilon, Timothy Lynch, and Robert A. Levy—as well as Cato friend Spencer Marsden—for valuable editorial contributions; David Lampo for producing the *Review*; research assistant Madison Kitchens for valuable work in preparing manuscripts for production; and interns Garrett Ard, Jason McCoy, Tanner Pittman, and Matthew Tievsky for all-around assistance.

Again, we reiterate our hope that this volume of the *Review* will aid and deepen understanding of our too often forgotten Madisonian first principles—individual liberty, secure property rights, federalism, and a government of delegated, enumerated, and thus limited powers. Our aim, again, is to advance the *Review*'s distinctive mission, unique among law journals: to give voice to a rich legal tradition—now eclipsed by the rise of the modern regulatory state—in which jurists understood that the Constitution reflects, and protects, natural rights of liberty and property, thereby serving as a bulwark against the abuse of government power.

We hope you enjoy the fourth volume of the *Cato Supreme Court Review*.

The Monopolistic Vices of Progressive Constitutionalism

*Richard A. Epstein**

I. Introduction: Three Challenges to Constitutional Interpretation

It is my great pleasure to be asked to deliver the Cato Institute's third annual B. Kenneth Simon Lecture in Constitutional Thought, and to follow on the heels of Judge Douglas Ginsburg and Professor Walter Dellinger, two of this nation's most distinguished constitutional thinkers. The connection here is especially fitting because I shall pick up on themes that are contained in both of those lectures. Judge Ginsburg's inaugural lecture was entitled "On Constitutionalism,"[1] dealing with interpretive issues inherent in a written constitution. Professor Dellinger spoke next on "The Indivisibility of Economic Rights and Personal Liberty,"[2] an issue especially vexing to modern constitutional thought.

Judge Ginsburg's essay addresses the difficult question of how one can keep faithful to the original Constitution once it is understood that the Constitution cannot be read as a self-contained document. That objective depends for its success on at least three related tasks. The first is the explication of the common but critical terms in

*James Parker Hall Distinguished Service Professor of Law, The University of Chicago; Peter and Kirsten Bedford Senior Fellow, The Hoover Institution, Stanford University. This article is an expanded version of the third annual B. Kenneth Simon Lecture in Constitutional Thought, delivered at the Cato Institute on September 17, 2004. My thanks to Rachel Kovner of the Stanford Law School, class of 2006, for her meticulous and insightful research assistance. The Cato Institute will publish my longer and more detailed treatment of this subject—*How Progressives Rewrote the Constitution*—later this year.

[1] Douglas H. Ginsburg, On Constitutionalism, 2002–2003 Cato Sup. Ct. Rev. 7 (2003).

[2] Walter Dellinger, The Indivisibility of Economic Rights and Personal Liberty, 2003–2004 Cato Sup. Ct. Rev. 9 (2004).

the document that resist easy analysis: commerce, private property, freedom of speech, impairment of the obligation of contract, as well as a host of more technical terms like "Letters of Marque and Reprisal,"[3] "any Office of Profit or Trust,"[4] and "Capitation, or other direct, Tax."[5]

The second task is to identify the appropriate level of scrutiny that should be brought to any particular legislative provision or administrative act that is challenged on judicial review. Is there a case for exacting strict scrutiny at one extreme or the most forgiving standard of rational basis review at the other? Or is the proper approach to somehow split the difference by adopting some intermediate standard that hovers uneasily between the poles? On this attitudinal issue, the Constitution itself is mute.

The third task is to articulate the implied doctrines and exemptions that should be read into the Constitution as a matter of either history or constitutional logic. There is no obvious theory of plain meaning, no set of dictionary definitions dealing with key building blocks of constitutional theory that are *not* stated in the text but must nonetheless be imported for that text to make any sense.

Problems such as those are not small. They are huge, and central to the entire enterprise of interpretation. State sovereign immunity against suits by individuals, for example, is nowhere mentioned in the Constitution but was clearly understood by the Framers as a background proposition, even if it is hotly disputed today;[6] intergov-

---

[3] U.S. Const. art. I, § 10, cl. 1.

[4] U.S. Const. art. I, § 9, cl. 8.

[5] U.S. Const. art. I, § 9, cl. 4.

[6] See, e.g., The Federalist Nos. 81, 82 (Alexander Hamilton). For an exhaustive discussion, see Hans v. Louisiana, 134 U.S. 1, 12–15 (1890) (affirming the general applicability of the doctrine, relying in part on Hamilton). It should be noted that modern constitutional lawyers have entered into enormous disputes over this question, in part because of distaste for the doctrine, which I share.

Much of the confusion, however, comes from the reading of the Eleventh Amendment, which states, "The judicial power of the United States shall not be construed to extend to any suit in law or equity, commenced or prosecuted against one of the United States by Citizens of another State, or by Citizens or Subjects of any Foreign State." U.S. Const. amend. XI. If this provision were the only source of sovereign immunity, then it would be hard to see how the doctrine could protect states from suits by their own citizens. But such is not the case. The key word here is "construed," which indicates that the Amendment is designed to correct some prior misapprehension as to the scope of the doctrine; here it was the then-recent decision in *Chisholm v. Georgia*, 2 U.S. (2 Dall.) 419 (1793), which allowed a suit by a South Carolina citizen

ernmental immunity has a similar status.[7] Likewise, as I shall note briefly in this lecture, the dormant Commerce Clause is absolutely critical to the constitutional design; but it arises, if at all, only by implication. And finally, an adequate theory of interpretation must find a place for the most ubiquitous concept in constitutional law, "the police power." Ernst Freund, perhaps the greatest cross between lawyer and political scientist of his generation, wrote that it should be understood "as meaning the power of promoting the public welfare by restraining and regulating the use of liberty and property."[8] Yet there is no specific textual reference to the police power in the Constitution, even though it influences the interpretation of many key clauses of the Constitution that deal with both individual rights and jurisdictional limitations.[9]

Choosing the proper modes of interpretation lies close to the core of this lecture, and forms the centerpiece of Professor Dellinger's lecture, whose theme of indivisibility of economic and property rights on one hand and personal liberties on the other has long been close to my own heart.[10] The argument here rests on two propositions. First, it is difficult in principle to draw a sharp line between these two categories, for rules that govern the workplace, for example,

---

against Georgia for a revolutionary war debt. *Id*. at 450–51 (Blair, J.); *id*. at 465–66 (Wilson, J.); *id*. at 475–77 (Jay, C.J.). But as *Hans* explained, the basic doctrine was not created by the Eleventh Amendment, nor limited in scope to it. 134 U.S. at 10–19. That said, *Hans* has been at the center of modern constitutional law debate. See, e.g., Seminole Tribe v. Florida, 517 U.S. 44, 69, 72 (1996) (rejecting the claim that Congress under its commerce power could abrogate the doctrine of state sovereign immunity). As should be evident, the contention that the commerce power could even reach state sovereign immunity depends heavily on the vast modern extensions of the power, which receive no support from either the text or the structure of the Constitution. For modern critiques of the doctrine, see Erwin Chemerinsky, Against Sovereign Immunity, 53 Stan. L. Rev. 1201 (2001); for a defense of *Hans*, see David P. Currie, The Constitution in the Supreme Court: The Second Century: 1888–1986, at 7–9 (1990).

[7] See, e.g., McCulloch v. Maryland, 17 U.S. (4 Wheat.) 316, 428, 435–36 (1819) (federal immunities); Collector v. Day, 78 U.S. (11 Wall.) 113, 126–27 (1871) (state immunities), discussed in David P. Currie, The Constitution in the Supreme Court: The First Hundred Years: 1789–1888, at 160–68 (1985).

[8] Ernst Freund, The Police Power: Public Policy and Constitutional Rights iii (1904).

[9] For discussion, see Richard A. Epstein, The "Necessary" History of Property and Liberty, 6 Chap. L. Rev. 1 (2003).

[10] See, e.g., Richard A. Epstein, The Indivisibility of Liberty Under the Bill of Rights, 15 Harv. J.L. & Pub. Pol'y 35 (1992).

could easily impact the way in which political or religious activities can take place through the firm. And banning discrimination in private clubs, to take another example, threatens both the exclusive right to possession on one hand and the freedom of association on the other.[11] Second, and ultimately more important, the judicial tendency to fragment liberties means that the lower level of respect accorded to economic liberties will often dilute the level of protection given to those personal rights (such as freedom of conscience) that are of tangential interest to business or commerce.

II. The Progressive Challenge to the Old Court

Both of those themes play an important role in this lecture, which concerns the vision of American constitutional law championed by the Progressive movement. That movement proved strong and vital in the period between 1900 and 1930 and set the agenda for many of the lasting New Deal reforms that were introduced in the 1930s, some of which remain centerpieces of American law and policy to this day. As a political matter, the Progressives backed an ambitious legislative agenda of extensive regulation on a wide range of issues: sometimes they had to do with rate regulation and the aggressive enforcement of antitrust laws; at other times they had to do with the regulation of the workplace in the form of maximum hours and minimum wage regulation on one hand and strong protection for unions on the other.

To achieve their goals, Progressives envisioned two fundamental transformations of constitutional law. The first was a bold expansion of federal power, seeking to bring all forms of productive activity under the mantle of the Commerce Clause, which provides that "Congress shall have Power . . . to regulate Commerce with foreign Nations, and among the several States, and with the Indian Tribes."[12] The second was a truncation of the scope of individual constitutional rights. To do this, Progressives had to reverse field on two key developments of the earlier law as fashioned by their intellectual and political adversaries on what is called (as part of winner's history) the "Old Court." The first thing that needed to be reversed was the Old Court's broad definition of liberty, which extended to cover liberty

[11]See, e.g., Boy Scouts of America v. Dale, 530 U.S. 640 (2000).
[12]U.S. Const. art. I, § 8, cl. 3.

of contract. The second was its conception of state police power; a broader conception was needed, to dovetail with the narrower class of liberties presumptively entitled to constitutional protection. The Old Court had sought to limit the police power so that it did not consume the very liberties it was intended mainly to protect; thus, the Court customarily held that the power reached only matters that advanced the "safety, health, morals, and general welfare of the public."[13]

Those two battles were fought over the entire period from the end of the Civil War to the climactic 1937 Supreme Court term. The common view is that the Progressives were sound on both fronts and were therefore justly entitled to the fruits of their labors. I disagree with that assessment and think that both constitutional law and the American polity would have been far better off if we had stuck with the two doctrines of the Old Court that were so criticized by the Progressives. Let there be a thousand rationales for the shift; on the ground, they all boil down to one: the Progressives thought they could tell a good monopoly from a bad one; thus, they constantly propped up monopolies in labor, goods, and services for their select clientele. The Old Court was not perfect in articulating its own position, but it clearly and rightly saw state-created monopolies as a threat to be constrained rather than a social advance to be welcomed.

To set the framework for the constitutional debate that follows, it is useful to note the tenets of the Progressive position in support of state-created monopolies. Chief among those was the view that the transformation of the means of economic production had rendered obsolete all the optimistic predictions of traditional classical liberal thinkers such as John Locke, David Hume, William Blackstone, Adam Smith, David Ricardo, and Jeremy Bentham.[14] The earlier

---

[13] Lochner v. New York, 198 U.S. 45, 53 (1905).

[14] For a sympathetic critique of this position, see Jacob Viner, The Intellectual History of Laissez Faire, 3 J.L. & Econ. 45 (1960), which ultimately rejects laissez faire for its inability to deal with the problems of monopoly and wealth distribution. Yet the regulation of monopolies was accepted by the versions of laissez faire that influenced the United States Supreme Court; and the Court showed little resistance to the introduction of progressive taxation—done, of course, with an eye toward the redistribution of income and wealth. See, e.g., Brushaber v. Union Pac. R.R., 240 U.S. 1 (1916). The purest versions of laissez faire never gained a foothold within the Supreme Court.

writers had all stressed, in their own way, three propositions. The first is that a system of strong property rights is necessary to allow individuals to plan for the future and to internalize the benefits of their own labor. The maxim that "only those who sow should reap" was agricultural in its origins, but its implications were far broader: the point was that no one will make any investment in resources unless he can be confident of a return. The ability to own and protect land over time allowed this condition to be satisfied. Any insecurity in the title to land, whether it came through taxation or regulation, would reduce the incentive to invest. The second proposition stressed by the earlier writers was that voluntary contract allowed individuals to pool their talents, combine their resources, and swap goods and services in ways that worked to their mutual benefit. The third was that the state had to develop a limited and consistent system of taxation and regulation to defend property rights and facilitate voluntary exchange. Included in those functions were the supply of infrastructure that was difficult for individuals to assemble through voluntary means, and the control and regulation of monopolies, first in connection with common carriers and other network industries, and later in connection with large industrial complexes that sought to use mergers and cartels to advance their ends.

The Progressives did not oppose the classical liberal agenda to the extent that it sought to supply infrastructure or to allow for taxation. But they clearly thought that the mix of public and private power had to be radically shifted in favor of broader government control to meet the challenges of an industrial age. On matters of taxation, for example, the Progressives rejected the "benefit theory" of taxation, which sought to tax individuals only to the extent that they benefited from the services government provided. They championed instead a system of progressive taxation, where the marginal rates increased with income, on the explicit ground that it would redistribute wealth from rich to poor, based on some ability to pay.[15] More important for these purposes, they thought that an antitrust law was not sufficient to deal with the fundamental imbalances of

---

[15] See generally Henry Simons, Personal Income Taxation (1938), for the most sophisticated statement. The progressive tax itself was upheld by the Old Court. See Brushaber, 240 U.S. at 25–26. I shall not discuss questions of taxation further here. For my general views, see Richard A. Epstein, Can Anyone Beat the Flat Tax?, 19 Soc. Phil. & Pol'y 140 (2002), answering no.

industrialization. To their minds, large firms in nominally competitive industries exerted a dominance of bargaining power with both workers and consumers. As Felix Frankfurter wrote: "These are not days of Hans Sachs, the village cobbler and artist, man and meistersinger. We are confronted with mass production and mass producers; the individual, in his industrial relations, but a cog in the great collectivity."[16]

To redress this imbalance, strong legislative measures were necessary in labor and consumer markets. The older belief in freedom of contract was thought to be manifestly unequal to the challenges of the day. What John Dewey wrote in 1927 of labor relations really applied to any transaction in which big business was on one side and the little man on the other:

> In general, labor legislation is justified against the charge that it violates liberty of contract on the ground that the economic resources of the parties to the arrangement are so disparate that the conditions of genuine contract are absent; action by the state is introduced to form a level on which bargaining takes place.[17]

One would never know from this gloomy assessment that between 1900 and 1930 real wages at the bottom of the economic pyramid turned upward by a factor of about two, while the number of hours worked by unskilled laborers declined from around sixty per week to fifty.[18] For all their insistence on realism, the Progressives never were concerned with the actual level of advancement of the ground. Rather, they took their self-evident propositions about the conditions of modern social life to validate the expansion of government intervention.

Those deep, well-nigh unshakable, convictions led Progressives to move on both fronts previously mentioned. Broad federal power was needed to forestall various forms of competition among states; and narrow conceptions of individual liberty, coupled with a broad view of state police power, were needed to cabin that dangerous "formal" conception of freedom of contract, given that "genuine"

---

[16] Felix Frankfurter, Law and Order, 10 Yale Rev. 225, 233–34 (1920).

[17] John Dewey, The Public and Its Problems 62 (1927).

[18] U.S. Bureau of the Census, Historical Statistics of the United States: Colonial Times to 1957, at 91 (Series D 589–602).

freedom of contract was not possible due to the inequality of bargaining power between the individual and the new industrial firm. The doctrines of the Old Court, which stood in the path of "progress," had to go by one means or another.

What follows is a quick trip through the demise of the traditional doctrines of limited federal power and broad individual rights. That demise opened the door for the Progressive agenda, which at root knew only one way to combat the social dangers against which the Progressives railed: the substitution of state-monopolies and cartels for competitive markets.[19] Let us begin with the commerce power and then move to individual rights.

III. The Ever-Expanding Commerce Power

Under the original conception of the Constitution, the states held the vast body of unenumerated powers to regulate the behavior of their citizens, while the federal government was one of enumerated powers to deal with such matters as bankruptcy, immigration, patents and copyrights, post roads, and, of course, commerce among the several states.[20] The exact meaning of the Commerce Clause was not tested until *Gibbons v. Ogden*[21] was decided in 1824, and even then the meaning was tested only by indirection, for at issue in that case was not the validity of any federal legislation but an act by New York that gave to Robert Fulton (who assigned his rights to Ogden) the exclusive right to use steam power in New York waters. Gibbons had set up a steam run from Elizabethtown, New Jersey, to New York City, and his claim was that the federal power over interstate commerce trumped the state power to assign monopolies on what was unquestionably a journey that crossed state lines. Chief Justice Marshall had to do some fast stepping in order to find a conflict between the federal laws and state power, which he did by holding that the 1793 federal licensing acts for ships in interstate waters were inconsistent with the state-created local monopoly.[22]

---

[19] I address these themes at length in Richard A. Epstein, Free Markets Under Siege (Institute of Economic Affairs 2004), reprinted in an American edition (Hoover Institution 2005).

[20] For a more detailed statement of my views, see Richard A. Epstein, The Proper Scope of the Commerce Power, 73 Va. L. Rev. 1387 (1987).

[21] 22 U.S. (9 Wheat.) 1 (1824).

[22] *Id.* at 211–12.

On the facts of this decision, he no doubt advanced a coherent procompetitive agenda. But by the same token, his major concern was with the delineation of national power, not economic theory. In all likelihood, that is, he would have decided the case in favor of federal power even if the United States had sought to create a monopoly for an interstate run that a state opposed.

Yet there were limits to the extent to which Marshall was prepared to promote federal power, for his view of the commerce power only touched "commerce," and commerce "among" the several states. As he wrote concerning the latter, "Comprehensive as the word 'among' is, it may very properly be restricted to that commerce which concerns more States than one."[23] The point of this was to make it clear that there were forms of "commerce"—by which he meant navigation, trade, and, more generally, business intercourse of all sorts—that were wholly within a given state, and to them the federal commerce power did not reach. The point here was critical, for if all commercial transactions counted as commerce among the several states, then the United States could have limited contracts for the sale of slaves within the antebellum south—which, however welcome on moral grounds, would have destabilized the Union long before 1860.[24] But once it was accepted that this domain of *intrastate* commerce lay beyond the reach of federal power, then it necessarily followed that those productive activities one step removed from commerce, including manufacture, mining, and agriculture, fell outside the scope of the federal commerce power. It is easy to infer that this was Marshall's understanding, for he also insisted that states, in exercise of their police power, had the exclusive right to conduct the inspections of goods that either preceded or followed the shipment

[23] *Id.* at 194.

[24] Note that Article I, Section 9, Clause 1 provides that "[t]he Migration or Importation of such Persons as any of the states now existing shall think proper to admit, shall not be prohibited by the Congress prior to [1808]." U.S. Const. art I, § 9, cl. 1. That clause was protected from amendment under Article V. Only after the expiration of the provision could Congress regulate this trade under its power to control foreign commerce. It is odd to think that before 1808 the Commerce Clause allowed Congress to regulate in-state sales. The issue here is not the ugliness of slavery. It concerns what the knowledge of slavery does to highlight key constitutional structures. Stated otherwise, the extension of citizenship to all former slaves under Section 1 of the Fourteenth Amendment does not change the scope of the commerce power.

of goods in commerce.[25] The marginal case on this view was whether a journey that took two ships instead of one could count as a single interstate journey subject to federal regulation, if the entire trip crossed state lines, as was later held in *The Daniel Ball*.[26]

Thus, the decision in *Gibbons* upholding federal regulation of commerce across state lines was hostile to state regulation that could interfere with the operation of a national competitive market. That view survived and, indeed, flourished during the Progressive Era,[27] often under the judges who, unlike Marshall, believed in the inexorable expansion of federal power. The important movement from *Gibbons* that expanded federal regulatory power took place in two stages. First, the Court rejected Marshall's proposition that there was a discrete subset of commerce that could be described as internal to any state. That change was completed before the New Deal. Second, that principle was later expanded to all forms of manufacture and agriculture. That task was completed during the New Deal.

Concerning the first step, the key decision came in the *Shreveport Rate Cases*,[28] which allowed the Interstate Commerce Commission to regulate the rates of an in-state railroad that was competing with an interstate run.[29] The clear impact of this decision was a reduction in the level of competition that could otherwise have taken place if the Commerce Clause had been kept to its earlier contours. The anticompetitive nature of this expansion was made even more clear by the decision nearly a decade later in *Railroad Commission of Wisconsin v. Chicago, Burlington & Quincy Railroad Co.*[30] That decision allowed the regulation of a wholly intrastate line that was *not* in

---

[25] Gibbons, 22 U.S. (9 Wheat.) at 203 ("They [inspection laws] act upon the subject before it becomes an article of foreign commerce, or of commerce among the States, and prepare it for that purpose.").

[26] 77 U.S. (10 Wall.) 557, 565 (1870).

[27] See, e.g., Dean Milk Co. v. City of Madison, 340 U.S. 349, 356 (1951) (invalidating local ordinance that required all milk sold within the city to be processed within fifty miles of Madison, Wisconsin); H.P. Hood & Sons v. Du Mond, 336 U.S. 525, 530–31, 545 (1949) (invalidating licensing system that prohibited new plants in order to protect local interests); Baldwin v. G.A.F. Seelig, Inc., 294 U.S. 511, 523–25 (1935) (striking down differential tax on out-of-state milk intended to stabilize prices).

[28] 234 U.S. 342 (1914).

[29] *Id.* at 350–52.

[30] 257 U.S. 563 (1922).

competition with an interstate run; it introduced a general rate-of-return regime for the entire railroad system—government cartelization.[31] The simple insight here is that the broader the scope of the federal power, the more comprehensive and effective the federal cartel. The Commerce Clause was a two-edged sword, which during this period was used to increase the scope of national cartelization along lines congenial to the Progressives rather than to take competition into the bowels of the state.

Note, however, that these railroad cases left untouched the distinction in *United States v. E.C. Knight Co.*:[32] "Commerce succeeds to manufacture, and is not a part of it."[33] The same of course applied to agriculture and mining. Those limitations made it harder for the United States government to exert its power in favor of two groups that wielded inordinate influence in the Progressive period, labor and agriculture. Both groups benefited from the first Progressive initiative, section 6 of the Clayton Act, which held, in so many terms, that combinations among workers or farmers did not amount to combinations "in restraint of trade."[34] But that protection against private suits did not protect these organizations against defection by their own members; nor did it prevent outsiders from entering the market and lowering wages or lowering the prices for agricultural commodities. Those objectives required the ability to restrict entry into the market. For labor markets, the National Labor Relations Act of 1935[35] achieved that goal because it imposed on management a duty to bargain with

[31] *Id.* at 588–90.

[32] 156 U.S. 1 (1895).

[33] *Id.* at 12. *E.C. Knight* itself could be opposed on its facts given that the merger involved corporations in different states. But the major premise was good even if the minor premise was bad, and long before the New Deal, the justices of the Old Court, dealing with an issue that Chief Justice Marshall had not anticipated, accepted that the commerce power reached nationwide cartels. See, e.g., Addyston Pipe & Steel Co. v. United States, 175 U.S. 211, 241–42 (1899).

[34] 15 U.S.C. § 17 (2000) ("The labor of a human being is not a commodity or article of commerce. Nothing contained in the antitrust laws shall be construed to forbid the existence and operation of labor, agricultural, or horticultural organizations, instituted for the purposes of mutual help, and not having capital stock or conducted for profit, or to forbid or restrain individual members of such organizations from lawfully carrying out the legitimate objects thereof; nor shall such organizations, or the members thereof, be held or construed to be illegal combinations or conspiracies in restraint of trade, under the antitrust laws.").

[35] 49 Stat. 449 (1935) (codified as amended at 29 U.S.C. §§ 151–69).

a union, as the exclusive representative of employees, if that union had been selected in local elections. And to sustain the statute, the Supreme Court in *NLRB v. Jones & Laughlin Steel Corp.*[36] overturned quite recent case law[37] to hold that all manufacture was part of interstate commerce because of the effects that local disturbances in production could have on nationwide activities[38]—a point that was as true in 1787 as it was in 1937, but apparently had gone unnoticed for 150 years.

This expansion of federal power continued inexorably with respect to agriculture, where the New Deal policy was to create strong output restrictions in an effort to keep prices above world market levels. But the effort to regulate either the prices or the quantities of grain and dairy products shipped in interstate commerce would not be equal to the task, as savvy farmers shifted to various in-state uses of their grain rather than suffer the loss of production. Hence the Court inverted the maxim of Chief Justice Marshall: no longer was the commerce power *restricted* to *that* commerce that involved more states than one; instead, it was *extended* to *all* commerce, period. Thus, in *United States v. Wrightwood Dairy Co.*,[39] the Court held that Congress could regulate the sale of milk within a single state.[40] In *Wickard v. Filburn*[41] the Court finished the job by holding that Congress could limit farmers' right to feed their own grain to their own cows on the ground that the amount of grain they consumed locally could influence the interstate price of grain.[42] The objective of the scheme was to keep the price of grain in the United States at $1.16 per bushel when the world price was $.40.[43] The same administration that could enforce the antitrust laws with one breath could with another create the very cartels that are exhibit A of illegal collective action (inviting treble damages and criminal sanctions under the

---

[36] 301 U.S. 1 (1937).

[37] See A.L.A. Schechter Poultry Corp. v. United States, 295 U.S. 495 (1935) (overturning codes of fair competition for poultry industry).

[38] 301 U.S. at 36–41.

[39] 315 U.S. 110 (1942)

[40] *Id.* at 121.

[41] 317 U.S. 111 (1942).

[42] *Id.* at 127–29.

[43] *Id.* at 126.

antitrust laws, which the Progressives also favored). The labor and agriculture cases make clear how the Progressive program operated on the ground. All the talk about fair relationships between parties had only one real consequence: the preference for cartels over competition, even when every standard economic theory cries out for the opposite. The source of the error was the deep belief that firm size is the key determinant of prices and wages, when in fact the number of available alternatives is, and always has been, the key. The images of big-little conflicts that dominated the likes of Frankfurter and Dewey translated into deeply antisocial results.

There has been much talk of a revival of the Commerce Clause limitation because the Supreme Court has in the last decade struck down some statutes as outside the scope of the commerce power. But the current synthesis leaves matters largely unchanged, for the decision in *United States v. Lopez*,[44] which invalidated a Texas law that forbade the possession of guns near schools,[45] and that in *United States v. Morrison*,[46] which invalidated a provision of the Violence Against Women Act that would have created federal causes of action for local crimes against women,[47] are in fact only tiny deviations of doctrine. Both decisions affirmed the basic teaching of *Wickard* regarding economic affairs, and the Supreme Court has just reaffirmed that position emphatically in *Gonzales v. Raich*,[48] which dealt with claims of state autonomy allowing the medical use of marijuana that was either home-grown or supplied for free from in-state sources.[49] Today, the strong impulse to comprehensive legislation is not only a Progressive inclination. It also dominates modern social conservative thought, which is why defenders of the classical liberal tradition of limited government, like myself, feel ever more isolated now that both political parties have thrown in the towel on the Commerce Clause limitations. But justices are not politicians: why they should *want* to move heaven and earth to give an expansive

[44] 514 U.S. 549 (1995).
[45] *Id*. at 583.
[46] 529 U.S. 598 (2000).
[47] *Id*. at 614–17.
[48] 125 S. Ct. 2195 (2005).
[49] *Id*. at 2200.

reading of the Commerce Clause to prop up nationwide cartels is a question that the Progressives have never satisfactorily answered.

IV. Individual Rights and the Police Power

The second set of issues on which the Old Court drew the ire of the Progressives involves the interaction between liberty and property on one hand, and the legitimate scope of the police power on the other. As noted earlier, throughout the Progressive Era, the key question never concerned the existence of the police power, but rather the scope of its operation as recognized by the Old Court. For these purposes, it is correct to say that the dominant impulse of the Old Court insofar as it related to the regulation of economic affairs, broadly conceived, was more libertarian than it was conservative. The Court certainly showed little sign of being influenced by any Social Darwinist or religious attitudes, for example.[50] The judges who operated within that framework did not treat the phrase "safety, health, morals, and [the] general welfare" as being so broad as to authorize anything, for such a treatment would have meant that an unexpressed police power could nullify explicit constitutional protections. That was most definitely not the case in this period, and the point is most clearly brought home by seeing the kinds of government laws and actions that fell *outside* the scope of the police power. Three types of statutes immediately come to mind: those that work a confiscation of property of firms not "affected with the public interest"; those "labor" statutes that are defined in opposition to statutes that deal with health and safety; and statutes concerning the right of labor organizations to engage in collective bargaining on behalf of employees.

A. Businesses Affected with the Public Interest

In dealing with this issue, it is useful to note why this category of business was thought special by the Old Court. The question was whether the state had the power to regulate the rates that certain firms charged for their goods and services. The traditional English view on this subject did not rest on constitutional grounds, but nonetheless became the basis of the American constitutional law on the subject. The doctrine originated with Sir Matthew Hale, writing

---

[50]James W. Ely Jr., The Fuller Court 192–93 (2003).

in the seventeenth century,[51] and his views were adopted almost wholesale by Lord Ellenborough in *Allnut v. Inglis* in 1810.[52] The basic position was that in most markets everyone is entitled to charge what the market will bear, but that this principle did not apply in those cases in which a firm had either a legal or a natural monopoly. At that point some form of rate regulation was permissible to counteract the use of monopoly power, and much ingenuity had been used by both the Old Court and the Progressives to decide exactly what form of rate regulation was appropriate. There is room for debate on a question for which there is really no first-best answer. The Supreme Court over the years has had learned debates over which formula best regulates these activities and to this day gives extensive latitude to the scope of their regulation, even though it is keenly aware of the risk that rates could be set so low as to confiscate the investment that private firms commit to the regulated industry.[53]

It should be evident, therefore, that no member of the Old Court thought that the conception of businesses affected with the public interest was empty. Regarding such firms, the narrower conception sought to limit their power to engage in monopolistic practices, either alone or in conjunction with others. The upshot was that conservative justices such as Rufus Peckham were prepared to enforce the Sherman Antitrust Act against nationwide cartels.[54]

---

[51] Sir Matthew Hale, De Portibus Maris, reprinted in A Collection of Tracts Relative to the Law of England (Francis Hargrave ed., 1787). The original work was written around 1670.

[52] 12 East. 527, 530, 104 Eng. Rep. 206, 208 (K.B. 1810).

[53] For a summary of these views, see Duquesne Light Co. v. Barasch, 488 U.S. 299 (1989). For the view that the system of regulation undercuts dynamic innovation that uses technology to undercut natural monopolies, see Harold Demsetz, Why Regulate Utilities?, 11 J.L. & Econ. 55 (1968); Richard A. Posner, Natural Monopoly and Its Regulation, 21 Stan. L. Rev. 548 (1969). One vindication of this view is the unfortunate history of rate regulation under The Telecommunications Act of 1996, Pub. L. No. 104-104, 110 Stat. 58 (codified at 47 U.S.C. § 151 et seq.). When the Act was passed, the local Bell Companies had monopolies over "the last mile" of telephone service. Today that monopoly has been eroded not only by cell phones, but also by Internet and cable providers, which will soon be joined by electricity providers. Modern technology has led to the fusion of what used to be separate industry spaces, leading to enhanced competition within the broader market. In the meantime, the system of direct regulation of landlines has created a nightmare that could have been avoided with a little bit of patience.

[54] Addyston Pipe & Steel Co. v. United States, 175 U.S. 211, 241–45, 247–48 (1899).

Accordingly, both state and federal court judges accepted systems of rate regulation against natural monopolies.

The key question, therefore, was whether these restrictions would be enforced against those firms that did not possess monopoly power. The Progressives generally were dismissive of the view that regulation was not needed in cases of this sort. A 1932 case that shows the differences in the two positions was *New State Ice Co. v. Liebmann*,[55] where the Old Court, speaking through Justice Sutherland, invalidated a statute that required any new entrant into the ice business to obtain a certificate of public interest and necessity from the state.[56] The Old Court's view stems from the sensible conclusion that the only reason why such permission might be denied is to build a legal monopoly on behalf of the first entrant into any market. Justice Brandeis, in dissent, offered up an eloquent but misguided argument to the effect that the state has a legitimate interest in protecting producers against the "ruinous competition" of new entrants even though the very survival of a market economy depends on the ability of new firms to win customers away from their established rivals by offering a mix of lower prices and superior quality.[57] But the urge for cartelization that drove the Progressives on Commerce Clause issues carried over here as well.

The coup de grace came with *Nebbia v. New York*,[58] which involved a challenge to a New York statute that imposed minimum prices on milk in order to stop "ruinous competition" in the dairy industry. The Supreme Court, through Justice Roberts, sustained this exercise of government power on the ground that, for constitutional purposes, it made no difference whether the legislation was aimed at limiting the prices that could be charged by a natural monopoly or at propping up the prices of a competitive industry.[59] The adverse consequences of this misguided policy should not be difficult to see. Consumers, many of whom were in dire straits, now had to pay more for dairy products. And farmers who might have exited the industry in an orderly fashion were now encouraged to hang on

---

[55] 285 U.S. 262 (1932).
[56] *Id.* at 278–80.
[57] *Id.* at 292 (Brandeis, J., dissenting).
[58] 291 U.S. 502 (1934).
[59] *Id.* at 534–39.

through thick and thin, in ways that impeded the rationalization of the dairy industry in the face of rising productivity. The upshot was another round of agricultural and dairy subsidies with the usual distortions: extra burdens on those taxed, and over-production by those receiving the tax. The anticompetitive schemes that discriminated against foreign sellers were not tolerated under the dormant Commerce Clause, but under an expanded conception of the police power those equally counterproductive schemes that impacted local and out-of-state sellers alike received a constitutional imprimatur, and the dislocations that have followed dominate the Byzantine field of agricultural subsidies to this day.

B. Wages and Hours Regulation

A second great battle between the Old Court and the Progressives was over labor regulation—specifically, over state initiatives that sought to impose maximum hours or minimum wages for industrial workers in various industries. Within the classical framework, such regulations could not be justified by claiming that the relevant businesses were affected with the public interest, for there was virtually no evidence of natural monopolies in, for example, the bakery business. But there was an extended question of whether the regulations could be justified as health or safety measures under the police power. One defensible view is that the regulations are justified only in those cases where the harms in question are to strangers, as in nuisance cases, or where the dangers to the protected class of workers stem from undisclosed conditions that pose dangers for people in their ordinary employment. That position, which leaves it to workers to decide the level of known risks that they wish to take as part of their employment, is quite consistent with general principles of laissez faire. And it was defended on just those grounds by its most diligent advocates.[60]

But the members of the Old Court did not push this line consistently, for in areas of dangerous employment, they were in general willing to override freedom of contract even when informed parties

---

[60]See, e.g., Smith v. Baker & Sons, [1891] A.C. 325, 344 (Lord Bramwell, J.) ("It is a rule of good sense that if a man voluntarily undertakes a risk for a reward which is adequate to induce him, he shall not, if he suffers from the risk, have a compensation for which he did not stipulate.").

might have been prepared to assume the risk.[61] The Federal Employer Liability Act, which removed the defense of assumption of risk for railroad employees involved in accidents, was challenged on the ground that it applied to intrastate journeys that were (at least before 1914 and the *Shreveport Rate Cases*)[62] arguably in intrastate commerce, but no challenge was mounted to the substantive provision that removed the assumption of risk defense on what was indisputably, after all, a matter of safety. And it is possible to find many cases in this period that upheld decisions to override the common law's fellow-servant rule (whereby a firm could not be held vicariously liable for the injuries that one worker suffered at the hands of a fellow servant).[63] It was similar reasoning that led Justice Pitney to write a unanimous opinion for the Court sustaining the constitutionality of the New York workmen's compensation statute in *New York Central Railroad Co. v. White*.[64] The decisions here are hardly remarkable. Once health and safety entered as justifications under the police power, the terms were construed in their ordinary sense.

In dealing with these issues, there is good reason to think that the Old Court may not have placed the various safety statutes under sufficient scrutiny.[65] Although the point is not widely appreciated, the original workers' compensation plans were not introduced by statute but were entered into on a voluntary basis by various firms in the mining and transportation industries, where the high rate of accidents in large establishments made it possible to bear the fixed costs associated with putting one of these plans into action. The celebrated Wainwright Commission recommended their mandatory

---

[61]See, e.g., Holden v. Hardy, 169 U.S. 366, 393–96 (1898) (upholding maximum hour law for miners).

[62]See note 28, *supra*.

[63]See, e.g., Second Employer Liability Cases, 223 U.S. 1, 50 (1912). For the leading exposition of the fellow-servant (or common employment rule), see Farwell v. Boston & Worcester R.R. Corp., 45 Mass. 49 (1842) (Shaw, J.).

[64]243 U.S. 188, 200–02, 205 (1917).

[65]For key elements of this history, see Richard A. Epstein, The Historical Origins and Economic Structure of Workers' Compensation Law, 16 Ga. L. Rev. 775 (1982); Price V. Fishback, Liability Rules and Accident Prevention in the Workplace: Empirical Evidence from the Early Twentieth Century, 16 J. Legal Stud. 305 (1987); Price V. Fishback & Shawn Everett Kantor, A Prelude to the Welfare State: The Origins of Workers' Compensation (2000).

adoption in New York State.[66] But in the famous case of *Ives v. South Buffalo Railway Co.*,[67] the New York Court of Appeals struck down the initial version of the law on state constitutional grounds.[68] This reversal led to a prompt change in the New York Constitution to allow workmen's compensation statutes. But the willingness of large players (such as General Electric, the B&O Railroad, and International Harvester) to support these schemes should not be read as proving that whatever schemes enlightened firms adopt voluntarily should be imposed on others as a matter of statute. The cost of implementing these plans often makes sense for large firms with team production, which these companies are. The size matters because it allows the firm to spread the costs of introducing the plan over many workers. The team production matters because these firms do not suffer an efficiency loss from collectivizing the loss: it is less likely that any worker will be the sole cause of his own loss. Little firms are not likely to have either of these advantages.[69] The economic logic shows how even health and safety statutes can garner support for anticompetitive reasons. But the Old Court did not wish to deal with these mixed motives in cases challenging laws that had a clear and evident relation to workplace safety.

When the discussion turned to maximum hours and minimum wage laws, the question of mixed motivations remained, but the connection to safety was more attenuated and the anticompetitive and paternalistic aspects of the statutes were more evident. The famous 1905 decision in *Lochner v. New York*[70] sustained a constitutional challenge to a criminal conviction for violating a statute that provided:

> No employee shall be required or permitted to work in a
> biscuit, bread, or cake bakery or confectionery establishment

---

[66] The commission, chaired by J. Mayhew Wainwright, produced the *First Report to the Legislature of the State of New York by the Commission Appointed Under Chapter 518 of the Laws of 1909 to Inquire into the Question of Employer's Liability and Other Matters* (1910).

[67] 99 N.E. 431 (N.Y. 1911).

[68] *Id.* at 448.

[69] For a discussion of these cross-subsidies with the Occupational Safety and Health Administration (OSHA), see Ann P. Bartel & Lacy Glenn Thomas, Predation Through Regulation: The Wage and Profit Effects of the Occupational Safety and Health Administration and the Environmental Protection Agency, 30 J.L. & Econ. 239 (1987).

[70] 198 U.S. 45 (1905).

> more than sixty hours in any one week, or more than ten
> hours in any one day, unless for the purpose of making a
> shorter work day on the last day of the week.[71]

Clearly there were signs that something was amiss from the face of the statute itself. It applied not to all bakers, but only to those who worked "in a biscuit, bread, or cake bakery or confectionery establishment."[72] It exempted self-employed bakers, even though they faced the same health risks.[73] And the provision on maximum hours follows in the statute one that regulates sleeping quarters.[74]

This last point is telling because the immigrant bakers in Mr. Lochner's establishment worked more than sixty hours per week because they had to quite literally "sleep on the job" as part of their routine work cycle, during which time any exposure to dust and other particles would be at a minimum. The statute would have no effect on firms that used different modes of production—one crew bakes bread in the evening, say, and another packs and distributes it in the morning. The statute looks as though its apparent paternal gaze was really an effort to upset the competitive balance between different firms, yet that did not stop the Progressives from denouncing the decision for its "ill-conceived" interference in the workplace. Needless to say, *Lochner* was an easy casualty when the Court upheld the Fair Labor and Standards Act of 1938,[75] which imposed major restrictions on all forms of employment practices. Once again, the net effect of these decisions is to allow firms and unions to resist competition from new upstarts that might offer more efficient modes of production.

The decision in *Lochner* was close because the safety and health issues could not be ignored. It was for that reason that the dissent of Justice Harlan went to such lengths to validate this statute as a

[71] *Id.* at 46 n.1 (quoting 1897 N.Y. Laws art. 8, ch. 415, § 110).

[72] *Id.*

[73] Brief of Appellant at 8, Lochner v. New York, 198 U.S. 45 (1905) (No. 292).

[74] *Id.* (quoting 1897 N.Y. Laws art. 8, ch. 415, § 113) ("*Wash-rooms and closets; sleeping places.*—. . . No person shall sleep in a room occupied as a bake-room. Sleeping places for the persons employed in the bakery shall be separate from the rooms where flour or meal food products are manufactured or stored.") (emphasis in original).

[75] United States v. Darby, 312 U.S. 100, 116–17 (1941) (overruling Hammer v. Dagenhart, 247 U.S. 251 (1918)).

health measure, in sharp contrast to Justice Holmes' dissent, which inveighed against the Court for its reflexive adherence to laissez faire, but which could not command the support of even one other justice. If the connection between maximum hours legislation and safety is tenuous at best, the connection between a minimum wage statute and safety is altogether absent, which makes such statutes' anticompetitive aspects all the more clear: workers with minimum skills cannot compete for a place on the first rung by offering their services at lower rates. This anticompetitive effect is the best justification for why *Adkins v. Children's Hospital*,[76] which struck down a minimum wage law,[77] was defensible as a matter of first principle, then as now.

Nor did the Old Court's effort to distinguish between health and safety statutes on one hand and "labor" statutes on the other stop with minimum wage laws. In a series of well-publicized decisions, including *Coppage v. Kansas*,[78] the Old Court struck down on constitutional grounds statutes barring "yellow-dog" contracts that required workers not to join unions while they remained in the service of their employer.[79] In addition, as a common law matter, in *Hitchman Coal & Coke Co. v. Mitchell*,[80] the Old Court held that employers were entitled to obtain an injunction against any union that sought to induce individuals to join (or even promise to join) a union while remaining on the job in violation of that stipulation of undivided loyalty.[81] Here again the decision makes good sense. The tort of inducement of breach of contract is carefully limited so that anyone is entitled to offer a higher wage to lure an at-will employee away from his or her current position. But the yellow-dog provision has the important social advantage that it cuts down on the power of a labor union to organize a devastating strike that can be timed to generate maximum disruption of the business. Workers of course remain free to leave their jobs at any time to throw their lot in with the union, but their gradual departure will allow replacements to

---

[76] 261 U.S. 525 (1923).

[77] *Id.* at 561–62.

[78] 236 U.S. 1 (1915).

[79] See, e.g., *id.* at 26; Adair v. United States, 208 U.S. 161, 179–80 (1908).

[80] 245 U.S. 229 (1917).

[81] *Id.* at 261–62.

be hired in a wider labor market. There is no evidence whatsoever that Justice Pitney extended the tort of inducement of breach to impose special burdens on unions. Nor is there any public policy reason to dislike a result that strengthens competitive forces in labor markets. As noted earlier, in the long run workers benefit from these rules, as the consistent upward movement in wages and downward movement in hours can be traced to only one cause: the consistent increase in productivity translated into high wages just as the old school economists such as Smith and Ricardo had argued.

At this point, it is imperative to mention one case in which the Old Court deviated, with tragic consequences, from its effort to rein in the scope of the police power. On matters of race relations, the Court did not take the narrow view of the police power that it adopted in *Lochner*; rather, it used a far broader conception to sustain racial segregation in transportation, marriage, and, in *Plessy v. Ferguson*,[82] schooling. The discussion of the race cases in Freund is all too cryptic, occupying only five pages of the 800-page text.[83] It expresses some uneasiness but no outrage at a set of decisions that depended on a broad conception of the police power to hold that the separation of the races was little different from the separation of the sexes, and could be justified in order to protect against the dangers of miscegenation, mixed carriage on rails, or integrated schools. The level of deference here is far greater than in *Lochner*. The only opposition that Freund expressed to these decisions was that they could operate in an unfortunate fashion as a limitation on freedom of association, which of course is liberty of contract in yet another guise.[84]

The tension between the *Lochner* and the *Plessy* lines of thought posed a dilemma for Progressives. Once committed to legislative supremacy, they could do little to oppose *Plessy* at the same time they championed the reversal of *Lochner*. It is a pity that Progressives did not see in this any reason to slow down their attacks on the classical liberal conception that speaks of the protection of the like liberties of all. Clearly, that rule would allow for freedom of association and would call into question any exercise of public power that

---

[82] 163 U.S. 537 (1896).

[83] Freund, *supra* note 8, at 717–21.

[84] *Id.* at 720.

discriminates among individuals, requiring a clear public justification related to health and safety. But that was not meant to be. It was, after all, a Progressive and former Princeton professor and president, Woodrow Wilson, who led the successful effort to segregate the federal civil service once he became president of the nation, and he did so without any judicial resistance, precisely because the decision in *Plessy* gave such a broad account of the police power as to foreclose judicial challenge. At this point, the dangers of "science" and "expertise" should become clear. They allow for a degree of discretion in government behavior that can be put to bad as well as good purposes. Nor did the Progressives stay their hand only on race relations. In *Meyer v. Nebraska*[85] and *Pierce v. Society of Sisters*,[86] it was members of the Old Court who gave a broad definition of liberty to protect the rights of parents and children as well as private and religious schools. Justice Holmes had followed his *Lochner* line and was willing to allow the state to limit foreign language instruction,[87] as was Felix Frankfurter who, while opposed to the legislation in *Meyer* and *Pierce*, was reluctant to advocate striking it down lest he slow down the judicial demise of *Lochner, Adair,* and *Coppage*.[88]

So in the end, all other interests were subordinate to the labor questions. On these matters, *Lochner, Adair,* and *Coppage* were anathema to the Progressive movement, which saw in labor relations the key test of its conviction that state power on the side of labor was necessary to redress the imbalance of power that existed in labor markets. To make their case, the Progressives pounded on two related claims. The first was that the narrow (for so they seemed) categories of the police power under the old law did not reflect the full nature of the public interest that properly limited the scope of property and liberty. In their view a worker who had a weaker bargaining position than the employer might not be able to advance himself through private agreement. Progressives insisted that the Old Court had held to the contrary based upon outmoded and weak

---

[85] 262 U.S. 390, 403 (1923) (striking down statute that forbade the instruction of foreign languages in schools to students who had not passed the eighth grade).

[86] 268 U.S. 510, 536 (1925) (striking down statute that banned private education, secular or religious, for children between eight and sixteen years of age).

[87] Bartels v. Iowa, 262 U.S. 404, 412 (1923) (Holmes, J., dissenting).

[88] Felix Frankfurter, Can the Supreme Court Guarantee Toleration?, The New Republic, June 17, 1925, at 85.

formal or mechanical claims that did not stand the test of modern social science. In arguments that prefigured the rise of the administrative state, they claimed that good science leads to the abandonment of old formalities and to an increased trust of experts in dealing with a wide range of social and economic issues. The theme was expressed by Freund, and even more forcefully by Roscoe Pound in his well-known essay *The Need of a Sociological Jurisprudence.*[89] The same theme was of course adopted by Louis Brandeis in his famous brief in *Muller v. Oregon*[90] in support of maximum hours legislation for women—yet another misguided result that should not have survived the Progressive period because the ostensible protection it provided worked chiefly to prevent competition by women.

The Progressive cause, then, must make peace with the deleterious consequences of the laws it supported. But oddly enough Progressives were often more concerned with attacking laissez faire than with developing their own substantive theories of market behavior. For example, the explicit target of Roscoe Pound was "[t]he individualist conception of justice as the liberty of each limited only by the like liberties of all," which, he noted, sociologists regarded as the celebration of an outmoded conception of "legal justice" in opposition to the richer sociological conception of justice to which the legal system should aspire.[91] But Pound and his followers had not a clue as to what a system of sociological justice would entail, or why it performed better than the so-called formal or legal justice it aimed to displace. Not only could Progressives not explain the improvement in wages and prosperity under the regime they despised, but they could not offer any theoretical explanation for their broad conception of inequality of bargaining power and employer exploitation. It was clear that most employers did not enjoy any position of monopoly power and that the Old Court had accepted the application of the antitrust laws to cartel-like behaviors. But while the Old Court had applied the same conception to labor and management

---

[89] Roscoe Pound, The Need of a Sociological Jurisprudence, 19 The Green Bag 607 (1907) [hereinafter Pound, Sociological Jurisprudence]; see also Roscoe Pound, Mechanical Jurisprudence, 8 Colum. L. Rev. 605 (1908).

[90] Brief for Defendant in Error, Muller v. Oregon, 208 U.S. 412 (1908) (No. 107), in Landmark Briefs and Arguments of the Supreme Court of the United States: Constitutional Law 63–178 (Philip B. Kurland & Gerhard Casper eds., 1975).

[91] Pound, Sociological Jurisprudence, *supra* note 89, at 612, 615.

alike,[92] the Progressives had by 1914 secured the exemption of labor and agriculture from the antitrust laws altogether—a clear case of partisan advantage covered up by sociological high jinx that took no note of the adverse social consequences of monopoly behavior.

With monopoly to one side, the question is whether workers would take jobs that left them worse off than they were before. To avoid that unhappy result, they do not need to form coalitions. They simply need to have the power to refuse to deal, which was a cardinal element of the synthesis of the Old Court. As Justice Pitney (who on these issues was far more astute than Justices Holmes and Brandeis combined) insisted in *Coppage v. Kansas*, contracts for labor, like other contracts, were formed only when each side felt that it was better off than before.[93] That conclusion holds, moreover, notwithstanding any real or apparent disparity in wealth at the outset of the transaction. And any effort to insist that the worker receive, as by some unexplained metric, the larger fraction of the surplus generated by employment contracts is sure to disrupt one mechanism of progress on which overall prosperity depends. Mutual gain does not depend on the parity of wealth of the parties in their initial positions. No matter how great the disparity in wealth, the poorer party will not enter into a transaction that makes him worse off than before. Remember, despite their "empirical" and "sociological" bent, it was the Progressives who lacked any overall social conception of justice. They were concerned only with union members; not with those excluded from unions; not with those who paid higher prices; and not with those whose welfare was disrupted by strikes and other forms of job actions.

None of this of course had any effect on the defenders of unionization. Felix Frankfurter expressed the dominant position well when he insisted: " 'Collective bargaining' is the starting point of the solution and not the solution itself. This principle must, of course, receive ungrudging acceptance. It is nothing but belated recognition of economic facts—that the era of romantic individualism is no more."[94]

However misguided it was, this campaign enjoyed success when the main causes of the Depression—the currency deflation and the

[92] See Loewe v. Lawlor, 208 U.S. 274 (1908).

[93] 236 U.S. 1, 17 (1915).

[94] Felix Frankfurter, Law and Order, *supra* note 16, at 233–34.

Smoot-Hawley tariff—wreaked massive damage to the overall economic system. But those measures were no product of industrialization as such; rather, they were calculated policy choices by Congress that were inconsistent with the views of the Old Court, but beyond its capacity to review. The tariff marked a massive interference with voluntary exchange, and deflation counted as a major, if tacit, transfer of wealth from debtors (who have to pay back fixed denomination loans with more valuable dollars) to creditors.

Nonetheless, such was the dominant Progressive ethos of the time that the Progressives thought that the best way to deal with these legislative interventions was to disrupt the system of voluntary exchange yet a third time by the adoption of rules that displaced the pro-competitive constitutional rules of the Old Court with major systems of monopoly power. The Norris-LaGuardia Act of 1932 declared that the yellow-dog contract was against public policy, and rested that view on a finding that freedom of contract was not a viable ideal in the absence of full equality of bargaining power.[95] In a similar vein, a key finding of the National Labor Relations Act of 1935 (NLRA) took a page out of the Progressive handbook:

> The inequality of bargaining power between employees who do not possess full freedom of association or actual liberty of contract, and employers who are organized in the corporate or other forms of ownership association, substantially burdens and affects the flow of commerce, and tends to aggravate recurrent business depressions, by depressing wage rates and the purchasing power of wage earners in industry and by preventing the stabilization of competitive wage rates and working conditions within and between industries.[96]

This finding was an effort to allow labor unions to stabilize the wages of their members, but to do so in a fashion that put all the burden of economic fluctuation on other workers and firms. The Act offers no explanation as to how free competition could be the source of depression, or why the steady increase in wages should not be attributed to market forces. And its effort to stabilize wage rates within industries amounts to little more than an effort to extend

[95] 29 U.S.C. §§ 102–103.
[96] 29 U.S.C. § 151.

36

the scope of cartels across the full range of markets. As a statement of economic principle, the entire NLRA is riddled with economic blunders whose effect is to introduce a costly system of collective bargaining, replete with organizational struggles and strikes. Yet there is not a single word on how any of these measures would, or could, counter the effects of tariffs and deflation.

There is, on balance, little doubt that the Supreme Court, which sustained this statute, has read it as it was intended, giving full effect to the important modifications introduced by the Taft-Hartley Act that control the ability of unions to enter into various secondary boycotts of those firms that do business with another firm that is subject to a unionization drive or strike. And yet, the rate of unionization continues to plunge from a high of about thirty-five percent of the private sector in the 1950s to well under ten percent today. Many try to find in this decline some story about the efforts of judges and firms to subvert the Act, but that claim rings hollow given the remarkably constant interpretation the Act has received over the past fifty years. Rather, the decline in unionization should be read as a vindication of the view that most unions do not supply workers with value that equals the costs associated with membership. For the hope of getting a short-term profit, a union worker takes the risk that a strike will bring down an entire firm (as happened, for example, with Eastern Airlines) or that high labor costs will force firms into bankruptcy (as happened with United Airlines) or that foreign imports will simply take the ground out from American firms struggling to cope with inefficient labor practices and high wage costs. Make no mistake about it: Strong labor unions must work with their unionized employers to keep high tariff walls around their businesses. But over time these will erode through end-runs that even the wary cannot foresee. Still, it seems as though neither courts nor legislatures will learn the one lesson that this history has to teach, which is that the overinflated claims of the Progressives make no sense today. Many will give the Progressives the benefit of doubt on these issues by saying that unions are not necessary today even though they were critical to social advancement years ago. But that claim to social relativism should fall on deaf ears unless someone is prepared to explain which local circumstances made monopoly superior to competitive industries.

V. Conclusion

At the end of the day, no matter where we look, it is this one stark question—whether we have a constitutional preference for competition or monopoly—that defines the difference between classical liberalism and the Old Court on one hand and modern social welfare liberalism and Progressivism on the other. The blunt truth here is that for all their efforts to cloak themselves in advanced learning and social sophistication, the Progressives were wrong on just about every point on which they differed from their classical liberal rivals. In the end, the most secure route to a safe and prosperous society lies not in the rejection of the principles of Locke, Smith, Hume, and Bentham as being the work of "romantic individualists." Rather, it lies in understanding that their powerful and coherent theories can be applied with precision and understanding to circumstances that lay far outside their comprehension. The invisible hand, as it were, has its place in intellectual history.

"Poor Relation" Once More: The Supreme Court and the Vanishing Rights of Property Owners

*James W. Ely Jr.**

I. Introduction

In three cases during its 2004–2005 term—*Lingle* v. *Chevron U.S.A., Inc.*,[1] *Kelo* v. *City of New London*,[2] and *San Remo Hotel* v. *City and County of San Francisco*[3]—the Supreme Court addressed related issues pertaining to the constitutionally protected rights of property owners. The justices sought to clarify aspects of their confused and contested takings jurisprudence. Unfortunately, the Court followed its recent trend of curtailing ownership rights in the face of economic regulations and governmental acquisition by eminent domain.[4] After a line of cases that began to put teeth into the Takings Clause of the Fifth Amendment, the Court seems to have lost its way and backtracked. For all their once bright promise, therefore, property rights decisions of the Court under Chief Justice William H. Rehnquist are ending, to paraphrase T.S. Eliot, with a whimper, not a bang.[5]

The Court has not demonstrated a sustained commitment to meaningful enforcement of individual property rights. Notwithstanding

*Professor of Law, Vanderbilt University School of Law. I am grateful to Jon W. Bruce for his helpful comments on a draft of this article.

[1]125 S. Ct. 2074 (2005).

[2]125 S. Ct. 2655 (2005).

[3]125 S. Ct. 2491 (2005).

[4]See, e.g., Tahoe-Sierra Preservation Council, Inc. v. Tahoe Regional Planning Agency, 535 U.S. 302 (2002); Brown v. Legal Foundation of Washington, 538 U.S. 216 (2003).

[5]"The Hollow Men," in T.S. Eliot, The Complete Poems and Plays, 1909–1950, 56–59 (1952).

scholarly and journalistic talk of a "conservative" Rehnquist Court,[6] the justices have been unwilling to break free of the New Deal constitutional hegemony that radically weakened traditional judicial solicitude for economic rights.[7] Despite some piecemeal moves to enhance the protection afforded property owners by reinvigorating the Takings Clause,[8] the overall record of the Rehnquist Court on economic liberties has been disappointing and marked by lost opportunities.

II. Historical Framework

To understand this term's trilogy of property rights decisions in context, it will be helpful to briefly review the historical role of property rights in our constitutional order. The conviction that private property was essential for self-government and political liberty was long a central tenet of Anglo-American constitutionalism.[9] Heirs of that tradition, the Framers of the Constitution and Bill of Rights were motivated in large part by the desire to establish safeguards for property. They felt that property rights and liberty were indissolubly linked. "Perhaps the most important value of the Founding Fathers of the American constitutional period," Stuart Bruchey observed, "was their belief in the necessity of securing property rights."[10] Thus, James Madison asserted at the Philadelphia convention that "the

[6]As the more liberal justices have gained ascendancy, the Rehnquist Court in recent years has disappointed conservatives and libertarians in a series of high-profile cases including those involving college affirmative action programs, limits on campaign contributions, the scope of congressional commerce power, and the rights of property owners.

[7]James W. Ely Jr., The Guardian of Every Other Right: A Constitutional History of Property Rights (2nd ed. 1998). See also Walter Dellinger, The Indivisibility of Economic Rights and Personal Liberty, 2003–2004 Cato Sup. Ct. Rev. 9, 13 (2004) (concluding that "the New Deal Court swept far too broadly in repudiating the protection of economic liberties").

[8]See, e.g., First English Evangelical Lutheran Church v. County of Los Angeles, 482 U.S. 304 (1987); Nollan v. California Coastal Commission, 483 U.S. 825 (1987); Lucas v. South Carolina Coastal Council, 505 U.S. 1003 (1992); Dolan v. City of Tigard, 512 U.S. 374 (1994); Eastern Enterprises v. Apfel, 524 U.S. 498 (1998).

[9]Ely, *supra* note 7, at 10–58. For a sweeping study that stresses the necessity of private property as a prerequisite for individual liberty, see Richard Pipes, Property and Freedom (1999).

[10]Stuart Bruchey, The Impact of Concern for the Security of Property Rights on the Legal System of the Early American Republic, 1980 Wis. L. Rev. 1135, 1136.

primary objects of civil society are the security of property and public safety."[11]

From the beginning of the New Republic, courts curtailed legislative infringement of property and contractual rights. In 1795 in *Vanhorne's Lessee* v. *Dorrance*[12] Justice William Paterson, who had been an important member of the constitutional convention, revealingly declared that "the right of acquiring and possessing property, and having it protected, is one of the natural, inherent and unalienable rights of man."[13] As is well known, there was a close affinity between the jurisprudence of John Marshall and the defense of economic rights. The property-conscious dimensions of Marshall's constitutionalism primarily found expression in a famous string of cases broadly construing the Contracts Clause.[14] Other prominent antebellum jurists stressed the association between private property and political liberty. As Justice Joseph Story explained:

> [I]n a free government almost all other rights would become utterly worthless, if the government possessed an uncontrolled power over the private fortune of every citizen. One of the fundamental objects of every good government must be the due administration of justice; and how vain it would be to speak of such an administration, when all property is subject to the will or caprice of the legislature and the rulers.[15]

Industrialization and urbanization posed new challenges to the legal system in the decades following the Civil War. Adoption of the Fourteenth Amendment in 1868 created new avenues for federal judicial review of state legislation. The Supreme Court began in the late nineteenth century to scrutinize regulatory legislation under the Due Process Clause.[16] More important for our purposes, however, was the extension of the just compensation principle to the states.

---

[11]1 The Records of the Federal Convention of 1787, at 147 (Max Farrand ed., 1937).

[12] 2 U.S. (2 Dall.) 304 (C.C. Pa. 1795).

[13] *Id*. at 310.

[14]See Charles F. Hobson, The Great Chief Justice: John Marshall and the Rule of Law 72–110 (1996); James W. Ely Jr., The Marshall Court and Property Rights: A Reappraisal, 33 J. Marshall L. Rev. 1023, 1029–47 (2000) (discussing the Marshall Court's Contracts Clause jurisprudence).

[15]3 Joseph Story, Commentaries on the Constitution of the United States 664 (1833).

[16]Ely, *supra* note 7, at 82–100.

In 1833 in *Barron* v. *Baltimore*[17] the Court had ruled that the Bill of Rights, including the Fifth Amendment, was binding only on the federal government.[18] In the leading 1897 case of *Chicago, Burlington and Quincy Railroad Company* v. *Chicago*,[19] however, the justices held that the payment of compensation when private property was taken for public use was an essential element of due process as guaranteed by the Fourteenth Amendment.[20] Attesting to the high standing of property rights, the *Chicago Burlington* case marked the initial move to incorporate specific provisions of the Bill of Rights into the Fourteenth Amendment's Due Process Clause.

The Supreme Court, during the tenure of Melville W. Fuller as chief justice (1888–1910), established several other vital bedrock principles governing takings jurisprudence.[21] First, the justices made clear that the power of eminent domain did not authorize government to acquire the property of one person for transfer to another, even upon payment of compensation. In other words, government could take private property only for public use.[22] Second, the Court underscored the fundamental fairness norm implicit in the Takings Clause. It pointed out that the purpose of the clause was to prevent "the public from loading upon one individual more than his just share of the burdens of government, and says that when he surrenders to the public something more and different from that which is exacted from other members of the public, a full and just equivalent shall be returned to him."[23] In this classic statement the Court cut to the heart of the basic inquiry underlying takings jurisprudence— how far can society single out individuals to contribute a disproportionate amount toward providing social goods? In other words, when should society, through taxation, rather than individual owners bear the cost of achieving desired social goals?

By the late nineteenth century courts and commentators were considering whether a regulation might so diminish the value or

[17]32 U.S. (7 Pet.) 243 (1833).

[18]*Id.* at 250–51.

[19]166 U.S. 226 (1897).

[20]*Id.* at 238–39.

[21]See generally James W. Ely Jr., The Fuller Court and Takings Jurisprudence, 2 J. of Sup. Ct. Hist. 120 (1996).

[22]Missouri Pacific Railway Company v. Nebraska, 164 U.S. 403, 417 (1896).

[23]Monongahela Navigation Company v. United States, 148 U.S. 312, 325 (1893).

usefulness of property as to be tantamount to a taking without physical interference or acquisition of title. Property ownership had long been understood to encompass use and enjoyment, not mere title. In his famous 1792 essay James Madison perceptively warned people against government that *"indirectly* violates their property, in their actual possessions."[24] Although Madison anticipated the regulatory takings doctrine, the modern doctrine began to take shape in the last decades of the nineteenth century.[25] For example, in a treatise on eminent domain published in 1888, John Lewis declared that when a person was deprived of the possession, use, or disposition of property "he is to that extent deprived of his property, and, hence ... his property may be taken, in the constitutional sense, though his title and possession remain undisturbed."[26] Likewise, in 1891 Justice David J. Brewer pointed out that regulation of the use of property might destroy its value and constitute the practical equivalent of outright appropriation.[27] While on the Supreme Judicial Court of Massachusetts, Oliver Wendell Holmes also recognized that regulations might amount to a taking of property. "It would be open to argument at least," he stated, "that an owner might be stripped of his rights so far as to amount to a taking without any physical interference with his land."[28] As a member of the Supreme Court in 1908 Holmes insisted that a height restriction on buildings that rendered a building lot useless would constitute a compensable taking.[29] In short, the famous 1922 decision of *Pennsylvania Coal v. Mahon*,[30] in which the Court endorsed the emerging concept of a regulatory taking, was hardly an innovation. Rather, it reflected the desire of the Framers for robust protection of the rights of property

[24]James Madison, Property, National Gazette (March 29, 1792), reprinted in 14 The Papers of James Madison 266–68 (Robert A. Rutland & Thomas A. Mason eds., 1983) (emphasis in original).

[25]Adam Mossoff, What Is Property? Putting the Pieces Back Together, 45 Ariz. L. Rev. 371, 428–36 (2003) (examining cases from late nineteenth century in which courts treated restrictions on use or diminution in value of property as a taking).

[26]John Lewis, A Treatise on the Law of Eminent Domain 40–46 (1888).

[27]David J. Brewer, Protection to Private Property from Public Attack, 55 New Englander and Yale Rev. 97, 102–05 (1891).

[28]Bent v. Emery, 53 N.E. 910, 911 (Mass. 1899).

[29]Hudson Water Company v. McCarter, 209 U.S. 349, 355 (1908).

[30]260 U.S. 393 (1922).

owners and marked the culmination of years of discussion about the impact of regulation on property ownership.

The issue of regulatory takings has been most frequently litigated in the context of land use controls. Two trends became apparent early on. First, the Court sometimes conflated takings challenges with the deprivation of property without due process in violation of the Fourteenth Amendment.[31] Superficially similar, these concepts are in reality quite different. A law that constitutes a deprivation of property without due process is simply void. On the other hand, the Takings Clause does not prevent governmental interference with existing property relationships. It only mandates that owners receive just compensation for any property taken by governmental action. In an age of tight budgets and tax cutting initiatives, however, legislators all too often are inclined to provide public benefits by imposing regulatory burdens on a small group of landowners rather than by taxing society as a whole. In this light, land use regulations may represent an attempt to circumvent the just compensation command of the Fifth Amendment.

Second, for decades after *Pennsylania Coal* the Court was reluctant to actually invoke the regulatory taking doctrine to invalidate land use controls. Part of the problem was that the Court found it hard to differentiate between appropriate regulations and an unconstitutional regulatory taking. The standard set forth by Holmes in *Pennsylvania Coal Company v. Mahon*[32]—"[t]he general rule at least is, that while property may be regulated to a certain extent, if regulation goes too far it will be recognized as a taking"[33]—was not much help in deciding particular cases. Proceeding in an essentially ad hoc manner, the Court wrestled for decades to articulate a comprehensible formula to govern regulatory takings claims. A review of this line of cases is, for the most part, outside of this study. Eventually, in 1978 in *Penn Central Transportation Co. v. New York City*,[34] the Court declined to establish set rules and instead endorsed a multi-factor approach to assess whether a land use restriction amounted to a

[31]See generally Lawrence Berger, Public Use, Substantive Due Process and Takings—An Integration, 74 Neb. L. Rev. 843 (1995).

[32]260 U.S. 393 (1922).

[33]*Id.* at 415.

[34]438 U.S. 104 (1978).

taking of property. Of particular significance were the "economic impact of the regulation on the claimant," the extent to which the regulation unduly frustrated "distinct investment-backed expectations," and "the character of the governmental action."[35] Those indeterminate factors provide little guidance to individuals and in practice are heavily balanced in favor of the government and against compensation. Efforts to fashion per se takings tests to govern land use exactions afford only narrow protection to landowners and have added to the doctrinal confusion.[36]

To fully appreciate the problems with contemporary takings jurisprudence, one must take account of the diminished constitutional status of property in the wake of the political triumph of the New Deal. Protection of property rights was a central theme in American constitutionalism before 1937.[37] In the early twentieth century, however, the Progressive movement began urging a more active role for state and federal governments in regulating the economy, leading to an assault on the high constitutional standing of property. Legal theorists associated with the Progressives argued that constitutional doctrine overstated the importance of property and contractual rights.[38] This intellectual challenge to property rights came to fruition in the 1930s.

The Great Depression and the New Deal program of President Franklin D. Roosevelt constituted a watershed in constitutional history. The New Deal legislative program ran directly counter to traditional constitutional principles emphasizing a limited federal government and a high regard for the rights of property owners. The bitter struggle between the New Dealers and the Supreme Court is well known and cannot be treated in detail here. A profound change of direction by the Court, often called the constitutional revolution

---

[35]*Id.* at 124.

[36]Laura S. Underkuffler, On Property: An Essay, 100 Yale L.J. 127, 130 (1990) ("Various tests . . . have been used to determine whether a constitutionally cognizable property interest exists. The resulting incoherence is profound.").

[37]Ely, *supra* note 7, at 3–134.

[38]Morton J. Horwitz, The Transformation of American Law, 1870–1960, at 33–63, 145–67 (1992); Mossoff, *supra* note 25, at 372–76 (discussing attempts in early twentieth century to reformulate the concept of property). See generally Morton Keller, Regulating a New Economy: Public Policy and Economic Change in America, 1900–1933 (1990).

of 1937, significantly undermined judicial solicitude for private property.[39] A key feature of New Deal constitutionalism was a judicially fashioned dichotomy between the rights of property owners and other personal liberties. This novel approach was set forth in 1938 in the famous footnote four of *United States v. Carolene Products Co.*,[40] in which the Court signaled that it would give a higher degree of due process scrutiny to a preferred class of individual rights, such as free speech and religious freedom, than to property rights.[41] The rights of owners were relegated to a secondary status, entitled to just a low level of due process review. Economic regulations were presumed to be valid and, henceforth, received only cursory judicial review under a "rational basis" test highly deferential to government. It is hard to square this subordination of property rights with either the expressed views of the Framers or the language of the Constitution and Bill of Rights. But the reduced status of property rights well served the political agenda of the New Deal. Today the Court remains fixated on hierarchical rights with property on the bottom tier.

The wholesale abandonment of federal judicial review of economic legislation under due process had ramifications for the other property clauses of the Constitution. Both the once powerful Contracts Clause and the Takings Clause were virtually ignored for decades. The security of economic interests was left to the political arena, in marked contrast to other claims of individual rights. This sweeping change in the Court's philosophy cannot be explained solely by reference to political pressure emanating from the New Deal. Instead, it reflected a skeptical attitude toward private property, an attitude that permeated modern legal culture. Property, deemed an impediment to expanded government authority and redistributive

---

[39] William E. Leuchtenburg, The Supreme Court Reborn: The Constitutional Revolution in the Age of Roosevelt (1995); Pipes, *supra* note 9, at 241 ("Roosevelt and his advisors encouraged a fundamental and longlasting change in attitude toward private property: laws conceived and presented as emergency measures were subtly transformed into innovative principles which fundamentally altered first governmental and then judicial attitudes toward ownership.").

[40] 304 U.S. 144 (1938).

[41] *Id.* at 152–53, 153 n.4.

policies, was no longer viewed as worthy of serious judicial protection.[42] Modern constitutional law had moved far from the position espoused by the Framers, that property was a bulwark of individual liberty.

With this brief history as background to draw from we can now analyze the three important takings cases the Court decided during its 2004–2005 term. Those cases, in order, addressed the following broad questions:

(1) How does one determine when a government regulation effects a taking of property?

(2) Does the "public use" restraint in the Takings Clause permit government to transfer property from one private party to another, under its eminent domain power, in order to promote economic development?

(3) Are owners who claim that a state or local regulation amounts to a taking of property precluded from presenting their claim in federal court by a judicially crafted requirement that they must first seek compensation through state procedures?

III. The Narrowing of the Regulatory Takings Doctrine in *Lingle*

A. Background of the Litigation

The *Lingle* litigation grew out of the Supreme Court's continuing struggle to formulate coherent standards governing regulatory takings. In 1980 in *Agins v. City of Tiburon*,[43] a case involving a facial attack on a municipal zoning ordinance, the Court held, in an opinion by Justice Lewis Powell, that a land use law "effects a taking if the ordinance does not substantially advance legitimate state interests . . . or denies an owner economically viable use of his land."[44] This language was repeated in a number of subsequent takings decisions

---

[42]See Richard A. Epstein, Takings: Descent and Resurrection, 1987 Sup. Ct. Rev. 1 ("Today there are many who are openly hostile to private property, and who would gravitate toward the pole that sharply limits its role in social, economic, or political affairs. This skeptical attitude toward property has been reflected by the sharply reduced protection that private property has received in modern American constitutional law.").

[43]447 U.S. 255 (1980).

[44]*Id.* at 260.

by the Court.[45] Over time the "substantially advances" wording was treated as a separate regulatory takings test, and was invoked by lower federal courts to strike down rent control ordinances in several cases.[46]

At issue in *Lingle* was a 1997 Hawaii statute that set the maximum rent that oil companies could charge dealers who leased company-owned service stations.[47] The expressed legislative rationale behind this measure was a desire to reduce retail gasoline prices, yet it was agreed that Chevron was free to raise wholesale gasoline prices to offset any loss resulting from the rent reduction.[48] Chevron did not challenge the constitutionality of the statute on the ground that it could not earn a reasonable return on investment. Rather, its attack was predicated squarely on the contention that Hawaii's law did not "substantially advance" its purpose of reducing gasoline prices, and thus effected a regulatory taking.[49] Lengthy litigation ensued. The federal district court found as a fact that the act would not achieve the goal of lowering gasoline prices for consumers, and might indeed cause prices to increase. Concluding that the statute constituted an unconstitutional taking of property, the trial court granted summary judgment to Chevron.[50]

A divided panel of the Ninth Circuit Court of Appeals affirmed, reasoning that the act did not in fact substantially advance the state's objective.[51] It rejected Hawaii's argument that the rent control measure should be evaluated under the Due Process Clause of the Fourteenth Amendment rather than the Takings Clause.[52] Dissenting,

[45]See, e.g., Tahoe-Sierra Preservation Council, Inc. v. Tahoe Regional Planning Agency, 535 U.S. 302, 334 (2002); City of Monterey v. Del Monte Dunes at Monterey, Ltd., 526 U.S. 687, 704 (1999); United States v. Riverside Bayview Homes, Inc., 474 U.S. 121, 126 (1985).

[46]See, e.g., Richardson v. City and County of Honolulu, 124 F.3d 1150, 1165–66 (9th Cir. 1997), cert. denied, 525 U.S. 871, 525 U.S. 921, and 525 U.S. 1018 (1998); Cashman v. City of Cotati, 374 F.3d 887, 892–93, 896 (9th Cir. 2004).

[47]It is noteworthy that the statute prohibited companies from refusing to renew leases so long as local dealers continued to pay the below-market rents, yet it allowed those same dealers to sublet the stations and charge market rents. For an analysis of the takings implications, see Brief of Amicus Curiae Cato Institute in Support of Respondent, Lingle v. Chevron U.S.A., Inc., 125 S. Ct. 2074 (2005) (No. 04-163).

[48]Lingle v. Chevron U.S.A., Inc., 125 S. Ct. 2074, 2078 (2005).

[49]*Id.* at 2082.

[50]Chevron U.S.A., Inc. v. Cayetano, 198 F. Supp. 2d 1182, 1193 (D. Haw. 2002).

[51]Chevron U.S.A., Inc. v. Lingle, 363 F.3d 846 (9th Cir. 2004).

[52]*Id.* at 850.

Judge William A. Fletcher maintained that the "substantially advances" test was unsuitable for reviewing a rent control statute.[53]

Before analyzing the Supreme Court's decision, a few general observations are in order. The Hawaii statute would appear a curious measure to trigger an important takings decision. Commercial rent control is unusual in the United States. Moreover, the act is perhaps best viewed as an indirect price control law, since the object of the legislature was to reduce retail gasoline prices. Hence, cases dealing with land use and zoning issues may not be entirely pertinent in resolving the constitutionality of the statute. As the trial court accurately ascertained, the act is highly unlikely to produce lower gasoline prices. The international oil market and Hawaii's isolated geographic location are doubtless the principal factors in determining prices in the state, and neither can be regulated by the legislature. So there is a pronounced shadow boxing quality to the contested statute. Indeed, Judge Fletcher, who dissented from the Ninth Circuit's opinion, nonetheless agreed that the state's argument was weak and that the trial court "did not err" in holding that the "substantially advances" test was not satisfied.[54] Put simply, the district court's analysis of the probable economic impact of the act was correct.

On the other hand, it was also unclear that Chevron had suffered much economic loss as a consequence of the statute. Indeed, Chevron conceded that earnings on its investment in lessee-dealer stations in Hawaii satisfied the constitutional standard of a reasonable return. Thus, the case did not fit easily within the protective function of the Takings Clause.

B. Supreme Court's Opinion

In *Lingle* Justice Sandra Day O'Connor, writing for a unanimous Court, reversed the Ninth Circuit and jettisoned the "substantially advances" formula as inappropriate for determining whether a regulation amounts to a taking.[55] O'Connor began her analysis by insisting that a direct governmental appropriation or physical occupation

---

[53]*Id.* at 859–61 (Fletcher, J., dissenting).

[54]*Id.* at 859.

[55]125 S. Ct. 2074 (2005).

represented the typical example of a taking under the Fifth Amendment.[56] She then repeated the historically dubious proposition set forth in 1992 in *Lucas v. South Carolina Coastal Council*[57] that before *Pennsylvania Coal* it was thought that the Takings Clause did not reach regulations at all.[58] As discussed above, jurists and commentators had long discussed whether regulations might be so onerous as to have the practical effect of a physical taking. Turning to the currently recognized categories of regulatory takings, O'Connor emphasized that the inquiry in each situation

> aims to identify regulatory actions that are functionally equivalent to the classic taking in which government directly appropriates private property or ousts the owner from his domain. Accordingly, each of these tests focuses directly upon the severity of the burden that government imposes upon private property rights.[59]

Turning to the "substantially advances" formula of *Agins*, O'Connor declared that such an inquiry is not tailored to measure the magnitude of the burden placed on private property by a regulation or to shed light on which regulations are functionally comparable to government appropriation.[60] Stressing that questions about the efficacy of a regulation did not address the extent of the owner's burden, she observed: "The notion that such a regulation nevertheless 'takes' private property for public use merely by virtue of its ineffectiveness or foolishness is untenable."[61] The wisdom of legislation, in her view, does not determine whether a regulation has so burdened property as to constitute a taking.

O'Connor pointed out that Chevron was not seeking to obtain compensation but rather to bar enforcement of a statute it viewed as irrational. Such a claim, she asserted, properly arises under the Due Process Clause of the Fourteenth Amendment.[62] Expressing concern that the "substantially advances" test would require judicial

---

[56]*Id.* at 2081.

[57]505 U.S. 1003 (1992).

[58]125 S. Ct. at 2081.

[59]*Id.* at 2082.

[60]*Id.* at 2084.

[61]*Id.*

[62]*Id.* at 2085.

scrutiny of a wide array of state and federal regulations, she emphasized the highly deferential review of economic legislation under
the rubric of due process since 1937.[63]

In conclusion, O'Connor said that future regulatory takings claims
should proceed on the other established theories—permanent physical invasion, deprivation of all economically viable use, violation of
the *Penn Central* guidelines, or land use exactions that amount to a
per se physical taking because not closely tied to the impact of the
proposed development.[64] It is unclear if this is a closed list of possible
regulatory takings, but the Court seems disinclined at the moment
to expand the regulatory takings doctrine.

Justice Anthony Kennedy, in a brief concurring opinion, noted
that the decision "does not foreclose the possibility that a regulation
might be so arbitrary or irrational as to violate due process."[65] He
added that "failure of a regulation to accomplish a stated or obvious
objective would be relevant to that inquiry."[66] In 1998 in *Eastern
Enterprises v. Apfel* Justice Kennedy, again concurring, had found a
statute imposing a retroactive exaction of money on a former
employer to violate due process principles.[67] Perhaps alone among
the justices, he appears willing to meaningfully review economic
legislation under the due process norm.

C. Analysis

Lingle must be seen as a setback for those interested in reviving
constitutional protection for the rights of property owners.[68] To be
sure, the opinion makes some valid points: a silly regulation does
not necessarily run afoul of the Takings Clause; the "substantially
advances" formula was imprecise and could have profitably been
refined; a regulatory takings inquiry should focus in large part on
the burden inflicted on the owner of private property, although the
irrational character of a regulation might well speak to the degree

---

[63]*Id.*

[64]*Id.* at 2081–82.

[65]*Id.* at 2087.

[66]*Id.*

[67]Eastern Enterprises v. Apfel, 524 U.S. 498, 539–50 (1998) (Kennedy, J., concurring).

[68]For a defense of the "substantially advances" test, see R.S. Radford, Of Course
a Land Use Regulation That Fails to Substantially Advance Legitimate State Interests
Results in a Regulatory Taking, 15 Fordham Envtl. L.J. 353 (2004).

of burden. Still, *Lingle* is disappointing on several scores and perpetuates the second class status of property rights.

First, the suggestion that Chevron's claim should be heard under the Due Process Clause is almost certainly futile. The Supreme Court has not invalidated an economic regulation as violative of due process since 1937. The notion that Chevron could gain a real consideration of a due process claim is fanciful. Federal courts no longer provide even cursory property rights review under due process. Indeed, O'Connor repeats the prevailing rule of broad judicial deference to legislative judgments. She asserts rather than explains that courts, in her language, "are not well suited" to scrutinize economic regulations.[69] The dismissive treatment accorded economic rights is in striking contrast with substantive protection extended to a variety of non-economic rights under due process. But this raises a fundamental question: Why are courts somehow competent to enforce non-economic rights, which often turn upon value judgments, but not economic rights? Worse yet, the New Deal dichotomy between property and other individual rights, although phrased in terms of judicial deference, masks a high level of judicial activism. Courts can pick and choose among those rights they will enforce depending on their subjective assessment of which claims are more worthy.

O'Connor's opinion clearly demonstrates the New Deal constitutional hegemony at work. She even cited *Ferguson v. Skrupa*,[70] a vintage expression of New Deal constitutionalism. In *Ferguson* the Supreme Court readily sustained a special interest law and virtually abdicated any judicial review of economic legislation under due process. So long as *Ferguson* holds sway, property owners cannot expect much from the Due Process Clause. O'Connor's relegation of Chevron's claim to due process review would be more credible if she had moved to abandon the subordination of property rights under due process. One can only hope that Kennedy's view gains adherents.

Second, although the *Lingle* opinion reaffirmed several regulatory takings tests, it made plain that the principal standard for deciding whether a taking has occurred continues to be the multi-factor

---

[69]Lingle v. Chevron U.S.A., Inc., 125 S. Ct. 2074, 2085 (2005).
[70]372 U.S. 726 (1963).

approach adopted in *Penn Central*.[71] This is unfortunate, because *Penn Central* is fraught with problems. As O'Connor noted, the *Penn Central* factors have each "given rise to vexing subsidiary questions."[72] Not only are the various factors identified in *Penn Central* vague, but there is no indication as to how each factor is to be weighted or how they are to be related. The result is a confused test that can be manipulated to justify any outcome. It is melancholy to reflect how little progress has been made in clarifying takings jurisprudence over the past quarter century. *Lingle* marks no advance in this regard.

Despite these reservations, *Lingle* contains a slender silver lining that warrants mention. A unanimous Supreme Court has now upheld the validity of several takings tests: permanent physical invasion (*Loretto*); deprivation of all economically viable use (*Lucas*); and land use exactions not closely related to the impact of proposed development (*Nollan* and *Dolan*).[73] This is a modest gain since the decisions establishing each of those tests were rendered by a divided Court. It now appears that those once-debated tests are on a firm constitutional footing.

IV. *Kelo* and the Evisceration of the Fifth Amendment's "Public Use" Requirement

A. *Background of Litigation*

The decision in *Kelo v. City of New London*[74] is the Supreme Court's most recent attempt to explicate the "public use" limitation on the exercise of eminent domain. Eminent domain is one of the most intrusive powers of government because it compels individual owners, without their consent, to relinquish their property. The extent of this power has long been contested, raising the underlying question of when the perceived needs of the public should trump the property rights of individuals. In 1795 Justice William Paterson

---

[71]438 U.S. 104 (1978).

[72]Lingle, 125 S. Ct. at 2082.

[73]See Loretto v. Teleprompter Manhattan CATV Corp., 458 U.S. 419, 434–35 (1982); Lucas v. South Carolina Coastal Council, 505 U.S. 1003, 1016 (1992); Nollan v. California Coastal Commission, 483 U.S. 825, 837 (1987); Dolan v. City of Tigard, 512 U.S. 374, 391 (1994).

[74]125 S. Ct. 2655 (2005).

famously characterized eminent domain as the "despotic power."[75] Although he acknowledged that the power of acquiring private property was an essential aspect of government, Paterson rejected private redistributions of property. "It is," he declared, "difficult to form a case, in which the necessity of a state can be of such a nature, as to authorize or excuse the seizing of landed property belonging to one citizen, and giving it to another citizen."[76] Paterson's opinion is informative as to the understanding of eminent domain held by the founding generation. Consistent with their high regard for private property as the bedrock of individual liberties, the Framers of the Bill of Rights restricted the exercise of eminent domain by imposing the "public use" and "just compensation" constraints in the Fifth Amendment. It seems a reasonable proposition, therefore, that the Public Use Clause was expected to have some meaning.

The Supreme Court had little occasion to address the "public use" requirement until the late nineteenth century. Nonetheless, prominent commentators as well as the Supreme Court insisted that it was illegitimate for government to take property from one private owner for the benefit of another. In 1829 in *Wilkinson v. Leland*,[77] for example, Justice Story observed: "We know of no case, in which a legislative act to transfer the property of A. to B. without his consent, has ever been held a constitutional exercise of legislative power in any state in the union."[78] Similarly, in his landmark 1868 treatise, the distinguished jurist Thomas M. Cooley asserted:

> The *public use* implies a possession, occupation, and enjoyment of the land by the public, or public agencies; and there could be no protection whatever to private property, if the right of government to seize and appropriate it could exist for any other use.[79]

In a later edition of the treatise, Cooley rejected specifically the notion that eminent domain could be utilized to transfer property

[75]Vanhorne's Lessee v. Dorrance, 2 U.S. (2 Dall.) 304, 311 (C.C. Pa. 1795).

[76]*Id.* See also Calder v. Bull, 3 U.S. (3 Dall.) 386, 388 (1798) (Chase, J.) (declaring that legislature could not legitimately enact "a law that takes property from A. and gives it to B.").

[77]27 U.S. (2 Pet.) 627 (1829).

[78]*Id.* at 658.

[79]Thomas M. Cooley, A Treatise on the Constitutional Limitations Which Rest Upon the Legislative Power of the States of the American Union 531 (1868).

to another private party "on vague grounds of public benefit to spring from the more profitable use to which the latter may devote it."[80] As early as 1872 the Supreme Court asserted that "[t]he right of eminent domain nowhere justifies taking property for a private use."[81]

Notwithstanding these developments, however, in the late nineteenth century both state and federal courts gradually adopted a broader reading of governmental authority to acquire private property. The constitutional norm of "public use" was increasingly equated with the more expansive concept of "public benefit" or "interest." Moreover, judicial review of legislative decisions about the need to exercise eminent domain grew slack. In the face of such trends the significance of the "public use" requirement steadily eroded.[82] The decline of the "public use" limitation was hastened by the larger jurisprudential shift associated with the political triumph of the New Deal. As discussed above, the new constitutional orthodoxy marginalized economic rights and strengthened governmental authority over private property. A shriveled Public Use Clause, therefore, was simply one aspect of the diminished constitutional rights of property owners generally. In 1949 one commentator declared that the doctrine of "public use" was virtually dead.[83]

Subsequent decisions by the Supreme Court validated that prediction. In 1954 in *Berman v. Parker*[84] the Court sustained the taking of land from one owner for transfer to a private development agency as part of a comprehensive urban renewal plan. It insisted that "[t]he role of the judiciary in determining whether [eminent domain] power is being exercised for a public purpose is an extremely narrow

[80]Thomas M. Cooley, A Treatise on the Constitutional Limitations Which Rest Upon the Legislative Power of the States of the American Union 663 (4th ed. 1878). For a discussion of Cooley's views about the appropriate use of eminent domain, see James W. Ely Jr., Thomas Cooley, "Public Use," and New Directions in Takings Jurisprudence, 2004 Mich. St. L. Rev. 845, 846–50.

[81]Olcott v. The Supervisors, 83 U.S. (15 Wall.) 678, 694 (1872).

[82]Lawrence Berger, The Public Use Requirement in Eminent Domain, 57 Or. L. Rev. 203, 204–25 (1978).

[83]Comment, The Public Use Limitation on Eminent Domain: An Advance Requiem, 58 Yale L.J. 599 (1949).

[84]348 U.S. 26 (1954).

one."[85] The opinion also likened the eminent domain power to the very different police power, the basic power of government to secure rights.[86] That mischief has confused courts and plagued analysis of the "public use" limitation ever since. The Court went a step further in 1984 in *Hawaii Housing Authority v. Midkiff*,[87] upholding a land redistribution scheme that entailed the transfer of fee simple title from a landowner to tenants to overcome the perceived problem of concentrated land ownership. Highly deferential to legislative determination of "public use," the Court indicated that it would uphold any exercise of eminent domain "rationally related to a conceivable public purpose."[88]

State courts by and large followed suit. Although some state judges were more inclined to carefully review the exercise of eminent domain, most followed the Supreme Court's deferential path. Indeed, the "public use" requirement reached something of a nadir with the Michigan Supreme Court's decision in 1981 in *Poletown Neighborhood Council v. City of Detroit*.[89] There the Michigan court ruled that the condemnation and subsequent transfer of private homes and businesses to the General Motors corporation for construction of a new plant satisfied the "public use" norm. The court reasoned that the private economic development the company promised would serve a public purpose by providing jobs and enhancing tax revenue in the Detroit community.[90] In effect, the *Berman, Midkiff,* and *Poletown* decisions gutted the "public use" requirement and seemingly justified an almost unlimited power to transfer property from one private party to another. *Poletown*, in particular, was highly influential. It opened the door to taking property for economic development by private enterprise and was widely followed nationwide.[91]

---

[85]*Id*. at 32.

[86]*Id*. ("We deal, in other words, with what traditionally has been known as the police power.").

[87]467 U.S. 229 (1984).

[88]*Id*. at 241.

[89]304 N.W.2d 455 (Mich. 1981).

[90]*Id*. at 458–59.

[91]Adam Mossoff, The Death of Poletown: The Future of Eminent Domain and Urban Development After County of Wayne v. Hathcock, 2004 Mich. St. L. Rev. 837, 841 (pointing out that "many other states" followed *Poletown* and found that private economic development constituted "public use").

Such aggressive exercise of eminent domain for development purposes fed the perception that governmental power was being employed to take property from the politically weak for predominantly private advantage. Critics charged that powerful interest groups controlled the eminent domain process for their own gain. Moreover, the public benefits that motivated the condemnations were in fact rarely delivered, they said.[92] Then, in a surprising development, the Michigan Supreme Court overruled *Poletown* in 2004 in *County of Wayne v. Hathcock*, holding that economic development was not a "public use" justifying acquisition of private property.[93] That dramatic reversal gained national attention, highlighting the controversy over the use of eminent domain to transfer property to private parties for commercial development.

When the U.S. Supreme Court agreed to hear the *Kelo* case shortly after *Hathcock* came down, many observers expressed hope that the stage was set at last for a new and more restrictive reading of "public use." Unfortunately, that hope was short lived. At issue in *Kelo* was a development plan fashioned to revitalize economically distressed areas of New London, Connecticut. The New London Development Corporation (NLDC), a private organization, was authorized by the city council to purchase or acquire by eminent domain real estate within a ninety-acre area. Under the plan the acquired space was to be used for the construction of a hotel, new residences, stores, and recreational facilities. It was announced that some of the parcels would be leased to private developers who would utilize the land in accordance with the development plan. The rationale behind this scheme was the promise of new jobs and increased tax revenue.[94] When the *Kelo* petitioners declined to sell their property, NLDC instituted eminent domain proceedings. The petitioners, residential owners, sought then to enjoin the proposed takings. There was no

---

[92]See Ilya Somin, Overcoming Poletown: County of Wayne v. Hathcock, Economic Development Takings, and the Future of Public Use, 2004 Mich. St. L. Rev. 1005, 1011–16 (noting that the economic benefits cited to justify the *Poletown* condemnation never materialized and questioning the evidence presented to support economic development takings).

[93]684 N.W.2d 765, 782 (Mich. 2004).

[94]See, e.g., Kelo v. City of New London, 125 S. Ct. 2655, 2658–60 (2005) (summarizing facts).

indication that any of the parcels was blighted. They were condemned only because they were located within the development
area. The petitioners alleged that the proposed taking of their property would violate the "public use" limitation in the Fifth Amendment. By a vote of four to three, the Supreme Court of Connecticut
rejected this contention, holding that economic development was a
valid "public use" under both federal and state constitutions.[95]

B. Supreme Court's Opinion

A sharply divided U.S. Supreme Court affirmed this determination, sustaining the exercise of eminent domain for purposes of
economic development. Writing for the majority, Justice John Paul
Stevens emphasized deference to legislative judgments regarding
the exercise of eminent domain.[96] He relied heavily on *Berman* and
Midkiff to observe that "our public use jurisprudence has wisely
eschewed rigid formulas and intrusive scrutiny in favor of affording
legislatures broad latitude in determining what public needs justify
the use of the takings power."[97] Declining to impose a rule that
courts should adopt a heightened standard in reviewing economic
development takings, he expressed concern that requiring a "reasonable certainty" that the public would actually benefit from development schemes would put courts in the position of second-guessing
the desirability of economic legislation.[98] Substantively, Stevens
brushed aside a literal interpretation of the "public use" requirement
as meaning use by the general public, maintaining instead that promoting economic development was a traditional function of government.[99] Nor was Stevens impressed with the argument that economic
development takings opened the door to conferring benefits on private parties,[100] reasoning that the public interest could sometimes
be best served by private enterprise.[101]

---

[95]Kelo v. City of New London, 843 A.2d 500, 528 (Conn. 2004).
[96]125 S. Ct. 2655, 2663–64 (2005).
[97]*Id*. at 2664.
[98]*Id*. at 2667–68.
[99]*Id*. at 2665.
[100]*Id*. at 2666.
[101]*Id*.

After quoting the famous language of Justice Samuel Chase in the 1798 case of *Calder v. Bull*[102] that a law cannot take property from A and give it to B, Stevens evidently felt a need to give lip service to that principle. He agreed that "a one-to-one transfer of property, executed outside the confines of an integrated development plan," would raise a suspicion that eminent domain was being used for a private purpose.[103] Stevens also acknowledged that "the necessity and wisdom of using eminent domain to promote economic development are certainly matters of legitimate public debate."[104] And he stressed that states were free to adopt stricter "public use" standards by statute or by interpretations of state constitutional law.[105]

Justice Kennedy joined the majority but added a murky concurring opinion. He insisted that courts, even under a deferential standard of review, should invalidate "a taking, that by a clear showing, is intended to favor a particular party, with only incidental or pretextual public benefits."[106] It remains unclear, however, how a court is to ascertain whether a particular taking is only pretextual without the very sort of careful inquiry into public purpose that the majority opinion forecloses. Kennedy also whimsically asserted that *Berman* and *Midkiff* imposed some meaningful limit on governmental power to condemn property.[107] At best, Kennedy's concurrence suggests some narrow and ill-defined role for the federal courts in reviewing "public use" in particular situations.

Speaking for the four dissenters, Justice O'Connor authored a blistering dissent.[108] "Under the banner of economic development," she charged, "all private property is now vulnerable to being taken and being transferred to another private owner."[109] She maintained that if incidental public benefits arising from economic development constituted "public use," then the Court had effectively deleted "the words 'for public use' from the Takings Clause of the Fifth

---

[102]3 U.S. (3 Dall.) 386, 388 (1798), quoted in Kelo, 125 S. Ct. at 2661 n.5.
[103]Kelo, 125 S. Ct. at 2667.
[104]*Id.* at 2668.
[105]*Id.*
[106]*Id.* at 2669 (Kennedy, J., concurring).
[107]*Id.* at 2670.
[108]*Id.* at 2671–77 (O'Connor, J., dissenting).
[109]*Id.* at 2671.

Amendment."[110] O'Connor pointed out that the Fifth Amendment placed two distinct limits on the exercise of eminent domain—that any taking must be for a "public use," and that the owner must be paid "just compensation."[111] Those requirements, she explained, "ensure stable property ownership by providing safeguards against excessive, unpredictable, or unfair use of the government's eminent domain power—particularly against those owners who, for whatever reasons, may be unable to protect themselves in the political process against the majority's will."[112] O'Connor identified three categories of takings that satisfied the "public use" requirement: transfers to public ownership, such as for roads or military bases; transfers to private parties, such as common carriers, who make the property available to the public; and transfers in unusual circumstances to private use where "the extraordinary, precondemnation use of the targeted property inflicted affirmative harm on society," such as for the elimination of blight or land oligopoly.[113] She expressed concern that the majority opinion "significantly expands the meaning of public use," and insisted that, realistically, this new understanding does not impose any restraint on the eminent domain power.[114]

Several additional points in O'Connor's dissent warrant comment. First, she sharply criticized the "errant language" in *Berman* that equated "public use" with the scope of the police power.[115] Second, she highlighted the far-reaching nature of eminent domain as conceived by the majority. "The specter of condemnation," she declared, "hangs over all property. Nothing is to prevent the State from replacing any Motel 6 with a Ritz-Carlton, any home with a shopping mall, or any farm with a factory."[116] Third, she noted the perverse implications of enlarged eminent domain power. "The beneficiaries," she aptly pointed out, "are likely to be those citizens with

[110]*Id.*

[111]*Id.* at 2672.

[112]*Id.*

[113]*Id.* at 2673–75.

[114]*Id.* at 2675.

[115]*Id.*

[116]*Id.* at 2676.

disproportionate influence and power in the political process, including large corporations and development firms."[117]

Justice Clarence Thomas joined the O'Connor dissent, but also wrote a separate opinion in which he raised deeper concerns about the Court's "public use" jurisprudence.[118] He maintained that the Court over the years had gone seriously astray in its construction of "public use," thus reducing the restraint to "a virtual nullity, without the slightest nod to its original meaning."[119] Considering at length the original understanding of the phrase "public use" and a series of early judicial opinions, Thomas urged the Court to return "to the original meaning of the Public Use Clause: that the government may take property only if it actually uses or gives the public a legal right to use the property."[120] Echoing O'Connor, he predicted that the losses and indignities inflicted by economic development takings "will fall disproportionately on poor communities."[121]

C. Analysis

Since the Public Use Clause of the Fifth Amendment had been largely drained of vitality before the *Kelo* decision, *Kelo* could be seen simply as administering the last rites. Nonetheless, the decision is profoundly disquieting because of its flawed reasoning and dismissive attitude toward the constitutional rights of property owners. It represents a lost opportunity to put the Court back in the business of policing government's eminent domain power.

The majority opinion by Justice Stevens presented an inadequate historical analysis of the Public Use Clause. Stevens gave no attention to the views of the Framers or the observations of leading commentators. Likewise, he did not probe the wording or purpose of the clause. Nor did he consider the costs imposed by condemnation, an issue that might call into question whether the taking served any public use. Rather, he contented himself with a discussion of Supreme Court decisions that purported to adopt a broad reading of "public use." He gave a cursory glance at some Court opinions from the late nineteenth and early twentieth centuries, focusing on

---

[117]*Id*. at 2677.

[118]*Id*. at 2677–87 (Thomas, J., dissenting).

[119]*Id*. at 2678.

[120]*Id*. at 2686.

[121]*Id*. at 2686–87.

language plucked from context rather than looking at the facts of those cases.[122] Not remotely do the fact patterns of those early cases match the circumstances of *Kelo*.[123] Suffice it to say that the Court of that era never endorsed the view that legislative determinations of "public use" were entitled to supine deference, nor did that Court ever approve such a sweeping use of eminent domain as is presented in *Kelo*.[124] In fact, Stevens's opinion rests almost entirely on *Berman* and *Midkiff*. Without considering whether those decisions were faithful to the constitutional text, he simply applied their holdings rather mechanically to economic development projects.

Nor did Stevens come to grips with the longstanding rule that questions about "public use" are for the judiciary to decide.[125] "It is well established," the Court declared in 1930, "that . . . the question [of] what is a public use is a judicial one."[126] The public use requirement is a constitutional standard that is an integral part of the Bill of Rights. It should not be erased in the guise of deference to legislative determinations.

Indeed, the whole question of judicial deference regarding "public use" warrants a fresh look. The Supreme Court does not defer to legislative decisions regarding criminal procedures or the enjoyment of free speech. In fact, among all the guarantees of the Bill of Rights, only the public use limitation is singled out for heavy deference to legislatures. It is highly unlikely that the Framers intended such an anomalous result.

---

[122]*Id.* at 2662–63.

[123] For example, both *Fallbrook Irrigation District v. Bradley*, 164 U.S. 112 (1896), and *Clark v. Nash*, 198 U.S. 361 (1905), cited by Stevens, upheld statutes authorizing condemnation for constructing public irrigation ditches across neighboring land. See, e.g., Fallbrook, 164 U.S. at 159; Clark, 198 U.S. at 367–68. Neither involved the acquisition of large tracts of land or the wholesale displacement of residential owners and small businesses.

[124]See generally Ely, *supra* note 21, at 127–29 ("[J]udicial deference, however strong, was not the same as abdication. The Fuller Court did assess the public use rationale in eminent domain cases . . .").

[125]Fallbrook, 164 U.S. at 159 (insisting that the determination of what is a public use is a judicial question that the justices "must decide . . . in accordance with our views of constitutional law"); *id.* at 159–60 (observing that state legislative declarations are not conclusive).

[126]Cincinnati v. Vester, 281 U.S. 439, 446 (1930). The Court added: "[T]he question remains a judicial one which this Court must decide in performing its duty of enforcing the provisions of the Federal Constitution." *Id.* at 446.

It is instructive to compare the Supreme Court's refusal to supervise the Public Use Clause with its handling of the other constitutional check on eminent domain, the just compensation requirement. Federal courts have long insisted that the determination of just compensation for a taking of property is a judicial, not a legislative, responsibility.[127] Justice David J. Brewer strongly articulated this position in the leading case of *Monongahela Navigation Company v. United States*:

> It does not rest with the public, taking the property, through Congress or the legislature, its representative, to say what compensation shall be paid, or even what shall be the rule of compensation. The Constitution has declared that just compensation shall be paid, and the ascertainment of that is a judicial inquiry.[128]

In that statement there is no deference to legislators, who have every incentive to minimize the obligation to pay. The need for judicial oversight seems obvious in order to uphold the constitutional norm of just compensation.

Why then does the Court review the just compensation but not the public use restraint on eminent domain? Both are constitutional standards designed to limit government's power. Why is almost insurmountable deference to legislators appropriate regarding the decision to take property but not regarding the necessary compensation? Stevens never addresses those questions.

Surely the same level of judicial review is merited for both limits. Otherwise all property is held at the pleasure of the legislature, a result at odds with the Framers' design. To be sure, there is no precise test to decide whether a particular exercise of eminent domain is for a public use.[129] But that is no excuse for judicial abdication of the kind we see in *Kelo*. One should bear in mind that there is no

---

[127]Vanhorne's Lessee v. Dorrance, 2 U.S. (2 Dall.) 304, 312 (C.C. Pa. 1795) (declaring that the legislature "cannot constitutionally determine upon the amount of the compensation, or value of the land").

[128]148 U.S. 312, 327 (1893).

[129]But see the distinctions drawn in the Cato Institute amicus brief in *Kelo*, articulating four rationales for public use condemnations—public projects, network and common carrier undertakings, blight reduction, and economic development—and analyzing the merits of each. Brief of Amicus Curiae Cato Institute in Support of Petitioners, Kelo v. City of New London, 125 S. Ct. 2655 (2005) (No. 04-108).

ready formula for just compensation, either, but that does not prevent judges from tackling the issue.[130] Surely courts could devise working rules to effectuate the public use norm, much as they have done with respect to just compensation. Indeed, the dissenting opinions by O'Connor and Thomas contain useful guidelines to frame further debate along these lines.

The unhappy outcome in *Kelo*, the forced displacement of residents from their homes, also underscores the fact that a principled respect for individual property rights often serves to safeguard the weak and vulnerable. Reflecting the lingering influence of the Progressive movement and the New Deal, many scholars are prone to disparage judicial solicitude for economic rights as favoritism to the wealthy and business interests. The *Kelo* decision puts the lie to that canard. By eviscerating the public use limitation the Court majority has opened the door for powerful corporations and developers, in league with local government, to condemn private property for any vague public purpose.[131] *Kelo* sustained a redistributive scheme that operated, as O'Connor and Thomas perceived, in favor of the developers at the expense of politically weak individual homeowners. This is a classic example, as the Framers saw, of how constitutional protection of property serves as a barrier against arbitrary and excessive government.

Where do we go from here? Short of a change of heart by the Court majority, homeowners must look to Congress or the states for relief. The *Kelo* decision aroused a firestorm of criticism crossing partisan lines. Stevens's majority opinion has triggered intense public debate, generating a national dialogue on eminent domain. In an extraordinary move, the House of Representatives, by a vote of 365 to 33, adopted a resolution expressing its "grave disapproval" of the majority opinion in *Kelo* and asserting that the decision "effectively

---

[130]See Glynn S. Lunney Jr., Compensation for Takings: How Much Is Just?, 42 Cath. U.L. Rev. 721 (1993) (discussing compensation methodologies and rationales for requiring compensation).

[131]See, e.g., Donald J. Kochan, "Public Use" and the Independent Judiciary: Condemnation in an Interest-Group Perspective, 3 Tex. Rev. L. & Pol. 49, 115 (1998); Joseph J. Lazzarotti, Public Use or Public Abuse, 68 UMKC L. Rev. 49, 51 (1999) (expressing concern that without meaningful judicial review "big government and powerful corporations can condemn private property for any public use or purpose they can rationalize, provided just compensation is paid").

negate[s] the public use requirement of the takings clause."[132] The House has also passed a bill that prevents the expenditure of federal funds in support of projects that utilize eminent domain for economic development purposes,[133] and a similar bill has been introduced in the Senate. In Connecticut the legislature asked local governments to observe an unofficial moratorium on current or planned eminent domain proceedings.[134] Connecticut legislators are considering a special session to take up the broad issue, while Governor M. Jodi Rell criticized *Kelo*, comparing the outcry over economic development condemnations to the Boston Tea Party and endorsing the call for a moratorium.[135] Even former President Bill Clinton expressed his disagreement with the ruling.[136] It is rare that a Supreme Court decision dealing with property rights generates such widespread attention and condemnation. Some states already bar economic development condemnations.[137] No doubt there will be additional moves in state legislatures to curb economic development condemnations. But those efforts, however welcome, are no substitute for a Supreme Court that enforces the Public Use Clause of the Fifth Amendment.

[132]H.R. 340, 109th Cong., 1st Sess. (2005).

[133]Joi Preciphs, Eminent-Domain Ruling Knits Rivals, Wall Street J., July 8, 2005, at 4A.

[134]New London agency agrees to moratorium on eminent domain, Hartford Courant (Online), July 26, 2005, available at http://www.courant.com/news/local/statewire/hc-26014446.apds.m0724.be-ct—sizjul26,0,6496088.story (visited August 11, 2005).

[135]Statement of Governor Rell on Call for Legislative Hearing on Eminent Domain (July 11, 2005), available at http://www.ct.gov/governorrell/cwp/view.asp?A=1761&Q=296184 (visited August 11, 2005).

[136]Josh Gerstein, Clinton: Court Was "Wrong" on Eminent Domain, New York Sun, July 14, 2005, available at http://www.nysun.com/pf.php?id=16974 (visited August 14, 2005).

[137]See, e.g., County of Wayne v. Hathcock, 684 N.W.2d 765 (Mich. 2004). Two other state courts have not categorically rejected the use of eminent domain for economic development purposes but have ruled, on the facts presented, that taking property for transfer to a private business did not constitute a valid public use under state constitutions. Southwestern Illinois Development Authority v. National City Environmental, LLC, 768 N.E.2d 1, 9–11 (Ill. 2002), cert. denied, 537 U.S. 880 (2002); Bailey v. Myers, 76 P.3d 898, 903–04 (Ariz. Ct. App. 2003).

V. *San Remo Hotel* and the Heightened Bar to Regulatory Takings Claims in Federal Court

A. Background of Litigation

In *San Remo Hotel* the Supreme Court revisited the question of bringing regulatory takings cases in the federal courts.[138] To put this decision in perspective, it is necessary to consider the ripeness doctrine annunciated in 1985 in *Williamson County Regional Planning Commission v. Hamilton Bank*.[139] In that case the Court prevented the claimant from bringing a regulatory taking action in federal court on the ground that the claim was not ripe. The Court held that a claimant must satisfy a two prong ripeness test before instituting a federal court challenge. He must obtain a "final decision" from the appropriate local government agencies on his land use application.[140] He must have sought and been denied compensation in state court.[141] Over the years, government officials bent on denying owners their rights to use their property have become skilled at delay—believing, often rightly, that the owner will exhaust his time and financial resources before any "final decision" is issued. As a practical matter, the *Williamson County* ripeness test virtually closes the door on claimants trying to use the federal courts to assert a takings claim. More troublesome still, the federal courts are precluded by the federal full faith and credit statute, which encompasses the doctrine of res judicata, from relitigating issues that have been resolved in state court actions.[142] Thus, regulatory takings claimants are typically left with no access to a federal forum.[143]

---

[138]125 S. Ct. 2491 (2005).

[139]473 U.S. 172 (1985).

[140]*Id.* at 190–94.

[141]*Id.* at 194–95.

[142]28 U.S.C. § 1738 (providing that "judicial proceedings . . . shall have the same full faith and credit in every court within the United States and its Territories and Possessions as they have by law or usage in the courts of such State . . .").

[143]The *Williamson County* ripeness requirements have long been the subject of criticism. See, e.g., Thomas E. Roberts, Ripeness and Forum Selection in Fifth Amendment Takings Litigation, 11 J. Land Use & Envtl. L. 37 (1995); Stephen E. Abraham, Williamson County Fifteen Years Later: When is a Takings Claim (Ever) Ripe?, 36 Real Prop. Prob. & Tr. J. 101, 104 (2001) ("*Williamson County* is regarded as posing formidable hurdles because of its two-part ripeness requirement, finality and compensation, that ultimately may block takings claims."); Max Kidalov & Richard Seamon, The Missing Pieces of the Debate Over Federal Property Rights Litigation, 27 Hastings Const.

In the *San Remo Hotel* case, a San Francisco city commission granted the petitioners, who owned the San Remo Hotel, a permit to operate as a tourist hotel on condition that they pay a $567,000 "conversion fee" for converting residential rooms to tourist rooms.[144] Lengthy administrative and judicial appeals ensued in both state and federal courts, the claimant alleging a regulatory taking. A federal court ruled that key portions of the case were not ripe under *Williamson County*.[145] Eventually the Supreme Court of California rejected the takings claim and upheld the conversion fee.[146] Having satisfied the *Williamson County* ripeness test, the petitioners now found their return to federal district court barred by the full faith and credit statute. Because the petitioners' federal claims were the same as those already adjudicated in the California courts, they were precluded from relitigating the issue in federal court. The Ninth Circuit Court of Appeals affirmed,[147] and the U.S. Supreme Court agreed to decide the narrow question of whether it should fashion an exception to the full faith and credit statute for claims arising under the Takings Clause of the Fifth Amendment.

B. Supreme Court's Opinion

The petitioners argued, in essence, that federal courts should not apply preclusion rules where a case is forced into state court in order to satisfy the ripeness test of *Williamson County*. The Court unanimously rejected this contention in two opinions.

Justice Stevens, speaking for five members of the Court, declined to create an exception to the full faith and credit statute absent an expression of congressional intent. Stressing the importance of finality and comity, Stevens was unimpressed with the notion that claimants necessarily "have a right to vindicate their federal claims in a federal forum."[148] He admitted that, in practice, most takings

L.Q. 1, 5 (1999) ("The U.S. Supreme Court has developed rules that make it almost impossible for federal courts to remedy violations of the Just Compensation Clause.").

[144]San Remo Hotel v. City & County of San Francisco, 125 S. Ct. 2491, 2495–96 (2005).

[145]San Remo Hotel v. City & County of San Francisco, 145 F.3d 1095, 1102 (9th Cir. 1998) (holding as-applied takings claim to be unripe and dismissing facial takings challenge based on *Pullman* abstention doctrine).

[146]San Remo Hotel v. City & County of San Francisco, 41 P.3d 87, 106–11 (Cal. 2002).

[147]San Remo Hotel v. City & County of San Francisco, 364 F.3d 1088, 1098–99 (9th Cir. 2004).

[148]125 S. Ct. at 2504.

claimants will be compelled to litigate their federal claims in state court.[149] Finding "scant precedent" for takings claims in the federal district courts, Stevens opined that "state courts undoubtedly have more experience than federal courts do in resolving the complex factual, technical and legal questions related to zoning and land use regulations."[150]

Chief Justice William Rehnquist, writing for four members of the Court, agreed in a concurring opinion that the petitioners were precluded by the full faith and credit statute from litigating their claim in federal court.[151] However, he urged the Court to revisit the second prong of the *Williamson County* ripeness test—that a takings claimant must seek compensation in state court before instituting a federal court action. Although Rehnquist had joined the opinion in *Williamson County*, further reflection caused him to question the justification for the state-litigation requirement. He pointedly observed that claimants challenging land use regulations on First Amendment grounds could proceed directly to federal court. He was puzzled "why federal takings claims in particular should be singled out to be confined to state court, in the absence of any asserted justification or congressional directive."[152] Those underlying issues were not before the Court because of the limited grant of certiorari.

C. Analysis

The majority opinion is a further manifestation of the Court majority's disdain for the rights of property owners. As a consequence of *San Remo Hotel*, takings claimants will have almost no opportunity to have their case even heard in a federal court. By shutting the door to a federal forum, the Supreme Court has significantly handicapped takings plaintiffs. So once again property rights are downgraded and given second-class treatment. The issue in *San Remo Hotel* was technical, but the outcome speaks volumes about the Court's lack of interest in enforcing property rights. No other important right is dealt with in such a shabby manner. One might have thought that

---

[149]*Id.* at 2506.

[150]*Id.* at 2506–07.

[151]*Id.* at 2507–10 (Rehnquist, C.J., concurring).

[152]*Id.* at 2509.

all the provisions of the Bill of Rights were entitled to protection in the federal courts. Unfortunately, that will not be the case unless the Court, at some future point, decides to pursue Rehnquist's invitation and modifies the *Williamson County* ripeness test.

VI. Conclusion

It remains to consider why the Supreme Court in *Lingle, Kelo,* and *San Remo Hotel* placed such a crabbed interpretation on the Takings Clause and the rights of takings claimants. As discussed above, the Court has abandoned the vision of the Framers, who believed that robust protection of the rights of property owners affirmed liberty by diffusing power and shielding individuals from governmental control. Indeed, the Court generally ignores the express property clauses in the Constitution and Bill of Rights while discovering a variety of novel non-economic rights. The blunt fact is that an abiding dislike of property rights, derived from New Deal constitutionalism, continues to hold intellectual sway. It is revealing, for example, that the majority opinions in *Lingle, Kelo,* and *San Remo Hotel* rest almost entirely on post-1937 decisions. The long history of judicial solicitude for the rights of property owners is simply discarded as unwanted baggage from our constitutional past, much like out-of-favor politicians were removed from official photographs in the Soviet Union. Unless the Supreme Court breaks free of statist thinking about property, there is little prospect that the property rights of individuals will be restored.

In 1994 Chief Justice Rehnquist proclaimed: "We see no reason why the Takings Clause of the Fifth Amendment, as much a part of the Bill of Rights as the First Amendment or the Fourth Amendment, should be relegated to the status of a poor relation."[153] The promise implicit in this comment—that the Takings Clause should receive the same level of judicial protection as other provisions of the Bill of Rights—has never been realized in the post–New Deal era and now seems further away than ever. It is a sad day for individual liberty and American constitutionalism.

---

[153]Dolan v. City of Tigard, 512 U.S. 374, 392 (1994).

Gonzales v. Raich: Wickard v. Filburn Displaced

*Douglas W. Kmiec**

I. Introduction

Over the last decade, the Supreme Court gave the impression that Congress' power "[t]o regulate Commerce . . . among the several States"[1] was not unlimited. In its 1995 *Lopez*[2] and 2000 *Morrison*[3] decisions, the Court made an attempt to re-establish a link between the Constitution and modern "constitutional law." The Court said "to here, but no further." In *Lopez*, for example, Chief Justice William Rehnquist recurred to James Madison's observation in *Federalist No. 45* that "the powers delegated by the proposed Constitution to the federal government are few and defined. Those which remain in the State governments are numerous and indefinite."[4] The powers remaining in the state governments are still indefinite, but after *Gonzales v. Raich*[5] they are also less numerous.

Raich involved a challenge not to the federal Controlled Substances Act (CSA)[6] itself but to the application of the Act to those Californians who by state law[7] are authorized to use marijuana under a doctor's care for relief of symptoms that do not respond to conventional medicines.[8] Even though the marijuana provided was grown entirely

---

*Caruso Family Chair and Professor of Law, Pepperdine University

[1] U.S. Const. art. I, § 8, cl. 3.

[2] United States v. Lopez, 514 U.S. 549 (1995).

[3] United States v. Morrison, 529 U.S. 598 (2000).

[4] Lopez, 514 U.S. at 552 (quoting The Federalist No. 45, at 292–93 (James Madison) (Clinton Rossiter ed., 1961)).

[5] Gonzales v. Raich, 125 S. Ct. 2195 (2005).

[6] Controlled Substances Act, 21 U.S.C. § 801 et seq. (hereinafter "CSA").

[7] The California law is not displaced or preempted by the decision in *Raich*, but the state law does not preclude federal prosecution.

[8] Raich, 125 S. Ct. at 2219.

71

within California and was provided to patients without being bought, sold, or bartered, six members of the Court upheld the application of the CSA to such patients as a valid exercise of Congress' regulatory power over interstate commerce. Writing for the Court's majority, Justice John Paul Stevens relied heavily on *Wickard v. Filburn*,[9] a 1942 decision, which, by the Court's own characterization, pressed the outer limits of federal power.[10] In *Raich*, the Court extended federal power even beyond those limits by holding that Congress could prevent a woman with a brain tumor from using a homegrown substance to survive.[11]

Harsh? Yes. Unconstitutional? Apparently not to six members of the Court. Congress itself made no findings about the effect of medicinal marijuana use on federal efforts to control the recreational use of marijuana. Unnecessary, said Justice Stevens. The Court need only conclude that Congress could have so concluded, even if it didn't and even if no actual proof was offered that it could. It was enough to suppose that Congress could have believed that allowing individual medical uses of marijuana would complicate enforcement of the CSA.[12] As explained more fully below, the majority claimed that it was not overruling *Lopez* and *Morrison*.[13] Those cases, said the Court, involved facial challenges to freestanding statutes—statutes that reached beyond regulating interstate commerce in all their applications—whereas here the CSA was conceded to be a *facially* valid comprehensive law prohibiting the purchase and sale of certain covered drugs; the CSA was only alleged to have been unconstitutionally *applied*. For the Court majority, it was beside the point that the litigation centered on a discrete class of medicinal use that had nothing to do with interstate commerce.[14]

---

[9]Wickard v. Filburn, 317 U.S. 111 (1942) (upholding a federal law that limited the amount of wheat a farmer could grow on his own farm for his own family's consumption on the theory that any wheat so self-reliantly produced reduced the need for wheat in the commercial market and by the law of supply and demand also reduced the market price for wheat).

[10]The *Lopez* Court characterized *Wickard* as "perhaps the most far reaching example of Commerce Clause authority over intrastate activity." See United States v. Lopez, 514 U.S. 549, 560 (1995).

[11]Raich, 125 S. Ct. at 2206–07.

[12]*Id*. at 2211–12.

[13]*Id*. at 2209–11; see *infra* notes 82–85 and accompanying text.

[14]125 S. Ct. at 2211.

Justice Antonin Scalia, who has argued powerfully for the interpretation of the Constitution by means of discerning its "original understanding,"[15] concurred in the judgment. Justice Scalia wrote separately, offering what he said was a more "nuanced" opinion. Unfortunately, it does not rely on original understanding, and it is not nuanced.[16] In a nutshell, Scalia concedes that intrastate, noncommercial medicinal drug use is not interstate commerce, but then proceeds to argue that intrastate noncommercial activities can be regulated under the Constitution's Necessary and Proper Clause in order to make the regulation of interstate commerce effective.[17] For years, Justice Clarence Thomas, from a similar originalist perspective, has argued that the modern "substantial effects" test, made explicit in *Wickard*, has no constitutional basis. Scalia's opinion addresses that problem in an unexpected way. For him, it seems that the substantial effects test, far from *overstating* Congress' authority, actually *understates* it. "Where necessary to make a regulation of interstate commerce effective," Scalia writes, "Congress may regulate even those intrastate activities that do not themselves substantially affect interstate commerce."[18] In Scalia's view "purely local" activities can be reached by Congress if Congress reasonably believes they must be reached to vindicate its "comprehensive scheme."[19] More on Scalia's argument below. Suffice it to say here that it is a far cry from the Madison of *Federalist No. 45*.[20] It arguably goes beyond even Justice Stephen Breyer, who in dissent in *Lopez* wrote: "[T]he specific question . . . is not whether the 'regulated activity sufficiently affected interstate commerce,' but, rather, whether Congress could have had '*a rational basis*' for so concluding."[21]

Justice Sandra Day O'Connor dissented in *Raich* for herself, Chief Justice Rehnquist, and Justice Thomas,[22] arguing that both the majority and Scalia ignored each of the factors articulated in *Lopez* and

[15]See generally Antonin Scalia, A Matter of Interpretation (1997).

[16]125 S. Ct. at 2215 (Scalia, J., concurring).

[17]*Id.* at 2215–20; see also *infra* notes 45–49, 90–96 and accompanying text.

[18]125 S. Ct. at 2216.

[19]*Id.* at 2218.

[20]See *supra* note 4.

[21]United States v. Lopez, 514 U.S. 549, 617 (1995) (Breyer, J., dissenting).

[22]125 S. Ct. at 2220–29 (O'Connor, J., dissenting).

Morrison: whether the regulation involves economic activity; whether the statute has a jurisdictional element requiring proof of a connection to interstate commerce; whether Congress made express legislative findings enabling the Court to understand the substantial effect of the regulated activity on interstate commerce; and whether in all events the purported regulatory authority was based on more than a mere inference that the national economy might be adversely affected. None of those factors were adequately addressed, said O'Connor.[23] In response to Scalia, she observed that

> the Necessary and Proper Clause does not change the analysis significantly. Congress must exercise its authority under the Necessary and Proper Clause in a manner consistent with basic constitutional principles. . . . [S]omething more than mere assertion is required when Congress purports to have power over local activity whose connection to an int[er]state market is not self-evident. Otherwise, the Necessary and Proper Clause will always be a back door for unconstitutional federal regulation.[24]

Justice Thomas dissented separately, thinking it useful to bolster O'Connor's precedent-based dissent with direct reference to constitutional text and history.[25] He supplies the historical definition of "commerce" as related to "trade or exchange—not all economic or gainful activity";[26] urges that the Necessary and Proper Clause not be seen as a license to either overstate or understate federal enumerated power; and suggests that there must be an "'obvious, simple, and direct relation' between the intrastate ban and the regulation of interstate commerce."[27] Here, he says, "Congress presented no evidence in support of its conclusions, which are not so much findings

---

[23]*Id*. at 2221 (O'Connor, J., dissenting) (noting the *Raich* majority opinion is "irreconcilable" with the reasoning of *Lopez* and *Morrison*).

[24] *Id*. at 2226 (citing Garcia v. San Antonio Metropolitan Transit Authority, 469 U.S. 528, 585 (1985) (O'Connor, J., dissenting)); see also *infra* notes 97–103 and accompanying text.

[25]125 S. Ct. at 2229–39 (Thomas, J., dissenting).

[26]*Id*. at 2230.

[27]*Id*. at 2231 (quoting Sabri v. United States, 541 U.S. 600, 613 (2004) (Thomas, J., concurring)).

of fact as assertions of power. Congress cannot define the scope of its own power merely by declaring the necessity of its enactments."[28]

Before more fully exploring the interplay among the justices in *Raich*, it is useful to canvass some of the Court's earlier efforts at interpreting the federal commerce power. It is a meandering course, resulting in ever expanding power.

II. Background: Original Motivation

A. Early Bright Lines

Congress did not truly exercise its affirmative commerce power until it passed the Interstate Commerce Act (ICA) in 1887[29] and the Sherman Antitrust Act in 1890.[30] Before passage of those acts, "interstate commerce" primarily involved removing artificial trade barriers among the states, a task most often addressed by the courts, without benefit of federal legislation. Toward the end of the nineteenth century, however, federal legislation was motivated by the rise of private trusts, concentrating the economic activities of local firms for the purpose of monopoly. Justice John Marshall Harlan, a conservative Republican, would remark: "The conviction [became] universal that the country was in real danger from another kind of slavery . . . that would result from the aggregations of capital in the hands of a few individuals and corporations controlling, for their own profit and advantage exclusively, the entire business of the country."[31]

The Interstate Commerce and Sherman Acts were intended to meet that concern. The ICA required railroads traveling through more than one state to charge a "just and reasonable" rate. The Sherman Act, which will be discussed shortly, was aimed at "restraints in trade" among the several states and efforts or attempts to monopolize. To the extent that the ICA sought to limit the power of the railways as natural monopolies, it was economically defensible and consistent with the original understanding of the commerce

---

[28]*Id.* at 2233.

[29]Interstate Commerce Act, ch. 104, 24 Stat. 379 (1887).

[30]Sherman Antitrust Act, ch. 647, 26 Stat. 209 (1890) (codified, as amended, at 15 U.S.C. § 2 et seq.).

[31]Standard Oil of New Jersey v. United States, 221 U.S. 1, 83–84 (1911) (Harlan, J., concurring and dissenting in part).

power as a power to remove artificial barriers to trade among the states. And while claims of natural monopoly can be overstated by regulators, during this period the rail companies could and did set rates to exclude competitors, especially regarding short distances. This was particularly irksome to local farmers who lacked the volume to command competitive rates, and the Granger Movement of the late nineteenth century convinced more than a few states to attempt to prevent discrimination between long and short haul shipment rates.[32] States, however, were incompetent to regulate beyond their borders, a point the Supreme Court made in invalidating Illinois' attempted regulation of long and short hauls that crossed state lines in *Wabash, St. Louis & Pacific Railway Co. v. Illinois.*[33]

The ease with which the *Wabash* Court differentiated intrastate from interstate commerce in 1886 is worth noting. The Court opined:

> It has often been held in this court, and there can be no doubt about it, that there is a commerce wholly within the State which is not subject to the constitutional provision; and the distinction between commerce among the States and the other class of commerce between the citizens of a single State, and conducted within its limits exclusively, is one which has been fully recognized in this court . . . .[34]

Thus, the Court in *Wabash* held that rates wholly within Illinois, between Alton and Chicago for example, would be subject to the state's authority.[35] However, the federal government could regulate rail service originating or terminating *external* to the prairie state. The Court at that time did not rely on any theory about internal commercial activity "affecting" interstate commerce since a legion of cases had already disclaimed federal authority over such local commercial endeavors. For example, wharves and warehouses that facilitated interstate commerce, but were within a single state, were the regulatory province of that state. To drive home that point, the Court in *Wabash* observed:

---

[32] For a discussion of the background and economic rationale of the ICA, see Richard A. Epstein, The Proper Scope of the Commerce Power, 73 Va. L. Rev. 1387, 1413–14 (1989).

[33] 118 U.S. 557, 565 (1886).

[34] *Id.*

[35] *Id.* at 577.

It was very properly said, in the case of the *State Tax on Railway Gross Receipts* . . . that "it is not everything that affects commerce that amounts to a regulation of it, within the meaning of the Constitution." The warehouses of these plaintiffs in error are situated, and their business carried on, exclusively within the limits of the State of Illinois. They are used as instruments by those engaged in State as well as those engaged in interstate commerce, but they are no more necessarily a part of commerce itself than the dray or cart by which, but for them, grain would be transferred from one railroad station to another. Incidentally they may become connected with interstate commerce, but not necessarily so.[36]

The Interstate Commerce and Sherman Acts likewise did not depend on an "affecting commerce" rationale, but on the reality of commercial activity that in fact involved more states than one being impeded by local rule. The *Wabash* decision, rendered a few months prior to the passage of the ICA, drew an analogy to commerce on the Mississippi.[37] The Court wrote:

The river Mississippi passes through or along the borders of ten different states, and its tributaries reach many more. The commerce upon these waters is immense, and its regulation clearly a matter of national concern. If each state was at liberty to regulate the conduct of carriers while within its jurisdiction, the confusion likely to follow could not but be productive of great inconvenience and unnecessary hardship. Each state could provide for its own passengers, and regulate the transportation of its own freight, regardless of the interests of others. Nay, more, it could prescribe rules by which the carrier must be governed within the state in respect to passengers and property brought from without. On one side of the river or its tributaries he might be required to observe one set of rules; and on the other, another. Commerce cannot flourish in the midst of such embarrassments.

The applicability of this language to the case now under consideration, *of a continuous transportation of goods* from New York to central Illinois, or from the latter to New York, is obvious, and it is not easy to see how any distinction can be made. Whatever may be the instrumentalities by which this

---

[36]*Id.* at 566 (quoting Munn v. Illinois, 94 U.S. 113, 135 (1876)).
[37]*Id.* at 572–73.

transportation from the one point to the other is effected, *it is but one voyage*—as much so as that of the steam-boat on the Mississippi river.[38]

B. Early Confusion

It was with *United States v. E.C. Knight Co.*[39] that matters started to get confused. In *Knight*, the Court refused to apply the Sherman Act to a wholly intrastate stock acquisition that resulted in a monopoly on sugar refining.[40] *Knight* is often understood to have drawn a distinction between manufacturing and commerce, with the former outside federal power and the latter within it.[41] This is a misreading of *Knight*.

The disagreement between the majority and the dissent in *Knight* was not over whether manufacturing and commerce both fell under federal power, but over whether the combinations sought to be regulated by the Sherman Act related to buying and selling among the states *post*-manufacture. Thus, Justice Harlan, who would have upheld the application of the Act, states his disagreement with the *Knight* majority as follows:

> It is said that manufacture precedes commerce, and is not a part of it. But it is equally true that when manufacture ends, that which has been manufactured becomes a subject of commerce; that buying and selling succeed manufacture, come into existence after the process of manufacture is completed ... and are as much commercial intercourse, where articles are bought to be carried from one state to another, as is the manual transportation of such articles after they have been so purchased.[42]

Harlan reminds the *Knight* majority that it is committing error when it fails to understand why Chief Justice John Marshall included navigation as part of the federal commerce power in the seminal

---

[38]*Id.* (quoting Hall v. DeCuir, 95 U.S. 485 (1877) (emphasis added)).

[39]United States v. E.C. Knight Co. 156 U.S. 1 (1895).

[40]*Id.* at 18.

[41]For example, this is how Justice Anthony Kennedy reads the case in his *Lopez* concurrence before he proceeds to disavow the distinction. See United States v. Lopez, 514 U.S. 549, 570 (1995) (Kennedy, J., concurring).

[42]E.C. Knight Co., 156 U.S. at 35–36 (Harlan, J., dissenting).

case of *Gibbons v. Ogden*.[43] Commerce included navigation in *Gibbons*, not because it was buying, selling, or bartering. Navigation is not that. Rather, the point of the federal power asserted and sustained in *Gibbons* was the facilitation of buying, selling, or bartering of goods across state lines. Harlan saw the Sherman Act in *Knight* as doing the same. If Congress can prevent New York from issuing exclusive navigational licenses in *Gibbons*, then it can prevent a stock purchase in a single state from sheltering an exclusive (monopolistic) combination of sugar refining. Consistent with the Court's earlier Mississippi River analogy made a few years before the passage of the Sherman Act, Harlan writes:

> Whatever improperly obstructs the free course of interstate intercourse and trade, as involved in the buying and selling of articles to be carried from one state to another, may be reached by Congress under its authority to regulate commerce among the states. The exercise of that authority so as to make trade among the states in all recognized articles of commerce absolutely free from unreasonable or illegal restrictions imposed by combinations is justified by an express grant of power to Congress, and would redound to the welfare of the whole country. I am unable to perceive that any such result would imperil the autonomy of the States, especially as that result cannot be attained through the action of any one State.[44]

Note well what Harlan did not do by this remark: he did not claim that manufacturing and commerce were the same; he did not extend Congress' power beyond that dealing with commerce (buying, selling, bartering); he did not disregard the need to limit federal authority to commercial activity involving more states than one. He did, of course, insist that Congress could reach an intrastate commercial activity if it was a "necessary and proper" means to advance interstate commerce.

[43]Gibbons v. Ogden, 22 U.S. (9 Wheat.) 1 (1824) (finding a federal law licensing ships to engage in the "coasting trade," under which Gibbons operated, to preempt a New York law granting a 30-year monopoly to Ogden to ply the waters between New York and New Jersey. Before the Court acted, the effect of New York's monopoly grant was to preclude Gibbons from operating under his federal license.).

[44]E.C. Knight Co., 156 U.S. at 37.

C. Early Confusion Begets Later Confusion—Only Worse

There is more of the history of the commerce power to tell, but it is worthwhile at this point to pause in order to compare Harlan's dissent in *Knight* with Scalia's far broader "necessary and proper" claims in his concurrence in *Raich*. Scalia writes:

> Congress's regulatory authority over intrastate activities that are not themselves part of interstate commerce (including activities that have a substantial effect on interstate commerce) derives from the Necessary and Proper Clause. And the category of "activities that substantially affect interstate commerce," is *incomplete* because the authority to enact laws necessary and proper for the regulation of interstate commerce is not limited to laws governing intrastate activities that substantially affect interstate commerce. Where necessary to make a regulation of interstate commerce effective, Congress may regulate even those intrastate activities that do not themselves substantially affect interstate commerce.[45]

Scalia's assertion is way beyond the Mississippi River analogy and far broader than Harlan's reasoning in *Knight*, even as Harlan was urging a broad conception of federal power to sustain the application of the Sherman Act to the formation of a sugar refining monopoly in a single state.

Harlan noted that the Constitution, in granting the commerce power, avoided defining the specific means for placing this legitimate authority into effect. On this, Harlan and Scalia would surely agree. However, nowhere does Harlan make the argument that congressional freedom over *means* (subject to their being "necessary and proper") confers freedom over *ends*. To the contrary, Harlan's dissent recurs to the sound instruction from John Marshall: "Let the end be legitimate, let it be within the scope of the constitution, and all means which are appropriate, which are plainly adapted to that end, which are not prohibited, but consist with the letter and spirit of the constitution, are constitutional."[46] It was thus pivotal to Harlan's claim for the application of federal antitrust power to establish that "[t]he end proposed to be accomplished by the act of 1890 is the

---

[45]Gonzales v. Raich, 125 S. Ct. 2195, 2216 (2005) (Scalia, J., concurring) (emphasis in original) (citations omitted).

[46]McCulloch v. Maryland, 17 U.S. (4 Wheat.) 316, 421 (1819).

protection of trade and commerce among the States against unlawful restraints."[47] There was no one in Court disputing that monopolies restrain interstate trade. There was no one in Court denying that the sugar being refined was destined for a national market and that sugar was a commercial product being actively bought and sold. In *Raich*, by contrast, it was beyond dispute that the medicinal marijuana in issue was *not* a commercial product; and it was vigorously disputed whether noncommercial, medicinal use of marijuana had any effect on commercial marijuana being illegally bought and sold outside California.

Harlan could easily step on the necessary and proper platform to defend the use of a federal cause of action as a means to diminish "combinations, conspiracies, and monopolies which, by their inevitable and admitted tendency, improperly restrain trade and commerce among the States."[48] By comparison, Scalia's journey is not a step but a leap, transforming the constitutional authorization of necessary and proper means into a defense of unconstitutional ends. To make the point as plainly as possible, simply substitute the *Raich* facts into Harlan's rhetorical conclusion: "Who can say that [federally prosecuting individuals who are not undertaking any commercial activity and who are acting wholly intrastate pursuant to state authority] is not appropriate to attain the end of [limiting the illegal interstate commercial market in drugs]?" Such a prosecution is neither necessary nor proper to that end. How is arresting and prosecuting a discrete class of sick people necessary to win the "war on drugs," when law enforcement, itself, disclaims this as a necessity?[49]

As unfortunate as *E.C. Knight's* misstep of not understanding the true commercial nature of the Sherman Act's application in that case, it did not do great harm to John Marshall's reasoning in *Gibbons*. Unlike Scalia's *Raich* concurrence, the focus of federal power remained wholly upon commerce. Even if there was disagreement

---

[47]E.C. Knight Co., 156 U.S. at 39 (Harlan, J., dissenting).

[48]*Id.*

[49]Responding to the decision in *Raich*, federal drug authorities seemed to disclaim that which had been pleaded by the acting solicitor general: "We have never targeted the sick and dying, but rather criminals engaged in drug trafficking," Drug Enforcement Administration spokesman Bill Grant said. See Crackdown on Medical Marijuana Users Unlikely, Associated Press (June 7, 2005), available at http://www.msnbc.msn.com/id/8118123 (last visited August 15, 2005).

in *Knight* about what intrastate activity could be reached by federal law, both the majority and dissent in *Knight* agreed that for an activity to be federally regulated that activity still had to be clearly established as part of a larger interstate commercial universe. Moreover, within a decade much of the *Knight* disagreement was resolved. For example, in *Swift & Co. v. United States*,[50] the Court coined a "stream of commerce" or "current of commerce" metaphor that returned the Court to the Mississippi River analogy and allowed Congress to regulate the slaughterhouse business in Chicago.[51] Looked at formally, the slaughterhouse business in Chicago was completely *intra*state and, under the *Knight* majority, might have been thought to be beyond the reach of Congress. But the Court took note of the fact that the slaughterhouse business was just one way station in an interstate industry that encompassed everything from ranching to the retailing of beef.[52]

The *Shreveport Rate Cases*[53] confirmed and slightly expanded Congress' power by expressly inviting the national legislature to contemplate the *effect* of *intra*state rate setting on *inter*state rates—but again, the focus was solely on commerce. Of course, it was conceded that Congress, via the Interstate Commerce Commission (ICC), could set minimum rail cargo transportation rates for trains that actually moved in interstate commerce. But that was not the problem. *Wabash* involved price discrimination between intrastate and interstate components of a single interstate journey. In *Shreveport*, the ICC's desired regulation sought to address local shipping rates for hauls that were not part of an interstate journey. By staying in Texas, shippers adjacent to the Louisiana state line could ship their goods more inexpensively to markets across Texas than to closer Louisiana markets. That disparity in rates had a substantial economic *effect* on interstate commerce, and the Court held that Congress could reach into the purely intrastate rail traffic in Texas in order to impose its higher minimum federal rate schedule on that traffic as well.[54] That was an

---

[50]196 U.S. 375 (1905) (Holmes, J.).

[51]*Id.* at 399.

[52]*Id.* at 398–99.

[53]Houston, East & West Texas Railway Co. v. United States, 234 U.S. 342 (1914) (hereinafter the "Shreveport Rate Cases").

[54]*Id.* at 353–54.

incremental increase in federal authority, but *Shreveport*, like *Swift*, kept Congress' power focused on commercial activity, thereby arguably vindicating the constitutional text, while not permitting state lines to be asserted in a formalistic way that would balkanize the national market.

D. Taking the Commerce Power Beyond Commerce

Champion v. Ames[55] took the commerce power beyond commerce, by permitting it to be employed to prohibit sending lottery tickets across state lines, not because doing so restricted or burdened interstate commerce, but because lotteries were perceived as morally evil. Here too, as with the *Knight* case, the modern version of *Champion* suffers from revisionism. Thus, writing for the *Raich* majority, Stevens notes that, "[i]n the *Lottery Case* [*Champion v. Ames*], the Court rejected the argument that Congress lacked [the] power to prohibit the interstate movement of lottery tickets because it had power only to regulate, not to prohibit."[56] Scalia echoes that characterization of *Champion* in his *Raich* concurrence.[57] Yet the real significance of *Champion* was not its distinction between regulatory promotion or restriction but an unfortunate acceptance of judicial abdication— the notion that the Court had no duty to inquire whether either means, promotion, or restriction, was legitimately aimed at the subject matter of interstate commerce.

By this judicial complacency, the commerce power was extended to non-commerce purposes in the early twentieth century. Mistakenly, the constitutionality of the question became popularly inseparable from the underlying policy issues. Thus, for example, the federal regulation of child labor was disavowed in 1918 in *Hammer v. Dagenhart*;[58] yet by the time of the New Deal it was found constitutional in *United States v. Darby*,[59] which overruled *Hammer* on its way toward sustaining federal minimum wage and maximum hour laws. Arguing from text alone, the *Hammer* majority reasoned that working conditions

---

[55]188 U.S. 321 (1903).

[56]Gonzales v. Raich, 125 S. Ct. 2195, 2207 n.29 (2005) (quoting United States v. Lopez, 514 U.S. 549, 571 (1995) (Kennedy, J., concurring) (third alteration in original)).

[57]*Id.* at 2219 (Scalia, J., concurring).

[58]247 U.S. 251 (1918).

[59]312 U.S. 100 (1941).

could not be regulated by Congress because they were not "commerce"—that is, buying and selling or trade. Working conditions were matters of health, safety, and morals—the province of the states. As Justice William Day wrote for the *Hammer* majority, Congress' power over interstate commerce "was to enable it to regulate such commerce, and not to give it authority to control the States in their exercise of the police power over local trade and manufacture. The grant of authority over a purely federal matter was not intended to destroy the local power always existing and carefully reserved to the states in the Tenth Amendment to the Constitution."[60]

In his dissent in *Hammer*, Justice Oliver Wendell Holmes elides the non-commerce nature of the regulation by suggesting that "[t]he act does not meddle with anything belonging to the States. They may regulate their internal affairs and their domestic commerce as they like. But when they seek to send their products across the state line they are no longer within their rights."[61] Keeping children out of sweatshops is a salutary policy objective, but it cannot fairly be said to relate to the act of buying, selling, or bartering. Holmes tries to escape this textual boundary by declaring that no single state has authority over the national market, while Congress does. But again, with the exception of *Champion*, Congress was thought to have this authority as it related to buying, selling, or bartering, not generally with respect to bad acts.[62] *Champion* weakened that supposition, but the case was seen by the *Hammer* majority as merely keeping an evil thing (a lottery ticket) out of a national market, not as a wholesale invitation to regulate working conditions that did not directly implicate buying, selling, or bartering and that had until then been under the supervision of the states. Holmes countered sweepingly: "[Congress] may carry out its views of public policy whatever indirect effect they may have upon the activities of the States."[63]

[60]Hammer, 247 U.S. at 273–74.

[61]*Id.* at 281 (Holmes, J., dissenting).

[62]Compare, for example, Harlan's reasoning in *Knight* that the intrastate monopoly dampened the sale of sugar outside the single state where the monopoly was secured by stock acquisition; likewise, the finding that intrastate rate setting undermined interstate rates in the *Shreveport Rate Cases* arguably established a necessary linkage between intrastate practice and the capacity to buy, sell, or barter that was missing in *Hammer*. The chief justice would revive this inquiry in *Lopez* by insisting that there be a logical stopping point, rather than the obfuscation of what is national and what is local by the piling up of inference upon inference.

[63]*Id.*

With the onset of the Great Depression, Holmes' view became the law of the land. Notably, in *National Labor Relations Board v. Jones & Laughlin Steel Corp.*,[64] the Supreme Court voted five to four to sustain federal labor legislation regulating management and union activity at manufacturing plants. After that, the Court would no longer make any serious effort to keep the commerce power focused on commerce, and the interstate limitation would soon disappear. As briefly noted earlier, the Court in *Wickard*[65] was concerned with the restrictions imposed by the Agricultural Adjustment Act on the activities of farmer Filburn. The idea behind the Act's acreage restrictions was to keep farm prices up by limiting supply. When Filburn grew on more acreage than his quota allowed, intending the surplus for his noncommercial home consumption, the Court sustained the Act.[66] It did not matter that Filburn's activity was local and not regarded as commerce. It could be reached if Congress could rationally believe it exerted a substantial economic effect on interstate commerce. It did not matter if the effect was "direct" or "indirect" or if Filburn's surplus was insubstantial in terms of the overall wheat market. Congress could consider the similar activity of thousands of "Farmer Filburns" across the country in its assessment of the economic effects of that activity on interstate commerce. In other words, a principle of aggregation was built into the "substantial economic effects" test.

And what remained of state authority? State powers were no longer "numerous," as Madison promised, but the ever diminishing residue of the federal regulatory enterprise. Ignoring the very point of the Tenth Amendment—to secure the Constitution's premise of delegated, enumerated, and thus limited powers—the *Darby* Court said the Amendment stated "but a truism."[67] That rather meaningless truism persisted unassailed until the mid-1990s.

III. The Tide Turns? *Lopez* and *Morrison* after *Raich*

In 1995, in *United States v. Lopez*,[68] the Court put a brake on its nearly sixty years of Commerce Clause deference to Congress. *Lopez*

---

[64]301 U.S. 1 (1937).
[65]Wickard v. Filburn, 317 U.S. 111 (1942).
[66]*Id.* at 113–17 (summarizing facts); *id.* at 128–29 (holding).
[67]United States v. Darby, 312 U.S. 100, 124 (1941).
[68]514 U.S. 549 (1995).

arose when a twelfth-grade student carried a concealed handgun into his high school, and was subsequently charged with violating the federal Gun-Free School Zones Act of 1990, which forbids "any individual knowingly to possess a firearm at a place that [he] knows . . . is a school zone."[69] A five to four Court, per Chief Justice Rehnquist, found that, in passing the Act, Congress had exceeded its power under the Commerce Clause. Reverting to the constitutional text, the Court said that possession of a gun in a local school zone was in no sense an economic activity.[70] Seeming to limit the aggregation principle in *Wickard*, the Court resolved that even through repetition of the activity elsewhere, school gun possession would not have a substantial effect on interstate commerce.[71] Nor had Congress made any effort to limit the scope of the statute by incorporating a jurisdictional element, which would ensure, through case-by-case inquiry, that the firearms possession in question had the requisite factual nexus with interstate commerce.[72] There were indeed no facts to indicate that the student had recently moved in interstate commerce or that he had come into possession of the firearm via interstate commerce.[73] While those defending the Act speculated about higher insurance costs and lower educational achievement, the Court called this piling "inference upon inference," all in a manner calculated to transform the Commerce Clause into a general police power, which it is not.[74]

Five years later the Court decided *United States v. Morrison*,[75] a challenge to a section of the Violence Against Women Act (VAWA),[76] which provided a federal civil remedy for victims of gender-motivated violence. Echoing its *Lopez* considerations, a five to four Court again held the statute to be beyond Congress' authority under the Commerce Clause. The regulated activity was not commercial

---

[69]Gun-Free School Zones Act, 18 U.S.C. § 922(q)(2)(A) (1990).

[70]514 U.S. at 561, 567.

[71]*Id.*

[72]*Id.* at 561–62.

[73]*Id.* at 567.

[74]*Id.* at 567–68.

[75]United States v. Morrison, 529 U.S. 598 (2000).

[76]Violence Against Women Act, 42 U.S.C. § 13981.

or economic.[77] The statute contained no jurisdictional element limiting its application to certain factual circumstances involving interstate commerce.[78] The only difference between *Morrison* and *Lopez* was that Congress had held hearings that attempted to document a "but-for" causal chain from the initial occurrence of violent crime to its attenuated effects on interstate commerce.[79] But the Court saw that evidence as without a meaningful stopping point or limiting principle since, were it accepted, the reasoning would allow Congress to regulate any crime whose nationwide, aggregated impact had substantial effects on employment, production, transit, or consumption. Proclaiming that it was important to separate what is local from what is national, the Court did not see how it could sustain the Act without also inviting and approving federal displacement of state law over marriage, family law, and child rearing, all of which could likewise be said to have, in the aggregate, effects on the national economy.[80] In the end, the Court concluded that Congress may not regulate intrastate, noneconomic, criminal conduct based solely on the conduct's aggregate effect on interstate commerce.[81] After *Raich*, that conclusion is open to considerable question. Here is why.

A. Do Lopez *and* Morrison *Survive* Raich?

As a formal matter, Justice Stevens, writing for the *Raich* majority, distinguishes but does not overrule *Lopez* and *Morrison*. Specifically, he notes that "in both *Lopez* and *Morrison* the parties asserted that a particular statute or provision fell outside Congress' commerce power in its entirety."[82] Here, Raich and other seriously ill patients without another effective medicinal remedy asked merely to excise an individual application of the Controlled Substance Act to their unique circumstance—namely, to patients under a doctor's care who, with explicit state approval, were being given marijuana that all agreed had never traveled interstate or been part of a commercial transaction. To save *Lopez* and *Morrison*, the majority had to argue

[77]529 U.S. at 611–12.
[78]*Id.*
[79]*Id.* at 612.
[80]*Id.* at 615–16.
[81]*Id.* at 617.
[82]Gonzales v. Raich, 125 S. Ct. 2195, 2197 (2005).

that Raich's "as applied" challenge failed, unlike the facial challenges mounted in *Lopez* and *Morrison*. Indeed, the distinction, said Justice Stevens, was "pivotal."[83]

It may be rhetorically pivotal, but it is constitutionally perverse. It would be far more respectful of the delicate balance between the federal and state governments to invalidate isolated, excessive applications of otherwise legitimate federal power than to invalidate whole statutes wholesale. Nevertheless, Stevens attempts to justify the distinction doctrinally as a part of commerce power precedent going back to *Wickard*, holding that "[w]here the class of activities is regulated and that class is within the reach of federal power, the courts have no power 'to excise, as trivial, individual instances' of the class."[84] That statement may be faithful to pre-*Lopez* and pre-*Morrison* case law, but it is unfaithful to the Court's structural obligation to separate local from national activities.

The Court's refusal to consider Raich's as-applied challenge is especially puzzling since it obviously anticipated doing as-applied analyses when it complained in both *Lopez* and *Morrison* about the absence of jurisdictional elements that would make as-applied case-by-case examination possible.[85] Nor can the *Raich* opinion be explained by invoking the judicial restraint that gives deference to policy choices made by political branches, for there are two such branches in play here. After all, not just Congress but the people of California and the California Assembly made policy choices, too. A restrained judicial posture is not the same as a policy of federal deference, which prompts the ultimate question—to which government does the Constitution assign the policy choice? Only Thomas addresses that question directly, looking at original understanding as he does so.

B. Was it Economic? Was it Commerce? Did it Matter?

Stevens also attempts to distinguish *Lopez* and *Morrison* by noting that neither dealt with an economic transaction, whereas *Raich* involves activities that are "quintessentially economic."[86] It is hard

---

[83]*Id.*

[84]*Id.* at 2197–98 (quoting Perez v. United States, 402 U.S. 146, 154 (1971)).

[85]United States v. Lopez, 514 U.S. 549, 561 (1995); United States v. Morrison, 529 U.S. 598, 609–13 (2000).

[86]Raich, 125 S. Ct. at 2211.

to take that argument seriously on a record that establishes only medicinal use, coupled with a total absence of buying, selling, or bartering. If donative transactions were commercial, the argument might work, but then large bodies of common law would have to be rewritten.

The majority's definition of what is "economic," which it finds in a modern dictionary, is quite broad: "'Economics' refers to 'the production, distribution, and consumption of commodities,'"[87] Stevens writes. In her dissent, O'Connor finds the definition to be so broad that nothing is left out:

> [I]t will not do to say that Congress may regulate noncommercial activity simply because it may have an effect on the demand for commercial goods, or because the noncommercial endeavor can, in some sense, substitute for commercial activity. Most commercial goods or services have some sort of privately producible analogue. Home care substitutes for daycare. Charades games substitute for movie tickets. Backyard or windowsill gardening substitutes for going to the supermarket. To draw the line wherever private activity affects the demand for market goods is to draw no line at all, and to declare everything economic.[88]

Thomas, in turn, thinks the whole exercise is off-point. The constitutional text speaks of commerce, not economics, and the meaning of that term at the founding was "selling, buying, and bartering, as well as transporting for these purposes,"[89] none of which is involved in the present case. Remarkably, however, Scalia thinks the economic/noneconomic distinction unimportant. He would allow Congress to regulate even noneconomic activities if doing so were necessary and proper for the regulation of interstate commerce.

C. *Does the Judiciary Have Any Role in Deciding What Is Local and What Is National?*

The majority sustains the federal law's application by invoking a deferential, rational basis standard—i.e., Congress could have rationally believed, without any showing of evidence other than its litigation pleading, that intrastate medicinal use would harm the federal

---

[87]*Id.* (quoting Webster's Third International Dictionary 720 (1996)).

[88]*Id.* at 2225 (O'Connor, J., dissenting).

[89]*Id.* at 2230 (Thomas, J., dissenting) (citing Lopez, 514 U.S. at 586–69 (Thomas, J., concurring)).

regulatory program in the sense of having a "substantial effect" on interstate commerce. Scalia seems to accept that deferential understanding of "substantial effect," but then adds a separate basis for sustaining federal control that is unrelated to the substantial effect inquiry. Specifically, he thinks noncommercial, noneconomic, wholly intrastate activity can be federally regulated, with or without substantial effect, if that regulation is a reasonable means to accomplishing some federal interest. "[T]he means chosen [simply must be] 'reasonably adapted' to the attainment of a legitimate end under the commerce power."[90]

Scalia references the venerable precedent of *McCulloch v. Maryland*,[91] but it is far from evident that he follows it. *McCulloch* reminds us that even when the end is constitutional and legitimate, the means must be "appropriate" and "plainly adapted" to it. Moreover, those means must not be "otherwise prohibited" and must be "consistent with the letter and spirit of the constitution."[92] Those phrases— Scalia says they are not "merely hortatory"[93]—suggest that a fairly rigorous standard of review is called for. Yet no such rigorous review is evident in Scalia's opinion. Nor is the majority's review rigorous. It is satisfied not by evidence but by assertion. The federal government asserted that marijuana was fungible and that some would inevitably find its way to the national market. On that mere assertion, the Court sustained a non-textual exercise of federal authority over a noncommercial, intrastate activity. In dissent, Thomas articulates a far more demanding standard for interpreting the Necessary and Proper Clause. "In order to be 'necessary,'" said Thomas, "the intrastate ban must be more than 'a reasonable means [of] effectuating the regulation of interstate commerce.' It must be 'plainly adapted' to regulating interstate marijuana trafficking—in other words, there

---

[90]*Id.* at 2217 (Scalia, J., concurring). Thus, he contends that in *Darby* the imposition of a federal minimum wage is sustained, under the Commerce Clause, because intrastate wages substantially affect the interstate market, whereas intrastate federal record keeping requirements are sustained not because of that effect but, under the Necessary and Proper Clause, as reasonable means to accomplish the regulatory end of the federal control of wages and hours. *Id.* at 2217–18.

[91]17 U.S. (4 Wheat.) 316 (1819).

[92]Raich, 125 S. Ct. at 2218–19 (quoting McCulloch, 17 U.S. (4 Wheat.) at 421–22).

[93]*Id.* at 2219.

Gonzales v. Raich: Wickard v. Filburn *Displaced*

must be an 'obvious, simple, and direct relation' between the intrastate ban and the regulation of interstate commerce."[94]

To be sure, Scalia exhibits some residual sympathy for the federal commerce power being "otherwise limited," citing the opinions in *Printz v. United States*[95] and *New York v. United States*,[96] which held that Congress cannot order states to undertake the administration of federally enacted programs or to legislate as the federal government wishes. Those limits are traced to the Tenth Amendment; they stand for the Constitution's limiting principle of "state sovereignty." The three dissenters in *Raich* would agree, but they believe the federal-state balance is to be maintained not just when the Tenth Amendment is interpreted but when the scope of the federal commerce power is discerned as well. It is fair to say that the majority, and Scalia in concurrence, divide from the dissent on this specific and very important point: *the majority and Scalia think it is not up to the Court to be cognizant of state sovereignty in its interpretation of the federal commerce power, whereas the dissenters see this as a matter of judicial duty.*

D. The Camel's Nose—Medicine or Legalization?

The majority's strongest rhetorical flourish is in the claim that if states can regulate the intrastate medicinal use of marijuana, they will soon assert the power to regulate intrastate recreational use as well. O'Connor responds in dissent that medical and nonmedical (i.e., recreational) uses of drugs are realistically distinct and can be segregated for purposes of regulation.[97] This is a factual claim, which the federal government disputes. Assuming the dispute, O'Connor's dissent notes that all the parties in this litigation agree that only medicinal use is at issue in this as-applied challenge, and the Court has always understood itself obligated to speak only as broadly as necessary.[98] But just as good arguments hang together, so too do bad ones: here, the majority's perverse and rather selective preference for

[94]*Id.* at 2231 (Thomas, J., dissenting) (quoting McCulloch, 17 U.S. (4 Wheat.) at 421, and Sabri v. United States, 541 U.S. 600, 613 (2004) (Thomas, J., concurring)).
[95]521 U.S. 898 (1997).
[96]505 U.S. 144 (1992).
[97]125 S. Ct. at 2223–24 (O'Connor, J., dissenting).
[98]*Id.* at 2224.

wholesale invalidation over as-applied adjudication[99] aligns with its unwillingness to examine the facts as they actually exist.

Defining the scope of the commerce power has always been an indirect means of preserving traditional state functions. Shortly before Kennedy and Scalia took their seats, the Court had tried but then gave up defining what those functions were directly.[100] Rehnquist and O'Connor vowed that the Court would one day return to the effort.[101] Yet the *Raich* majority, including Kennedy and Justice Scalia by concurrence, has now abandoned the effort to revive enumerated powers federalism even by indirect means. Ignoring both the limits on federal power and the state interest in protecting the health and safety of its citizens—to which the "States lay claim by right of history and expertise"[102]—the Court rests supine. For the majority and Scalia, federal power over interstate commerce marijuana is without limit, even if the state has identified a discrete subpart (noncommercial, medicinal uses) over which federal power is not appropriate. It is hard to understand why it believes this to be the case. As the dissent noted, in *Wickard v. Filburn*, previously identified by the Court as the outer limit of federal power, the statute at issue had exempted small quantities of wheat. Thus, as a matter of law, "*Wickard* did not hold or imply that small-scale production of commodities is always economic, and automatically within Congress' reach."[103]

E. Can Justice Thomas Be Serious?

The Thomas dissent goes deeper than that of O'Connor and Rehnquist. Thomas repeats his consistent criticism of the non-originalist nature of the "substantial effects" test.[104] He calls the test "rootless"

---

[99]Cf. United States v. Raines, 362 U.S. 17, 20–22 (1960) (describing the Court's preference for as-applied rather than facial challenges).

[100]Compare National League of Cities v. Usery, 426 U.S. 833 (1976), with Garcia v. San Antonio Municipal Transit Authority, 469 U.S. 528 (1985).

[101]See Garcia, 469 U.S. at 570–77 (Powell, J., joined by Rehnquist and O'Connor, JJ., dissenting).

[102]Raich, 125 S. Ct. at 2224 (O'Connor, J., dissenting) (quoting United States v. Lopez, 514 U.S. 549, 583 (1995)).

[103]*Id.* at 2225–26 (O'Connor, J., dissenting).

[104]*Id.* at 2235–37 (Thomas, J., dissenting); see also Lopez, 514 U.S. at 584 (Thomas, J., concurring), and United States v. Morrison, 529 U.S. 598, 627 (2000) (Thomas, J., concurring).

because it is tethered to neither the Commerce nor the Necessary and Proper Clause. "Under the Commerce Clause, Congress may regulate interstate commerce, not activities that substantially affect interstate commerce,"[105] he writes. And, as noted earlier, he employs a narrower, more originalist definition of commerce—"selling, buying, and bartering, as well as transporting for these purposes."[106] That definition is resisted because it implicates the basis for federal environmental laws, wage and hour laws, and the like. Civil rights laws premised on Congress' commerce power would be similarly vulnerable.[107]

In his *Raich* dissent, Thomas does not discuss how he would reconcile the commerce power, properly limited, and the modern regulatory state, but he clearly indicates that if a satisfactory answer is to be found, it is best guided by original understanding.[108] An

---

[105]Raich, 125 S. Ct. at 2235 (Thomas, J., dissenting).

[106]*Id.* at 2230 (quoting Lopez, 514 U.S. at 585).

[107]The concern for civil rights legislation might be avoided by re-anchoring the authority for such to the Thirteenth or Fourteenth Amendments. See generally Douglas W. Kmiec, Stephen B. Presser, John C. Eastman & Raymond B. Marcin, The American Constitutional Order 602 (2d ed. 2004). Cf. Richard A. Epstein, Forbidden Grounds 10 (1992) ("So great were the abuses of political power before 1964 that, knowing what I know today, if given an all-or-nothing choice, I should still have voted in favor of the Civil Rights Act in order to allow federal power to break the stranglehold of local government on race relations.").

[108]A satisfactory answer becomes less elusive with candid acknowledgment that some problems are national. As discussed more fully in the Cato Institute's amicus brief in *Gonzales v. Raich*, interpreting the commerce power in light of its original understanding (in particular, with reference to the Virginia Resolution) better delimits the scope of federal power, for it helps reveal when, for example, trans-boundary air and water resources must be protected on a national level. The federal government has that power so long as Congress sufficiently identifies that its legislative interest is in this type of migratory resource—which is inherently plagued by conflicting state regulatory schemes. Cf. Solid Waste Agency v. U.S. Army Corps of Engineers, 531 U.S. 159 (2001) (finding the federal interest not precisely identified, but suggesting it could be). Air and water resources rarely inhabit one state. It is the common nature of the resource that makes these environmental questions, absent a national solution, collapse into a costly and wealth-minimizing regulatory war between conflicting state jurisdictions. Similarly, Congress' power to reach private discrimination on the basis of race is not contradicted by purposive reliance on the Virginia Resolution. Federal laws banning discrimination at public accommodations, such as motels and restaurants, vindicate a constitutional interest (racial nondiscrimination) legally held by the nation as a whole. A national interest of this magnitude need not rest upon awkward inquiries into the quantities of goods and services held in trade. Cf. Heart

originalist would assume that the Constitution's text is the locus of interpretative effort, and other short-hand doctrinal rubrics ("channels," "instrumentalities," "substantial effects") ought to be understood in a way that is faithful to that text. "[T]he Framers could have drafted a Constitution that contained a 'substantially affects interstate commerce' Clause had that been their objective."[109] They did not. Instead, the Framers drafted a Constitution that gave Congress the power "to regulate Commerce . . . among the several States . . ."[110] The textual meaning of that grant of power is crystallized only when the clause is interpreted in harmony with its *purpose*. That underlying purpose is revealed by examining John Marshall's seminal opinion in *Gibbons v. Ogden*;[111] Daniel Webster's oral argument in that case; and the Virginia Resolution, which was the genesis of the Commerce Clause. Looking at each, here is what can be found.

In *Gibbons*, we are given the following rule of construction: "If . . . there should be serious doubts respecting the extent of any given power, it is a well settled rule, that the objects for which it was given . . . should have great influence in the construction."[112] And similarly, "We know of no rule for construing the extent of such powers [as the commerce power], other than is given by the language of the instrument which confers them, taken in connexion [sic] *with the purposes* for which they were conferred."[113] Substantively, Marshall's opinion in *Gibbons* rather quickly deduced that the federal commerce power included authority not just over the buying and selling of goods but also over navigation. That is an analytical jump not resolvable by text alone.[114] If it is to be explained, we must dig deeper.

of Atlanta Motel, Inc. v. United States, 379 U.S. 241 (1964); Katzenbach v. McClung, 379 U.S. 294 (1964).

[109]Lopez, 514 U.S. at 588 (Thomas, J., concurring).

[110]U.S. Const. art. I, § 8, cl. 3.

[111]Gibbons v. Ogden, 22 U.S. (9 Wheat.) 1 (1824).

[112]*Id.* at 188–89.

[113]*Id.* at 189 (emphasis added).

[114]As scholars have pointed out, Marshall short-cuts the analysis. See Roger Pilon, Freedom, Responsibility, and the Constitution, 68 Notre Dame L. Rev. 507, 533–37 (1993). Rather than elaborating the complete inquiry, he rather quickly reaches the conclusion that "commerce" includes navigation, not mere "traffic" or the interchange of commodities. He is correct, of course, but the closest he comes to overtly identifying the functional account of the Commerce Clause is to say that "[t]he power over commerce, including navigation, was one of the primary objects for which the people of America adopted their government. . . ." Gibbons, 22 U.S. (9 Wheat.) at 190. That

Not surprisingly, it turns out that Webster highlighted the problems of conflicting navigational licenses issued by the federal government and the states. Webster spent little time trying to do what the majority and concurrence belabor in *Raich*, namely, asserting that something is "commerce," or an activity that substantially affects it. Webster termed it vain to look for a precise or exact definition of commerce.[115] That, he said, was not the way the Constitution proceeded. Instead, the extent of the power was to be measured by its object.

And what was the object or prevailing purpose of the commerce power? To rescue (Webster's word) the general Union from "the embarrassing and destructive consequences, resulting from the legislation of so many different States, and to place it under the protection of a uniform law."[116] Webster did not envision a commerce power

is true, and important, but it doesn't fully disclose the functional account; for Marshall's use of "objects" here anticipates, but only suggests—without full elaboration—why federal regulation of navigation coincides with the constitutional purpose of the commerce power. Nevertheless, it is obvious that to reach his result, Marshall employed both the text and the purpose underlying the text to fairly consider both the federal *and* state sides of the commerce power. As discussed below, the underlying purpose or object of the Commerce Clause is informed by the Virginia Resolution, and recourse to it reveals how Marshall was able to so quickly ascertain the scope of federal power in *Gibbons* and how that outcome coincided with Madison's own proposition that the national government was to have "compleat authority in all cases which require uniformity." Letter from James Madison to George Washington (Apr. 16, 1787), reprinted in 2 The Writings of James Madison 344–45 (1900–1910). Under the Virginia Resolution, "among the several states" can be understood as a synonym for power directed at either vindicating a national commercial interest— that is, one held by the nation as a whole like interstate movement and transportation, communication, or national defense, or a commercial subject that cannot be addressed by an individual state without undermining the policies of other states.

[115]The tangled academic debates over the word "commerce," in isolation, tend to wax and wane, depending on one's ideology, between plenary power and the limited power that is strictly necessary to manage the concerns of the eighteenth century. See generally Arthur B. Mark III, Currents in Commerce Clause Scholarship, 32 Cap. U. L. Rev. 671 (2004); see also Grant S. Nelson & Robert J. Pushaw, Jr., Rethinking the Commerce Clause: Applying First Principles to Uphold Federal Commercial Regulations but Preserve State Control Over Social Issues, 85 Iowa L. Rev. 1 (1999); and Randy E. Barnett, The Original Meaning of the Commerce Clause, 68 U. Chi. L. Rev. 101 (2001). Professor Barnett splendidly argued on behalf of *Raich* before the Supreme Court and his historical research was singled out for special reliance by Justice Thomas. 125 S. Ct. 2195, 2230 (2005) (Thomas, J., dissenting).

[116]Gibbons, 22 U.S. (9 Wheat.) at 11 (syllabus) (summary of Daniel Webster's arguments for the plaintiff). Notice how similar Webster's argument is to the Mississippi River analogy that would still be guiding the Court in *Wabash* over eighty years later.

without limit. Indeed, the commerce power was not to consume the state's separate sovereignty; rather, the Court was to interpret the power to keep the interests of the two governments "as distinct as possible," said Webster. "The general government should not seek to operate where the states can operate with more advantage to the community; nor should the states encroach on ground, which the public good, as well as the constitution, refers to the exclusive control of Congress."[117] The rule of thumb from Webster is that federal commercial power is to apply where the general interests of the union would otherwise be jeopardized by conflicting state regulation, *but* state regulation is to be preferred where that is not true and states have the better vantage from which to address a public problem. Is this simply advocacy, or does it have constitutional root?

Webster's argument, and Marshall's acceptance of it in *Gibbons*, flows directly from the Virginia Resolution underlying the commerce power. The Sixth Virginia Resolution of 1787 (Virginia Resolution) provides:

> [T]hat the National Legislature ought to possess the Legislative Rights vested in Congress by the Confederation; and moreover, to legislate in all cases for the general interests of the union, and also in those cases to which the States are separately incompetent, or in which the harmony of the United States may be interrupted by the exercise of individual Legislation.[118]

That Resolution was sent to the Committee on Detail. What emerged was the enumerated federal commerce power. It was not intended to change the resolution's meaning. As Robert L. Stern has commented:

> Significantly, the Convention did not at any time challenge the radical change made by the committee [of detail] .... It accepted *without discussion* the enumeration of powers made by the committee which had been directed to prepare a constitution based upon the general propositions that the federal government was "to legislate in all cases for the general

---

[117]*Id.* at 17.

[118]Records of the Debates in the Federal Convention of 1787 as Reported by James Madison 389 (Charles C. Tansill ed., Legal Classics Library 1989) (1927); also found in Notes of Debates in the Federal Convention of 1787 Reported by James Madison 380 (W.W. Norton & Co. ed., 1966).

interests of the Union . . . and in those to which the states are separately incompetent." . . . This absence of objection to or comment upon the change is susceptible of only one explanation — that the Convention believed that the enumeration conformed to the standard previously approved, and that the powers enumerated comprehended those matters as to which the states were separately incompetent and in which national legislation was essential.[119]

Does this assist the Court, or just substitute new words? At a minimum, it clarifies why Marshall could so easily construe commerce to include navigation, which on its face seems a non sequitur. The obscurity drops away when navigation is linked not to commercial activity per se, but to an interest that must be held by the union of the states in order to avoid imperiling national interests. Indeed, Marshall's decisional words in *Gibbons* directly connect the concerns of the Virginia Resolution to the scope of the commerce power, and in so doing they state a faithful constitutional understanding of *both* the federal *and* state sides of the commerce power. He wrote:

> The genius and character of the whole government seem to be, that its action is to be applied to all the external concerns of the nation, and to those internal concerns which affect the States generally; but not to those which are completely within a particular State, which do not affect other States, and with which it is not necessary to interfere, for the purpose of executing some of the general powers of the government. The completely internal commerce of a State, then, may be considered as reserved for the State itself.[120]

If navigation across state lines or even navigation that is internal to a state is to be treated as "commerce" when it "affects the States generally," is the noncommercial medicinal use of marijuana to be so treated? It strains credulity to conclude that such use is of national interest—or that it "affects the States generally" in comparison to, say, preventing racial distinctions from impeding commercial action.

---

[119]Robert L. Stern, That Commerce Which Concerns More States Than One, 47 Harv. L. Rev. 1335, 1340 (1934); see also Douglas W. Kmiec, Rediscovering a Principled Commerce Power, 28 Pepp. L. Rev. 547, 560–62 (2001).

[120]Gibbons, 22 U.S. (9 Wheat.) at 195.

"National interest" is not synonymous with a "very important political topic." Reliance on the modern cumulative or substantial effects tests alone obscures that. To ask whether an individual action "substantially affects" interstate commerce, without reference to the purpose of the granted power, is to ask an incomplete question. By contrast, a principled inquiry seeks to identify the presence or absence of an interest that can be claimed only by the nation as a whole or that must be addressed nationally because of demonstrated state incapacity. And demonstrated state incapacity must be theoretically as well as *practically* grounded, not merely rhetorically asserted. Incapacity should mean that an individual state's regulatory activity would actually be defeated by the competing regulatory policies of other states.

IV. Implications and Conclusion

A majority of the present Court finds no judicially enforceable limit on the federal commerce power. It is enough that Congress could rationally believe that regulating the activity (whether wholly local or not, and whether commercial or not) was part of a comprehensive regulatory scheme or, in *Congress' sole judgment*, was necessary to make interstate regulation effective. Those "tests" are without teeth. Now, only where Congress makes the "drafting mistake" of regulating a local, noncommercial subject on a freestanding basis is there a slight chance that a majority of the Court will honor the *Lopez* and *Morrison* precedents to question and, possibly, invalidate that isolated exercise of power. The *Raich* majority's deferential posture is inconsistent with those precedents and in tension with the Court's recent efforts to revive federalism generally.

Kennedy, the author of an ambivalent concurrence in *Lopez*, returned to the federal fold when he joined the *Raich* majority in silence. In *Lopez* he had said that he was influenced by an often identified chief virtue of federalism, that it promotes innovation: "a single courageous State may, if its citizens choose, serve as a laboratory; and try novel social and economic experiments without risk to the rest of the country."[121] Apparently he now prefers uniformity to diversity.

---

[121]New State Ice Co. v. Liebmann, 285 U.S. 262, 311 (1932) (Brandeis, J., dissenting).

Unlike Kennedy, Scalia openly separated himself from the federalist structure of the Constitution without any inquiry into the original understanding of the commerce power and with an understanding of the Necessary and Proper Clause that begs the essential question about where power had actually been assigned. It is often appropriate for the Court to be restrained and to give deference to legislative judgments about how best to implement policy; that deference is unwarranted, however, if the Court has not first satisfied itself that the right sovereign has acted. But for that to be more than a meaningless inquiry, there must be a richer understanding of the Commerce and Necessary and Proper Clauses than was demonstrated by the *Raich* majority or the Scalia concurrence.

To conclude let me compliment the majority and dissent. Federalism is frequently labeled a doctrine of convenience, but it cannot be assailed here that the Court elevated politics over principle. In deciding against state authority, Stevens expresses sympathy for the state's policy allowing medicinal marijuana use; in writing her dissent in support of state authority, O'Connor observes that she would not have favored its policy.[122] Of course, this makes it all the more regrettable (if not ironic) that it was a mistaken conception of constitutional principle that kept Stevens and the majority from allowing California to extend compassion to seriously ill neighbors. In truth, California's medicinal use exception was highly limited and respectful of federal interests, especially as state law otherwise dovetailed and reinforced the federal regulation of controlled substances. The subsidiarity and federalism values of allowing individual states to meet the unique needs of its citizens did not impress

---

[122]Wrote Justice Stevens: "The case is made difficult by respondents' strong arguments that they will suffer irreparable harm because, despite a congressional finding to the contrary, marijuana does have valid therapeutic purposes. The question before us, however, is not whether it is wise to enforce the statute in these circumstances; rather, it is whether Congress' power to regulate interstate markets for medicinal substances encompasses the portions of those markets that are supplied with drugs produced and consumed locally." Gonzales v. Raich, 125 S. Ct. 2195, 2201 (2005). By comparison, Justice O'Connor commented: "If I were a California citizen, I would not have voted for the medical marijuana ballot initiative; if I were a California legislator I would not have supported the Compassionate Use Act. But whatever the wisdom of California's experiment with medical marijuana, the federalism principles that have driven our Commerce Clause cases require that room for experiment be protected in this case." *Id.* at 2229 (O'Connor, J., dissenting).

the majority and Justice Scalia. For them, federal power cannot be contingent on the happenstance of state concurrence. Perhaps not, but federal power had been thought to be contingent on constitutional text as originally understood at the time of its ratification.[123] Only Thomas paid direct attention to the Constitution's words and the well-documented purpose of the Commerce Clause.

In short, *Wickard v. Filburn* has been displaced as the "outer limit" of federal power.

[123]Antonin Scalia, A Matter of Interpretation (1997).

Town of Castle Rock v. Gonzales: Executive Indifference, Judicial Complicity

*Roger Pilon**

I. Introduction

We came in out of the state of nature, so the story goes, in order better to protect ourselves. There is safety in numbers, we said, and justice too. Thus, we gave up our rights of self-enforcement, in most cases, and asked the state to do it for us.[1] But what if the state fails in that most basic of its functions? What recourse do we have?

The tragic case that brought those questions before the Supreme Court this term, *Town of Castle Rock v. Gonzales*,[2] arose out of divorce proceedings in which one Mrs. Jessica Gonzales sought and obtained a temporary restraining order (TRO) against her estranged husband. Made permanent shortly thereafter and served that day on Mr. Gonzales, the order commanded him not to "molest or disturb the peace" of Mrs. Gonzales or their three daughters, ages ten, nine, and seven, and to remain at least 100 yards from the family home at all times. In bold letters on the back it gave him ample "WARN-ING" that a knowing violation was a crime and that he may be arrested without notice if a law enforcement officer had probable cause to believe he had knowingly violated the order.

Most important for our purposes, the order also included a "NOTICE TO LAW ENFORCEMENT OFFICIALS" that read in part:

YOU SHALL USE EVERY REASONABLE MEANS TO ENFORCE THIS RESTRAINING ORDER. YOU SHALL ARREST, OR, IF AN ARREST WOULD BE IMPRACTICAL

---

*Vice President for Legal Affairs; Director, Center for Constitutional Studies, Cato Institute.

[1]Those are the opening lines in Roger Pilon, Criminal Remedies: Restitution, Punishment, or Both? 88 Ethics 348 (1978), responding to Randy E. Barnett, Restitution: A New Paradigm of Criminal Justice, 87 Ethics 279 (1977).

[2]125 S. Ct. 2796 (2005).

UNDER THE CIRCUMSTANCES, SEEK A WARRANT FOR
THE ARREST OF THE RESTRAINED PERSON WHEN YOU
HAVE INFORMATION AMOUNTING TO PROBABLE
CAUSE THAT THE RESTRAINED PERSON HAS VIO-
LATED OR ATTEMPTED TO VIOLATE ANY PROVISION
OF THIS ORDER AND THE RESTRAINED PERSON HAS
BEEN PROPERLY SERVED WITH A COPY OF THIS ORDER
OR HAS RECEIVED ACTUAL NOTICE OF THE EXIS-
TENCE OF THIS ORDER.[3]

A few weeks later, at about 5:00 or 5:30 p.m. on a weekday after-
noon, without notice or advance arrangements, Mr. Gonzales
abducted the three daughters while they were playing outside the
family home in Castle Rock, Colorado. When Mrs. Gonzales noticed
the children were missing, she suspected her husband had taken
them, given his history of suicidal threats and erratic behavior. At
about 7:30 p.m. she called the Castle Rock Police Department, which
dispatched two officers. As the Court describes:

> When [the officers] arrived . . . she showed them a copy of
> the TRO and requested that it be enforced and the three
> children be returned to her immediately. [The officers] stated
> that there was nothing they could do about the TRO and
> suggested that Mrs. Gonzales call the Police Department
> again if the three children did not return home by 10:00 p.m.
> At approximately 8:30 p.m., Mrs. Gonzales talked to her
> husband on his cellular telephone. He told her "he had the
> three children [at an] amusement park in Denver." She called
> the police again and asked them to "have someone check
> for" her husband or his vehicle at the amusement park and
> "put out an [all points bulletin]" for her husband, but the
> officer with whom she spoke "refused to do so," again telling
> her to "wait until 10:00 p.m. and see if" her husband returned
> the girls.
> At approximately 10:10 p.m., Mrs. Gonzales called the
> police and said her children were still missing, but she was
> now told to wait until midnight. She called at midnight and
> told the dispatcher her children were still missing. She went

---

[3]That notice and the quoted facts that follow are taken from the opinion of the
Court, *id.* at 2801–02. The quoted facts are taken by the Court from the complaint
respondent Mrs. Gonzales filed in federal district court. Because the case comes to
the Court on appeal from a dismissal of the complaint, the Court assumes its allega-
tions are true.

to her husband's apartment and, finding nobody there, called the police at 12:10 a.m.; she was told to wait for an officer to arrive. When none came, she went to the police station at 12:50 a.m. and submitted an incident report. The officer who took the report "made no reasonable effort to enforce the TRO or locate the three children. Instead, he went to dinner." At approximately 3:20 a.m., Mrs. Gonzales' husband arrived at the police station and opened fire with a semiautomatic handgun he had purchased earlier that evening. Police shot back, killing him. Inside the cab of his pickup truck, they found the bodies of all three daughters, whom he had already murdered.[4]

A layman reading and reflecting on those horrific facts would most likely have little difficulty concluding that the Castle Rock police officers had a clear legal duty on behalf of Mrs. Gonzales to enforce the restraining order; that they were grossly negligent, at least, in failing to do so; and that, accordingly, they and the town of Castle Rock, their employer, were liable to Mrs. Gonzales for the losses she suffered as a result of that failure. At bottom, after all, the protection at issue here is the very thing we created government in the first place to provide. Our founding document, the Declaration of Independence, states that plainly: "That to secure these Rights [to Life, Liberty, and the Pursuit of Happiness], Governments are instituted among Men."

Indeed, does anyone doubt that a private firm would be held liable if it had contracted to enforce that order and its agents had been as derelict as the Castle Rock police were? The layman understands a contract. And he has an intuitive understanding of the social contract as well. Are public officials, unlike their private counterparts, insulated from responsibility and hence, to that extent, "above the law"? Principle aside, as a practical matter it goes without saying that it is far more effective to hold officials accountable in a targeted way than to try to do so through the broad brush of periodic elections. The political remedy favored by many conservatives of the judicial restraint school—Mrs. Gonzales' right to vote every so often—is cold comfort here. In the end, therefore, this case is not difficult.

Unfortunately, that common sense eluded seven members of the Supreme Court this term. Led by Justice Antonin Scalia, with a

[4]*Id.* at 2801–02.

brief concurrence by Justice David Souter, joined by Justice Stephen Breyer, the Court followed a strained course of reasoning to deny Mrs. Gonzales her claim for relief under section 1983 of the Civil Rights Act of 1871,[5] which spells out the right of individuals to sue state officials they believe have violated their constitutional rights under color of state law. In a word, Scalia could find no constitutional right to be violated and hence no violation. Only Justice John Paul Stevens, joined by Justice Ruth Bader Ginsburg, came close to the first principles of the matter. They would have upheld the six members of the en banc Tenth Circuit Court of Appeals that had found for Mrs. Gonzales.[6]

Because Scalia's opinion for the majority is tightly argued, I will follow and analyze it point by point. To better ground and frame the analysis, however, it will be useful at the outset to recur to those first principles on which the common sense view rests, the better also to see how far today we have strayed from them. This will be no wild-eyed excursion into the hoary reaches of natural rights theory, let me note. I will not be inventing rights with abandon. Neither did the two justices or six judges below who found for Mrs. Gonzales. Rather, I want simply to outline the principles that pretty much everyone in the founding generation and most in the generation that wrote and ratified the Civil War Amendments agreed on. Representations to the contrary notwithstanding, it is a foundation at some remove from the one upon which many "originalists" like Scalia rest.[7]

II. First Principles

A. In the Beginning

"We start with first principles," Chief Justice William Rehnquist famously said in 1995 in *United States v. Lopez*.[8] "The Constitution creates a Federal Government of enumerated powers."[9] Invoking the Tenth Amendment, which makes the doctrine of enumerated powers explicit, he might more fully have said that the Constitution

---

[5]42 U.S.C. § 1983.

[6]366 F.3d 1093 (10th Cir. 2004).

[7]See, e.g., Antonin Scalia, A Matter of Interpretation 138–41 (1997).

[8]514 U.S. 549 (1995).

[9]*Id.* at 552.

creates a government of *delegated,* enumerated, and thus limited powers. For the Tenth and Ninth Amendments together, the final documentary evidence from the founding period, recapitulate the theory of government and governmental legitimacy that was first set forth in the Declaration and is implicit throughout the Constitution. Grounded in Lockean state-of-nature theory,[10] the idea is that we are all born with certain natural rights, as reflected largely in the English common law:[11] the right to property, broadly understood as "Lives, Liberties, and Estates" as Locke put it;[12] the right to change that world of natural rights through contract; and the instrumental, second-order right to secure or enforce those substantive, first-order natural and contractual rights through what Locke called the "Executive Power" that each of us enjoys in the state of nature.[13]

That three-part theory of rights is implicit in the Declaration and is employed by the Tenth Amendment, which tells us that power is legitimate only insofar as it has been delegated to the government by those who first have it, "we the people," the powers not so delegated being reserved to the states or to the people. And the Ninth Amendment makes it clear that we have far more rights than the few that could have been enumerated in the original Constitution and the Bill of Rights. In a nutshell, the Constitution is a social contract through which the founding generation created a government whose powers are limited to those that have been delegated to it, which makes them legitimate, leaving individuals otherwise free to pursue happiness as they think best, exercising all the rights they've retained. And as the powers enumerated in the Constitution indicate, most are drawn from Locke's Executive Power: in one way or another, that is, most are aimed at securing our first-order substantive rights.[14]

[10]John Locke, The Second Treatise of Government, in Two Treatises of Government (Peter Laslett ed., 1960) (1690).

[11]Edward S. Corwin, The "Higher Law" Background of American Constitutional Law 26 (1955) ("[T]he notion that the common law embodied right reason furnished from the fourteenth century its chief claim to be regarded as higher law.").

[12]Locke, *supra* note 10, at ¶ 123.

[13]*Id.* at ¶ 13.

[14]I have discussed those issues more fully in Roger Pilon, The Purpose and Limits of Government, in Limiting Leviathan 13–37 (Donald P. Racheter & Richard E. Wagner eds., 1999), reprinted as Cato's Letter No. 13 (Cato Institute 1999). See also Scott Douglas Gerber, To Secure These Rights: The Declaration of Independence and Constitutional Interpretation (1995).

To be sure, the great bulk of that executive or police power was left with the states, but state constitutions follow the same Lockean theory of legitimacy as the federal Constitution. In particular, government officials are our agents, charged by constitutional contract with exercising the power we've delegated to them. Cast negatively, the idea of "inherent sovereignty," other than in the people, and "discretionary power," other than for practical reasons, is utterly foreign to our system of government. Thus, of particular relevance here, officials may have some discretion as a practical matter, but when that discretion is clearly removed, they must act as charged.

B. Completing the Constitution

But even after the Bill of Rights was added in 1791, the original design was flawed by the Constitution's oblique recognition of slavery, made necessary to ensure union. Thus, as the Court held in 1833,[15] the Bill of Rights applied not against the states but only against the government created by the document it amended, the federal government. And slavery, far from withering away, as most Framers had hoped it would, was ended only by the Civil War and the ratification of the Civil War Amendments.

With the ratification of those Amendments, however, the relationship between the federal government and the states was fundamentally changed. Especially through Section 1 of the Fourteenth Amendment—defining citizenship, protecting the privileges or immunities of United States citizens against state violations, and ensuring due process and equal protection by the states—individuals at last had federal remedies against state violations of their rights. As has rightly been said, the Civil War Amendments "completed" the Constitution, finally incorporating into the document the grand founding principles of the Declaration of Independence.[16]

But the Court has never come to grips with that fundamental change. The problem began in 1873, barely five years after the Fourteenth Amendment was ratified, when a deeply divided five to four Court effectively eviscerated the Privileges or Immunities Clause

---

[15]Barron v. Mayor of Baltimore, 32 U.S. (7 Pet.) 243 (1833).

[16]See especially Robert J. Reinstein, Completing the Constitution: The Declaration of Independence, Bill of Rights and Fourteenth Amendment, 47 Temp. L. Rev. 361 (1993).

from the Amendment in the infamous *Slaughterhouse Cases*.[17] Thereafter the Court would attempt to do under the Due Process Clause what was meant to be done under the more substantive Privileges or Immunities Clause. The effort has been uneven at best, largely because the Court seems never to have grasped that the rights "incorporated" against the states *ab initio* by the Fourteenth Amendment included not simply most of those in the Bill of Rights but the whole body of rights that stands behind the Constitution, drawn not simply from the Bill of Rights but from the common law and natural rights traditions—rights we never gave up. Those rights, "more tedious than difficult" to enumerate, were *constitutionalized* by the Fourteenth Amendment.[18]

Thus, such subsequent federal and state legislation as the Civil Rights Act of 1871, *provided it is faithful to the Fourteenth Amendment as originally understood*, does not "create" any new rights. Rather, it simply recognizes and clarifies the rights and procedures the Amendment had already constitutionalized. It is positive law, yes, but law that reflects not simply the will of the legislature that enacts it but that of the generation that wrote and ratified the Amendment, which itself reflected the "higher law" from which it was drawn, as the debates in the thirty-ninth Congress that passed the Amendment and the debates surrounding ratification make clear.[19]

[17]83 U.S. (16 Wall.) 36 (1873). See Kimberly C. Shankman and Roger Pilon, Reviving the Privileges or Immunities Clause to Redress the Balance Among States, Individuals, and the Federal Government, 326 Cato Policy Analysis (Nov. 23, 1998), reprinted in 3 Tex. Rev. L. & Pol. 1 (1998).

[18]The quoted phrase is from Justice Bushrod Washington's authoritative interpretation of Article IV's Privileges and Immunities Clause: Corfield v. Coryell, 6 F. Cas. 546, 541 (C.C.E.D. Pa. 1823). Washington's opinion was among the sources relied on by those who drafted the Fourteenth Amendment.

[19]In the House, Rep. John Bingham, the author of Section 1, said its provisions would protect "the inborn rights of every person." Cong. Globe., 39th Cong., 1st Sess. 2542 (statement of Rep. Bingham). In the Senate, Luke Poland, a former state chief justice, said that Section 1 "is the very spirit and inspiration of our system of government. The absolute foundation upon which it is established. It is essentially declared in the Declaration of Independence and in all the provisions of the Constitution." Id. at 2961 (statement of Sen. Poland). After Speaker of the House Schuyler Colfax presided over the debates in that chamber, he told his constituents that Section 1 is "going to be the gem of the Constitution. . . . it is the Declaration of Independence placed immutably and forever in the Constitution." Cincinnati Commercial, Aug. 9, 1866, at 2, col.3.

The failure of the Court to fully or clearly grasp those points continues to this day, of course. In fact, today, on a wide range of issues, the Fourteenth Amendment is the main ground on which modern judicial "liberals" and "conservatives" so often wage war. Armed with the "law-as-politics" agenda set by the New Deal Court in 1937 and 1938,[20] modern liberals recognize rights under the Amendment episodically, largely ignoring genuine rights like property and contract while inventing specious "rights" from whole cloth—like the "right" to procure or perform an abortion, a matter for criminal law line-drawing that properly falls under the general police power of the states. In reaction, modern conservatives too often recoil at the very idea of judges recognizing rights not found explicitly in the constitutional text.[21] Dubious "originalists" and "textualists," they ignore or disparage the plain text (the Ninth Amendment, the Privileges or Immunities Clause), the true original understanding, and the structure that reflects that understanding.

C. Modern Confusions

Not surprisingly, the checkered history of Fourteenth Amendment interpretation has led to several confusions and erroneous doctrines. One was just mentioned: the Amendment is not a mere invitation to legislators, much less judges, to legislate at will; rather, it is "complete," yet it binds those who interpret it. And it "completes" the Constitution in the sense that it incorporates the Declaration's principles and applies them at last against the states. Thus, legislators and judges do not have to "create" new rights; they simply have to recognize, clarify, and make explicit the rights that are already there,

---

[20]Following President Franklin Roosevelt's infamous Court-packing scheme early in 1937, the New Deal Court eviscerated the doctrine of enumerated powers in *Helvering v. Davis*, 301 U.S. 619 (1937), and *NLRB v. Jones & Laughlin Steel Corp.*, 301 U.S. 1 (1937). Then in 1938 the Court bifurcated the Bill of Rights, effectively distinguishing "fundamental" and "nonfundamental" rights, and invented a bifurcated theory of judicial review in famous (or infamous) footnote four of *United States v. Carolene Products Co.*, 304 U.S. 144 (1938). I have discussed those issues more fully in Roger Pilon, Restoring Constitutional Government, 2001–2002 Cato Sup. Ct. Rev. vii (2002). For a penetrating analysis of the political machinations that surrounded the Court-packing scheme, see William E. Leuchtenburg, The Supreme Court Reborn: The Constitutional Revolution in the Age of Roosevelt (1995).

[21]See, e.g., Scalia, Matter of Interpretation, *supra* note 7; Robert H. Bork, The Tempting of America: The Political Seduction of the Law (1990); Lino Graglia, It's Not Constitutionalism, It's Judicial Activism, 19 Harv. J.L. & Pub. Pol'y 293 (1996).

if only by implication. That takes sound lawmaking and judge-crafting, to be sure: it means that legislators and judges must appeal more to reason than to will or politics, but that is nothing less than what the oath of office requires. Lawmakers and judges are not free, therefore, to stray beyond their authority, as too many modern liberals, proponents of unbounded legal positivism, would have them do. But neither may they shirk from their responsibilities to faithfully clarify through legislation, or interpret and apply through adjudication, the Amendment's principles and broad language, as too many modern conservatives, proponents of a narrow legal positivism, would have them do.

A closely related point follows: Far from *requiring* federal or state legislation to effect the changes wrought by the Fourteenth Amendment, Section 1 of the Amendment was drafted to be *self-executing*—to enable individuals to bring actions against states without Congress having first to authorize it or to articulate their rights. In fact, Rep. John Bingham, one of the Amendment's chief sponsors in the thirty-ninth Congress and the author of Section 1, introduced two versions of Section 1 that were *not* self-executing, only to be remonstrated from the floor that those versions would leave the enjoyment of rights "to the caprice of Congress."[22] A third version of Section 1, the present version, cured that problem by making the Section self-executing.

Finally, for present purposes, the early loss of the Privileges or Immunities Clause and the Court's subsequent reliance on the Due Process Clause to do so much of the Amendment's work has led to a spurious distinction, with serious consequences, between "substantive" and "procedural" due process. Due process clauses have a long and glorious history of protecting substantive rights stretching back at least to Magna Carta.[23] Thus, the narrow view of the clause

---

[22]"But this amendment proposes to leave it to the caprice of Congress; and your legislation on the subject would depend upon the political majority of Congress, and not upon two thirds of Congress and three fourths of the States." Cong. Globe, 39th Cong., 1st Sess. 1095 (statement of Rep. Hotchkiss) (quoted in Reinstein, *supra* note 16, at 393 n.179).

[23]See, e.g., Bernard H. Siegan, Property Rights: From Magna Carta to the Fourteenth Amendment (2002). In *Solesbee v. Balkcom*, 339 U.S. 9, 16 (1950), Justice Felix Frankfurter wrote in dissent, "It is now the settled doctrine of this Court that the Due Process Clause embodies a system of rights based on moral principles so deeply imbedded in the traditions and feelings of our people as to be deemed fundamental to a civilized society as conceived by our whole history."

held today by many modern conservatives—that "substantive due process" is something of an oxymoron and that government may deprive a person of life, liberty, or property, provided only that the process due is accorded—is wrong historically as well as in theory.

The theory of the matter, in a nutshell, is this: *all* rights, including procedural rights, are ultimately substantive; in a state of nature, the procedural rights that arise when first-order substantive rights are threatened or violated—i.e., the second-order enforcement rights (the "Executive Power"), and rights against wrongful enforcement— are derived from those first-order substantive rights. We call them "procedural" rights simply because they pertain to and arise in the context of enforcing or securing our first-order substantive rights of property and contract, a context essentially procedural. By virtue of their derivation from our first-order substantive rights, however, those procedural rights, once they arise or "kick in," are every bit as "substantive" as the underlying rights they are meant to secure. After all, the state-of-nature procedural right "to prosecute," whether to punish or to seek restitution, is a liberty—which arises only when a wrong is alleged.[24] Similarly, the procedural right against unreasonable searches and seizures is also a liberty, derived straightforwardly from the right to be free. Were we not to have lost the Privileges or Immunities Clause, this spurious dichotomy might never have arisen. But the loss has "forced" the Court, so to speak, to make the Due Process Clause do double duty—to serve as a source of both substantive and procedural rights, a duty that might better have been, and doubtless was meant to be, split between the two clauses.

III. Applying the Principles

With that brief background, especially concerning the Fourteenth Amendment, we can now turn to the case at hand and then to Scalia's opinion for the Court. As noted above, but for the history of the Amendment's interpretation and the confusions that have ensued, *Castle Rock*, like *Slaughterhouse* long before, should have been an easy case. As explained and justified by the social contract theory on which the nation rests, when Mrs. Gonzales entered civil society she yielded up, in most situations, her state-of-nature Executive

---

[24] I have discussed those issues more fully in Pilon, Criminal Remedies, *supra* note 1.

Power to enforce her rights—contracting mainly with the state, but also with the federal government, to have those governments exercise that right for her and on her behalf. And with the ratification of the Fourteenth Amendment she authorized a federal check on the states. All of that is evidenced by the Declaration, the federal and state constitutions, the statute at issue, and the restraining order issued under it.

The precise terms of that contract are no small matter, of course, especially for the case at hand, about which more in a moment. But concerning the principle at issue, there is nothing extraordinary in the arrangement itself. In a state of nature Mrs. Gonzales might have contracted for the same protection with a private protective agency.[25] Having contracted instead with the state, her right to have government protect her—derived from her former right to protect herself—amounts simply to one of the "privileges" of citizenship meant to be protected under Section 1's Privileges or Immunities Clause.[26] Having abridged one of her privileges by failing to protect her, the town, a subsidiary of the state, is liable, at least in principle.

Alternatively, under the Due Process Clause Mrs. Gonzales had a property interest in the above-noted contractual right to be protected by the state. Since all rights are reducible to property,[27] once

---

[25]See, e.g., Robert Nozick, Anarchy, State, and Utopia, Part I (1974).

[26]Speaking in the Senate, Jacob Howard said the most important feature of Section 1 of the Fourteenth Amendment was the Privileges or Immunities Clause. He addressed the scope of the clause by drawing on Justice Washington's explication of Article IV's Privileges and Immunities Clause (see note 18, *supra*), listing "protection by the Government" first among our privileges. Cong. Globe., 39th Cong., 1st Sess. 2765 (statement of Sen. Howard). That the Constitution leaves such protection with the states, in most cases, is immaterial since the object of the privilege is the same whether the power of protection was delegated by Mrs. Gonzales to the federal government, as in some cases, or reserved to the states, as with the general police power. The change wrought by the Fourteenth Amendment, which the *Slaughterhouse* majority was unwilling to acknowledge, was to make the privilege one of *national* citizenship, which no state might thereafter abridge. Thus were states restricted; and thus was federalism fundamentally changed by the ratification of the Fourteenth Amendment.

[27]Locke, *supra* note 10, at ¶ 123 ("Lives, Liberties, and Estates, which I call by the general Name, *Property*"); James Madison, Property, National Gazette, March 29, 1792, at 175, reprinted in 6 The Writings of James Madison 101 (Gaillard Hunt ed., 1906) ("In a word, as a man is said to have a right to his property, he may be equally said to have a property in his rights.").

she entered civil society the property she formerly held in her state-of-nature right to protect herself became simply the property she now holds through contract, the right to be protected. In failing to protect her, the town deprived her of her property—there having been no process forthcoming that might have shown that she had somehow forfeited that property. Here too, then, the town is liable for that deprivation, at least in principle.

That general theory needs to be tempered, however, by practical considerations of the kind that would likely arise in any contractual setting, private or public, involving enforcement. For just as no one in the state of nature would be able to provide absolute security for himself, so too no prudent party offering such services, private or public, would contract to provide absolute security. Thus it is that in civil society, law enforcement officials enjoy a measure of discretion as to whether and how they exercise the authority that has been delegated to them. As we negotiated the social contract, we did not charge officials with providing *absolute* security. But neither did we give them absolute discretion.

All of that was left only implicit in the Constitution and its amendments, of course, to be clarified and made explicit later, consistent with the underlying principles, through either judicial discovery or statute. That there is a measure of indeterminacy here should not surprise: law has numerous such areas. But neither should it lead to judicial deference bordering on abdication. Notwithstanding the indeterminacy that is inherent in the enforcement context, therefore, it is the underlying principles that we need to keep foremost in mind as we analyze the Court's handling of this case.

IV. Justice Scalia's Opinion for the Court

That deductive approach to the case, grounded in first principles and in the theory of the Constitution, sits uneasily among those accustomed to a world of mere positive law. Thus, Scalia, generally a textualist, rarely invokes that underlying theory, which does what inescapably incomplete text alone cannot do—give a complete account. All three opinions issuing from the Court ignore the Privileges or Immunities Clause, of course, focusing instead on the Due Process Clause. And all three wrestle with the spurious and distracting distinction between "substantive" and "procedural" due process—in part because a 1989 decision, *DeShaney v. Winnebago*

County,[28] had ruled out "substantive due process" relief for Mrs. Gonzales, but also because they're working within a positivist framework whereby states "create" rights to life, liberty, and property, then "create" various procedures to guard against deprivation of those positive rights. Thus are "substantive" and "procedural" rights separated, both the creations of positive law—of mere will. Accordingly, none of the opinions conceives of process rights as being substantive because entailed by substantive rights, as discussed above, although Stevens does make an effort to cut through the artificial distinction in a note responding to Souter's concurrence.[29]

A. Framing the Issue

Scalia frames the case as follows: "whether an individual who has obtained a state-law restraining order has a constitutionally protected property interest in having the police enforce the restraining order when they have probable cause to believe it has been violated."[30] As noted above, Mrs. Gonzales sued under section 1983, "claiming that the town violated the Due Process Clause because its police department had 'an official policy or custom of failing to respond properly to complaints of restraining order violations' and 'tolerate[d] the non-enforcement of restraining orders by its police officers.'"[31]

Beginning with the text of both the Fourteenth Amendment's Due Process Clause and section 1983, which creates a federal cause of action for the deprivation of rights "secured by the Constitution and laws," Scalia first distinguishes *DeShaney*: "We held [there] that the so-called 'substantive' component in the Due Process Clause does not 'requir[e] the State to protect the life, liberty, and property of its citizens against invasion by private actors.'"[32] With the grammatical overkill of "so-called" plus sneer quotes, we cannot miss Scalia's well-known contempt for the idea of "substantive due process." That leaves "procedural due process." But the "procedural component" of the clause doesn't protect every "benefit," Scalia says,

---

[28]489 U.S. 189 (1989).
[29]Town of Castle Rock v. Gonzales, 125 S. Ct. 2796, 2824 n.20 (2005) (Stevens, J., dissenting).
[30]*Id.* at 2800.
[31]*Id.* at 2802.
[32]*Id.* at 2803.

thereby inviting us to look upon Mrs. Gonzales as claiming a mere "benefit," not a right. A property interest entails "more than an abstract need or desire," he continues. It requires "a legitimate claim of entitlement." And that is "created" not by the Constitution, he says, but by some "independent source such as state law."[33]

B. U.S. Constitution or State Statute?

All right, grant for the moment that this claim must be created by state law, not by the Constitution. But "a benefit is not a protected entitlement if government officials may grant or deny it in their discretion,"[34] Scalia says, thus planting the theme he will try to develop for pretty much the rest of the opinion. He notes that the court below found no such discretion; thus, it held that Colorado law *did* create an entitlement "because the 'court-issued restraining order . . . specifically dictated that its terms must be enforced' and a 'state statute command[ed]' enforcement . . . ."[35] Scalia will work that issue of discretion shortly, but first he addresses Mrs. Gonzales' contention that the Court must give deference to the Tenth Circuit's analysis of Colorado law. And in the course of doing so he wrestles with the question of whether Colorado law has given Mrs. Gonzales a property interest "for purposes of the Fourteenth Amendment."

As noted above, this case fits more naturally under the Privileges or Immunities Clause. But "for purposes of" procedural due process, Scalia asserts that, despite its "state-law underpinnings," that question is ultimately one of federal constitutional law and hence one for the High Court to determine by asking whether the underlying substantive interest created by state law "rises to the level of" a legitimate claim of entitlement—again, "for purposes of" procedural due process.[36]

Just what "rises to the level of" means here, or in any rights context for that matter, is hard to know. However common, the idiom mixes values and rights, degree and kind, uncritically; thus, it sits uncomfortably in discussions about rights. Presumably, we're invited to believe that if an "interest" is, perhaps, "important

[33]*Id.*
[34]*Id.*
[35]*Id.*
[36]*Id.* at 2803–04.

enough," it "rises to the level of" a right. If so, that bespeaks profound confusion about the theory of rights. Moreover, here it suggests that an interest may be a *right* under state law (if the Tenth Circuit is right), yet not have "risen" to that level "for purposes of" procedural due process (if Scalia is right). And that would seem to contradict Scalia's earlier claim that entitlements enjoying due process protection are created not by the Constitution but by state law.[37] Or is it rather that Mrs. Gonzales has a *right* under state law, but a mere "benefit" under federal law, even though federal law here depends on state law? Is it surprising that the layman has difficulty following these hermeneutics?

But there's more. The deference the Court owes a circuit court interpreting state law in its jurisdiction "can be overcome," Scalia says. The problem here, it seems, is that the court below relied primarily on the "language from the restraining order, the statutory text, and a state-legislative-hearing transcript"—that from Scalia the textualist—rather than "a deep well of state-specific expertise." And because those texts "say nothing distinctive to Colorado, but use mandatory language that . . . appears in many state and federal statutes," deference to the circuit court's reading is unwarranted, presumably.[38] Stevens too puzzles over what he calls that "odd" reasoning, which he says "makes a mockery of our traditional practice."[39] Be that as it may, Scalia adds that if the circuit court's analysis were to be accepted, "we would necessarily have to decide conclusively [the] federal constitutional question"[40]—i.e., the due process question. And that he is unprepared to do.

C. Right or Mere Benefit?

Thus does Scalia begin his own altogether conclusory analysis of whether Colorado law created a right or simply a benefit. Pointing to the notice to law enforcement personnel that was printed on the

---

[37]*Id.* at 2803. ("Such [due process] entitlements are 'of course . . . not created by the Constitution. Rather, they are created and their dimensions are defined by existing rules or understandings that stem from an independent source such as state law.'") (citing Paul v. Davis, 424 U.S. 693, 709 (1976) (quoting Board of Regents v. Roth, 408 U.S. 564, 577 (1972)).

[38]*Id.* at 2804.

[39]*Id.* at 2815 n.2 (Stevens, J., dissenting).

[40]*Id.* at 2804.

back of the restraining order, which effectively restates the statutory provision, he quotes from that statutory text, which reads, in relevant part:

(a) A peace officer shall use every reasonable means to enforce a restraining order.

(b) A peace officer shall arrest, or, if an arrest would be impractical under the circumstances, seek a warrant for the arrest of a restrained person when the officer has information amounting to probable cause [to believe that the order has been violated].

(c) A peace officer shall enforce a valid restraining order whether or not there is a record of a restraining order in the registry.[41]

Scalia then cites briefly from the legislative history of the statute. As if the "shall" above were not enough (for a textualist), that history, cited far more extensively in the Stevens dissent, makes it unmistakably clear that in this area involving domestic violence, Colorado, like a number of other states in recent years, meant precisely to remove virtually all law enforcement discretion, especially given the well-documented evidence that absent such mandatory requirements, police underenforcement tended to be the rule, often with tragic results, which is just what happened here.

Yet Scalia dismisses the text, uncharacteristically, and the legislative history too, which he is ordinarily more inclined to do. He baldly asserts, "[w]e do not believe that these provisions of Colorado law truly make enforcement of restraining orders *mandatory*," claiming that "[a] well established tradition of police discretion has long coexisted with apparently mandatory arrest statutes."[42] Doubtless to the surprise of many Scalia watchers, text here is trumped by "tradition," as reflected in, of all things, the "ABA Standards for Criminal Justice" that he cites.[43] Those standards give three reasons for not interpreting mandatory statutes literally: (1) "legislative history," which goes the other way here; (2) "insufficient resources"; and (3) "sheer physical impossibility," neither of which was an issue here.

---

[41]*Id*. at 2805.

[42]*Id*. at 2805–06.

[43]*Id*. at 2806 (citing 1 ABA Standards for Criminal Justice 1–4.5, commentary, 1-124-1-125 (2d ed. 1980) (footnotes omitted)).

Continuing in this vein, Scalia next cites the Court's treatment of the "shall order" language at issue in a recent case involving a Chicago crowd dispersal ordinance: "[I]t is, the Court proclaimed, simply 'common sense that *all* police officers must use some discretion in deciding when and where to enforce city ordinances.'"[44] Scalia could have illustrated at length, of course, this "tradition" of police discretion coexisting side-by-side with apparently mandatory text, but none of that would have distracted one bit from the fact that in *this* area, concerning domestic violence, the Colorado legislature meant precisely to *eliminate* police discretion, as the evidence adduced by the dissent makes overwhelmingly clear. Thus, when Scalia says that "a true mandate of police action would require some stronger language from the Colorado Legislature than 'shall use every reasonable means to enforce a restraining order' (or even 'shall arrest . . . or seek a warrant'),"[45] we have to ask, what more could the legislature have done? Stevens, too, remarks that "it is hard to imagine what the Court has in mind . . ." by way of stronger language.[46] Perhaps the four words could have been added that many believe should have been added at the end of the Constitution: "And we mean it."

Scalia himself gives no indication of what more the Colorado legislature could have done. Instead, he now starts, in effect, to split hairs. He avers that "[i]t is hard to imagine that a Colorado peace officer would not have *some* discretion," given the "circumstances of the violation or the competing duties of the officer . . . ."[47] But even if such "circumstances" had obtained in this case, and none did, that argument, of course, poses a straw man: the legislature could hardly have expected to eliminate discretion *absolutely*. The impossible standard Scalia implicitly erects would render legislatures impotent, officers immune, and citizens disarmed and vulnerable.

Next, Scalia notes that discretion is needed especially when the whereabouts of the suspected violator are unknown, which again was not the case here once Mrs. Gonzales had located her husband. Scalia continues to work variations of the absent-offender situation,

---

[44]*Id.* (citing Chicago v. Morales, 527 U.S. 41, 62 n.32 (1999)) (emphasis added).
[45]*Id.*
[46]*Id.* at 2818 (Stevens, J., dissenting).
[47]*Id.* at 2806 (emphasis added).

concluding by noting that the statute at issue requires, when arrest is impractical, that the officer seek a warrant rather than an arrest. But of course the Castle Rock police did not do that either.

At this point Scalia complains that Mrs. Gonzales did not specify "the precise means of enforcement that the Colorado restraining-order statute assertedly mandated," adding that "[s]uch indeterminacy is not the hallmark of a duty that is mandatory."[48] But neither, of course, did the statute permit the Castle Rock police to do nothing, which is what they did. Stevens gives the complaint short shrift, analogizing the statutory duty of the police and the correlative right of the citizen to any other entitlement that might be satisfied in various ways.[49] Scalia's argument here is simply too precious to be credible.

Yet he presses the point. In answer to the dissent's contention that the entitlement in question is ultimately quite precise—"either make an arrest or (if that is impractical) seek an arrest warrant"—Scalia claims that "the seeking of an arrest warrant would be an entitlement to nothing but procedure," which could hardly be "the basis for a property interest" since it remains in the discretion of a judge to grant it and of the police to execute it.[50] Note first that "the making of an arrest" is every bit as "procedural" as "the seeking of an arrest warrant." Both are processes executed in service of underlying substantive rights. Second, notice that Scalia seems unable to conceive of a procedural right as being a substantive right, derived from an underlying substantive right, as discussed earlier. For him, perhaps (it is unclear here), a right is either substantive, and hence an entitlement, or procedural, and hence not an entitlement. Finally, while it is true that there is an element of discretion involved in a judge's granting a warrant and in the police executing it—just as there is in the police making an arrest when it is practical to do so—the statutory context here reduces that discretion nearly to a nullity. Once again, then, we're back to the statutory text and legislative history, which Scalia is trying desperately to "what if" away. It is passing strange, at least, to find Scalia, for whom judicial restraint is all but a commandment, looking for light that would enable a

[48]*Id.* at 2807.
[49]*Id.* at 2820 (Stevens, J., dissenting).
[50]*Id.* at 2808.

judge ruling on a warrant request to ignore the plain text before him and substitute his own judgment.

In a final effort to show that Colorado has not created an entitlement, Scalia mounts an argument that soon brings us back to first principles. He asks us to suppose that enforcement of the restraining order were in fact mandatory rather than discretionary: it would still not follow, he claims, that the *beneficiary* of the order had an entitlement to its enforcement. Making officials' duties mandatory can serve various ends, he says. In fact, it's the "normal course" of the criminal law to serve public "rather than" private ends, because criminal acts strike at "the very being of society." Mrs. Gonzales' alleged interest stems "only" from the statutory scheme, he continues. Although the statute speaks of "protected persons," it does so respecting only ministerial matters, not enforcement. Most important, Scalia concludes, the statute speaks of the protected person's power to *initiate* civil proceedings; but on the criminal side, it speaks only of her power to *request* the prosecuting attorney to initiate proceedings. And it is silent about any power to request, much less demand, that an arrest be made.[51]

In that argument, Scalia works, for all it is worth, the modern split between civil and criminal law. To oversimplify considerably, and set aside overlaps, civil law deals with wrongs between private individuals, redressed by private suits; criminal law deals with wrongs against the public, redressed by prosecutions by the state. Centuries ago there was no such split: a wrong against an individual, whether accidental or intentional, was redressed through private suits. But among other reasons, as the king's peace grew in importance as a "public interest," he took on responsibility for redressing those "spill-over" wrongs against the public, and two distinct proceedings evolved—civil for private matters, criminal for public matters.

Nevertheless, state-of-nature theory is able to account for both, since there are two sets of interests at stake when an ordinary crime occurs—those of the victim and those of the public. When the state emerges from the state of nature, the victim of crime retains his right to be made whole by suing the criminal for restitution, while the state assumes the right to prosecute the criminal to redress the

[51]*Id.* at 2808–09.

separate wrong to the community the crime occasions—a right that belonged to mankind in general in the state of nature but was yielded up to the state once men left the state of nature and created the state.[52]

Clearly, then, the right of the state to prosecute and punish is parasitic upon and grows out of the right of the victim to seek restitution and, if the wrong is intentional, punish. The state's right, that is, was not created from whole cloth; rather, the state got that right by delegation from the people who first had it, then yielded it up to the state to exercise on their behalf. Thus, when Scalia says the "normal course" of the criminal law is to serve public *rather than* private ends, he overstates the matter substantially. The criminal law serves both ends. For victims of crime have an interest in restitution from the criminal; but they also have an interest in seeing the criminal punished as well as incapacitated by incarceration or restraint, as the case may be, even if those are public interests too.

Indeed, the interest of the victim, as distinct from that of the public, looms especially large here; for the statute making it a crime to violate a restraining order is meant almost entirely to protect a particular individual, not the public in general. Since the private end served by this criminal law dwarfs the public end, Scalia could not be more wrong on this point. Likewise, Mrs. Gonzales' "alleged interest" does not stem "only" from the statutory scheme. It stems from her natural right against "molestation" and her natural right to secure that right, which she yielded up to the state to exercise on her behalf, as reflected in and given effect by Colorado's statutory scheme. That the statute speaks of "protected persons" only in the context of ministerial matters is utterly irrelevant: the very fact that it speaks of "protected persons" implies that there are persons with rights to be protected. Finally, that a protected person may *initiate* civil proceedings but only *request* the initiation of criminal proceedings speaks simply to the division of labor we instituted through constitutions when we left the state of nature.[53] Before leaving the

---

[52]For a fuller discussion, see Pilon, Criminal Remedies, *supra* note 1; Barnett, Restitution, *supra* note 1.

[53]Stevens drives that point home when he notes: "Indeed, for a holder of a restraining order who has read the order's emphatic language, it would likely come as quite a shock to learn that she has no right to demand enforcement in the event of a violation. To suggest that a protected person has no such right would posit a lacuna between a protected person's rights and an officer's duties—a result that would be hard to reconcile with the Colorado Legislature's dual goals of putting an end to police

state of nature Mrs. Gonzales could initiate criminal proceedings herself; she now buys that service, paying for it through taxation, from the state, which is duty-bound to provide it as of right, (social) contractual right—at least here, where her representatives have made that duty so crystal clear.

D. For Due Process Purposes?

Having disposed, he believes, of the argument that Mrs. Gonzales was entitled under state law to have the restraining order enforced, Scalia returns finally and briefly to the question of whether, *assuming otherwise*, her right to enforcement could constitute a property interest for purposes of the Due Process Clause. One would think that question settled in the affirmative by earlier remarks in the opinion.[54] After all, why else would Scalia have directed most of his energies toward showing that Colorado had *not* created an entitlement?

Nevertheless, at this juncture he argues, for due process purposes, that a right to have a restraining order enforced, unlike traditional conceptions of property, "does not 'have some ascertainable monetary value,' as even [the Court's] '*Roth*-type property-as-entitlement' cases have implicitly required."[55] Stevens responds that Mrs. Gonzales could certainly have hired a private security firm, which would have monetized the value of the protection.[56] Scalia replies that the analogy is not precise because a private party would not have the power to arrest if the crime had not occurred in his presence.[57] Stevens answers that the abduction was ongoing (thus removing that restraint), so a private arrest would have been legal.[58] To such lengths does Scalia go to try to disprove what should be clear to all—that there is very little that cannot be monetized.

Scalia then raises a second argument to show that, for due process purposes, Mrs. Gonzales' entitlement does not constitute a property interest: "the alleged property interest here arises *incidentally*," he

indifference and empowering potential victims of domestic abuse." Castle Rock, 125 S. Ct. at 2821 n.16 (Stevens, J., dissenting).

[54]See note 37, *supra*.

[55]Castle Rock, 125 S. Ct. at 2809 (discussing Board of Regents v. Roth, 408 U.S. 577 (1972)).

[56]*Id*. at 2823 n.19 (Stevens, J., dissenting).

[57]*Id*. at 2809 n.12.

[58]*Id*. at 2823 n.19 (Stevens, J., dissenting).

says, "not out of some new species of government benefit or service" but as a function of what governments have always done—arrest suspected criminals. Were *direct* benefits withheld, due process protections would be triggered, he continues. But here the benefits are *indirect*. Quoting the 1980 case of *O'Bannon v. Town Court Nursing Center*,[59] Scalia says, "'[t]he simple distinction between government action that directly affects a citizen's legal rights . . . and action that is directed against a third party and affects the citizen only indirectly or incidentally, provides a sufficient answer to' [Mrs. Gonzales'] reliance on cases that found government-provided services to be entitlements."[60]

No, it is not a sufficient answer. Scalia asks us here to think of the government's action as being "directed against a third party," i.e., Mr. Gonzales, with Mrs. Gonzales, the beneficiary, affected only "indirectly" or "incidentally." Doubtless, Mrs. Gonzales would be surprised to learn that the failure of the police to enforce the restraining order affected her only indirectly or incidentally. Scalia would be right if we were talking about the "incidental" benefits we all lose when the police fail to enforce, say, traffic laws, but that is hardly the situation here. Stevens notes, moreover, that Scalia's reliance on *O'Bannon* is mistaken since the Court there concluded that the regulations at issue had *not* created an entitlement, whereas here Scalia is assuming the opposite "for due process purposes."[61] More directly, however, it simply strains credulity to think of Mrs. Gonzales as a mere incidental beneficiary of this statute. Here again, it is the precise character of the statutory scheme the state created that Scalia is unwilling to acknowledge.

V. Conclusion

Unable to recognize the property right Mrs. Gonzales had under the Due Process Clause, as made clear by Colorado's statute and particularized by the restraining order she obtained, much less the privilege she enjoyed under the Privileges or Immunities Clause, Scalia concludes, quite naturally, that it is unnecessary for the Court to determine whether "the town's custom or policy prevented the

[59]447 U.S. 773 (1980).
[60]Castle Rock, 125 S. Ct. at 2809–10.
[61]*Id.* at 2823 n.18 (Stevens, J., dissenting).

police from giving her due process when they deprived her of that alleged interest."[62] Thus, the Court reversed the decision of the court below.

Summarizing the state of the law that results, and invoking the analogy above, Scalia observes that *Castle Rock* and, before that, *DeShaney* stand for the proposition that "the benefit that a third party may receive from having someone else arrested for a crime generally does not trigger protections under the Due Process Clause, neither in its procedural nor in its 'substantive' manifestations."[63]

True, that is an accurate statement of the law as the Court has now decided it. And as the Court *should* have decided such cases, being faithful to the Constitution, Scalia's statement may also be "generally" true; but the facts of a given case can and often should lead a court to override that presumption. In this case, however, where the legislature has clearly overridden the presumption by recognizing a right arising under a particular set of circumstances, any indeterminacy there might otherwise have been has been removed. To be sure, the state might have gone even further: it might have provided victims with "personally enforceable remedies," as Scalia next suggests,[64] thus making Mrs. Gonzales' right even more explicit. But its failure to take that further step does not mean that Mrs. Gonzales, unlike an ordinary crime victim unprotected by something like the Colorado statutory scheme, does not have a remedy under the Fourteenth Amendment.

Waxing more broadly, Scalia says this decision reflects the Court's "continuing reluctance to treat the Fourteenth Amendment as 'a font of tort law.'"[65] But this case sounds in contract, not in tort. Mrs. Gonzales isn't a "stranger" to the police. She's in a special relationship with them, created by the legislature and particularized by the judge who signed the restraining order.

The tragedy of the Court's Fourteenth Amendment jurisprudence over the years, starting with the *Slaughterhouse Cases*, is its failure to recognize that the Amendment, for the second time in the nation's history, created "a more perfect union." Not that it ended federalism,

---

[62]*Id.* at 2810.
[63]*Id.*
[64]*Id.*
[65]*Id.*

123

by any means, but it did erect far-reaching limits on what states could do—saying here, for example, that especially if states clarify rights under the Amendment and put in place a set of particularized protections for their citizens, they cannot then walk away from enforcing those protections with impunity. The indifference of the Castle Rock police to their responsibilities under that regime led directly to the death of three little girls. The repeated failures of the Court over so many years to articulate and secure the guarantees against that kind of indifference that were crafted in the aftermath of the Civil War makes it complicit in that tragedy.

Do We Have a Beef With the Court? Compelled Commercial Speech Upheld, but It Could Have Been Worse

*Daniel E. Troy**

Johanns v. Livestock Marketing Association expanded the "government-speech doctrine" at the expense of commercial speech. In upholding the Beef Promotion and Research Act of 1985, the Court weakened the protections afforded businesses compelled to fund commercial messages with which they disagree. Although the Court sidestepped application of the *Central Hudson* test for regulations of commercial speech, the opinion nevertheless continues the jurisprudential mistake of treating commercial messages as "lower value" speech. That proposition is easily established by asking what would have been the reaction to the decision had *Johanns* involved a hot button political issue rather than a beef checkoff program.

The result, however, may not be all negative. First, the Court did not apply the *Central Hudson* test, which affords reduced constitutional protection to commercial speech. Second, the Court adopted a new rule that, at least facially, appears to treat commercial speech as more equal to other forms of expression. Also, by moving away from the *Glickman* and *United Foods* line of precedents, the Court abandoned a test that created an incentive for the government to regulate more rather than less. Meanwhile, *Johanns* leaves open the possibility of selected challenges to invocations of the government-speech doctrine. Such challenges may ultimately impose a limit on what seems now like a boundless doctrine.

*Daniel E. Troy is a partner in the Washington, D.C., and New York offices of Sidley Austin Brown & Wood, where he practices food and drug law, as well as constitutional and appellate litigation. From 2001 to 2004, he was Chief Counsel of the U.S. Food and Drug Administration. He wishes to thank Kurt Kastorf, a summer associate at Sidley, for his invaluable assistance in preparing this article.

I. Introduction

Imagine that the federal government were to impose a special tax exclusively on abortion clinics and used the revenue generated to launch a national advertisement campaign with the slogan "Abortion Providers: Murderers for Hire." On each advertisement is emblazoned "Paid for by America's Abortion Providers." Further imagine that pro-choice groups, understandably upset by such a campaign, push to have the tax repealed. Then, to defeat the repeal effort, government officials respond by funneling the money collected from the abortion providers into a propaganda campaign to build public and legislative support for the tax. Such a campaign would result, at minimum, in a public outcry. Most citizens and politicians to the left of the political spectrum, as well as many on the right, would be outraged and characterize the program as an impermissible compulsion of speech and an inappropriate use of federal funds.

Yet, in *Johanns v. Livestock Marketing Association*,[1] the Supreme Court approved an analogous program and barely made the news. What accounts for the lack of outcry over *Johanns*? The answer is obvious: unlike the hypothetical abortion campaign, which involves compelling controversial political speech, *Johanns* concerned commercial speech.

Specifically, *Johanns* involved a First Amendment challenge to the Beef Promotion and Research Act of 1985.[2] The Act directed the secretary of agriculture to impose a dollar-per-head assessment ("checkoff") on all sales or importation of cattle and a proportional assessment on imported beef products.[3] It also required the secretary to appoint a Cattlemen's Beef Promotion and Research Board. That Board, in turn, convened an Operating Committee composed of ten board members and ten representatives named by a federation of state beef councils.[4] The Operating Committee spent the majority of the assessment on beef-related promotional campaigns. These campaigns typically included the familiar slogan: "Beef. It's What's

---

[1] 125 S. Ct. 2055 (2005).
[2] 99 Stat. 1597 (codified at 7 U.S.C. § 2901 et seq.).
[3] 125 S. Ct. at 2058.
[4] *Id.*

for Dinner."[5] Many of the promotional messages bear the attribution "Funded by America's Beef Producers."[6]

The challengers to the program included two associations representing members who collect and pay the checkoff, as well as individual cattle producers and dealers also subject to the assessment.[7] Before bringing their suit, the plaintiffs invoked a provision of the Act allowing beef producers to petition the secretary of agriculture to hold a referendum on the continuation of the beef checkoff program.[8] These producers opposed promoting beef as a generic commodity. They contended such a campaign impeded their ability to promote superior subclasses of beef such as American beef, grain-fed beef, and certified Angus or Hereford beef.[9]

The secretary never even held the referendum.[10] Instead, the Beef Promotion and Research Board responded to the petition attempt by using the very money collected through the assessment to promote the Beef Act to cattle producers and legislators and, thus, perpetuating its own existence.[11] The U.S. Department of Agriculture, meanwhile, delayed processing the petition. It then declared the petition's signatures invalid.[12]

The plaintiffs responded by filing suit in federal district court. They alleged, among other things, that the Act violated their First Amendment rights by compelling them to fund a commercial message with which they disagreed.[13] The district court and the U.S. Court of Appeals for the Eighth Circuit agreed with the plaintiffs, finding a violation of the First Amendment.[14] The Supreme Court, however, vacated and remanded. It determined that the promotional

[5] *Id.* at 2059.

[6] *Id.*

[7] *Id.*

[8] Livestock Marketing Association v. United States Department of Agriculture, 132 F. Supp. 2d 817, 820 (D. S.D. 2001).

[9] Johanns, 125 S. Ct. at 2060.

[10] Livestock Marketing Association, 132 F. Supp. 2d at 821–22.

[11] *Id.* at 821.

[12] *Id.* at 821–22.

[13] Johanns, 125 S. Ct. at 2059.

[14] Livestock Marketing Association v. United States Department of Agriculture, 335 F.3d 711, 725–26 (8th Cir. 2003); Livestock Marketing Association v. United States Department of Agriculture, 207 F. Supp. 2d 992, 1002 (D. S.D. 2002).

campaign was government speech, and hence not susceptible to a First Amendment challenge.[15]

Interpreting the implications of *Johanns* for commercial speech requires some background about commercial speech generally as well as about commodity checkoff programs specifically. Part II of this article examines the history of the commercial-speech doctrine, as well as the litigation over commodity checkoff programs preceding the *Johanns* decision. Part III questions the logic underlying the decision. Part IV, however, tempers criticism of *Johanns*. Although lovers of freedom should view the decision with disappointment, the message may not be quite as bad as it could have been. The "government-speech" rationale may have been preferable to the other grounds on which the Court could have found for the government, and the majority opinion's language leaves open the possibility of attaching meaningful limits to the scope of the doctrine in future decisions. Finally, the Court rejected the Eighth Circuit's invitation to apply the *Central Hudson* test, which treats commercial speech as deserving of less-than-full constitutional protection.

II. Background

A. The History of Commercial Speech

1. "Lower Value" Speech

The Supreme Court has long treated commercial speech, such as advertisements placed in a newspaper or magazine, differently than other content.[16] Generally, the government may impose reasonable restrictions on the time, place, or manner of speech, but only if it does so in a content-neutral way.[17] In sharp contrast, the Court allows restrictions on commercial speech, even of truthful information concerning lawful products, if that regulation "directly advances" a "substantial governmental interest" in a manner "not more extensive than is necessary to serve that interest."[18] Employing this test

---

[15] Johanns, 125 S. Ct. at 2066.

[16] Daniel E. Troy, Advertising: Not "Low Value" Speech, 16 Yale J. on Reg. 85, 88 (1999).

[17] Content-neutral speech restrictions are those that apply to all speech, regardless of subject matter. See, e.g., Firsby v. Schultz, 487 U.S. 474, 481 (1988).

[18] Central Hudson Gas & Electric Corp. v. Public Service Commission, 447 U.S. 557, 573 (1980).

gives the government more control over the content of advertisements than it has over other communications, such as those concerning political, scientific, or artistic issues.[19]

Scholars are sharply divided over the Court's approach to commercial speech. Some believe that commercial speech need not be afforded status under the First Amendment equal to other speech.[20] Others find little logical or historical justification for concluding that commercial speech is of "lower value" than other modes of expression.[21]

The First Amendment itself provides no basis for affording commercial speech second-class status. It reads: "Congress shall make no law . . . abridging the freedom of Speech, or of the Press."[22] That the language of the First Amendment is categorical, however, is not sufficient to demonstrate that commercial speech ought to enjoy full constitutional protection. Few would argue, for example, that the Amendment prohibits imposing limits on speech that creates an imminent and grave danger.[23] Examining the original understanding

---

[19]Troy, *supra* note 16, at 88.

[20]See, e.g., Cass R. Sunstein, Democracy and the Problem of Free Speech 123–24 (1993); Alexander MeikleJohn, Political Freedom (1960); Akhil Reed Amar, Intratextualism, 112 Harv. L. Rev. 747, 812–18 (1999); C. Edwin Baker, Commercial Speech: A Problem in the Theory of Freedom, 62 Iowa L. Rev. 1 (1976); Lillian R. BeVier, The First Amendment and Political Speech: An Inquiry into the Substance and Limits of Principle, 30 Stan. L. Rev. 299, 352–55 (1978); Vincent Blasi, The Pathological Perspective and the First Amendment, 85 Colum. L. Rev. 449, 484–89 (1985); Thomas H. Jackson & John Calvin Jeffries, Jr., Commercial Speech: Economic Due Process and the First Amendment, 65 Va. L. Rev. 1 (1979); Frederick Schauer, Commercial Speech and the Architecture of the First Amendment, 56 U. Cin. L. Rev. 1181, 1187 (1988); William Van Alstyne, Remembering Melville Nimmer: Some Cautionary Notes on Commercial Speech, 43 UCLA L. Rev. 1635, 1640 (1996).

[21]44 Liquormart, Inc. v. Rhode Island, 517 U.S. 484, 522 (1996) (Thomas, J., concurring). See also Troy, *supra* note 16, at 89. See, e.g., Alex Kozinski & Stuart Banner, Who's Afraid of Commercial Speech, 76 Va. L. Rev. 627, 628 (1990); Martin H. Redish, The First Amendment in the Marketplace: Commercial Speech and the Values of Free Expression, 39 Geo. Wash. L. Rev. 429, 431 (1971); Rodney A. Smolla, Information, Imagery, and the First Amendment: A Case for Expansive Protection of Commercial Speech, 71 Tex. L. Rev. 777, 780, 782 (1993). Cf. Kathleen M. Sullivan, Cheap Spirits, Cigarettes, and Free Speech: The Implications of 44 Liquormart, 1996 Sup. Ct. Rev. 123, 147–60.

[22]U.S. Const. amend. I.

[23]See, e.g., Schenck v. United States, 249 U.S. 47 (1919) (clear and present danger).

of the First Amendment is thus necessary to determine the categories of speech that warrant constitutional protection.

2. Commercial Speech in Historical Context

As I have shown at length elsewhere, the colonial history preceding the passage of the First Amendment demonstrates that government efforts to regulate commercial speech should be judged by the same searching inquiry employed in assessing restrictions on other forms of speech.[24] Several factors show that the Framers believed that the right to advertise was encompassed within the "freedom of the press." First, the Founders viewed freedom of speech and property rights as the essential components of individual liberty.[25] In *Cato's Letters*, the authors articulated the inextricable link between free speech and property rights, writing: "This sacred privilege is so essential to free government, that the security of property; and the freedom of speech, always go together; and in those wretched countries where a man cannot call his tongue his own, he can scarce call anything else his own."[26] That view is echoed in the writings of James Madison, who drafted the First Amendment.[27]

Second, paid advertisements provided both the motive and means for the spread of the press across colonial America.[28] American newspapers emerged only as colonial business and industry began to expand.[29] These newspapers did not just depend on advertising for their support; they were the primary vehicles for disseminating commercial information.[30] Advertisements, like other forms of

---

[24] Troy, *supra* note 16, at 93–108.

[25] *Id.* at 93–96; John O. McGinnis, The Once and Future Property-Based Vision of the First Amendment, 63 U. Chi. L. Rev. 49, 58–63 (1996). See also John Locke, The Second Treatise on Government 4 (Thomas P. Peardon ed., Bobbs-Merrill 1st ed. 17th prtg. 1975) (1690) (defining the "state of perfect freedom" as the ability of people "to order their actions and dispose of their possessions and persons as they think fit").

[26] John Trenchard & Thomas Gordon, 1 Cato's Letters 110 (Ronald Hamow ed., Liberty Classics ed. 1995) (1720–23).

[27] See, e.g., James Madison, Property, The Nat'l Gazette, Mar. 27, 1792, reprinted in 14 The Papers of James Madison 266–68 (Robert A. Rutland et al. eds., 1983) (1792).

[28] Troy, *supra* note 16, at 97–101.

[29] See Edwin Emery & Michael Emery, The Press and America 18 (1978).

[30] James Playsted Wood, The Story of Advertising 85 (1958).

speech, were thought to inform the reading public.[31] Given the importance of advertising to colonial Americans, modern constitutional scholars are at odds with history when they characterize commercial speech as "lower value."

Third, the colonial American opposition to government interference with commercial speech proved a catalyst of the American Revolution.[32] The British Stamp Act of 1765 assessed a tax on each newspaper printed, as well as a per-advertisement fee.[33] This tax, perceived as an offense to property rights, galvanized the colonial press against the British government.[34] The successful repeal of the Stamp Act demonstrates the commitment of early Americans to an independent press and their willingness to fight against monetary restrictions on commercial speech.[35]

Finally, examining state statutes in place when the First Amendment was ratified reveals that early America did not restrict commercial messages about lawful products or services.[36] The only limitations placed on advertising concerned the promotion of unlawful activity.[37] These early statues in fact demonstrate that state legislatures viewed advertising as an important social tool, and sometimes

[31]See, e.g., History of Printing in America with a Biography of Printers, and an Account of Newspapers (1810), quoted in D. Boorstin, The Americans: The Colonial Experience 328 (1958).

[32]Troy, *supra* note 16, at 101–02.

[33]See Arthur Schlesinger, Sr., Prelude to Independence: The Newspaper War on Britain 1764–1776, at 68 (1966).

[34]See Kent R. Middleton, Commercial Speech in the Eighteenth Century, in Newsletters to Newspapers: Eighteenth-Century Journalism 277, 282 (Donovan H. Bond & W. Reynolds McLeod eds., 1977); see also Objections by A Son of Liberty, N.Y. J., Nov. 8, 1787, reprinted in 6 The Complete Anti-Federalist 34, 36 (Herbert J. Storing ed., 1981).

[35]See Eric Neisser, Charging for Free Speech: User Fees and Insurance in the Marketplace of Ideas, 74 Geo. L.J. 257, 264 (1985).

[36]Troy, *supra* note 16, at 103–06.

[37]See, e.g., Act for the Prevention of Lotteries, 1792, The Laws of Maryland 189–90 (1811); Act to Prevent Horse Racing, 1803, The Public Statute Laws of the State of Connecticut 381–82 (1808); Act Enabling the Town-Councils of Each Town in This State to Grant Licenses for Retailing Strong Liquors, and to Prevent the Selling of the Same without License, and against the Keeping of Signs at Unlicensed Houses, 1728, The Public Laws of the State of Rhode Island and Providence Plantations 391–95 (1798).

even required advertising as a means of protecting the property and legal rights of others.[38]

This "robust tradition of American commercial speech" continued through the Civil War and the ratification of the Fourteenth Amendment.[39] A review of state legislative practices around the time of the Fourteenth Amendment's ratification reveals that regulation of advertising remained limited to restrictions on promotion of illegal products and services.[40] Accordingly, incorporating the behavior of the post–Civil War states into an originalist examination of the First Amendment provides additional evidence that commercial speech ought to be afforded full constitutional protection.[41]

B. Modern Commercial-Speech Doctrine

1. The Decline of Equal Treatment for Advertisers

Given advertising's rich role in our nation's founding, it may appear surprising that the Supreme Court would afford commercial speech anything less than full First Amendment protection. The emergence of a schism between the commercial-speech doctrine and protections for other modes of expression is, to some extent, a historical accident. During the early twentieth century, courts began to analyze constraints on commercial speech under the rubric of substantive due process. This conflation of categories—restrictions placed on advertisements are infringements on speech, not mere economic regulations—has come back to haunt First Amendment jurisprudence. When the Court began to repudiate the *Lochner*-era

---

[38] Troy, *supra* note 16, at 105; see also Act for Amending, and Reducing into System, the Laws and Regulations Concerning Last Wills and Testaments, the Duties of Executors, Administrators and Guardians, and the Rights of Orphans and Other Representatives of Deceased Persons, 1798, Laws of Maryland 457–60 (1811).

[39] Troy, *supra* note 16, at 109.

[40] *Id.*

[41] The restrictions imposed by the First Amendment originally applied only to the federal government. The Supreme Court later considered those restrictions to have been "incorporated" against the states through the Fourteenth Amendment. See Gitlow v. New York, 268 U.S. 652 (1925). Thus, originalist jurists consider Reconstruction-era legislative practices to provide relevant evidence of the protections afforded commercial speech. See, e.g., 44 Liquormart, Inc. v. Rhode Island, 517 U.S. 484, 517 (1996) (Scalia, J., concurring) (treating post–Civil War state legislative practices as relevant to the commercial-speech inquiry).

notion that economic regulations violated the Due Process Clause, constitutional protections for advertising crumbled.[42]

The beginning of the twentieth century saw the Gilded Age give way to the Progressive Era as disenchantment with unfettered capitalism grew.[43] The Supreme Court pushed back against the Progressive movement, striking down social welfare programs on the belief that they infringed on natural rights of contract and property. In the early twentieth century's most famous case, *Lochner v. New York*,[44] the Court struck down a state law that capped the work week at sixty hours for bakery employees.

Although the early twentieth century saw some push for advertising reform, commercial speech remained well-protected. Legislative efforts to clean up false or misleading commercial ads essentially codified the existing common law.[45] World War I helped to glorify the advertising industry, as ample marketing helped to sell $24 billion in war bonds and raise $400 million for the Red Cross.[46] Both the Supreme Court and state courts protected commercial speech when it was threatened, invoking the due process right to economic liberty.[47]

The national mood changed in the wake of the Great Depression. Advertising took a hard hit, losing out both in terms of income and public esteem.[48] Public outcry against commercialism resulted in best-selling exposés of advertising practices and a widespread call for increased restrictions on commercial speech.[49]

The Supreme Court, meanwhile, had begun backing away from its *Lochner*-era jurisprudence, allowing states to expand their police

[42] Troy, *supra* note 16, at 114–22.

[43] See, e.g., Matthew Josepson, The Robber Barons 445–53 (1934); Rudolph J.R. Peritz, Competition Policy in America 1888–1992: History, Rhetoric, Law 11 (1996).

[44] 198 U.S. 45 (1905).

[45] See Wood, *supra* note 30, at 336 (describing the Advertising Federation of America's model antifraud statute).

[46] Frank Presbrey, The History and Development of Advertising 565 (1929).

[47] See, e.g., American School of Magnetic Healing v. McAnnulty, 187 U.S. 94 (1902), discussed in Peritz, Competition Policy in America, *supra* note 43, at 102–03 (describing how the *McAnnulty* decision showed "solicitude towards commercial speech"); Ware v. Ammon, 278 S.W. 593, 595 (Ky. Ct. App. 1925).

[48] See Wood, *supra* note 30, at 417–24.

[49] *Id.* at 419–26.

powers over commerce.[50] The advertising industry, having relied on economic due process arguments to protect itself in court, had the rug pulled out from under its feet. In the Supreme Court's first case assessing whether the First Amendment protected advertising, the Court quickly concluded that "purely commercial" speech deserved no constitutional protection.[51]

In *Valentine v. Chrestensen*,[52] the City of New York had warned Mr. Chrestensen that his handbills soliciting people to visit a submarine for a fee violated the city's anti-litter ordinance.[53] In response, Chrestensen added a protest to the back of the circular, criticizing the city for refusing to let him use the public pier to display his submarine.[54] When New York nonetheless threatened to enforce the ordinance, Chrestensen brought suit alleging a violation of the First Amendment.[55] Justice Owen Roberts, writing for the Court, rejected Chrestensen's claim, declaring that "the Constitution imposes no such restraint on government as respects purely commercial advertising."[56] The Court rejected Chrestensen's inclusion of the protest on his handbill as a mere ruse.[57]

2. The Central Hudson *Approach*

Fortunately, *Chrestensen* has never been interpreted as strictly as its literal reading would appear to require. Almost immediately, scholars called the Supreme Court's distinction between commercial and noncommercial speech into question.[58] The Court itself later expressed some reservation about the three-page opinion. Justice

---

[50] See Lincoln Federal Labor Union v. Northwestern Iron & Metal Co., 335 U.S. 525, 535–36 (1949) (noting that the Court no longer followed the *Lochner* line of cases). See, e.g., People v. Pennock, 293 N.W. 759, 762 (Mich. 1940) (upholding statute banning advertisement of contraceptives); Allen v. McGovern, 169 A. 345, 345–46 (N.J. 1933) (upholding ordinance banning unsolicited advertising); Semler v. Oregon State Board of Dental Examiners, 34 P.2d 311, 315 (Or. 1934) (upholding ordinance placing advertisement restrictions on dentists).

[51] Valentine v. Chrestensen, 316 U.S. 52 (1942).

[52] *Id.* at 54.

[53] *Id.* at 53.

[54] *Id.*

[55] *Id.* at 54.

[56] *Id.*

[57] *Id.* at 55.

[58] Troy, *supra* note 16, at 122.

William O. Douglas, who had joined the opinion, wrote that "[t]he ruling was casual, almost offhand. And it has not survived reflection."[59] The most immediate doctrinal problem created by *Chrestensen* was definitional. When is speech commercial? In *New York Times Company v. Sullivan*,[60] the Court held that an editorial advertisement protesting civil rights abuses by Alabama officials did not lose its First Amendment protection simply because it was a paid advertisement.[61] Twelve years later, the Court narrowed the definition of commercial speech to speech that "propose[s] a commercial transaction."[62]

In the 1970s, the Court began to reconsider its approach to advertisements. The resurrection of commercial speech rights began with *Bigelow v. Virginia*.[63] In this politically charged case, the Court reversed the conviction of a Virginian editor who accepted an ad describing the availability of low-cost abortions in New York.[64] Justice Harry Blackmun, writing for the Court, found that speech contained within paid advertisements "is not stripped of First Amendment protection merely because it appears in that form."[65] Instead, because commercial speech receives some First Amendment protection, the Court reasoned, the interests of the publisher, reader, and consumer must be balanced against the state interest in prohibiting the dissemination of publications promoting abortion.[66] The Court deemed Virginia's interest to be small, because *Roe v. Wade*[67] had deemed legal the activity that Virginia sought to proscribe.[68]

The Court could have limited *Bigelow* to the narrow proposition that states may not prohibit advertising related to an activity that is a constitutional right. Instead, in *Virginia State Board of Pharmacy v. Virginia Citizens Consumer Council*,[69] Justice Blackmun wrote that

[59] Cammarano v. United States, 358 U.S. 498, 514 (1959) (Douglas, J., concurring).
[60] 376 U.S. 254 (1964).
[61] *Id.* at 265–66.
[62] Virginia State Board of Pharmacy v. Virginia Citizens Consumer Council, Inc., 425 U.S. 748, 776 (1976).
[63] 421 U.S. 809 (1975).
[64] *Id.* at 811–13.
[65] *Id.* at 818.
[66] *Id.* at 826–27.
[67] 410 U.S. 113 (1973).
[68] Bigelow, 421 U.S. at 821–22.
[69] 425 U.S. 748 (1976).

even commercial speech, which does "no more than propose a commercial transaction," warranted some First Amendment protection.[70] The test for weighing the First Amendment values served by commercial speech would come four years later, in *Central Hudson Gas & Electric Corp. v. Public Service Commission of New York.*[71]

Central Hudson involved the constitutionality of a state regulation completely banning promotional advertising by an electric utility.[72] The Court adopted a four-part test that gives the government an opportunity to justify restrictions on entirely truthful commercial speech.[73] Under this test, a court must determine whether:

(1) the commercial speech concerns a lawful activity and is not misleading;
(2) the government interest asserted to justify the regulation is substantial;
(3) the regulation directly advances that government interest; and
(4) the regulation is no more extensive than necessary to serve that interest.[74]

The *Central Hudson* test rejected the "highly paternalistic" notion that the government can completely suppress commercial speech, but it "elevated *Virginia Pharmacy*'s hint of second-class status for commercial speech to the level of black-letter law."[75] This crabbed reading of the First Amendment has produced a fractured and unpredictable jurisprudence. The highly subjective nature of the test produces inconsistent results.[76] In the past, the Court has often

---

[70] *Id.* at 762.
[71] 447 U.S. 557 (1980).
[72] *Id.* at 558–59.
[73] *Id.* at 561–66.
[74] *Id.* at 564–66.
[75] *Id.* at 562; Troy, *supra* note 16, at 127.
[76] See Jay D. Wexler, Defending the Middle Way: Intermediate Scrutiny as Judicial Minimalism, 66 Geo. Wash. L. Rev. 298, 301 (1998) (defending the *Central Hudson* approach but conceding that "[n]ot only are the terms of the intermediate scrutiny test themselves indeterminate, but the test itself has also been particularly vulnerable to manipulation by the Supreme Court"). See also Van Alstyne, *supra* note 20, at 1637.

applied a weak version of intermediate scrutiny or deferred to self-serving legislative determinations that the restrictions serve a state interest.[77]

Posadas de Puerto Rico Association v. Tourism Company of Puerto Rico[78] best demonstrates the potential for *Central Hudson* to go awry.[79] Puerto Rico, after legalizing gambling, prohibited the advertising of gambling to the Puerto Rican public, but allowed casinos to promote gambling in the rest of the United States and to incoming tourists.[80] The law included a ban on printing the word "casino" on common items such as lighters, pencils, and napkins, which may be accessible to the Puerto Rican public.[81]

The Court upheld the restriction.[82] In doing so, it uncritically accepted the assessment of the Puerto Rican legislature that gambling would result in the "disruption of moral and cultural patterns," that advertising of gambling would increase these harms, and that the restrictions were "no more extensive than necessary to serve the government's interests."[83] While this approach of giving the elected government deference in its judgments is generally a sound policy, judicial review must be more rigorous when constitutionally protected rights are at stake. The purpose of the First Amendment, and of the Bill of Rights as a whole, is to empower the judiciary to scrutinize and, if necessary, invalidate legislation. The Court thus rejected a clear constitutional warrant to protect the speech at issue.

The ruling also potentially eviscerated the strength of the *Central Hudson* test. The Court wrote that the "greater power to completely ban casino gambling necessarily includes the lesser power to ban

---

[77] See, e.g., Zauderer v. Office of Disciplinary Counsel of the Supreme Court of Ohio, 471 U.S. 626, 651 (1985) (approving of a restriction where it is "reasonably related to the State's interest"); Friedman v. Rogers, 440 U.S. 1, 13 (1979) (upholding a ban on optometrists' use of trade names where "there is a significant possibility that the trade names will be used to mislead").

[78] 478 U.S. 328 (1986).

[79] See Sullivan, *supra* note 21, at 123; see generally Philip B. Kurland, Posadas de Puerto Rico v. Tourism Company: 'Twas Strange, 'Twas Passing Strange, 'Twas Pitiful, 'Twas Wondrous Pitiful, 1986 Sup. Ct. Rev. 1.

[80] Posadas, 478 U.S. at 331–34.

[81] *Id.* at 333.

[82] *Id.* at 348.

[83] *Id.* at 341–43.

advertising of casino gambling."[84] This notion is quite dangerous. Given the broad view that most courts have of the police power, state legislatures, as well as the U.S. Congress, can presumably outlaw a vast array of goods and services. If they correspondingly have the power to regulate all speech concerning those goods and services, the First Amendment would mean very little. The dissent in *Posadas*, in response to the majority's "greater-include-the-lesser" argument, aptly notes that "the 'constitutional doctrine' which bans Puerto Rico from banning advertisements concerning the lawful casino gambling is not so strange a restraint—it is called the First Amendment."[85]

Wisely, the Court has stepped back somewhat from *Posadas*.[86] In *44 Liquormart, Inc. v. Rhode Island*,[87] at least five members of the Court acknowledged the important role that advertising has played in American history.[88] Nonetheless, although the Court has been far more protective of commercial speech since *44 Liquormart*, the Court has not yet repudiated its doctrine of reduced protection for commercial speech.[89] However, by applying a standard in *Johanns* closer to that applied in noncommercial speech cases, it may have taken a step towards harmonizing the commercial-speech doctrine with the original meaning of the First Amendment.

C. *The Commodity Checkoff Litigation*

1. *The Rise of Modern Checkoff Programs*

Over the past decade, one of the cutting-edge issues of commercial-speech litigation has involved the constitutionality of agricultural "checkoff" programs. Since 1997, the Supreme Court has (amazingly) decided three such cases, assessing the constitutionality

---

[84] *Id.* at 345–46.

[85] *Id.* at 355 (Brennan, J., dissenting).

[86] See, e.g., 44 Liquormart, Inc. v. Rhode Island, 517 U.S. 484, 516 (1996); Rubin v. Coors Brewing Co., 514 U.S. 476, 491 (1995).

[87] See note 86, *supra*.

[88] 44 Liquormart, 517 U.S. at 495–96 (Stevens, J., joined by Kennedy, Souter, and Ginsburg, JJ.); *id.* at 522–23 (Thomas, J., concurring in part and concurring in judgment).

[89] See Daniel Halberstam, Commercial Speech, Professional Speech, and the Constitutional Status of Social Institutions, 147 U. Pa. L. Rev. 771, 792 (1999) (noting that "the still-dominant test devised by the Court is simply a quantitatively-reduced protection afforded to commercial speech, as compared to noncommercial speech").

of regulations on the advertisement of tree fruit,[90] mushrooms,[91] and beef,[92] respectively.

Since the New Deal, the federal government has heavily regulated agriculture.[93] The Florida Citrus Advertising Tax of 1935 became the prototype for hundreds of farm commodity promotion programs implemented by the states and the federal government.[94] Many of the early programs involved voluntary assessments. Producers marked a "checkoff" box if they wished to continue in the program.[95] Legislatures shifted to mandatory programs, as producers complained that nonparticipating members created a "free-rider" problem— i.e., nonparticipants benefited from the programs without paying any of the costs.[96] Congress created most of the mandatory programs during the 1980s and 1990s.[97] Currently, sixteen such programs are in place.[98]

Many producers support commodity checkoff programs. Generic advertising of commodities is often a cost-effective means of increasing gross sales of a good.[99] Making the program mandatory reduces the risk that some business competitors will free-ride off of the generic advertisement of others.[100] However, not all farmers feel that

---

[90] Glickman v. Wileman Brothers & Elliot, Inc., 521 U.S. 457, 477 (1997).

[91] United States v. United Foods, Inc., 533 U.S. 405, 412 (2001).

[92] Johanns v. Livestock Marketing Association, 125 S. Ct. 2055, 2066 (2005).

[93] See, e.g., Agricultural Marketing Agreement Act of 1937, 7 U.S.C. § 601 et seq. (2003); Agricultural Adjustment Act of 1938, 7 U.S.C. § 1281 et seq. (2003); Agricultural Act of 1949, 7 U.S.C. § 1421 et seq. (2003).

[94] Geoffrey S. Becker, Federal Farm Promotion ("Check-off") Programs, North County Small Engines 2 (July 12, 2002), available at http://www.ncseonline.org/NLE/CRS/abstract.cfm?NLEid=15966.

[95] Id.

[96] Hearings on H.R. 1776 et al. Before the Subcommittee on Domestic Marketing, Consumer Relations, and Nutrition of the House Committee on Agriculture, 101st Cong., 1st Sess. 95–96 (1989) (statement of James Ciarrocchi); see also Richard A. Posner, Economic Analysis of the Law 61 (6th ed. 2003).

[97] Becker, *supra* note 94, at 1.

[98] Id. See also Avocados Plus Inc. v. Veneman, 370 F.3d 1243, 1245–46 (D.C. Cir. 2004) (noting the creation of the Hass Avocado Promotion Program). The Department of Agriculture currently administers programs for avocados, beef, blueberries, cotton, dairy products, eggs, milk, honey, peanuts, lamb, mushrooms, popcorn, pork, potatoes, soybeans, and watermelons. See, e.g., Johanns, 125 S. Ct. at 2059 n.2.

[99] Becker, *supra* note 94, at 5.

[100] See note 96, *supra*.

the benefits of such programs outweigh the costs. Most gains from increased demand flow to retailers and distributors, rather than to the producers who foot the bill for the advertisements.[101]

Some producers also reject the premise behind generic marketing of a particular commodity. A primary argument in favor of generic advertisements is that attempts by particular producers to "brand" their goods are inefficient.[102] If most consumers notice no difference between various types of beef, and use all brands of beef interchangeably, then efforts by marketers to teach consumers to eat a particular brand merely add cost to the product without producing a corresponding benefit for consumers.[103] However, many beef producers vigorously contest the notion that their products are interchangeable.[104] Instead, they wish to promote the superiority of a particular subclass of beef such as American beef, grain-fed beef, or certified Angus or Hereford beef.[105]

Thus, mandatory assessment programs force some producers to provide financial support for commercial speech with which they disagree. Because the First Amendment imposes limits on the ability of the government to compel people to speak[106] or to pay for speech with which they disagree,[107] opponents of commodity checkoff programs began to file suit against the Department of Agriculture. The first of these cases to reach the Supreme Court was *Glickman v. Wileman Brothers & Elliott, Inc.*[108]

2. Glickman v. Wileman Brothers & Elliott, Inc.

In *Glickman*, a group of California fruit producers objected to a mandatory advertising scheme that used more than fifty percent of

---

[101] See Boyd Kidwell, The Checkoff Wars, Progressive Farmer (October 2004), available at http://www.progressivefarmer.com/farmer/business/article/0,19846, 749517,00.html. See also Ronald D. Knudson, Agricultural and Food Policy 308–11 (4th ed. 1998) (describing monopsony power of buyers in the agricultural sector).

[102] Becker, *supra* note 94, at 5–6.

[103] *Id.*

[104] Johanns v. Livestock Marketing Association, 125 S. Ct. 2055, 2059–60 (2005).

[105] *Id.*

[106] See West Virginia State Board of Education v. Barnette, 319 U.S. 624, 642 (1943); Wooley v. Maynard, 430 U.S. 705, 717 (1977).

[107] See Abood v. Detroit Board of Education, 431 U.S. 209, 234–35 (1977); Keller v. State Bar of California, 496 U.S. 1, 9–11, 16–17 (1990).

[108] 521 U.S. 457 (1997).

the advertising assessments to promote specific varieties of fruit grown only by a few producers.[109] The district court upheld the scheme and entered a judgment against the fruit producers for $3.1 million in past due assessments.[110]

On appeal, the U.S. Court of Appeals for the Ninth Circuit reversed.[111] The court applied the *Central Hudson* test, finding that the government had failed to prove both that generic advertising was more effective than individual advertising and that the program was narrowly tailored.[112] The Ninth Circuit opinion conflicted with a decision of the Third Circuit,[113] prompting the Supreme Court to grant certiorari.[114]

The California scheme presented the commercial-speech doctrine with a new twist. *Central Hudson* and its progeny dealt with affirmative restrictions on speech,[115] whereas the fruit growers were not banned from speaking. However, the growers had strong arguments by analogy to two related doctrines: compelled speech and compelled funding of speech.

The First Amendment prohibits the government from compelling political or ideological speech. In *West Virginia State Board of Education v. Barnette*,[116] the Court held that Jehovah's Witnesses could not be forced to stand and salute the American flag in violation of their religious beliefs.[117] In *Wooley v. Maynard*,[118] it set aside the conviction of a New Hampshire man who obscured a portion of his license plate that announced the state motto "Live Free or Die."[119] In *Hurley v. Irish-American Gay, Lesbian & Bisexual Group of Boston*,[120] it ruled that Boston could not compel a private association of veterans to

---

[109] *Id.* at 464.

[110] *Id.*

[111] Wileman Brothers & Elliot, Inc. v. Espy, 58 F.3d 1367, 1386 (9th Cir. 1995).

[112] *Id.* at 1379–81.

[113] See United States v. Frame, 885 F.2d 1119, 1137 (3d Cir. 1989).

[114] Glickman, 521 U.S. at 466–67.

[115] See *supra* notes 72–74 and accompanying text.

[116] See note 106, *supra*.

[117] 319 U.S. 624, 642 (1943).

[118] 430 U.S. 705 (1977).

[119] *Id.* at 716–17.

[120] 515 U.S. 557 (1995).

allow members of a gay, lesbian, and bisexual group to march in the veterans' parade.[121]

The First Amendment also protects individuals from forced financing of political or ideological speech. For example, in *Abood v. Detroit Board of Education*,[122] the Court limited unions from spending on ideological messages those funds received from nonunion employees as part of agency shop arrangements.[123] And the Court applied the union analogy to the law bar in *Keller v. State Bar of California*,[124] excusing members from contributing funds to political and ideological causes.[125]

None of these cases convinced the Supreme Court to apply the *Central Hudson* test to the California fruit growers. The Court reversed the decision of the Ninth Circuit, holding that the Department of Agriculture's requirement that the fruit producers finance generic advertising did not violate the First Amendment.[126] Indeed, the Court said it did not believe the case presented a free speech claim at all. Instead, it characterized the government's action as an extension of a legitimate market order.[127]

The Court cited three distinguishing "characteristics" of the advertising scheme that made application of the *Central Hudson* test inappropriate:

(1) The scheme did not prevent any producer from communicating any message;

(2) The scheme did not compel any producer to engage in actual or symbolic speech; and

(3) The scheme did not require any producer to endorse or finance any political or ideological views.[128]

This list of factors appeared to be a fatal blow to the prospect that the compelled speech and compelled funding of speech doctrines

---

[121] *Id.* at 580–81.

[122] 431 U.S. 209 (1977).

[123] *Id.* at 234–35.

[124] 496 U.S. 1 (1990).

[125] *Id.* at 16–17.

[126] See Glickman v. Wileman Brothers & Elliot, Inc., 521 U.S. 457, 477 (1997).

[127] *Id.* at 476.

[128] *Id.* at 469–70.

would be applied to commercial speech. Each factor appears to reaffirm the Court's perception of commercial speech as "lower value."

The Court cited no authority to substantiate the significance of the first characteristic. In fact, *Wooley v. Maynard*,[129] which the Court cites to support the third characteristic, indicates that the availability of other modes to express commercial speech has no constitutional significance at all. In *Wooley*, the Court noted that "[t]he right to speak and the right to refrain from speaking are complementary components of the broader concept of 'individual freedom of mind.'"[130] The Court thus had rejected as irrelevant the dissent's assertion that Mr. Maynard could have affixed a bumper sticker to his car disclaiming his belief in the New Hampshire state motto.[131] It is hard to distinguish *Glickman* from *Wooley*, other than on the ground that the Court believed commercial speech to be less deserving of constitutional protection than Mr. Maynard's speech.

The second characteristic, that the scheme does not compel any producer to engage in actual or symbolic speech, may be true, but seems to ignore the line of cases establishing that compelled funding of speech itself may run afoul of the Constitution. The Court distinguished *Abood* and other compelled funding cases by noting that requiring the fruit producers to pay the assessments "cannot be said to engender any crisis of conscience."[132] However, it is unclear whether the majority based this assessment on the notion that commercial speech can never produce a crisis of conscience, or on its suspicion that the fruit producers' First Amendment claim was a pretext to overturn the tax scheme.[133]

The third characteristic, that the scheme did not require the producers to endorse or finance a political or ideological view, leaves little doubt that the Court was affording greater protection to political and ideological speech than to commercial speech. Thus, after

---

[129]430 U.S. 705 (1977).

[130]*Id.* at 714.

[131]*Id.* at 722 (Rehnquist, J., dissenting).

[132]Glickman, 521 U.S. at 472.

[133]Some of the majority's language suggested that it doubted the sincerity of the respondents' claims. *Id.* at 471 ("With trivial exceptions on which the court did not rely, none of the generic advertising conveys any message with which respondents disagree.").

Glickman, the Court appeared to have rendered the First Amendment impotent to prevent compulsion of commercial speech.[134]

3. United States v. United Foods, Inc.

Only four years after *Glickman*, though, the Supreme Court granted certiorari on another checkoff case, *United States v. United Foods, Inc.*,[135] and (surprisingly) appeared to afford meaningful protection to farmers from programs compelling commercial speech.

United Foods objected to the Mushroom Act, passed by Congress in 1990, which authorized a "Mushroom Council" to research and market new uses for mushrooms.[136] The large agricultural company contended that generic mushroom advertisements disproportionately aided its competitors and refused to pay the assessment.[137] After United Foods lost an action brought before the secretary of agriculture, it filed a complaint seeking review of the adverse ruling.[138] The district court held that *Glickman* controlled, and dismissed the action.[139]

The U.S. Court of Appeals for the Sixth Circuit reversed the district court.[140] In the Sixth Circuit's view, the controlling factor in *Glickman* was the extensiveness of the government regulation of the California fruit industry. By contrast, the mushroom business was "unregulated" and thus "entirely different from the collectivized California tree fruit business."[141] The court concluded that, "in the absence of extensive regulation, the effort by the Department of Agriculture to force payments from plaintiff for advertising is invalid under the First Amendment."[142]

---

[134] See Edward J. Schoen, et al., United Foods and Wileman Bros.: Protection Against Compelled Commercial Speech—Now You See It, Now You Don't, 39 Am. Bus. L.J. 467, 496–97 (2002).

[135] 533 U.S. 405 (2001).

[136] Mushroom Promotion, Research, and Consumer Information Act, 7 U.S.C. § 6101 (1994).

[137] United Foods, 533 U.S. at 408–09.

[138] *Id.*

[139] United Foods, Inc. v. United States, 197 F.3d 221, 222 (6th Cir. 1999).

[140] *Id.* at 223–24.

[141] *Id.*

[142] *Id.*

This distinction between the cases ignores the fact that all of the characteristics that the Supreme Court had found to deprive the plaintiffs in *Glickman* of a First Amendment claim were present in *United Foods* as well.[143] The Mushroom Act did not prevent United Foods from producing its own advertisements. Nor did it require United Foods to engage in symbolic speech or to finance a political or ideological view.

Nonetheless, the Supreme Court affirmed the Sixth Circuit's decision.[144] Unlike in *Glickman*, the Court accepted the producers' analogy to the compelled speech cases, explaining that "[j]ust as the First Amendment may prevent the government from prohibiting speech, the Amendment may prevent the government from compelling individuals to express certain views, or from compelling certain individuals to pay subsidies for speech to which they object."[145] The Court was comparatively protective of commercial speech, noting that "[t]he fact that the speech is in aid of a commercial purpose does not deprive respondent of all First Amendment protection."[146]

The Supreme Court, like the Sixth Circuit, distinguished *Glickman* based on the comprehensiveness of the restrictions placed on California fruit growers. The fruit program "differs from the [mushroom program] in a most fundamental respect. In *Glickman* the mandated assessments for speech had been ancillary to a more comprehensive program restricting marketing autonomy."[147] By contrast, with the mushroom program, "for all practical purposes, the advertising itself, far from being ancillary [was] the principal object of the regulatory scheme."[148] The Court thus found it unnecessary to apply the *Central Hudson* test, because, "even viewing commercial speech as entitled to lesser protection," it found "no basis under either *Glickman* or [its] other precedents to sustain the compelled assessments."[149]

[143] See *supra* note 128 and accompanying text.

[144] United States v. United Foods, Inc., 533 U.S. 405, 417 (2001).

[145] *Id.* at 410 (citing Wooley v. Maynard, 430 U.S. 705 (1977); West Virginia State Board of Education v. Barnette, 319 U.S. 624 (1943); Abood v. Detroit Board of Education, 431 U.S. 209 (1977); and Keller v. State Bar of California, 496 U.S. 1 (1990)).

[146] *Id.*

[147] *Id.* at 411.

[148] *Id.* at 411–12.

[149] *Id.* at 410.

As the dissent points out, "it is difficult to understand why the presence or absence of price and output regulations could make a critical First Amendment difference."[150] That the plaintiffs in *Glickman* were subject to comprehensive regulations does nothing to reduce the impact upon them of being compelled to support a message with which they disagreed.

Nor could the difference have been "fundamental." The comprehensiveness of the California fruit program was not among the distinguishing characteristics listed by the Court in *Glickman*.[151] There is, in fact, some disagreement among members of the Court over whether such regulations were even in place at the time of the litigation.[152]

The *United Foods* decision provided some tangible protection from compelled commercial speech just four years after the Supreme Court appeared to have shut the door on such claims. However, the decision was not a total victory. The opinion yet again reiterated the Court's position that commercial speech deserves less vigorous protection than other expression.[153] Moreover, read in tandem with *Glickman, United Foods* establishes a rather murky criterion by which First Amendment claims are to be resolved: evidently, lower courts must assess the comprehensiveness of government programs.[154] Even worse, *United Foods* thereby provides an incentive for the government to regulate more, not less.

The Court's decision concluded by foreshadowing the *Johanns* case. In its brief on the merits before the Supreme Court, the government introduced for the first time the notion that the checkoff programs may comprise "government speech," and hence be immune from First Amendment scrutiny.[155] The Court rejected that argument as untimely raised, suggesting that it could be presented in a subsequent case.[156] The Department of Agriculture accepted the Court's invitation in *Johanns v. Livestock Marketing Association*.

---

[150] *Id.* at 421 (Breyer, J., dissenting).

[151] See Glickman v. Wileman Brothers & Elliott, Inc., 521 U.S. 457, 469–70 (1997); see also *supra* note 128 and accompanying text.

[152] See United Foods, 533 U.S. at 420–21 (Breyer, J., dissenting).

[153] *Id.* at 409.

[154] Schoen, *supra* note 134, at 519.

[155] United Foods, 533 U.S. at 416.

[156] *Id.* at 416–17.

III. *Johanns v. Livestock Marketing Association*

In the wake of *United Foods,* the Beef Promotion and Research Act of 1985 looked like a sitting duck. While *United Foods* had left open the question of precisely what constitutes a comprehensive regulatory scheme, there was little question that the Cattlemen's Beef Promotion and Research Board did not meet the test. The Beef Act was virtually identical to the Mushroom Act, which had not survived judicial scrutiny.[157]

Nonetheless, in *Johanns* the Court upheld the Beef Act. Just as *United Foods* came down four years after *Glickman,* swinging the pendulum toward greater protection for commercial speech, *Johanns* came down four years after *United Foods* and swung the pendulum back. The decision is hard to rationalize without concluding that it is driven in part by the continued belief of the majority of the Court that commercial speech is "lower value" speech. The view of government speech it espouses is so broad that it appears to displace most protections for compelled funding of speech.

But each time the pendulum swings, its arc may be a bit smaller. *United Foods* did not undo all of the damage to the commercial-speech doctrine wrought by *Glickman,* and *Johanns* does not bring the doctrine back to a pre-*United Foods* state. Ironically, a loss in *Johanns* may do more good for commercial speech in the long run than the win in *United Foods.* The *United Foods* decision appeared to usher in an age where legislatures have an incentive to regulate commodities as comprehensively as possible, to insulate the program from First Amendment scrutiny. That perverse incentive appears to be gone. Moreover, the Court will almost certainly have to impose some kind of a limitation on the government-speech doctrine it espoused in *Johanns.* Because this doctrine treats all forms of speech neutrally, these limits might ultimately help nudge commercial-speech protection toward greater parity with non-commercial-speech protection.

A. The Decision in Johanns

1. Lower Court Rulings

The plaintiffs in *Johanns* opposed promoting beef as a generic commodity, which they contended impeded their ability to promote

---

[157] See Livestock Marketing Association v. United States Department of Agriculture, 207 F. Supp. 2d 992, 1002 (D. S.D. 2002).

147

superior subclasses of beef such as American beef, grain-fed beef, and certified Angus or Hereford beef.[158] Before bringing their suit, the plaintiffs had attempted to use a provision of the Act allowing beef producers to petition the secretary of agriculture to hold a referendum on the continuation of the beef checkoff program.[159] When this effort failed, the producers filed suit, alleging, among other things, that the Act violated their First Amendment rights by compelling them to fund a commercial message with which they disagreed.[160]

The district court enjoined the program, concluding that the scheme was indistinguishable from the regulations in *United Foods*. The court found that "[t]he beef checkoff is, in all material respects, identical to the mushroom checkoff: producers and importers are required to pay an assessment, which assessments are used by a federally established board or council to fund speech."[161] It thus rejected the Department of Agriculture's attempts to distinguish the program, including the Department's claim that the advertisements were government speech.[162]

The U.S. Court of Appeals for the Eighth Circuit unanimously affirmed, on slightly different grounds.[163] Instead of rejecting the Department of Agriculture's contention that the beef advertisements were government speech, the court held that the origin of the speech did not matter.[164] In its view, government-speech status was only relevant to First Amendment challenges regarding the content of speech, not challenges to its compelled funding.[165]

2. The Majority Opinion

The Supreme Court vacated the Eighth Circuit's decision, accepting the government-speech defense.[166] It distinguished the decisions

---

[158] Johanns v. Livestock Marketing Association, 125 S. Ct. 2055, 2059–60 (2005).

[159] Livestock Marketing Association v. United States Department of Agriculture, 132 F. Supp. 2d 817, 820 (D. S.D. 2001).

[160] Johanns, 125 S. Ct. at 2060.

[161] Livestock Marketing Association v. United States Department of Agriculture, 207 F. Supp. 2d 992, 997 (D. S.D. 2002).

[162] *Id.* at 1002–07.

[163] Livestock Marketing Association v. United States Department of Agriculture, 335 F.3d 711, 726 (8th Cir. 2003).

[164] *Id.* at 720–21.

[165] *Id.*

[166] Johanns v. Livestock Marketing Association, 125 S. Ct. 2055, 2066 (2005).

barring compelled payment for speech, stating that "[o]ur com-
pelled-subsidy cases have consistently respected the principle that
'[c]ompelled support of a private association is fundamentally different from compelled support of the government.'"[167] Because the
secretary of agriculture had final say over the content of the advertisements, the program was "effectively controlled by the Federal
Government" and thus cannot "be the cause of any possible First
Amendment harm."[168]

The Livestock Marketing Association had argued that the advertisements did not constitute permissible government speech for two
reasons: First, the advertisements were designed by the Beef Board,
which was partially composed of members of private industry and
received only pro forma supervision from the secretary of agriculture.[169] Second, the Beef Act employed a targeted assessment, which
required individual beef producers to foot the cost of advertising.[170]
The Livestock Marketing Association argued that this funding mechanism was suspect both because it gives control of the beef program
to narrow interest groups and because it creates the perception
among the general public that the advertisements speak for the beef
producers.[171]

The Court rejected each point. It noted that the Beef Board included
members appointed by the secretary of agriculture and that the
secretary had final say over the content of each advertisement.[172]
That the assessment was targeted at beef producers in particular,
the Court concluded, made no constitutional difference. It noted
that "[c]itizens may challenge compelled support of private speech,
but have no First Amendment right not to fund government speech.
And that is no less true when the funding is achieved through
targeted assessments devoted exclusively to the program to which
the assessed citizens object."[173]

[167] *Id.* at 2062.
[168] *Id.* at 2062, 2064.
[169] *Id.* at 2062.
[170] *Id.* at 2063.
[171] *Id.*
[172] *Id.* at 2062–63, 2064.
[173] *Id.* at 2063.

Meanwhile, the Court interpreted the case as a "facial challenge"—i.e., an assertion that the statute would always operate unconstitutionally, on all sets of facts. Thus, the Court rejected the Livestock Marketing Association's claim that the public would falsely attribute the advertisements to its members.[174] Because nothing in the Beef Act required that the messages be attributed to the respondents, the facial challenge failed. The opinion left open the possibility that a claim of confusion might prevail "[o]n some set of facts."[175]

3. The Primary Dissent

Writing the primary dissent, Justice David Souter argued that the beef checkoff program could not qualify as government speech because the design of the program insulated the government from political accountability.[176] He noted that the majority's "error is not that government speech can never justify compelling a subsidy, but that a compelled subsidy should not be justifiable by speech unless the government must put that speech forward as its own."[177] In other words, political accountability is lost if the message comes from a self-interested private group currently favored by government.

Justice Souter contended that the government-speech doctrine is justified both by necessity and by the possibility that the political process will serve as a check on what the government chooses to say.[178] But the targeted nature of the assessment and the fact that the government did not take responsibility for its advertisements stymied the ability of the political process to serve as an effective check on the government.

To Justice Souter, that the government targeted the assessment at beef producers heightened the harm imposed by the advertisements. Justice Souter agreed with the majority that the government must be free to use generalized tax revenue to express its views, or else all government action would become subject to a heckler's veto.[179] Under a targeted assessment, however, "the particular interests of

---

[174] Id. at 2065–66.
[175] Id. at 2065.
[176] Id. at 2069 (Souter, J., dissenting).
[177] Id. at 2068.
[178] Id. at 2070–71.
[179] Id. at 2070.

those singled out to pay the tax are closely linked with the expression, and taxpayers who disagree with it suffer a more acute limitation on their presumptive autonomy as speakers to decide what to say and what to pay for others to say."[180]

Meanwhile, the advertisements in *Johanns* need not indicate that they were funded by the government, removing an important check on political accountability.[181] There is no reason that an individual consumer, watching a beef commercial, has any reason to believe that the advertisement is the work of the federal government. If the individual did wonder if the government paid for the ad, the tag line "Funded by America's Beef Producers" would strongly imply otherwise.[182]

B. Johanns *as a Setback for Commercial Speech*

The *Johanns* decision is a setback for commercial-speech interests. Most immediately, it weakens the protection that advertisers won in *United Foods*. More subtly, it again reaffirms the Supreme Court's view that commercial speech is "lower value."

1. An Expansive View of Government Speech

The government-speech doctrine, as announced by the *Johanns* court, seems unbounded, for two reasons: First, it is hard to constrain a doctrine that is based on a distinction without a difference. The majority distinguishes the compelled-speech line of cases by noting that those cases involved subsidizing private associations rather than government.[183] However, there is no inherent reason why forcing an organization to pay for speech with which it disagrees is worse when the speech is coordinated by a private association rather than by the government. If a woman who is pro-life were forced to contribute to a campaign to promote abortions, she would probably take little solace in the fact that the program is administered by the state rather than by a private party. If anything, the imprimatur of legitimacy attached to state-sponsored messages may make the coercion even more offensive.

---

[180] *Id.* at 2071.
[181] *Id.* at 2072.
[182] *Id.*
[183] *Id.* at 2061.

As both the majority and dissent agree, the government must have some ability to fund programs from the general tax revenue without being subject to a heckler's veto.[184] However, this argument merely explains why the government must have *some* ability to compel funding for speech. It does not support a hard rule in which all speech directly controlled by the government is immune from First Amendment inquiry.

By contrast, the dissent's position that targeted assessments should be held to greater First Amendment scrutiny is consistent with the Jeffersonian notion that "to compel a man to furnish contributions of money for the propagation of opinions which he disbelieves, is sinful and tyrannical."[185] Justice Souter, responding to the majority's contention that there is no principled way to distinguish between general and targeted taxes, refers to "the commonsense notion that individuals feel a closer connection to speech that they are singled out to fund with targeted taxes than they do to expression paid for with general revenues."[186]

Second, the government-speech doctrine as expressed in *Johanns* appears unbounded because the majority gave short shrift to the unique facts of the case. Consider: The Beef Board had carefully shielded itself from political accountability. The plaintiffs alleged that the secretary exercised only *pro forma* control over the Beef Board.[187] Moreover, there was no reason for the public to suspect that the government was footing the bill for the beef campaign. Consumers do not normally assume that the government is purchasing commercials demanding that they eat more meat. And even if consumers might otherwise have supposed government sponsorship, the commercials included the true but misleading tag line "Funded by America's Beef Producers."[188]

Even the democratic checks built into the Beef Act did not appear to work. As noted, before bringing their suit, the plaintiffs had attempted to invoke a provision of the Act allowing beef producers

---

[184] *Id.* at 2062; *id.* at 2070 (Souter, J., dissenting).

[185] A Bill for Establishing Religious Freedom 77, in 5 The Founders' Constitution § 37 (P. Kurland & R. Lerner eds., 1987).

[186] 125 S. Ct. at 2071 n.4 (Souter, J., dissenting) (citing Massachusetts v. Mellon, 262 U.S. 447 (1923)).

[187] *Id.* at 2072 n.5.

[188] *Id.* at 2072.

to petition the secretary of agriculture to hold a referendum on the continuation of the beef checkoff program.[189] The secretary never held the referendum.[190] The Beef Promotion and Research Board meanwhile responded to the petition attempt by using the very funds collected through the assessment to promote the Beef Act to cattle producers and legislators and thereby perpetuate its own existence.[191] If the beef checkoff program provides sufficient political accountability to satisfy the requirements of the government-speech doctrine, it is unclear what legislation would not.

The prospect that mere administrative oversight is sufficient to convert compelled subsidies of speech into government speech is troubling. It is easy to imagine how the states might restructure the programs struck down in *Abood* and its progeny to turn them into permissible subsidies. For example, had Michigan given its secretary of labor administrative control over local teachers unions, the ideological messages in *Abood* may have passed the *Johanns* test.[192] This possibility creates a situation antithetical to the First Amendment in which the more invasive state oversight becomes, the less likely it is to face First Amendment scrutiny.

2. A Dismissive View of Commercial Speech

The Court's dismissive attitude toward commercial speech in *Johanns* is just as troubling as the apparently weak limits set on government regulation. The Court rejected the Eighth Circuit's application of the *Central Hudson* test, considering the inquiry to be irrelevant if the advertisements satisfied the requirements for government speech.[193] Thus, the opinion does not discuss the value of commercial speech directly.

However, it is hard to analyze the ruling without concluding that it relies in part on the notion that compulsion of commercial speech is a less serious threat to the First Amendment than are government infringements on other modes of expression. The abortion analogy

---

[189] Livestock Marketing Association v. United States Department of Agriculture, 132 F. Supp. 2d 817, 820 (D. S.D. 2001).

[190] *Id*. at 821–22.

[191] *Id*. at 821.

[192] Compare Abood v. Detroit Board of Education, 431 U.S. 209, 235–36 (1977).

[193] 125 S. Ct. at 2066.

in the introduction to this article demonstrates this point.[194] If the government were to compel abortion clinics to pay for speech condemning abortions, a judicial decision upholding this imposition based on the government-speech doctrine would undoubtedly provoke public outrage. Moreover, it is quite likely that the Court would be hostile to a government scheme that attributed such messages to the abortion providers themselves, and then shielded the implementing officials from accountability.

Thus, even though the Court forswore any explicit references to the "lower value" it has accorded commercial expression, the *Johanns* decision nonetheless demonstrates that commercial speech is not being afforded equal protection with other modes of expression, despite the history and explicit text of the First Amendment.

IV. The Bright Side of *Johanns*

Even if *Johanns* is not a victory for advocates of commercial speech, it need not be seen as a total loss either. Ironically, the most positive aspect of the decision may be the Court's refusal to grant the speech at issue the review normally entitled to commercial speech under the *Central Hudson* test. By applying the government-speech doctrine instead of *Central Hudson*, the Court adopted a test that is facially neutral as between commercial and other modes of expression. The Court will likely refine and limit this doctrine as litigants attempt to apply it to other forms of speech. Because *Johanns* establishes that the government-speech doctrine applies to commercial speech, any limits that the Court places on the doctrine in non-commercial contexts should, one hopes, benefit commercial expression as well.

A. The Best of Bad Options

The good news is that the Court may have chosen a comparatively benign means of upholding the beef checkoff program. Had the Court applied *Central Hudson* but nonetheless found the beef checkoff program constitutional, the decision would likely have eroded the protections afforded by the third and forth prongs of the test,

---

[194] See Part I, *supra*.

which the Court has used recently to strike down a host of restrictions on advertising.[195] The government had not presented any evidence that generic advertising was more effective than individual advertising or that the program was narrowly tailored.[196]

Even a victory for the Livestock Marketing Association via analogy to *United Foods* would not have been entirely satisfying. To distinguish *United Foods* from *Glickman*, the Court had adopted a nebulous test focusing on the comprehensiveness of government regulation.[197] The juxtaposition of the two cases created an odd incentive for the government to protect against First Amendment violations by increasing government regulation. As Justice Stephen Breyer noted in his dissent in *United Foods*, less invasive laws that rely on self-regulation are "more consistent, not less consistent, with producer choice. It is hard to see why a Constitution that seeks to protect individual freedom would consider the absence of 'heavy regulation' to amount to a special, determinative reason for refusing to permit this less intrusive program."[198] Thus, to the extent that *Johanns* represents a shift away from the framework established by *Glickman* and *United Foods*, this shift may be desirable.

B. Limiting the Scope of the Doctrine

As the government-speech doctrine continues to develop, the Court may well place additional limits on its invocation. The majority opinion includes the possibility of one such limit: an "as-applied" challenge to regulations attributing government speech to private parties.[199] Although the Court concludes that *Johanns* presents a facial challenge, it leaves open the possibility that another litigant will prevail on an as-applied claim that the government is falsely crediting speech to the complaining party. The Court states that, "on some set of facts," the theory might "form the basis for an as-applied

[195] Lorillard Tobacco Co. v. Reilly, 533 U.S. 525, 555–60, 565–66 (2001); Greater New Orleans Broadcasting Association v. United States, 527 U.S. 173, 185–96 (1999); Rubin v. Coors Brewing Co., 514 U.S. 476, 483–91 (1995).

[196] Wileman Brothers & Elliot, Inc. v. Espy, 58 F.3d 1367, 1379–81 (9th Cir. 1995).

[197] See *supra* notes 147–51 and accompanying text.

[198] See United States v. United Foods, Inc., 533 U.S. 405, 422 (2001) (Breyer, J., dissenting).

[199] See Johanns v. Livestock Marketing Association, 125 S. Ct. 2055, 2065 (2005). As-applied challenges assert that a statute is unconstitutional on the facts of a particular case.

challenge—if it were established . . . that individual beef advertisements were attributed to [plaintiffs]."[200]

C. Achieving Equal Status for Commercial Speech

If the premise of this article is correct—that the decision in *Johanns*
reflects in part an unwillingness to afford commercial speech equal
status with other modes of protected expression—then invoking the
government-speech doctrine in cases involving political and ideological speech should force the Court to impose meaningful limits on
the doctrine. Because the Court did not delineate between advertisements and other modes of expression in *Johanns*, these limits should
arguably apply to commercial speech as well.

Just as politically charged cases drove the Court's original movement away from its complete renunciation of protection for commercial speech in *Chrestensen* toward the intermediate scrutiny of *Central
Hudson*, here, too, political and ideological issues may force the
Court to constrain the government-speech doctrine.[201] In *Bigelow* the
Court resurrected commercial speech rights in part because of its
desire to solidify the right to abortion.[202] Similarly, in *New York Times
Company v. Sullivan*, the Court narrowed the definition of commercial
speech to afford protection to civil rights advocates.[203] As the states
and the federal government begin to invoke the government-speech
doctrine to defend subsidies for political or ideological speech, the
Court may well begin to impose greater restraints on the doctrine.
Given that those limits apply to commercial speech as well, compelled speech in the commercial context might also benefit from
such a doctrinal shift.

The ultimate effect of *Johanns v. Livestock Marketing Association*
may thus depend on whether the Court views the government-
speech doctrine as an occasional defense against compelled subsidies
or as a shift away from the convoluted doctrine established by *Glickman* and *United Foods*. If the government-speech doctrine is simply
another means for the government to justify restrictions on commercial speech, then constraining the scope of the doctrine will limit
the harm caused by *Johanns*.

---

[200] *Id.*

[201] See *supra* notes 60–68 and accompanying text.

[202] See Bigelow v. Virginia, 421 U.S. 809, 818, 826–27 (1975).

[203] See New York Times Co. v. Sullivan, 376 U.S. 254, 265–66 (1964).

If, however, the Court intends *Johanns* as a shift away from *Glick-man* and *United Foods* toward a new mode of analysis for compelled commercial subsidy cases, then *Johanns* could actually work to the benefit of commercial speech. The government-speech doctrine facially affords commercial speech what it has always deserved—equal status with other modes of expression. Thus, if the government-speech doctrine were to become the dominant mode of analysis in compelled subsidy cases, and if later cases involving political and ideological expression were to force the Court to put some meaningful boundaries on the doctrine, the ironic result may be that a case that silently discriminated against commercial expression might nudge it back on the path toward equal status with other forms of speech.

The Establishment Clause During the 2004 Term: Big Cases, Little Movement

Marci A. Hamilton[*]

This was the term when the Supreme Court might have made Establishment Clause history. It was asked in the Ten Commandments cases to definitively reject the longstanding, though often maligned, *Lemon v. Kurtzman*[1] test, where the Court laid out three factors to consider in Establishment Clause cases: whether the law has a secular purpose, an improper effect of benefiting or burdening religion, or excessive entanglement with religion. While individual members of the Court, like Justice Scalia, have been grumbling about *Lemon* for quite a while,[2] it has been *the* standard in such cases since 1971. The Court was further confronted with the request, in *Cutter v. Wilkinson*,[3] to approve of legislative accommodation that dramatically increased religious prisoners' free exercise rights and would have created the broadest permissible accommodation of religious exercise to date. But neither of these dramatic requests was granted.

Instead, five members of the Court refused to abandon the "purpose" prong of *Lemon*—which requires that the government have a secular purpose for enacting the law. They left that issue to another day and, perhaps, to a new justice in the wake of Justice Sandra Day O'Connor's retirement. And a unanimous Court read the language of accommodation in the Religious Land Use and Institutionalized

*Paul R. Verkuil Chair in Public Law, Cardozo School of Law
[1]403 U.S. 602 (1971).

[2]See, e.g., Board of Education v. Grumet, 512 U.S. 687, 751 (1994) (Scalia, J. dissenting); Lamb's Chapel v. Center Moriches Union Free School District, 508 U.S. 384, 397–98 (1993) (Scalia, J. concurring) ("As to the Court's invocation of the *Lemon* test: Like some ghoul in a late-night horror movie that repeatedly sits up in its grave and shuffles abroad, after being repeatedly killed and buried, *Lemon* stalks our Establishment Clause jurisprudence once again, frightening the little children and school attorneys of Center Moriches Union Free School District.").

[3]125 S. Ct. 2113 (2005).

Persons Act (RLUIPA) narrowly, transforming the Act's seemingly drastic accommodation measures into a modest legislative accommodation. Its survival, therefore, worked little change in current Establishment Clause jurisprudence.

If these cases share any notable characteristic, it is that that they confirm the status quo understanding of the First Amendment's religion clauses, and, thus, mark a starting point for the reconfigured Court once Justice O'Connor's successor is confirmed. She has been an important vote in these cases, because she believes in the importance of government neutrality; yet, as was characteristic of her jurisprudence in general, she has been unwilling to take the neutrality principle to what she believed were absurd conclusions. Accordingly, while she has found unconstitutional a solitary crèche erected in a courthouse, she found no violation in either a more general holiday display or in the use of "under God" in the Pledge of Allegiance.[4] The absence of her moderating influence may well tip the balance against the separation of church and state closer to a political intertwinement between government and religion.

Below, I examine this term's Establishment Clause cases in turn, focusing first on *Cutter* and then on the Ten Commandments cases.

I. *Cutter v. Wilkinson*: Normalizing Legislative Accommodation of Religion

For the first time since 1990, when the Supreme Court decided *Employment Division v. Smith*,[5] the Supreme Court addressed the question of the permissible scope of legislative accommodation of religious practices. In *Smith*, the Court held that religious motivation does not excuse illegal conduct. In other words, the Free Exercise Clause does not mandate judicial accommodation of religious conduct, even though it may permit legislative accommodation of that conduct. As the *Smith* Court put it: "[T]o say that a nondiscriminatory religious-practice exemption is permitted, or even that it is desirable, is not to say that it is constitutionally required, and that

---

[4]Lynch v. Donnelly, 465 U.S. 668, 692 (1984) (O'Connor, J., concurring) (holiday display); County of Allegheny v. ACLU, 492 U.S. 573, 632–33 (1989) (O'Connor, J., concurring in part) (crèche in courthouse); Elk Grove Unified School District v. Newdow, 124 S. Ct. 2301, 2326–27 (2004) (O'Connor, J., concurring) (Pledge of Allegiance).

[5]494 U.S. 872, 890 (1990).

the appropriate occasions for its creation can be discerned by the courts."[6]

In dictum, the Court further stated that legislative accommodation could be permissible if it did not violate the Establishment Clause.[7] Thus, under *Smith*, judicial accommodation is not mandated, and legislative accommodation is potentially permissible, but only if it is squared with constitutional limitations.[8] Since *Smith*, many have had been awaiting further clarification of the Court's dictum regarding permissible legislative accommodation, and *Cutter* offered the Court an opportunity to further elaborate on the permissible scope of the legislative accommodation doctrine. The *Cutter* decision was carefully crafted, though, to the particular circumstances of the accommodation at issue, and, therefore, provided little new guidance regarding other accommodations.

Cutter dealt with section 3 of RLUIPA, which required state and local institutions to accommodate religious practices. The question presented asked whether section 3, in the prison context, was consistent with the Establishment Clause.[9] The Court answered in the affirmative.

A. Background: The Religious Freedom Restoration Act

Some background is necessary to understand the genesis of RLUIPA and its intention. After the *Smith* Court held that there is no free exercise defense to neutral, generally applicable laws, legal scholars and numerous religious and civil liberties organizations raised a hue and cry,[10] arguing vociferously that judicial accommodation was far preferable to legislative accommodation. These critics claimed (albeit incorrectly) that the Court had applied strict scrutiny to all free exercise cases up to that point and had therefore departed from prior precedent.[11] To "correct" free exercise doctrine, they

---

[6]*Id.*

[7]*Id.*

[8]*Id.*

[9]Cutter v. Wilkinson, 125 S. Ct. 2113, 2117 (2005).

[10]Marci A. Hamilton, God vs. the Gavel: Religion and the Rule of Law 223–27 (Cambridge 2005) (hereinafter God vs. the Gavel). See also Brief for Amicus Curiae The Tort Claimants' Committee at 25–26, Gonzales v. O Centro Espirita Beneficiente Uniao, No. 04-1084 (U.S. filed July 8, 2005).

[11]For a more detailed discussion of the actual free exercise doctrine preceding *Smith*, see God vs. the Gavel, *supra* note 10, at 214–23, 276–80.

urged Congress to enact the Religious Freedom Restoration Act (RFRA),[12] which purported to "restore" free exercise doctrine to where it was before *Smith*. And during the course of three years of hearings, Congress vehemently criticized the Court for its holding in *Smith*.[13]

RFRA's supporters—which included President Clinton—intended to overturn the rule announced in *Smith* through a simple legislative majority. During debate over the bill, the *Smith* decision was described as "a dastardly and unprovoked attack on our first freedom."[14] Then-Representative Schumer called it "a devastating blow to religious freedom, [which] we are trying to undo."[15] Congress was not reticent about making clear its intention to overrule *Smith*: "This landmark legislation," explained Representative Nadler, "will overturn the Supreme Court's disastrous decision, Employment Division versus Smith, which virtually eliminated the First Amendment's protection of the free exercise of religion."[16] President Clinton also understood RFRA as a provision that would overrule *Smith*, as he explained when he signed the Act into law: "[T]his act reverses the Supreme Court's decision Employment Division against Smith and reestablishes a standard that better protects all Americans of all faiths in the exercise of their religion in a way that I am convinced is far more consistent with the intent of the Founders of this Nation than the Supreme Court decision."[17]

[12]42 U.S.C. § 2000bb (2005).

[13]RFRA's legislative history contains over 400 pages explicitly criticizing *Smith*. See, e.g., The Religious Freedom Restoration Act of 1990: Hearings on H.R. 5377 Before the Subcommittee on Civil and Constitutional Rights of the House Committee on the Judiciary, 101st Cong., 2d Sess. 2, 8, 9, 11, 22, 28–29, 31–32, 35, 38, 41, 48, 49, 51, 61 (1990); The Religious Freedom Restoration Act of 1991: Hearings on H.R. 2797 Before the Subcommittee on Civil and Constitutional Rights of the House Committee on the Judiciary, 102d Cong., 2d Sess. 7, 8, 19, 23, 32, 39, 45, 63, 99, 136, 160, 175, 193, 201, 214, 249, 251, 271 (1992).

[14]137 Cong. Rec. E2422 (daily ed. June 27, 1991) (statement of Rep. Solarz).

[15]139 Cong. Rec. H2360 (daily ed. May 11, 1993) (statement of Rep. Schumer).

[16]139 Cong. Rec. H2359 (daily ed. May 11, 1993) (statement of Rep. Nadler). See also 139 Cong. Rec. H2361 (daily ed. May 11, 1993) (statement of Rep. Hoyer) ("This ruling did great mischief to the rights of all Americans. Religious liberty [is] no longer a fundamental constitutional right."); 139 Cong. Rec. S14464 (daily ed. October 27, 1993) (statement of Sen. Coats) ("The Court has effectively turned religious Americans into second class citizens.").

[17]Remarks on Signing the Religious Freedom Restoration Act of 1993, President William J. Clinton, Nov. 16, 1993, 29 Weekly Comp. Pres. Doc. 2377.

RFRA did not create specific exemptions from the Establishment Clause's neutrality principle for specific religious practices burdened by law, as Congress had with respect to anti-discrimination law in Title VII of the Civil Rights Act of 1964.[18] Rather, RFRA created a judicial standard of review that would be applicable to laws that burden religious exercise. Its scope, therefore, was constitutional: that is, RFRA mandated that every category of law in the country (local, state, and federal; legislative, executive, and judicial),[19] when applied to burden religious conduct in a significant way, must satisfy strict scrutiny as that standard has been characterized in the Court's First Amendment cases. Specifically, RFRA barred government from applying its laws in any way that "substantially burdened" religious conduct unless the government could prove the law existed to further a "compelling interest" and was the "least restrictive means" of accomplishing that interest.[20]

In *City of Boerne v. Flores*,[21] the Court held that RFRA was unconstitutional, reasoning that Congress cannot supplant the Supreme Court's interpretation of the Constitution through legislative action. The Court held that, in attempting to do so, Congress had violated separation-of-powers principles,[22] had exceeded Congress' power under Section 5 of the Fourteenth Amendment (which was the only congressional power that Congress considered as a source of its enacting authority),[23] and had violated Article V's mandated procedures to amend the Constitution.[24]

B. Round II: Religious Land Use and Institutionalized Persons Act

In the wake of *Boerne*, RFRA's proponents immediately returned to Congress to request further legislation to protect religious accommodation, preferably with RFRA's scope. First, Congress considered

---

[18]42 U.S.C. § 2000e-1

[19]"(1) [T]he term 'government' includes a branch, department, agency, instrumentality, and official (or other person acting under color of law) of the United States, or of a covered entity; (2) the term 'covered entity' means the District of Columbia, the Commonwealth of Puerto Rico, and each territory and possession of the United States . . ." 42 U.S.C. § 2000bb-2(1)-(2) (2005).

[20]42 U.S.C. § 2000bb-1 (2005).

[21]521 U.S. 507 (1997).

[22]God vs. the Gavel, *supra* note 10, at 236.

[23]*Id.* at 236–37.

[24]*Id.*

the Religious Liberty Protection Act (RLPA)—a proposal that met this demand—but members proved unwilling to pass another law that approached the sweep of RFRA.[25] Instead, Congress responded by attempting to protect religious accommodation in two relatively discrete arenas of law—land use law and the law governing state institutions. Thus, three years after the Court held RFRA unconstitutional in *City of Boerne v. Flores*,[26] and ten years after the Court's decision in *Smith*, Congress enacted, and President Bill Clinton signed, the Religious Land Use and Institutionalized Persons Act (RLUIPA),[27] a bill that imposes heightened scrutiny on regulation of religious exercise by programs that receive federal financial assistance when those programs regulate individuals' exercise of religion in a burdensome way.[28]

RLUIPA is in fact two distinct laws brought under one lengthy heading—one of these laws imposes strict scrutiny on federally assisted local and state land use programs that substantially burden religious conduct while the other imposes scrutiny on regulations in federally assisted state institutions, including prisons.[29] Only the provision imposing strict scrutiny in the prison context was at stake in the Supreme Court's unanimous decision in *Cutter v. Wilkinson*.

Applied to prisons, RLUIPA's language, taken by itself, is at a significant distance from the Court's pre-existing free exercise jurisprudence in the prison context. Before *Smith*, RFRA, and RLUIPA, the Court had applied low-level scrutiny to prison regulations and mandated deference to prison interests.[30] Justice O'Connor encapsulated the approach in her *Turner* opinion: "[A] [prison] regulation

---

[25]For further details, see Marci A. Hamilton, Federalism and the Public Good: The True Story Behind the Religious Land Use and Institutionalized Persons Act, 78 Ind. L.J. 311, 332–54 (2003).

[26]521 U.S. 507 (1997).

[27]42 U.S.C. § 2000cc (2005).

[28]*Id.*

[29]42 U.S.C. 2000cc-3(i) (2005) provides: "Severability.—If any provision of this Act or of an amendment made by this Act, or any application of such provision to any person or circumstance, is held to be unconstitutional, the remainder of this Act, the amendments made by this Act, and the application of the provision to any other person or circumstance shall not be affected."

[30]See O'Lone v. Estate of Shabazz, 482 U.S. 342 (1987); Turner v. Safley, 482 U.S. 78 (1987).

cannot be sustained where the logical connection between the regulation and the asserted goal is so remote as to render the policy arbitrary or irrational. Moreover, the governmental objective must be a legitimate and neutral one. We have found it important to inquire whether prison regulations restricting inmates' First Amendment rights operated in a neutral fashion, without regard to the content of the expression."[31] However, RLUIPA, on its face, appeared to demand far more exacting scrutiny.

C. Cutter v. Wilkinson: *A Victory for the Status Quo*

In *Cutter*, the Court was finally presented with an opportunity to address the scope of RLUIPA's language. Five Ohio state prisoners alleged that certain prison regulations impeded their religious freedom and therefore violated section 3. They included members of the Church of Jesus Christ Christian, which is a subdemonination of the Christian Identity Church (a white supremacist organization), as well as members of Wicca, Satanist, and Astaru religions. The Ohio prison regulations forbade certain reading materials and ceremonial items, and required adherence to religious dress and appearance mandates. The regulations also did not mandate a chaplain trained in their particular religions. The prisoners argued that RLUIPA required prisons to give prisoners access to white supremacist literature, conduct religious services, dress as their religion commands, and have a prison chaplain specifically trained in their religion.[32] The State of Ohio, in turn, challenged the constitutionality of RLUIPA under the Establishment Clause, arguing that the law did not have a secular purpose and that its effect was to give religious prisoners superior constitutional rights.[33]

The trial court held that RLUIPA's strict scrutiny test is constitutional, because it allows some safety and security claims to outweigh

---

[31]Safley, 482 U.S. at 89–90.

[32]Gerhardt v. Lazaroff, 221 F. Supp. 2d 827, 832–33 (S.D. Ohio 2001). Among the readings requested in *Gerhardt* were publications used as gang identifiers written in foreign languages prisoners were known to have utilized for codes. See Brief for Respondents, Cutter v. Wilkinson, 125 S. Ct. 2113 (No. 03-9877) (U.S. filed Feb. 11, 2005).

[33]For a summary of the facts of the case, see Gerhardt, 221 F. Supp. 2d at 833–34.

claims for religious accommodation and therefore does not imper-
missibly advance religion, as the Court's Establishment Clause forbids.[34] The court also held that RLUIPA was a proper exercise of
Congress' power under the Spending Clause, because, according to
the trial court, RLUIPA furthered the general welfare of the United
States and gave the states a meaningful choice to accept federal
funds knowing the attached conditions.[35]

The U.S. Court of Appeals for the Sixth Circuit reversed and held
that RLUIPA violates the Establishment Clause "because it favors
religious rights over other fundamental rights without any showing
that religious rights are at any greater risk of deprivation."[36] The
court relied on Justice Stevens's reasoning in his concurrence to
Boerne:

> If the historic landmark on the hill in Boerne happened to
> be a museum or an art gallery owned by an atheist, it would
> not be eligible for an exemption from the city ordinances
> that forbid an enlargement of the structure. Because the land-
> mark is owned by the Catholic Church, it is claimed that
> RFRA gives its owner a federal statutory entitlement to an
> exemption from a generally applicable, neutral civil law.
> Whether the Church would actually prevail under the statute
> or not, the statute has provided the Church with a legal
> weapon that no atheist or agnostic can obtain. This govern-
> mental preference for religion, as opposed to irreligion, is
> forbidden by the First Amendment.[37]

Justice Stevens's analysis in *Boerne* suggests that granting a special
privilege for the conduct of religious groups, and not for groups
engaged in other First Amendment–protected activities, violates the
Establishment Clause. As the Sixth Circuit recognized, that same
argument can be made with respect to RLUIPA, which operates

---

[34]*Id.* at 846–49.

[35]*Id.* at 839–44.

[36]Cutter v. Wilkinson, 349 F.3d 257, 262 (6th Cir. 2003).

[37]*Id.* at 261 (quoting City of Boerne v. Flores, 521 U.S. 507, 536–37 (1997)). The State
of Ohio also had challenged Congress' power to enact RLUIPA, but the Sixth Circuit
did not reach the issue: "For all the reasons set forth above, we hold that [RLUIPA]
violates the Establishment Clause. Because of this determination, we have no need
to consider the alternative grounds raised by defendants in their constitutional challenge to RLUIPA." *Id.* at 268–69.

identically to RFRA, though it does not, as RFRA would, apply to every law in the land.

The decision was appealed to the Supreme Court, where Justice Ginsburg issued a unanimous opinion, reversing the Sixth Circuit. On its face, the opinion may appear to be a win for the prisoners and RLUIPA's supporters. Closer reading of the opinion brings that conclusion into rather serious doubt. The Court characterized the question before it as one of permissible accommodation, and reaffirmed the principle that legislatures may accommodate religious conduct within certain parameters, a principle previously approved in dictum in *Smith*[38] and expressly in *Corporation of Presiding Bishop of the Church of Jesus Christ of Latter-Day Saints v. Amos.*[39] The *Amos* Court upheld Congress' exemption of religious employers from Title VII, which otherwise forbids employers from discriminating on the basis of religious belief (and which provides no exemption for discrimination on the basis of racial or gender-based classifications).[40] Aside from the peyote exemptions approved in dictum in *Boerne*, *Amos* is the Court's sole case upholding a legislative accommodation. In *Texas Monthly, Inc. v. Bullock*,[41] the Court had invalidated special tax treatment for religious publications, because the government directed a subsidy exclusively to religious writings that promulgate the teachings of religious faith.[42] *Cutter* essentially left the doctrine as it was.

Justice Ginsburg's unanimous decision found no Establishment Clause defect with RLUIPA, as applied, for two primary reasons. First, said Ginsburg, section 3 deals with whether a prisoner is able to worship *at all* and therefore "alleviates *exceptional* government-created burdens on private religious exercise."[43] For the framing generation, free "exercise" of religion referred primarily to worship. There is good reason to doubt that the Free Exercise Clause was intended to extend beyond worship. Thus, a situation that deprives

---

[38]Employment Division v. Smith, 494 U.S. 872, 890 (1990).

[39]483 U.S. 327, 338 (1987).

[40]Title VII of the Civil Rights Act of 1964, § 702, 42 U.S.C. §§ 2000e–2000e-17 (2005).

[41]489 U.S. 1 (1989).

[42]*Id.* at 5 (invalidating state tax that had an exclusive exemption for religious periodicals).

[43]Cutter v. Wilkinson, 125 S. Ct. 2113, 2121 (2005).

a believer of any possibility of worship is worse, as a constitutional matter, than burdens on conduct other than worship.[44] RLUIPA does not, by its terms, limit itself to worship, but the institutionalized person is not in a position to engage in other religious conduct beyond worship, such as proselytizing on street corners, by the very nature of his or her institutionalization. There are degrees of burdens on religious practice, from those that preclude worship altogether in the institutional setting to those, like land use laws, that affect only where—not whether—worship will occur. Institutional regulations encompassed by RLUIPA generated "exceptional" burdens on the right of worship, because section 3 operates in an arena where "the government exerts a degree of control unparalleled in civilian society" and "that is severely disabling to private religious exercise."[45]

Second, unlike the courts below, Justice Ginsburg reads RLUIPA to require *deferential* review of prison regulations, not strict scrutiny as it is understood in the realm of constitutional law. It is an understatement to say that the Court did not take RLUIPA's language of strict scrutiny at face value. Instead, the Court relied on legislative history that instructed courts to apply RLUIPA with "due deference to the experience and expertise of prison and jail administrators in establishing necessary regulations and procedures to maintain good order, security and discipline, consistent with consideration of costs and limited resources."[46]

Lest the lower courts applying *Cutter* misunderstand the Court's message, a footnote reiterated the directive to defer to prison officials' judgments: "It bears repetition . . . that prison security is a compelling state interest, and that deference is due to institutional officials' expertise in this arena."[47] Moreover, at the end of the opinion, the Court urged prison administrators to refuse to accommodate religious exercise in circumstances where "inmate requests for religious accommodations become excessive, impose unjustified burdens on other institutionalized persons, or jeopardize the effective

---

[44]See Arlin M. Adams & Charles J. Emmerich, A Heritage of Religious History, 137 U. Pa. L. Rev. 1559, 1582–94 (1989)

[45]125 S. Ct. at 2121.

[46]*Id.* at 2123 (quoting 139 Cong. Rec. 26190 (1993) (remarks of Senator Hatch) and Joint Statement S7775 (quoting S. Rep. No. 103–111, at 10 (1993))).

[47]*Id.* at 2124 n.13.

functioning of an institution . . . ."[48] Thus, far from establishing strict scrutiny with teeth, the *Cutter* Court read RLUIPA to require deference to prison interests and to prison authorities' expertise regarding those interests. It is not too much to say that the Court used RLUIPA's legislative history to gut its plain language. The Court's holding, therefore, did not so much reverse the Sixth Circuit, or affirm the trial court, as it re-interpreted the statute. Had the courts below read RLUIPA's language identically, they may well have reached the same legal conclusions as the Supreme Court.

In sum, the Court upheld RLUIPA because the statute merely requires accommodation when prison regulations create exceptional burdens, but did so with the proviso that courts must apply its ruling with deference to governing authorities. One is left to wonder precisely how far the import of section 3 now is from the low-level scrutiny constitutional precedents that pre-dated RLUIPA. The distance does not appear to be great at all. Far from being an opinion that opens the door to expansive accommodation, as some had feared, *Cutter* leaves the range of permissible accommodation rather narrow. Moreover, it reaffirms the principle that legislative accommodation must be examined to ensure it does not encroach on the establishment of religion. Thus, as interpreted, RLUIPA is significantly less onerous than Title VII's creation of a mandatory exemption from anti-discrimination principles for religious employers who discriminate in hiring on the basis of religious belief. In short, by emphasizing its legislative history, the Court's reading makes the statute less controversial than it might have been.

D. Ramifications

However, upholding RLUIPA, even on these terms, does introduce a new factor into legislative accommodation doctrine. While RLUIPA's imposition is not as onerous as Title VII's anti-discrimination exemption, it covers a significantly larger field of law. Whereas Title VII's exemption applies only to hiring practices, and not all of employment law (e.g., issues involving pensions or union seniority, for example), section 3 of RLUIPA imposes its terms on an entire category of law—prison regulation. Its terms potentially modify every aspect of prison regulation, to the extent that such regulation

---

[48]*Id.* at 2125.

burdens religious conduct. Thus, although the scope of permissible accommodation recognized in *Cutter* is narrow, the reach of the opinion is potentially quite wide. *Cutter*, however, does not answer whether applying strict scrutiny to burdens on religious conduct well beyond worship and within an entire arena of law is consistent with the Establishment Clause. That very question is working its way through the federal courts in litigation addressing section 2 of RLUIPA, which imposes strict scrutiny on another arena of law: neutral, generally applicable land use laws. Unlike the provisions at issue in *Cutter*, section 2 offers no legislative history requiring deference to local land use authorities, and, therefore, presents a harder disestablishment question than does section 3.[49] The *Cutter* Court explicitly declined to rule on any aspect of section 2.[50]

One of the more fascinating elements of *Cutter* is the Court's clear-headed treatment of RLUIPA's terms as "legislative" and not equivalent to "constitutional" language. Remember, Congress, when it enacted RLUIPA, borrowed constitutional language—that is, language from the Court's constitutional precedents construing the First Amendment; it incorporated that language into the statutory "strict scrutiny" test that RLUIPA applies to burdens on religious exercise. Thus, it lifted the Court's language and placed it within a statutory context. It would have been easy for the Court to interpret RLUIPA's terminology in the same way that that terminology is used in constitutional cases. That is certainly what the lower courts did. Yet, the Court deals with the language with due deference to the legislature and interprets RLUIPA's language of strict scrutiny according to the intent of Congress. It therefore treats RLUIPA's language like any other legislative enactment, to be interpreted according to the usual tools of statutory interpretation and congressional intent, rather than according to the Court's own understanding of the terms. This is driven by a praiseworthy sensitivity to the separation of powers.

[49]The legislative history does, to be sure, require religious landowners to complete the land use process at the local level, but it does not water down the strict scrutiny language.

[50]*Id.* at 2119 n.3 ("Section 2 of RLUIPA is not at issue here. We therefore express no view on the validity of that part of the Act."). The other issue deferred is Congress' power to enact RLUIPA, *id.* at 2120, which Justice Thomas, in concurrence, doubts: "[T]hough RLUIPA is entirely consonant with the Establishment Clause, it may well exceed Congress' authority under either the Spending Clause or the Commerce Clause." *Id.* at 2125 n.2 (Thomas, J., concurring).

One can see this interpretive move most clearly by focusing on the Court's reliance on legislative history regarding legislative intent—a distinctive method of *statutory* interpretation. The Court, to Justice Scalia's chagrin, often looks to legislative history to pinpoint the meaning of particular legislative terms[51]—and in the case of RLUIPA, that history plainly suggested that Congress intended the terms of the statute to be applied with deference to prison regulators. Thus, the *Cutter* Court (rightly) recognizes a dual interpretive track for the language of strict scrutiny: a constitutional meaning, when the language of strict scrutiny is used by the Court in the context of judicial interpretation of the Constitution, and a separate legislative meaning, which applies when the same language is employed by Congress with congressional gloss.[52]

Of course, it remains to be seen whether the application of the weaker legislative strict scrutiny language used in RLUIPA will undercut the strength of strict scrutiny in the constitutional context; in this common law system, one can expect some cross-pollination between the two doctrines. That would be unfortunate for those arenas where strict scrutiny is justified, e.g., cases of racial discrimination or government suppression of speech based on its message. It is also further evidence of the folly that results when a legislature adopts language drawn from a judicial standard of review as part of its own substantive legislation. In the constitutional context, a judicial standard of review is supposed to be a policy-free way of analyzing whether the legislature acted contrary to the Constitution.

---

[51]See Henry M. Hart Jr. et al., The Legal Process: Basic Problems in the Making and Application of Law (1994); Stephen Breyer, On the Uses of Legislative History in Interpreting Statutes, 65 S. Cal. L. Rev. 845 (1992); see also, e.g., Small v. United States, 125 S. Ct. 1752, 1757 (2005) (using legislative history to determine the meaning of "any"); Koons Buick Pontiac GMC v. Nigh, 125 S. Ct. 460, 467–68 (2005) (using legislative history to determine the meaning of "subparagraph"); Doe v. Chao, 540 U.S. 614, 622–23 (2004) (looking to drafting history to interpret terms).

[52]It is possible that Congress might borrow judicial language wholesale and intend it to be applied just as the court has applied it, but that is not what happened with section 3, and, as a practical matter, is highly unlikely as it requires Congress to add no additional gloss in the legislative history. It also invites separation of powers challenges as in *Boerne*, because the only reason Congress would enact a pure judicial standard of review is to displace the Court's existing standard. In any event, legislative meaning is likely to diverge from constitutional meaning; and the degree of divergence requires investigation into the intent of Congress.

Yet, legislation is policy by its very nature, and when incorporated into legislation, the language of the judicial standard of review can no longer function as it is supposed to function in the judicial context. Rather, it becomes an indicator of policy preferences—and the Supreme Court properly treated it as such in *Cutter*.

II. The Ten Commandments Decisions: Context Is Everything

RLUIPA, like RFRA, was a product of religious and civil rights interests pressuring Congress to obtain special treatment for religious actors. Also like RFRA, RLUIPA was not the subject of public debate, but rather was a creature of legal specialists in Congress and religious pressure groups. RLUIPA is a classic example of the type of legislative exemption I document in *God vs. the Gavel*, which occurs mostly sub rosa and is neither known nor understood by the general citizen.[53] As such, the *Cutter* ruling is a rather esoteric exercise in Establishment Clause interpretation and therefore is dramatically different from the rulings in the two Ten Commandments cases, *McCreary County v. ACLU*[54] and *Van Orden v. Perry*,[55] which were litigated and debated in the context of a vehement and large political debate over the role of government and religious messages. It is quite ironic that *Cutter*, which featured five fringe religions, brought to the forefront the deep pluralism of the United States, while, in the same term, the justices were asked to address whether this is a "Christian country" in the context of the Ten Commandments cases.[56]

A. Introductory Overview of the Ten Commandments Cases

The Ten Commandments cases, which involved Establishment Clause challenges to displays of the Ten Commandments on government property, came to opposite results and were expressed through a plethora of concurring opinions. For this reason, some critics have charged the Court with muddying the constitutional waters, but it is my view that the Court's decisions turn on one axis: whether the government's purpose in posting religious messages on its property

---

[53]God vs. the Gavel, *supra* note 10, at 273–305

[54]125 S. Ct. 2722 (2005).

[55]125 S. Ct. 2854 (2005).

[56]Van Orden, 125 S. Ct. at 2861–62; McCreary County, 125 S. Ct. at 2740–41.

is to further religion. In light of existing Establishment Clause precedent, that is neither a new nor inchoate concept.

Both cases were decided five to four, with Justice O'Connor voting to hold the displays unconstitutional in both cases and Justice Breyer serving as the swing vote. That means that replacing Justice O'Connor with someone who is opposed to a vigorous Establishment Clause will likely open the door to the continued melding of power between church and state already initiated by the Rehnquist Court,[57] which in turn threatens real religious liberty.

Although the Court's opinions fail to make the distinction sufficiently clear, it is important to point out that the Ten Commandments cases ask whether the government may post on its own property displays with religious content. They do not begin to deal with a separate question—whether religious messages may circulate in the "public square," which is composed of the many means of information exchange in our society, including all forms of media, including the Web, and of course the public exchange of private views. The concept of the "public square" comes from the Court's free speech cases, in which the First Amendment restrains government from regulating private speech in a location where, as a matter of tradition, there has been a robust exchange of private views. When the government creates an open "forum," it cannot then regulate the content of speech, regardless of the government's distaste for the ideas contained within it. "[T]he fact that society may find speech offensive is not a sufficient reason for suppressing it," the Court has held. "Indeed, if it is the speaker's opinion that gives offense, that consequence is a reason for according it constitutional protection. For it is a central tenet of the First Amendment that the government must remain neutral in the marketplace of ideas."[58] In an era with a diminishing number of used public squares, but a highly active Web and media, the public square concept logically extends well beyond

---

[57]See Zelman v. Simmons-Harris, 536 U.S. 639 (2002) (school voucher system is without constitutional defect); Mitchell v. Helms, 530 U.S. 793 (2000) (computers for parochial schools are not per se unconstitutional). See also Elk Grove Unified School District v. Newdow, 542 U.S. 1, 28 (2004) (Rehnquist, C.J., concurring) ("Under God" in the Pledge of Allegiance is constitutionally permissible).

[58]FCC v. Pacifica Foundation, 438 U.S. 726, 745–46 (1978).

government property to capture all those locations where exchanges of views take place in the presence of the public.[59] The constitutional question in the public square cases, and as a matter of principle, is whether the government is suppressing viewpoints with which it disagrees. "As a matter of constitutional tradition, in the absence of evidence to the contrary, we presume that governmental regulation of the content of speech is more likely to interfere with the free exchange of ideas than to encourage it. The interest in encouraging freedom of expression in a democratic society outweighs any theoretical but unproven benefit of censorship."[60] Thus, the government is kept from suppressing private viewpoints engaged in public debate, including religious speech.[61]

Unfortunately, those interested in having the government support their religious viewpoint have hijacked "public square" and its related imagery and emotional force to argue that the Court is shoving religious speech out of the public square, i.e., out of public discourse altogether. For example, forbidding government from posting the Ten Commandments on its property has been characterized as a move that "exile[s] faith from the public square."[62] James Dobson characterized such decisions as proof "there is a religious witch hunt underway" in America, with the court "allow[ing] liberal special interests to banish God from the public square."[63] But this is a perversion of what "public square" actually means in constitutional lore.

The Ten Commandments cases are about government speech, not private speech, which means the public square cases simply are not on point. Moreover, the Ten Commandments cases involve government property dedicated to government purposes, for example,

[59]The Court has wrestled with whether a private space made available to the public is the equivalent of the traditional public square for First Amendment purposes. See, e.g., Pruneyard Shopping Center v. Robins, 447 U.S. 74 (1980); Hudgens v. NLRB, 424 U.S. 507 (1976); Lloyd Corp. v. Tanner, 407 U.S. 551 (1972).

[60]Reno v. ACLU, 521 U.S. 844, 885 (1997).

[61]See, e.g., Capitol Square Review & Advisory Board v. Pinette, 515 U.S. 753 (1995); Rosenberger v. Rector & Visitors of the University of Virginia, 515 U.S. 819 (1995).

[62]Bishop Thomas Wenski, Editorial: Founding Fathers, Founding Faith, Orlando Sentinel, July 3, 2005, at G3.

[63]John Aloysius, Divided on Display of Commandments, Denver Post, June 28, 2005, at A1 (quoting Focus on the Family Action chairman James Dobson).

courthouses and not public squares dedicated to free expression by private citizens. By melding apples and oranges—i.e., by treating precedent regarding private speech in the "public square" as precedent for cases involving scrutiny of religious messages embedded in government speech—critics have managed to create the impression that the Court's Establishment Clause decisions are actually suppressing private religious speech in toto by secularizing the public square. In fact, however, the Court's decisions are *promoting* public exchange of a wide variety of views. After the Ten Commandments cases, the public square remains every bit as full of competing religious and nonreligous viewpoints as before. The only difference is that one viewpoint does not have the government's thumb on its side of the scale. Thus, these cases are about particular viewpoints co-opting government authority, not about government suppression of the free exchange of religious views.

It is a simple fact that religious speech is robust in the United States and that the country in the twenty-first century is a deeply religious country, far more so than most other post-industrial nations, with many professing religious belief and a rate of church attendance that well outstrips our allies in Europe.[64] It is also a country of mind-boggling diversity, with beliefs ranging from atheism and secular humanism to mainstream religions to schisms and cults.[65] By keeping the government and religion meaningfully separate and by enforcing the absolute right to believe whatever one

---

[64]"Religion is much more important to Americans than to people living in other wealthy nations. Six-in-ten (59%) of people in the U.S. say religion plays a very important role in their lives." The Pew Research Center, Among Wealthy Nations . . . U.S. Stands Alone in its Embrace of Religion (Dec. 19, 2002), available at http://people-press.org/reports/display.php3?ReportID = 167 (last visited July 29, 2005). Over 80% of Americans say they believe in God. See Therapy of the Masses, The Economist, Nov. 6, 2003, available at http://www.economist.com/surveys/PrinterFriendly.cfm?StoryID = 2172112 (last visited July 29, 2005). According to the Harris Poll of February 26, 2003, 90% of all American adults believe in the existence of God, with 84% believing in both miracles and the survival of the soul after death. See Humphrey Taylor, The Religious and Other Beliefs of Americans (2003), available at http://www.harrisinteractive.com/harrispoll/index.asp?PID = 359 (last visited July 29, 2005).

[65]Diana L. Eck, A New Religious America 3–4 (2001). See also Mission Statement, The Pluralism Project, available at http://www.pluralism.org/about/mission.php (last visited July 29, 2005).

chooses, the United States has crafted vibrant religious liberty like no other before it.

Before turning to the Court's opinions, it is worthwhile to sketch the phenomenon of religious diversity during the founding and framing eras, in order to better understand each justice's views on the meaning of the Establishment Clause. First, at the time of the founding, there was no monolithic set of religious beliefs that all citizens shared. It was a single-faith, "Christian" country only in the sense that the vast majority of believers were part of some faith that owed its origins either to the Roman Catholic Church or to the Reformation. Jews first settled the United States 350 years ago, so there can be no honest claim this was exclusively a Christian country. And, of course, the American polity has always included nonbelievers, or, as with Thomas Jefferson, Deists, who may feel some fealty to a God, but who do not believe in Christian theology.[66] Thus, America has exhibited significant religious diversity and a strong feeling among members of different faiths about the marked differences between competing beliefs.[67]

Religious diversity at the time did not necessarily entail religious tolerance, which is why disestablishment became a theme for oppressed religious groups. For example, the Puritans settled the United States to avoid oppression in England and landed here—only to practice their own form of oppression. If one wanted to live in the Massachusetts Puritan communities, one had to believe what they believed, or one could exercise one's right to leave.[68] The Baptists

[66]Nathan Schachner, Thomas Jefferson: A Biography 155–56 (1951).

[67]Edmund Sears Morgan, Roger Williams: The Church and the State 86–99 (1967); John Witte, Jr., Religion and the American Constitutional Experiment 46–48 (2005); James Madison, Memorial and Remonstrance, in 8 The Papers of James Madison 301–02 (William T. Hutchinson et al. eds., 1962) ("What influence in fact have ecclesiastical establishments had on Civil Society? In some instances they have been seen to erect a spiritual tyranny on the ruins of the Civil authority; in many instances they have been seen upholding the thrones of political tyranny: in no instance have they been seen the guardians of the liberties of the people. Rulers who wished to subvert the public liberty, may have found an established Clergy convenient auxiliaries."). Moreover, there are distinctive biblical traditions, so that there are competing versions of the Ten Commandments among the monotheistic faiths.

[68]See generally Morgan, supra note 67; Timothy L. Hall, Separating Church and State: Roger Williams and Religious Liberty (1998); Amy S. Lang, Prophetic Woman: Anne Hutchinson and the Problem of Dissent in the Literature of New England 4–7 (1987).

dissented from Puritan practice and bore the brunt of the Puritans' established religion. They became the most fervent backers of the "separation of church and state," because they experienced firsthand the oppression of a union of power between the church and the state.[69] Two of the most important contributors were the Rev. Isaac Backus and John Leland. The Rev. Backus' incessant prodding of the Congregationalist establishment in Massachusetts set the stage for the end of establishment there in 1833.[70] Along with Leland, he believed that Baptist theology mandated the freedom to believe. Leland took it one step further and declared that "[t]he notion of a Christian commonwealth should be exploded forever."[71] On Leland's terms, religious establishments were "all of them, anti-Christocracies."[72]

Thus, early on, there was a division not simply between religious persons and non-religious persons, but also a division between those religious groups that held and exercised state power (which enjoyed the privileges of religious establishments) and those that were oppressed by them (which did not). At the federal level, the former camp lost: The Establishment Clause formally foreclosed transferring this unequal power relationship into the federal arena. At the same time, the diversity of religious beliefs in the United States ensured that any permanent and formal establishment of religion was politically impracticable and, therefore, the state establishments fell by the wayside early in the nineteenth century.[73] A century later, the Supreme Court interpreted the Establishment Clause to apply to the states, because it was incorporated into the Fourteenth Amendment.

As the diversity of religious belief in the United States has become more pronounced over the centuries, the role of the Establishment Clause as a protector of those believers who lack political power has come to the fore. Justice O'Connor's endorsement test reinforces

---

[69]See Bernard Bailyn, The Ideological Origins of the American Revolution 261–67 (1967).

[70]See *id.*; Witte, *supra* note 67, at 28 n.11.

[71]Witte, *supra* note 67, at 29.

[72]Leonard Levy, The Establishment Clause 136 n.12 (2d ed. 1994).

[73]*Id.* at 25–26, 110–19.

this tradition.[74] "Endorsement sends a message to nonadherents that they are outsiders, not full members of the political community, and an accompanying message to adherents that they are insiders, favored members of the political community. Disapproval sends the opposite message."[75] In effect, she asks whether the outsider (translation: smaller religion or nonbeliever) is led to feel disenfranchised, in other words, less of a citizen, by the government's religious speech. It is a test that forces government to take into account the beliefs and nonbeliefs of all of its citizens, and not just those religious believers who happen to have contemporary access to power.

B. The Court's Clash of Establishment Clause Interpretations

I recount this history, because the debate at the heart of the Ten Commandments cases is whether the government may further mainstream religious beliefs. On this point, there is much disagreement on the current Court. Four members of the Court—Chief Justice Rehnquist and Justices Scalia, Kennedy, and Thomas—have found no constitutional fault when government explicitly embraces a pervasive religious viewpoint.[76] Indeed, they have treated such endorsement as the government's right.[77] By contrast, four members of the Court—Justices Stevens, O'Connor, Souter, and Ginsburg—have found constitutional error in the identical circumstance.[78] Thus, eight members embrace a bright-line rule with respect to the Ten Commandments. For the four conservatives, the Ten Commandments,

[74]See Lynch v. Donnelly, 465 U.S. 668, 687–90 (1984) (O' Connor, J., concurring) (coercive power in violation of the Establishment Clause measured by the purpose and effect of the conveyed message); County of Allegheny v. ACLU, 492 U.S. 573, 623–26 (1989) (O' Connor, J., concurring in part) (crèche displayed inside a courthouse conveys a message of non-inclusion to non-believers from the seat of state power). See also Lee v. Weisman, 505 U.S. 577, 609–11 (1992) (Souter, J., concurring) (Establishment Clause protections extend to the non-religious as part of the panoply of religious identity rights).

[75]Lynch, 465 U.S. at 688.

[76]Van Orden v. Perry, 125 S. Ct. 2854, 2861–64 (2005); McCreary County v. ACLU, 125 S. Ct. 2722, 2748 (2005) (Scalia, J., dissenting).

[77]Van Orden, 125 S. Ct. at 2861–62; McCreary County, 125 S. Ct. at 2750 (Scalia, J., dissenting).

[78]Van Orden, 125 S. Ct. at 2872 (Stevens, J., dissenting); McCreary County, 125 S. Ct. at 2747.

despite their patent religious content, can be endorsed by government. For the other four, the patent religious content of the Commandments means that government cannot not display them, except perhaps in extraordinary circumstances where the content makes it clear that the government is posting them for secular purposes.

Justice Breyer, who was the swing vote in the cases, rested his conclusions on whether the government was in fact endorsing a mainstream religious viewpoint in each case.[79] He certainly does not embrace the four conservative justices' suggested doctrine, which would give the government the right to engage in religious speech. But Justice Breyer also was not willing to go so far as to say that the Ten Commandments were so inherently religious that government posting on government property normally would be unconstitutional.

C. The Decisions

One case came out of Kentucky and the other out of Texas. The former involved government going out of its way to send a distinctly religious message to its citizens; while the latter involved a more passive, or innocuous, posting.

1. McCreary County v. ACLU

The Kentucky case, *McCreary County v. ACLU*,[80] involved the actions of two Kentucky counties that directed their courthouses to post the Ten Commandments in prominent locations. After being sued by the ACLU, the counties issued resolutions stating the Ten Commandments were the primary source of Kentucky law.[81] The resolutions expressed support for Alabama Judge Roy Moore's purchase and installation of a large Ten Commandments monument in the Alabama Supreme Court's foyer;[82] reiterated a 1993 statement

---

[79]In *Van Orden*, Justice Breyer stated that monument had a mixed purpose, but one that was primarily secular and therefore permissible. He goes on to agree with the evaluative principles laid out by Justice O'Connor in *McCreary*, but faults her application of those principles to the evidence in the Texas case. 125 S. Ct. at 2869–71 (Breyer, J., concurring).

[80]125 S. Ct. 2722 (2005).

[81]*Id.* at 2727.

[82]*Id.* at 2729.

by a unanimous Kentucky House of Representatives "in remembrance and honor of Jesus Christ, the Prince of Ethics";[83] and included a declaration that the "founding Fathers [had an] explicit understanding of the duty of elected officials to publicly acknowledge God as the source of America's strength and direction."[84] These resolutions, of course, did not dissuade the ACLU from pursuing its challenge, and the counties responded by hiring new lawyers.[85] Instead of removing the postings, they then added other documents, also chosen for their religious content, including the Magna Carta, the Declaration of Independence, the Bill of Rights, the lyrics of the Star Spangled Banner, the Mayflower Compact, the National Motto, the Preamble to the Kentucky Constitution, and a picture of Lady Justice.[86] Both the district court and the Court of Appeals for the Sixth Circuit enjoined the displays, because the obvious purpose of the displays was sectarian, not secular.[87] Even so, the counties never renounced their earlier resolutions.

Justice Souter, writing for five members of the Court, found that the Kentucky display violated the Establishment Clause, because the counties so obviously intended to send a religious message. "[T]he Commandments are an 'instrument of religion' and ... at least on the facts before it, the display of their text could presumptively be understood as meant to advance religion ...."[88] As Souter explained:

> Displaying that text is thus different from a symbolic depiction, like tablets with 10 roman numerals, which could be seen as alluding to a general notion of law, not a sectarian conception of faith. Where the text is set out, the insistence of the religious message is hard to avoid in the absence of a context plausibly suggesting a message going beyond an excuse to promote the religious point of view.[89]

---

[83]*Id.*

[84]*Id.*

[85]*Id.* at 2730.

[86]*Id.* at 2731.

[87]*Id.* at 2731–32.

[88]*Id.* at 2738 (quoting Stone v. Graham, 449 U.S. 39, 41 (1980)).

[89]*Id.*

Even though a number of amici in both cases invited the Court to reject *Lemon v. Kurtzman* as the governing standard in Establishment Clause decisions,[90] Justice Souter's opinion embraced the requirement first set forth in *Lemon* that government must have a "secular" purpose, saying "[e]xamination of purpose is a staple of statutory interpretation that makes up the daily fare of every appellate court in the country, and governmental purpose is a key element of a good deal of constitutional doctrine . . . [S]crutinizing purpose does make practical sense . . . in Establishment Clause analysis . . ."[91]

Four justices dissented. Justice Scalia, writing for Chief Justice Rehnquist and Justices Kennedy and Thomas, rejected the notion that government is forbidden from backing a particular religious viewpoint, stating that "the Court's oft repeated assertion that the government cannot favor religious practice is false . . . ."[92] He further caricatured and belittled the majority's reasoning, saying,

> That is one model of the relationship between church and state—a model spread across Europe by the armies of Napoleon, and reflected in the Constitution of France, which begins "France is [a] . . . secular . . . Republic." . . . Religion is to be strictly excluded from the public forum. This is not, and never was, the model adopted by America.[93]

---

[90]For examples, see Brief of Amicus Curiae Pacific Justice Institute in Support of Petitioners at 2–30, McCreary County v. ACLU, 125 S. Ct. 2722 (2005) (No. 03-1693); Brief for the States of Alabama, Florida, Idaho, Indiana, Kansas, Kentucky, Louisiana, Mississippi, Ohio, Pennsylvania, South Carolina, Texas, Utah, Virginia, and Wyoming as Amici Curiae in Support of Petitioners at 8–12, McCreary County v. ACLU, 125 S. Ct. 2722 (2005) (No. 03-1693); Brief of Amicus Curiae of Conservative Legal Defense and Education Fund, Joyce Meyer Ministries, Committee to Protect the Family Foundation, Lincoln Institute for Research and Education, American Heritage Party, Public Advocate of the United States, Radio Liberty, and Spiritual Counterfeits Project, Inc. in Support of Petitioners at 30, McCreary County v. ACLU, 125 S. Ct. 2722 (2005) (No. 03-1693); Brief of Amicus Curiae Judicial Watch, Inc. in Support of Petitioners at 9–14, McCreary County v. ACLU, 125 S. Ct. 2722 (2005) (No. 03-1693); Brief of Amicus Curiae Eagle Forum Education & Legal Defense Fund in Support of Petitioners at 3–8, McCreary County v. ACLU, 125 S. Ct. 2722 (2005) (No. 03-1693); Brief of Amicus Curiae The Rutherford Institute in Support of Petitioners at 13–19, McCreary County v. ACLU, 125 S. Ct. 2722 (2005) (No. 03-1693).

[91]McCreary County, 125 S. Ct. at 2734 (citations omitted).

[92]*Id.* at 2748 (Scalia, J., dissenting).

[93]*Id.* (citations omitted).

2. Van Orden v. Perry

In contrast to *McCreary*, the record in the Texas case, *Van Orden v. Perry*, did not contain evidence of overt government support for the religious content of the Ten Commandments.[94] The Texas government engraved the Commandments on a six-foot monument located on the Texas state capitol grounds, which was given to the state by the Fraternal Order of the Eagles (FOE) in order to deter juvenile delinquency.[95] The grounds surrounding the Texas State Capitol hold twenty-one historical markers and seventeen monuments, including the six-foot rendition of the Ten Commandments, which featured an inscription stating that it was donated by the FOE "to the people and youth of Texas."[96] A plurality of the Court characterized the posting as "passive."[97]

While the Court upheld the Texas display, no majority of the Court agreed on the reasoning. For the four *McCreary* dissenters, who now formed a plurality, government posting of the Ten Commandments was neither a violation of existing Supreme Court precedent nor in tension with the history behind the Establishment Clause. "Of course, the Ten Commandments are religious . . . [s]imply having religious content or promoting a message consistent with a religious doctrine does not run afoul of the Establishment Clause."[98]

Justice Breyer supplied the fifth vote to uphold the Texas display and reasoned that the government's purpose was secular enough:

> I believe that the Texas display—serving a mixed but primarily nonreligious purpose, not primarily "advancing" or "inhibiting religion," and not creating an "excessive government entanglement with religion"—might satisfy this Court's more formal Establishment Clause tests. But, as I have said, in reaching the conclusion that the Texas display falls on the permissible side of the constitutional line, I rely less upon a literal application of any particular test than upon

---

[94]Van Orden v. Perry, 125 S. Ct. 2722, 2871 (2005) (Breyer, J. concurring).
[95]*Id.* at 2870.
[96]*Id.* at 2858.
[97]*Id.* at 2861.
[98]*Id.* at 2863.

consideration of the basic purposes of the First Amendment's Religion Clauses themselves.[99]

In dissent, Justice Souter, writing for Justices Stevens, Ginsburg, and O'Connor, would have held that the display was frankly religious, because the Ten Commandments are, by their content, religious.

> [A] pedestrian happening upon the monument at issue here needs no training in religious doctrine to realize that the statement of the Commandments, quoting God himself, proclaims that the will of the divine being is the source of obligation to obey the rules, including the facially secular ones.
>
> . . . .
>
> To drive the religious point home, and identify the message as religious to any viewer who failed to read the text, the engraved quotation is framed by religious symbols: two tablets with what appears to be ancient script on them, two Stars of David, and the superimposed Greek letters Chi and Rho as the familiar monogram of Christ.[100]

D. Ramifications

These cases highlight the deep divide at the Court regarding government's power to set forth a particular religious message. On the one hand, it is quite clear that the chief justice and Justices Scalia, Thomas, and Kennedy would not only uphold, but applaud, any government display of a religious message that would have been relevant to the religious traditions of the founding era. It remains to be seen where their votes would fall if the religious message endorsed by government is not Christian and therefore not identifiable with the founding in some way. These justices have aligned themselves with a vocal segment of the political sphere, which argues vigorously that this is a "Christian country."[101]

---

[99]*Id.* at 2871 (Breyer, J., concurring) (citations omitted).

[100]*Id.* at 2893 (Souter, J., dissenting).

[101]Some, like Justice Scalia in dissent, have tried to make the Ten Commandments inherently neutral by identifying them with the great monotheistic religions, Christianity, Judaism, and Islam. But, as the *McCreary* case proves, each of these religions espouses a version of the Ten Commandments that reflects a separate religious tradition.

The justices in the majority of the *McCreary* case take a very different view of the American public. Their vision of this country encompasses every conceivable believer and nonbeliever. They hold government responsible to all of these citizens, with no special access for particular religious groups to government support of their messages. The majority further rejects the implicit, troubling argument of the conservatives: namely, that the government's posting of the Ten Commandments is justified because this is a "Christian country." It is an argument that works only at the most abstract level. To be sure, there were lots of Christians—some established, some oppressed, some tolerant, some not—but early America was hardly a big, happy Christian country. It included some Christian sects, like the Puritans (and other established religions), who oppressed those who did not agree with them. And it was a country with Jews and Catholics, who would not post the Protestant version of the Ten Commandments that was posted in the *McCreary* case. The *McCreary* Court was unwilling to fall into the "Christian country" solipsism.

These are stark differences, and the next justice of the Supreme Court, who replaces Justice O'Connor, will have the power to shift the doctrine either way.

III. Conclusion

The 2004 term did not break much new ground, if any, for the Establishment Clause. In the Ten Commandments cases in particular, it remains, as it was before, a context-dependent doctrine, which is driven by the facts of each case. Thus, there is no "Grand Unified Theory," to use Justice O'Connor's phraseology, but rather a pragmatic set of rules intended to keep the government neutral with respect to religion.[102] Of course, the conservative justices obviously have a different view of the matter, pressing first in *Mitchell v. Helms*,[103] and now in the Ten Commandments cases, for a bright-line rule that favors a stronger role for government endorsement. The question that remains to be answered is whether such a view can command a majority of the Court in the future. More to the

---

[102]Board of Education v. Grumet, 512 U.S. 687, 718 (1994) (O'Connor, J., concurring in part and in judgment).

[103]530 U.S. 793, 805 (2000) (plurality opinion).

point, the focus is now on how the next justice will mediate the play of power between state and the religious pluralism now entrenched in the United States.

The Significant Meaninglessness of
Arthur Andersen LLP v. United States

John Hasnas*

Although I hate to begin a serious article on an important Supreme Court case this way, the Court's recent decision in *Arthur Andersen LLP v. United States*[1] reminds me of nothing so much as the old Woody Allen line that "[s]ex without love is an empty experience . . . but as empty experiences go, it's one of the best."[2] This is because, for all practical purposes, *Andersen* is a meaningless decision, but as meaningless decisions go, it's one of the most significant. The Supreme Court's reversal of Andersen's conviction cannot revive the now-defunct firm, and the obstruction of justice statute that the Court is interpreting[3] has, in all ways relevant to Andersen's conviction, been superseded by the Sarbanes-Oxley Act of 2002.[4] And yet, by interpreting the language of the statute to require consciousness of wrongdoing, the Court may be indicating an important change of direction in the way it deals with the federal law of white collar crime. If so, *Andersen* may turn out to be a very important meaningless decision.

I. The Decision

In 2001, Arthur Andersen provided accounting, auditing, and consulting services to Enron Corporation, Andersen's largest single

*Associate Professor of Business, McDonough School of Business, Georgetown University; J.D. & Ph.D. in Philosophy, Duke University; LL.M in Legal Education, Temple University. The author wishes to thank Ann C. Tunstall of SciLucent, LLC, for her exceedingly helpful comments on a draft of this article and Annette Hasnas of the Montessori School of Northern Virginia for explaining how the apparently meaningless can carry great significance.

[1] 125 S. Ct. 2129 (2005).

[2] Love and Death (Metro-Goldwyn-Mayer 1975).

[3] 18 U.S.C. § 1512(b).

[4] See 18 U.S.C. § 1519 (prohibiting the destruction, alteration, or falsification of records).

account. At the end of August, the Securities and Exchange Commission (SEC) opened an informal investigation of Enron in response to newspaper reports of financial improprieties at the company. On October 16, Enron announced third quarter results that included a $1.01 billion charge to its earnings. On October 17, the SEC notified Enron that it had opened an investigation and requested various documents. On October 19, Enron forwarded that notification to Andersen. On October 30, the SEC opened a formal investigation of Enron and sent Enron a letter requesting accounting documents. On November 8, the SEC served both Enron and Andersen with subpoenas for documents. Therefore, between the end of August and November 8, Andersen had reason to know that the SEC may have wanted to examine documents in its possession relating to its audits of Enron.[5]

On October 10, Michael Odom, an Andersen partner, encouraged ten members of Andersen's Enron "engagement team" to comply with the firm's document retention policy. This policy instructed employees to retain "only that information which is relevant to supporting our work,"[6] but also stated that "in cases of threatened litigation . . . no related information will be destroyed."[7] On October 12, Nancy Temple, one of Andersen's in-house counsel, sent an e-mail to Odom recommending that he remind the Enron engagement team of Andersen's document retention policy. On October 16, Temple sent David Duncan, the head of the Enron engagement team, an e-mail responding to his draft memorandum concerning an Enron press release that characterized certain charges as non-recurring. In the e-mail, Temple recommended that he delete "language that might suggest that we have concluded the release is misleading."[8] On October 19, Temple sent an e-mail to a member of the Enron engagement team with the document retention policy attached, and on October 20, she instructed the members of Andersen's crisis-response team to follow the policy during a conference call. Following this call, Duncan instructed all members of the engagement

[5]For a summary of the chronology of the SEC's investigation of Arthur Andersen, see 125 S. Ct. at 2131–33.

[6]*Id.* at 2132.

[7]*Id.* at 2133 n.4.

[8]*Id.* at 2133 n.5.

team to comply with the policy. From then until November 9, the engagement team destroyed large numbers of both paper and electronic documents.[9]

Because, at the time, altering or destroying documents under such circumstances did not constitute obstruction of justice,[10] Andersen was not and could not be indicted for its employees' acts of document destruction and alteration. Instead, Andersen was indicted for and convicted of witness tampering in violation of 18 U.S.C. § 1512(b)(2), which prohibits "knowingly . . . corruptly persuad[ing] another person . . . with intent to cause or induce any person to (A) withhold testimony, or a record, document, or other object from an official proceeding; [or] (B) alter, destroy, mutilate, or conceal an object with intent to impair the object's integrity or availability for use in an official proceeding."[11] Thus, Andersen's offense consisted not in the alteration or destruction of documents, but in the efforts of its agents to persuade other employees to alter and destroy documents.

In defining what was required for one person to "corruptly persuade" another, the trial court instructed the jury that "[t]he word 'corruptly' means having an improper purpose. An improper purpose, for this case, is an intent to subvert, undermine, or impede the fact-finding ability of an official proceeding."[12] The court continued,

> Thus, if you find beyond a reasonable doubt that an agent, such as a partner, of Andersen acting within the scope of his or her employment, induced or attempted to induce another employee or partner of the firm or some other person to withhold, alter, destroy, mutilate, or conceal an object, and that the agent did so with the intent, at least in part, to

[9]For a full summary of Arthur Andersen's internal response to the SEC investigation, see United States v. Arthur Andersen LLP, 374 F.3d 281, 284–87 (5th Cir. 2004), and Arthur Andersen, 125 S. Ct. at 2131–33.

[10]See United States v. Aguilar, 515 U.S. 593, 599 (1995).

[11]Interestingly, despite the government's (and media's) focus on Andersen's document retention policy and the large amount of documents that were shredded pursuant thereto, Andersen's conviction appears to have been based solely upon Nancy Temple's recommendation to David Duncan to alter his draft memorandum. See Andersen's Motion for Judgment of Acquittal or a New Trial, United States v. Arthur Andersen LLP, Cr. No. H-02-121 (S.D. Tex. 2002), reprinted in Julie R. O'Sullivan, Federal White Collar Crime 449–52 (2d ed. 2003).

[12]Court's Instructions to the Jury, United States v. Arthur Andersen LLP, Cr. No. H-02-121 (S.D. Tex. 2002), reprinted in O'Sullivan, *supra* note 11, at 447.

subvert, undermine, or impede the fact-finding ability of an official proceeding, then you may find that Andersen committed the first element of the charged offense.[13]

Further, in defining what was required for one to act with the intent to impede an official proceeding, the court stated,

The government need only prove that Andersen acted corruptly and with the intent to withhold an object or impair an object's availability for use in an official proceeding, that is, a regulatory proceeding or investigation whether or not that proceeding had begun or whether or not a subpoena had been served.[14]

This instruction did not require the jury to find that the person who altered or destroyed documents had any particular proceeding in mind when he or she did so.

The Supreme Court granted certiorari because of a circuit split over the correct interpretation of what it means to knowingly corruptly persuade someone. The Second and Eleventh Circuits had adopted the interpretation given by the trial court that identified "corrupt" persuasion with persuasion motivated by an improper purpose.[15] The Third Circuit, in contrast, had explicitly rejected this interpretation,[16] holding that "more culpability is required for a statutory violation than that involved in the act of attempting to discourage disclosure in order to hinder an investigation."[17] Hence, the mens rea requirement[18] for § 1512(b) was in serious doubt.

In *Andersen*, the Supreme Court came down squarely on the side of the Third Circuit. It began its reasoning with the recognition that persuading someone to withhold testimony or documents from a government proceeding "is not inherently malign,"[19] illustrating this

---

[13]O'Sullivan, *supra* note 11, at 447.

[14]*Id.* at 447–48.

[15]See United States v. Thompson, 76 F.3d 442, 452 (2d Cir.1996); United States v. Shotts, 145 F.3d 1289, 1301 (11th Cir. 1998).

[16]See United States v. Farrell, 126 F.3d 484, 490 (3d Cir. 1997).

[17]*Id.* at 489.

[18] The mens rea requirement limits the state to punishing those who acted intentionally or recklessly. See *infra* note 50 and accompanying text.

[19]Arthur Andersen LLP v. United States, 125 S. Ct. 2129, 2134 (2005).

with the examples of a mother who persuades her son to exercise his Fifth Amendment right, a wife who persuades her husband not to disclose marital confidences, and an attorney who persuades a client to invoke his or her attorney-client privilege.[20] The Court then characterized the act of a manager who persuades his or her employees to comply with a valid document retention policy as a similarly benign form of persuasion, even though the policy may have been designed to keep information out of the hands of the government.[21] The Court continued by ruling that § 1512(b) did not criminalize such potentially benign forms of persuasion, but only "'*knowingly* ... corruptly persuading' another."[22] In doing so, it rejected the government's contention that "knowingly" did not modify the phrase "corruptly persuades" and held that the statute required the accused to act with the knowledge that he or she was engaging in an act of corrupt, as opposed to benign, persuasion.[23] The Court then completed its reasoning by interpreting the words "knowingly" and "corruptly" according to what it considered their "natural meaning."[24] Because "knowingly" is "normally associated with awareness, understanding, or consciousness," and "corruptly" with "wrongful, immoral, depraved, or evil," the Court held that "[o]nly persons conscious of wrongdoing can be said to 'knowingly ... corruptly persuade.'"[25] Because the trial court's instructions to the jury did not require it to find that Andersen's agents acted with such consciousness of wrongdoing, the Court held that they were fatally defective.

This did not constitute the only problem with the jury instructions, however. The Court also held that the trial court improperly neglected to inform the jury that it must find that the persuader acted with a particular official proceeding in mind. This requirement traced back to the Court's previous holding in the case of *United States v. Aguilar*,[26] in which the Court held that there must be a nexus

---

[20]*Id*. at 2135.

[21]*Id*.

[22]*Id*. (emphasis in original).

[23]*Id*. at 2135–36.

[24]*Id*. at 2135.

[25]*Id*. at 2135–36.

[26]515 U.S. 593 (1995).

between the act of obstruction and a particular official proceeding.[27] Thus, because "a 'knowingly . . . corrupt persuader' cannot be someone who persuades others to shred documents under a document retention policy when he does not have in contemplation any particular official proceeding in which those documents might be material," and because the trial court's instructions did not inform the jury of this, the Court again found the jury instructions to be defective, and on the basis of these defects, overturned Andersen's conviction.[28]

II. Its Meaninglessness

The *Andersen* decision is, of course, virtually meaningless to the human beings who once comprised the accounting firm. Prior to its indictment, Andersen was a $9 billion "big five" accounting firm with hundreds of partners and more than 28,000 employees.[29] This company ceased to exist long before its conviction as, even before its trial, its clients fled and the firm was forced to slash its workforce and sell off its component services in response. At present, the company consists of approximately 200 people employed to process the claims filed against it.[30] The reversal of its conviction cannot restore the partners' investments or the employees' jobs. The most it can do is add the $500,000 criminal fine to the pot of money available to pay Andersen's civil settlements and judgments and somewhat reduce the prospects of success for the civil litigants with suits against Andersen still outstanding. This is small consolation to those who saw their livelihoods destroyed.

The decision is also virtually meaningless with regard to the government's ability to pursue its campaign against white collar crime. The government charged Andersen with witness tampering only

[27]*Id.* at 599–600, cited in Andersen, 125 S. Ct. at 2137.

[28]125 S. Ct. at 2137.

[29]John C. Coffee, Jr., What Caused Enron? A Capsule Social and Economic History of the 1990s, 89 Cornell L. Rev. 269, 281 (2004) (profiling Andersen's value); Greg Farrell, A Posthumous Victory, USA Today Online (June 1, 2005), http://www.usatoday.com/money/industries/banking/2005-05-31-andersen-cover_x.htm.

[30]See Farrell, *supra* note 29.

because, at the time, it was not an offense to alter or destroy documents that may later be sought by the government. In effect, Andersen was charged with corruptly persuading its employees to do something that was not itself against the law. The Court's decision in *Andersen* means that one cannot be convicted of such an offense unless the government can establish that the persuader acted with consciousness of wrongdoing. This result might have been significant if the law had remained unchanged. However, long before the Court handed down its decision in *Andersen*, Congress had passed the Sarbanes-Oxley Act,[31] which rendered the point essentially moot.

In the first place, Sarbanes-Oxley added § 1512(c) to the witness tampering statute, punishing "[w]hoever corruptly (1) alters, destroys, mutilates, or conceals a record, document, or other object, or attempts to do so, with the intent to impair the object's integrity or availability for use in an official proceeding; or (2) otherwise obstructs, influences, or impedes any official proceeding, or attempts to do so."[32] This section renders the underlying act of document destruction or alteration a crime, making it unnecessary to go after a corrupt persuader to obtain a conviction. In any future case involving document destruction or alteration similar to that engaged in by Andersen's employees, the government may now indict the company for the destruction or alteration directly under § 1512(c). This, of course, makes any question regarding the mental state of those who encouraged the destruction or alteration entirely irrelevant. In addition, although § 1512(c) requires that one act corruptly, it does not require that one act knowingly, so the Court's holding that § 1512(b) requires consciousness of wrongdoing does not apply to § 1512(c). And despite thus having a weaker mens rea requirement than § 1512(b), § 1512(c) nevertheless carries twice the maximum penalty,[33] making its use even more attractive to the government.[34]

[31]Pub. L. No. 107-204, 116 Stat. 745 (codified in scattered sections of titles 11, 15, 18, 28, and 29 of the U.S. Code).

[32]18 U.S.C. § 1512(c).

[33]Violation of § 1512(c) is punishable by twenty years imprisonment, violation of § 1512(b) by ten. See 18 U.S.C. §§ 1512(b), (c).

[34]It could be argued that *Andersen* is still significant in that it requires consciousness of wrongdoing with regard to the portions of 18 U.S.C. § 1512(b) that do not concern document destruction or alteration, such as corruptly persuading someone not to testify (§ 1512(b)(1)), to evade legal process (§ 1512(b)(2)(c)), or not to communicate to a law enforcement officer (§ 1512(b)(3)). However, it is unlikely that *Andersen* has even this level of significance. The second clause of § 1512(c) criminalizes efforts to

Even more significantly, however, Sarbanes-Oxley added § 1519 to the United States Code, which subjects "[w]hoever knowingly alters, destroys, mutilates, conceals, covers up, falsifies, or makes a false entry in any record, document, or tangible object with the intent to impede, obstruct, or influence the investigation or proper administration of any matter within the jurisdiction of any department or agency of the United States . . . or in relation to or contemplation of any such matter" to twenty years imprisonment.[35] In contrast to §§ 1512(b) and (c), § 1519 does not require the defendant to have acted corruptly. It requires only that one knowingly destroy documents with the intent to impede a federal investigation. Further, § 1519 seems specifically designed to eliminate or at least attenuate the *Aguilar* nexus requirement that the Court affirmed in *Andersen*, since it does not require the document destruction to be closely tied to a pending official proceeding, but merely to be done "in contemplation of" any such proceeding. Thus, § 1519 allows prosecutors to visit twice the penalty on those who destroy or alter documents without having to establish either corrupt motivation or a close connection to an official proceeding.

Given the greater power, lower requirements of proof, and increased penalties of §§ 1512(c) and 1519, it is not surprising that prosecutors have put § 1512(b) into mothballs. For all intents and purposes, Sarbanes-Oxley has rendered it a dead letter. As a result, the Court's decision in *Andersen* requiring proof of consciousness of wrongdoing for a conviction under § 1512(b) is without practical effect. Since the government no longer needs § 1512(b) to pursue its campaign against white collar crime, strengthening § 1512(b)'s mens rea requirement can put no crimp in the campaign. *Andersen* makes it more difficult to obtain a conviction for an offense with which it is unlikely anyone will be charged, a textbook example of a meaningless decision.

III. Its Significance

Andersen is not entirely devoid of practical effect. It may be crucially important to Frank Quattrone (and anyone else who was convicted under § 1512(b) and whose appeal is still pending). Quattrone

"otherwise obstruct[], influence[], or impede[] any official proceeding"(§ 1512(c)(2)). This catch-all provision would subsume the other types of obstructive conduct covered by § 1512(b), again relieving the government of the burden of proving consciousness of wrongdoing.

[35]18 U.S.C. § 1519.

was a high-profile investment banker for Credit Suisse First Boston Corporation (CSFB) in December 2000 when CSFB was under investigation for its practices in allocating shares in initial public offerings. On December 5, he forwarded another CSFB employee's e-mail suggesting that CSFB's employees comply with the company's document retention policy and "catch up on file cleaning" with the added injunction, "having been a key witness in a securities litigation case in south texas [sic] i [sic] strongly advise you to follow these procedures."[36] On the basis of this conduct, he was convicted of witness tampering under § 1512(b) and two other counts of obstruction of justice.[37] Because Quattrone's trial court failed to instruct the jury that the government must prove that Quattrone was conscious of wrongdoing in sending the e-mail, *Andersen* could have great significance to Quattrone, who is appealing his conviction.[38]

But apart from this effect on the fate of Frank Quattrone (and others similarly situated), is there any reason to believe that the *Andersen* decision has any further significance? Standing alone, perhaps not. If *Andersen* is not an isolated decision, however, but an indication that the Court intends to subject the provisions of federal criminal law to a higher level of scrutiny than applied previously, then *Andersen* may prove to be as significant to the jurisprudence of white collar crime as *United States v. Lopez*[39] was to the jurisprudence of

---

[36]Indictment at 27–28, United States v. Quattrone, No. 03 Cr. 582 (S.D.N.Y. 2003).

[37]In addition to witness tampering, Quattrone was convicted of violating 18 U.S.C. §§ 1503 and 1505.

[38]In fact, the jury instructions in Quattrone's trial appear to be more defective than those the Court rejected in *Andersen*. As in *Andersen*, the trial court in Quattrone's case defined corrupt persuasion as persuasion motivated by an improper purpose, Trial Transcript at 2446, United States v. Quattrone, No. 03 Cr. 582 (S.D.N.Y. 2003); specifically instructed the jury that the government did not have to prove that Quattrone knew his conduct violated the law, Transcript, *supra*, at 2446–47; but failed to instruct it that the government had to prove that he acted with consciousness of wrongdoing. However, in Quattrone's case, the court went further and specifically instructed the jury that it did not have to find a nexus between Quattrone's conduct and any federal proceeding, Trial Transcript, *supra*, at 2450.

It is worth noting, however, that the reversal of Quattrone's conviction for witness tampering would not necessarily mean that his convictions on the other two counts of obstruction of justice would be reversed because neither § 1503 nor § 1505 require knowingly corrupt conduct.

[39]514 U.S. 549 (1995). Of course, given the limited application of the *Lopez* decision to date, especially in light of the Court's recent decision in *Gonzales v. Raich*, 125 S. Ct. 2195 (2005), this may be an ill-chosen analogy. On the other hand, given that

the Commerce Clause. To appreciate this possibility, however, we must take a moment to consider the nature of white collar crime.

A. The Difficulty of Enforcing White Collar Criminal Law

The common law evolution of criminal law produced a body of law designed to suppress actions that either directly harm or violate the rights of others or are inherently immoral (the so-called morals offenses or victimless crimes). This body of law, which is the subject of the typical first-year law school course on criminal law, is exemplified by offenses such as murder, rape, kidnapping, and theft, as well as prostitution, use of illegal narcotics, and, somewhat famously, taking a girl under the age of sixteen out of the care of her parents without their consent.[40] This is the "traditional" criminal law, which is prohibited by state law and, when the offenses transcend state boundaries or violate a federal interest, by federal law.

Over the course of the last century, Congress created a set of new federal offenses beyond those recognized by the traditional criminal law. These new offenses were designed to police the business environment for honest dealing and regulatory compliance. Thus, where a conviction for fraud under the traditional criminal law required proof that the "defendant obtained title or possession of money or personal property of another by means of an intentional false statement concerning a material fact upon which the victim relied in parting with the property,"[41] a conviction for the new federal offense of mail fraud required only proof that the defendant participated in a "deliberate plan of action or course of conduct by which someone intends to deceive or to cheat another."[42] This set of new offenses, which includes the federal fraud offenses,[43] the Racketeer Influenced and Corrupt Organizations Act (RICO),[44] the currency

significant changes in the Court's direction rarely occur suddenly or rapidly, perhaps it is entirely appropriate.

[40]See, e.g., Regina v. Prince, [1875] 2 L.R. Cr. Cas. Res. 154.

[41]People v. Drake, 462 N.E.2d 376, 377 (N.Y. 1984).

[42]Kevin F. O'Malley et al., Federal Jury Practice and Instructions § 47.13 (5th ed. 2000).

[43]18 U.S.C. §§ 1341, 1343–44, 1346–48.

[44]18 U.S.C. §§ 1961–63.

reporting[45] and money laundering[46] offenses, making false statements to federal investigators,[47] obstruction of justice,[48] and the violation of myriad specific federal regulations, may be somewhat imprecisely referred to as the law of white collar crime.[49]

The problem with this new body of criminal law was that it was impossibly difficult to enforce under the rules that governed the traditional criminal law. Having evolved in the context of the conflict between Parliament and the Crown for power and the struggle to preserve the "rights of Englishmen" against the prerogatives of the King, the traditional criminal law contained many civil libertarian features. Three such features that resided within the substantive criminal law were the mens rea requirement, which limited the state to punishing those who acted intentionally or recklessly,[50] the absence of vicarious criminal liability, which permitted punishment only for an individual's own actions,[51] and the principle of legality, which required that a criminal offense be clearly enough defined to give citizens adequate notice of what conduct is prohibited and to establish clear guidelines governing law enforcement.[52] The traditional criminal law also contained many procedural protections for liberty. The most famous of these were the twin requirements that the accused be presumed innocent until proven guilty and that the state establish the accused's guilt beyond reasonable doubt. The presumption of innocence placed the burden on the state to introduce evidence sufficient to establish every element of a criminal offense,[53] while

[45]31 U.S.C. §§ 5313, 5316, 5322, 5324; 26 U.S.C. § 6050I(a).

[46]18 U.S.C. §§ 1956–57.

[47]18 U.S.C. § 1001.

[48]18 U.S.C. §§ 1503, 1505, 1510, 1512, 1519, 1520.

[49]For a fuller description of the distinction between traditional and white collar crime, see John Hasnas, Ethics and the Problem of White Collar Crime, 54 Am. U. L. Rev. 579, 585–87 (2005).

[50]See Arnold N. Enker, Impossibility in Criminal Attempts—Legality and the Legal Process, 53 Minn. L. Rev. 665, 668 (1969). Of course, over the course of the twentieth century the mens rea requirement has been loosened to permit punishment for criminal negligence as well.

[51]See Francis B. Sayre, Criminal Responsibility for the Acts of Another: Development of the Doctrine Respondeat Superior, 43 Harv. L. Rev. 689, 702 (1930).

[52]See Joshua Dressler, Understanding Criminal Law 115 (3d ed. 2001).

[53]See, e.g., Model Penal Code § 1.12(1).

the requirement of proof beyond a reasonable doubt set the bar that the state must surmount to establish these elements exceedingly high. Also highly significant were the attorney-client privilege[54] and the Fifth Amendment right against self-incrimination,[55] both of which placed accurate and potentially incriminating information beyond the reach of the government. The latter was especially important because it helped ensure that the government honored the presumption of innocence by "forc[ing] the government not only to establish its case, but to do so by its own resources [rather than] simply calling the defendant as its witness and forcing him to make the prosecution's case."[56]

These inherent civil libertarian features of the traditional criminal law, when transferred to white collar crime prosecutions, rendered the white collar criminal law virtually unenforceable. Consider the effect of the presumption of innocence and the requirement of proof beyond reasonable doubt. White collar crime typically consists in deceptive behavior that is intentionally designed to be indistinguishable from non-criminal activity. Unlike traditional crime, there is no corpus delicti or smoking gun to introduce into evidence. As a result, considerable investigation may be required merely to establish that a crime has been committed, and even then, a great deal of legal and/or accounting sophistication may be required to unravel the deception. Under these circumstances, compliance with procedural rules that require "the government not only to establish its case, but to do so by its own resources"[57] can be extremely expensive. The assets that the government must expend to satisfy such liberal safeguards in each case it brings greatly reduces the total number of cases it can afford to bring, significantly reducing the deterrent value of white collar criminal statutes.

Further, in the absence of vicarious liability, the mens rea requirement means that to obtain a conviction, the government must show that a defendant intentionally or recklessly engaged in or authorized dishonest business practices or the violation of regulations. But in

---

[54]See Swidler & Berlin v. United States, 524 U.S. 399, 403 (1998) (describing the attorney-client privilege as one of the oldest recognized rights).

[55]U.S. Const. amend. V.

[56]Jerold H. Israel & Wayne R. LaFave, Criminal Procedure 26 (1985).

[57]Id.

the corporate context in which decision-making responsibility is diffused, this can be extraordinarily difficult, if not impossible, to do. Because "[c]orporations compartmentalize knowledge, subdividing the elements of specific duties and operations into smaller components,"[58] they frequently take actions that were never explicitly known to or authorized by any identifiable individual or individuals within the firm. This renders the mens rea requirement a significant impediment to conviction in white collar criminal cases.

In addition, the principle of legality requires that criminal offenses be defined clearly enough to give citizens adequate warning of what conduct is prohibited and, thus, that criminal statutes be narrowly construed. But the more definite the law's proscriptions, the more guidance it provides to "the ever-inventive American 'con artist'" in his efforts to come up with "new varieties of fraud" that are not technically illegal.[59] This narrow construction of criminal statutes, in effect, creates "loopholes" in the fabric of the white collar criminal law through which con artists can squeeze dishonest practices, putting them beyond the reach of the government.

Finally, the attorney-client privilege and the right against self-incrimination created serious obstacles to the successful prosecution of white collar criminal offenses. Because such offenses consist primarily in crimes of deception, the evidence upon which conviction for a white collar offense must rest will be almost entirely documentary in nature and will consist predominantly in the business records of the firm for which the defendant works. But to the extent that these records are in the personal possession of the defendant, contain communications between the defendant or other members of the firm and corporate counsel, or are the work product of corporate counsel, the right against self-incrimination and the attorney-client privilege render them unavailable to the government. Thus, to a much greater extent than in traditional criminal prosecutions, the evidence necessary to obtain a conviction for a white collar offense will be in the hands of those who cannot be compelled to produce it.

It is apparent that a federal prosecutor charged with enforcing the law of white collar crime within these constraints would be in an unenviable position. Effective enforcement clearly requires

---

[58]United States v. Bank of New England, M.A., 821 F.2d 844, 856 (1st Cir. 1987).
[59]United States v. Maze, 414 U.S. 395, 407 (1974) (Burger, C.J., dissenting).

escaping the civil libertarian bonds inherent in the traditional criminal law.

B. The Judicial Response to the Difficulty of Enforcement

For the past century, the federal judiciary has been cognizant of the difficulty the government faces in enforcing the white collar criminal law. Its response has been to erode the liberal constraints of the traditional criminal law when dealing with white collar crime. Consider, as a first illustration, the judicial creation and interpretation of the concept of corporate criminal liability. Nearly one-hundred years ago, the Court removed the bar to vicarious criminal liability when, in *New York Central & Hudson River Railroad Co. v. United States*,[60] it ruled that corporations, and hence their owners/shareholders, could be criminally punished for the actions of their employees.[61] The Court justified the abandonment of this liberal constraint purely on enforcement grounds, declaring that if "corporations may not be held responsible for and charged with the knowledge and purposes of their agents . . . many offenses might go unpunished."[62] Recognizing that maintaining the bar to vicarious criminal liability "would virtually take away the only means of effectually controlling the subject-matter and correcting the abuses aimed at [by the white collar criminal law],"[63] the Court simply abandoned the bar.

Once the Supreme Court endorsed vicarious corporate criminal liability, federal courts expanded and interpreted the concept to further curtail the effect of the liberal features of the traditional criminal law. Thus, they created an especially strict form of vicarious liability by holding corporations criminally liable for the conduct of their employees even when such conduct contravened official corporate policy and was contrary to explicit instructions directed to the employee himself or herself.[64] Further, they held that corporations could be charged with "the sum of the knowledge of all of

---

[60]212 U.S. 481 (1909).

[61]*Id.* at 493.

[62]*Id.* at 494–95.

[63]*Id.* at 495–96.

[64]See United States v. Hilton Hotels Corp., 467 F.2d 1000, 1007 (9th Cir. 1972).

[their] employees."[65] Under this collective knowledge doctrine, corporations could be convicted of a criminal offense even though no single employee had the requisite knowledge. Hence, the corporation could be guilty even though no individual member of the firm had committed a crime.

By allowing the criminal punishment of corporate entities, the courts not only abandoned the bar to vicarious criminal liability, but also greatly undermined the protections afforded by the presumption of innocence, the mens rea requirement, and right against self-incrimination. The respondeat superior/collective knowledge standard of corporate criminal liability reversed the presumption of innocence by conclusively presuming the firm to be guilty not only of any crime committed by any of its employees, but also of any crime that could have been committed if the firm had assembled the requisite collective knowledge, whether it did so or not. This standard effectively conscripted firms into becoming deputy law enforcement agencies because the only way for them to avoid criminal liability was to monitor the behavior of its employees to ensure both that none of them violates the law individually and that no laws are unintentionally violated as a result of employees' ill-informed or poorly-coordinated actions. It also eliminates the burden of establishing corporate mens rea in the form of a collective, corporate intention to engage in criminal activity by imputing the intention of any of its agents to the corporation even when the agent is acting contrary to corporate policy or instructions. Indeed, because the collective knowledge doctrine converts the unintentional and uncoordinated actions of the firm's individual employees into the intentional action of the firm, it essentially eliminates the mens rea requirement entirely. Finally, because corporations have no Fifth Amendment rights, corporate criminal liability creates a class of defendants shorn of the right against self-incrimination,[66] opening the door to evidence

---

[65]United States v. Bank of New England, 821 F.2d 844, 855 (1st Cir. 1987).

[66]The Court ruled that the Fifth Amendment right against self-incrimination did not apply to corporations in the 1906 case of *Hale v. Henkel*, 201 U.S. 43, 70 (1906). This made perfect sense at the time since, coming as it did three years before *New York Central, supra*, corporations were not then subject to criminal punishment. There would be no point in holding that an entity that could not be prosecuted had a right against self-incrimination. The situation changed when, three years later, corporations became liable to the criminal sanction. The point of extending the Fifth Amendment privilege to corporations would then be precisely the same as it is with regard to individuals, to preserve the liberal character of the criminal law embodied in the

that would otherwise be constitutionally unavailable to the government.[67]

Next consider the expansive reading the federal courts have given to the statutes directed against white collar crime. The federal fraud statutes, for example, prohibit devising "any scheme or artifice to defraud."[68] The courts have interpreted this to require neither that the victim rely on any statement of the defendant nor suffer any loss, ruling that "[b]y prohibiting the 'scheme to defraud,' rather than the completed fraud, the elements of reliance and damage would clearly be inconsistent with the statutes Congress enacted."[69] Further, the defendant is not required to make any misrepresentation of fact, since, under the fraud statutes:

> it is just as unlawful to speak "half truths" or to omit to state facts necessary to make the statements made, in light of the circumstances under which they were made, not misleading. The statements need not be false or fraudulent on their face, and the accused need not misrepresent any fact, since all that is necessary is that the scheme be reasonably calculated to deceive persons of ordinary prudence and comprehension.[70]

Indeed, the U.S. Court of Appeals for the Second Circuit itself recently declared the potential reach of the federal fraud statutes to be "virtually limitless."[71]

RICO, which was enacted explicitly for the purpose of enhancing federal law enforcement power,[72] supplies another example. Taking

presumption of innocence that "prohibits the state from easing its burden of proof by simply calling the defendant as its witness and forcing him to make the prosecution's case." Israel & LaFave, *supra* note 56, at 26. The Court, however, never revisited the issue with this in mind, but simply continued to cite *Hale* for what became known as the collective entity rule—the proposition that "for purposes of the Fifth Amendment, corporations and other collective entities are treated differently from individuals." Braswell v. United States, 487 U.S. 99, 104 (1988).

[67] For a fuller treatment of the effects of the doctrine of corporate criminal liability, see Hasnas, *supra* note 49, at 597–600.

[68] 18 U.S.C. § 1341.

[69] Neder v. United States, 527 U.S. 1, 25 (1999).

[70] United States v. Townley, 665 F.2d 579, 585 (5th Cir. 1982).

[71] United States v. Rybicki, 287 F.3d 257, 264 (2d Cir. 2002).

[72] Congress stated in its findings that it enacted RICO to remedy

> defects in the evidence-gathering process of the law inhibiting the development of the legally admissible evidence necessary to bring criminal and other sanctions or remedies to bear on the unlawful activities of those engaged in orga-

Congress at its word, the Supreme Court has held that "RICO is to be read broadly. This is the lesson not only of Congress' self-consciously expansive language and overall approach, but also of its express admonition that RICO is to 'be liberally construed to effectuate its remedial purposes.'"[73] Thus, the Court interpreted RICO to be applicable not merely to the efforts of organized crime to infiltrate legitimate businesses, but to any association of individuals that pursues criminal purposes.[74]

Further, the courts were willing to interpret regulatory offenses as requiring either no mens rea at all or mere negligence. Thus, for "public welfare offenses"[75] for which the penalty is relatively small, the Court dispensed with the mens rea requirement on the ground that to do otherwise would "impair[] the efficiency of controls deemed essential to the social order as presently constituted."[76] And even in cases in which the penalties are more substantial, the courts have been willing to uphold the convictions of individuals *and their supervisors* for acts of ordinary, as opposed to criminal, negligence.[77]

Courts gave a similarly broad interpretation to the "secondary" offenses that Congress enacted, offenses that consist entirely in actions that make it more difficult for the government to prosecute other substantive criminal offenses. Consider, for example, the money laundering statutes. 18 U.S.C. § 1956 makes it illegal to engage in financial transactions with the proceeds of unlawful activity with the knowledge that the transaction is intended to conceal information about the funds.[78] The courts have interpreted the language of this statute to mean that purchasing just about anything with money known to be the proceeds of unlawful activity will constitute a transaction designed to conceal information about the funds. Thus,

---

nized crime and because the sanctions and remedies available to the Government are unnecessarily limited in scope and impact.

Organized Crime Control Act of 1970, Pub. L. No. 91-452, 84 Stat. 922, 923 (1970). Thus, it is fairly clear that RICO was enacted to overcome the liberal impediments to prosecution embedded in the traditional criminal law.

[73]Sedima v. Imrex Co., 473 U.S. 479, 497–98 (1985) (citation omitted).

[74]United States v. Turkette, 452 U.S. 576 (1981).

[75]Morisette v. United States, 342 U.S. 246, 256 (1952).

[76]*Id.*

[77]United States v. Hanousek, 176 F.3d 1116, 1121 (9th Cir. 1999).

[78]See 18 U.S.C. § 1956(a)(1)(B)(i).

in *United States v. Jackson*,[79] the U.S. Court of Appeals for the Seventh Circuit upheld the money laundering conviction of an alleged drug dealer for writing checks to purchase cell phones and pay his rent, and for cashing checks for small amounts at his local bank.[80] Similarly, 18 U.S.C. § 1957 makes it illegal to engage in monetary transactions of more than $10,000 involving the proceeds of unlawful activity, regardless of the purpose for which the transaction is undertaken.[81] Several federal circuits have interpreted this statute to cover the withdrawal of more than $10,000 from any account that contains at least $10,000 in unlawful proceeds, regardless of how much untainted money the accounts also contain.[82] This interpretation of the statute criminalizes the use of more than $10,000 of one's own money, regardless of its source, once it has been commingled with illegal proceeds. This rendered the statute so broad in effect that it had to be amended in 1988 to permit criminal defendants to pay their attorneys.[83]

As another example, consider the offense of making false statements to a federal investigator. 18 U.S.C. § 1001 makes it a felony to lie to or otherwise deceptively conceal material information from officials investigating any matter within the jurisdiction of the federal government. The Supreme Court has interpreted this statute broadly enough to allow for conviction when one does no more than deny one's guilt of an offense.[84] In upholding the false statements conviction of a union official for responding "no" to two FBI agents who came to his home and asked him whether he had received unlawful cash payments, the Court was clear about the breadth of the statute's application, stating, "[b]y its terms, 18 U.S.C. § 1001 covers 'any' false statement—that is, a false statement 'of whatever kind.' The word 'no' in response to a question assuredly makes a 'statement.'"[85]

And, of course, the breadth with which the courts have interpreted the obstruction of justice statutes is illustrated by the facts of the

[79]935 F.2d 832 (7th Cir. 1991).

[80]*Id.* at 841.

[81]See 18 U.S.C. § 1957(a).

[82]See United States v. Moore, 27 F.3d 969, 976 (4th Cir. 1994); United States v. Johnson, 971 F.2d 562, 570 (10th Cir. 1992).

[83]See 18 U.S.C. § 1957(f)(1).

[84]Brogan v. United States, 522 U.S. 398 (1998).

[85]*Id.* at 400 (citation omitted).

Andersen and *Quattrone* cases themselves. A statute that allows criminal conviction for recommending that a co-worker revise a *draft* memorandum or for forwarding a co-worker's suggestion that employees "catch up on file cleaning" is one that has been broadly interpreted indeed.

The willingness of the federal judiciary to expansively interpret white collar criminal statutes went a long way toward eliminating the enforcement impediments posed by the principle of legality, the mens rea requirement, and the twin requirements of the presumption of innocence and proof beyond reasonable doubt. The broad interpretation of the substantive offenses such as the federal fraud offenses and RICO greatly ameliorated the inconveniences arising from the principle of legality's requirement that criminal offenses be definitely defined and narrowly construed. Because it is a feature of the common law, the principle of legality may be overridden by statute as long as the legislation is not unconstitutionally vague. And since the courts themselves determine when a statute is void for vagueness, it is unsurprising that their broad interpretations of white collar criminal statutes have passed constitutional muster.[86] Further, the judicial endorsement of public welfare offenses either eliminated the mens rea requirement outright or reduced it to insignificance, since allowing criminal conviction for ordinary negligence, which requires only the violation of the objective, reasonable person standard, eliminates the need for the government to introduce any

---

[86]On the other hand, the federal fraud statutes are so broadly defined that some of the federal judiciary appear to be ready to declare that they cross the constitutional boundary. Consider, for example, the recent dissenting opinion of Judge Jacobs in *United States v. Rybicki*, 354 F.3d 124 (2d Cir. 2003), suggesting that the vagueness issue may be ripe for consideration by the Supreme Court because:

> the vagueness of the statute has induced court after court to undertake a rescue operation by fashioning something that (if enacted) would withstand a vagueness challenge. The felt need to do that attests to the constitutional weakness of section 1346 as written. And the result of all these efforts—which has been to create different prohibitions and offenses in different circuits— confirms that the weakness is fatal. Judicial invention cannot save a statute from unconstitutional vagueness; courts should not try to fill out a statute that makes it an offense to "intentionally cause harm to another," or to "stray from the straight and narrow," or to fail to render "honest services."

Id. at 163–64 (Jacobs, J., dissenting).

evidence of what was actually in the defendant's mind. Most significantly, however, the courts' broad interpretation of the secondary offenses greatly reduces the government's burden of proof. Because conviction for a secondary offense does not require proving that the defendant is guilty of any underlying substantive offense, the government may use the secondary offenses as vehicles to punish those whom they suspect, but cannot convict, of substantive crimes. Thus, as two federal prosecutors themselves point out,

> [i]n addition to higher sentences in white collar cases, there are other advantages to federal prosecutors in pursuing money laundering charges against defendants, including: . . . the ability to prosecute a wrongdoer when there is either insufficient evidence of the underlying criminal conduct or insufficient evidence connecting the wrongdoer to the underlying criminal conduct . . . . [T]he money laundering statutes allow prosecutors to prosecute wrongdoers who very probably were involved in the underlying crime without enough evidence of this involvement to prosecute it directly. Thus evidence of the underlying crime which may be insufficient to prove all the elements of the underlying crime may still be enough to show that a specified unlawful activity occurred— leading to a money laundering conviction even if the defendant is acquitted of the underlying crime.[87]

Indeed, in *United States v. Jackson*,[88] the defendant's conviction on money laundering charges was upheld despite the fact that he was acquitted on the underlying substantive charge of drug trafficking.[89] That the false statements and obstruction of justice statutes may used for the same purpose is amply illustrated by the recent conviction of Martha Stewart for both offenses despite the fact that, as one who was neither an insider nor had misappropriated confidential information, she could not be charged with the underlying offense of insider trading.

---

[87]B. Frederick Williams, Jr. & Frank D. Whitney, Federal Money Laundering: Crimes and Forfeitures 14–16 (1999). Other advantages the authors mention include the ability to introduce potentially prejudicial evidence of wealth and "big spending" at trial and the ability to avoid the statute of limitations on the underlying offense by charging a defendant with a recent monetary transaction. *Id.* at 15.

[88]983 F.2d 757 (7th Cir. 1993).

[89]*Id.* at 766–67.

C. Andersen *as a Harbinger of Change?*

Against this background, *Andersen* appears to buck a nearly century-old judicial trend of reducing the burden on the prosecution in white collar cases. For decades, the federal courts have been steadily reducing the level of mens rea required by such offenses. Yet, in *Andersen*, the Court rejected the government's interpretation of § 1512(b) to require only knowledge that one was impeding an official proceeding in favor of an interpretation that required knowledge that one was acting wrongfully in doing so.[90] For decades, the federal courts have been interpreting white collar criminal statutes expansively. Yet, in *Andersen*, the Court specifically held that *Aguilar's* nexus requirement applied to § 1512(b).[91] What is the significance of this? Is there any evidence to suggest that *Andersen* is not simply an isolated, aberrant decision, but an indication of a judicial change of direction?

The honest answer to this question would be, "Some, but not much." Although a frank assessment would probably conclude that, in the context of white collar crime, the erosion of the liberal elements of the traditional criminal law is likely to continue, there is some reason to believe that the pro-prosecution tide has turned. Having thus admitted that the evidence is thin, let me nevertheless try to make the case that *Andersen* presages an increasing level of judicial scrutiny of the government's efforts to suppress white collar crime.

In 1995, the Court held in *United States v. Lopez*[92] that the Gun-Free School Zones Act of 1990[93] was unconstitutional because it exceeded the scope of power invested in Congress by the Commerce Clause.[94] In so ruling, the Court recognized that if the conduct the Act outlawed, possessing a firearm in a school zone, was not beyond the reach of the Commerce Clause, nothing was.[95] In effect, the Court

---

[90]125 S. Ct. 2129, 2136 (2005).

[91]*Id.* at 2137.

[92]514 U.S. 549 (1995).

[93]Pub. L. No. 101-647, title 17, § 1702, 104 Stat. 4844–45 (1990).

[94]514 U.S. at 567–68.

[95]In justifying its holding, the Court stated,

> To uphold the Government's contentions here, we would have to pile inference upon inference in a manner that would bid fair to convert congressional authority under the Commerce Clause to a general police power of the sort retained by the States. . . . To [so rule] would require us to conclude that the Constitution's enumeration of powers does not presuppose something not

found itself with its back against the wall. It either had to find some limit to Congress' power under the Commerce Clause or forthrightly declare that there was none. Faced with this choice, and unwilling to abandon the conception of the federal government as one of enumerated powers, the Court departed from its seventy year old practice of reading the Commerce Clause ever more expansively.

It may be that over the course of the past decade, the Court has come to believe that a similar point has been reached in its expansion of the federal government's power to combat white collar crime. The Court may now feel that it has relaxed the liberal safeguards of the traditional criminal law to such an extent that to continue to do so would be to essentially invest federal prosecutors with plenary power. As was the case in *Lopez*, the Court may again have its back against the wall in that it must either reinvigorate some of the libertarian protections of the traditional criminal law or forthrightly declare that the public's only protection against the federal government's power to police the business environment lies in the good faith of the prosecutors themselves.

The first glimmering that this may be the case can be found in the Court's decision in *United States v. Aguilar*.[96] In that case, a United States district judge had been convicted of obstructing a grand jury proceeding in violation of § 1503 by lying to two FBI agents.[97] In affirming the circuit court's reversal of this conviction, the Court held that a conviction under § 1503 required that the government demonstrate a "nexus" between the defendant's conduct and a judicial proceeding—that is, "a relationship in time, causation, or logic with the judicial proceedings [such that the conduct has] the 'natural and probable' effect of interfering with the due administration of justice."[98] Contrary to its prior practice of interpreting white collar criminal statutes broadly so as to ease the government's burden of proof,[99] in *Aguilar* the Court created a new hurdle for the government

enumerated and that there never will be a distinction between what is truly national and what is truly local.

Id. (citations omitted).

[96]515 U.S. 593 (1995).

[97]*Id.* at 595.

[98]*Id.* at 599 (citations omitted).

[99]See, for example, the discussion of the federal fraud offenses *supra* notes 68–71 and accompanying text.

to overcome. Apparently, the Court was not willing to invest federal prosecutors with the power to indict anyone who acted in a way that merely *might* later impede a judicial proceeding.

A second reason to suspect that change is in the offing can be found in the Court's decision in *Neder v. United States*.[100] In that case, the defendant appealed his convictions for mail, wire, and bank fraud on the ground that the trial court did not require the jury to find that any of his false statements were material.[101] Despite its recognition that "based solely on a 'natural reading of the full text,' materiality would not be an element of the fraud statutes,"[102] the Court nevertheless rejected the government's argument that "by punishing, not the completed fraud, but rather any person 'having devised or intending to devise a scheme or artifice to defraud,'"[103] Congress intended "criminal liability [to] exist so long as the defendant *intended* to deceive the victim, even if the particular means chosen turn out to be immaterial, *i.e.*, incapable of influencing the intended victim."[104] In holding "that materiality of falsehood is an element of the federal mail fraud, wire fraud, and bank fraud statutes,"[105] the Court again departed from its prior practice of interpreting the federal fraud statutes broadly and saddled the government with an additional element of proof. And again, the Court was apparently unwilling to invest prosecutors with the power to indict a citizen for doing *anything* with an intent to deceive.

Additional support can be found in the Court's recent decision in *United States v. Hubbell*.[106] In 1976, the Court held in *Fisher v. United States*[107] that the Fifth Amendment privilege against self-incrimination does not prevent the government from introducing the contents of documents acquired from a defendant pursuant to a subpoena duces tecum into evidence against him or her.[108] Rather, with regard

---

[100]527 U.S. 1 (1999).

[101]*Id.* at 6.

[102]*Id.* at 21 (citations omitted).

[103]*Id.* at 24.

[104]*Id.* (emphasis in original).

[105]*Id.* at 25.

[106]530 U.S. 27 (2000).

[107]425 U.S. 391 (1976).

[108]*Id.* at 414.

to voluntarily created documents, the Fifth Amendment protects only the testimonial aspects of the act of producing them. Specifically, it protects only the tacit communications that the defendant makes by producing the documents—i.e., communications that the documents exist, that they are in the possession or control of the defendant, and that the defendant believes the documents in his or her possession or control to be those described by the subpoena— and then, only when these communications are not "forgone conclusion[s]."[109] In *Hubbell*, the defendant had been compelled to turn over a large number of business documents pursuant to a subpoena dues tecum and a grant of immunity for his act of producing them. The government argued that as long as it made no use of Hubbell's tacit assertions that the documents existed, were in his possession, and were those described in the subpoena, it could introduce the contents of the documents into evidence against him without violating his grant of immunity. The Court rejected this argument and held that use of the contents of the document under such circumstances constituted an immunized derivative use.[110]

Given the importance of documentary evidence to the successful prosecution of white collar crime, the Court had been whittling away at citizens' ability to use the Fifth Amendment to keep such evidence out the hands of prosecutors for decades.[111] In *Hubbell*, the Court was confronted with a situation in which to reduce the scope of the privilege even further would be to render it vacuous. Similar to *Lopez*, the Court either had to reverse its direction or openly declare that the Fifth Amendment did not protect documents. And similar to *Lopez*, the Court was not ready to declare that there were no constitutional limits on the government's power to gather documentary evidence against its citizens. Thus, in *Hubbell*, the Court indicated that it was unwilling to invest federal prosecutors with the unchecked power to sift though citizens' records in search of evidence of criminal activity.

Against the backdrop of *Aguilar*, *Neder*, and *Hubbell*, it is possible to read the Court's unanimous decision in *Andersen* as an indication

---

[109]*Id.* at 411.

[110]530 U.S. at 40, 45–46.

[111]In addition to *Fisher*, see, e.g., Doe v. United States, 487 U.S. 201, 218 (1988); Braswell v. United States, 487 U.S. 99, 108–10 (1988).

of an institutional change of direction in its construction of white collar criminal statutes. Recognizing that these statutes could not be effectively enforced within the civil libertarian confines of the traditional criminal law, the Court has been loosening these restrictions for nearly a century. Perhaps it has now recognized that in doing so, it has crossed the line from facilitating effective law enforcement to undermining the rule of law.

The federal courts have largely dispensed with the principle of legality in order to give white collar criminal statutes the broad interpretations necessary to "close the loopholes" in the law against dishonest business conduct.[112] In doing so, however, they have invested federal prosecutors with exceedingly broad discretion to determine what constitutes a criminal offense. The Court cannot help but be aware, for example, that Martha Stewart was recently charged with securities fraud for publicly proclaiming her innocence of trading stocks on non-public information.[113] Similarly, the courts have created an inescapably strict form of corporate criminal liability in order to permit the resource-effective prosecution of white collar offenses.[114] But in doing so, they have invested federal prosecutors with vast powers to coerce desired behavior from corporations with the threat of criminal indictment. It cannot be lost on the Court that the Department of Justice now regularly demands that corporations fire certain executives, waive their attorney-client privilege, refrain

---

[112]See *supra* text accompanying note 59.

[113]In its indictment, the government alleged that because "Martha Stewart's reputation, as well as the likelihood of any criminal or regulatory action against Stewart, were material to Martha Stewart Living Omnimedia, Inc. ('MSLO') shareholders because of the negative impact that any such action or damage to her reputation could have on the company which bears her name" (Indictment ¶ 57, United States v. Stewart, No. 03 Cr. 717 (S.D.N.Y. June 4, 2003), available at http://news.findlaw.com/hdocs/docs/mstewart/usmspb60403ind.pdf), she had committed fraud by attempting to

> stop or at least slow the steady erosion of MSLO's stock price caused by investor concerns [by making or causing] to be made a series of false and misleading public statements during June 2002 regarding her sale of ImClone stock on December 27, 2001 that concealed that Stewart had been provided [non-public] information . . . and that Stewart had sold her ImClone stock while in possession of that information.

Id. at ¶ 60.

[114]See *supra* text accompanying notes 61–67.

from reimbursing their employees' legal fees, refuse to enter into joint-defense agreements with employees, and otherwise fully cooperate with the government in its prosecution of the firm's employees if the corporation wishes to avoid indictment, which, as the *Andersen* case demonstrates, can itself be a corporate death sentence.[115] Under these circumstances, it is not unreasonable to read the *Andersen* case as indicating that the Court believes that the pendulum has swung too far in favor of the prosecution.

Additional supporting evidence can be found within *Andersen* itself. After decades of weakening the mens rea requirements for conviction of white collar offenses, the Court was willing to adopt what it admits is "an inelegant formulation"[116] of the language of § 1512(b) to interpret the statute as requiring consciousness of wrongdoing. The Court justified this strengthened mens rea requirement on the ground that thus "limiting criminality to persuaders conscious of their wrongdoing sensibly allows § 1512(b) to reach only those with the level of 'culpability . . . we usually require in order to impose criminal liability.'"[117] The use of the word "usually" in this statement is quite suggestive. For, although consciousness of wrongdoing is the level of culpability that is usually required for liability under the *traditional* criminal law, it assuredly is not the level usually required under the white collar criminal law. Here, then, is another reason to read *Andersen* as indicating that the Court intends to realign the government's burden in white collar prosecutions with what it had been under the traditional criminal law.

This represents the evidence that can be marshaled in support of the proposition that *Andersen* foreshadows an increasing level of judicial scrutiny of the federal government's campaign against white collar crime. As I admitted at the outset, it is a bit thin. However, if what it suggests is, in fact, the case, if *Andersen* is a bellwether of the Court's revival of some of the libertarian features of the traditional criminal law, then, despite appearances, *Andersen* may prove to be a highly significant decision indeed.

---

[115]See Memorandum from Deputy Attorney General Larry Thompson, U.S. Dep't of Justice, to Heads of Department Components, Principles of Federal Prosecution of Business Organizations (Jan. 20, 2003), available at http://www.usdoj.gov/dag/cftf/corporate_guidelines.htm.

[116]125 S. Ct. 2129, 2135 (2005).

[117]*Id.* at 2136.

IV. Conclusion

Having presented my strongest case for *Andersen's* greater jurisprudential significance, I must concede that it rests on some rather weak reeds. Indeed, if the Court was truly resolved to rein in the discretion it had previously given to federal prosecutors, it could have done so much more effectively by reading a materiality requirement into § 1512(b), just as it read such a requirement into the federal fraud statutes in *Neder*.[118] Requiring obstructive conduct to be material to the government's ability to establish an underlying offense permits the government to prosecute genuine efforts to impede its law enforcement efforts, but restrains prosecutors' discretion to charge obstruction of justice when their ability to pursue the substantive offense could not have been affected and when the choice of charge is therefore "a mere shortcut to acquire a quick criminal conviction."[119] Overturning Andersen's conviction on the ground that the government failed to establish that the alleged obstructive conduct was material would have had significance beyond the instant case because it would have applied to §§ 1503, 1505, 1510, 1512(c), and 1519 as well as the now dormant § 1512(b).

But perhaps it is too much to expect the Court to have decided *Andersen* on a ground that was not argued to it. Under such circumstances, a decision that applies only to the instant case (and perhaps Frank Quattrone's), but that also indicates that consciousness of wrongdoing is the "level of 'culpability . . . we usually require in order to impose criminal liability,'"[120] may be the best that could be hoped for. In truth, given its limited range of application, there is not much in *Andersen* for one concerned about excessive prosecutorial power to love. Yet, it is pleasant to think of it as a precursor of similar decisions with wider application.

So perhaps *Andersen* really is a lot like sex without love. And just as sex without love is an empty experience, so *Andersen*, as a case

---

[118]See *supra* notes 100–05 and accompanying text.

[119]Ellen S. Podgor, Arthur Andersen, LLP and Martha Stewart: Should Materiality Be an Element of Obstruction of Justice?, 44 Wash. L.J. 583, 584 (2005). The author is grateful to Professor Podgor for pointing out this possibility to him.

[120]125 S. Ct. at 2136.

without prospective application, is a meaningless decision. But, to paraphrase Woody Allen, as meaningless decisions go, it's one of the best.

One Cheer for *United States v. Booker*

Timothy Lynch*

I. Introduction

There is a sharp philosophical split among the justices of the Supreme Court with respect to what the Constitution has to say about the administration of criminal law.[1] One faction contends that the Constitution establishes a paradigm of criminal justice that reflects the common law tradition.[2] The heart and soul of that paradigm is that the criminal law will be administered through an adversarial trial in which a jury of laypeople will make the pivotal decision as to whether the person accused will lose his liberty. The opposing faction rejects the proposition that the Constitution entrenched the common law paradigm into our fundamental law. Other paradigms are constitutionally permissible—and even more desirable—including a "non-adversarial" truth-seeking process in which government officials, not juries, find and declare facts.[3] The two opposing factions have clashed several times in recent years with respect to whether the Sixth Amendment right to trial by jury can fit within a sentencing system that allows judges to vary sentences according to facts that were not found by juries. Those factions clashed again in *United States v. Booker*,[4] a landmark sentencing ruling that has already had

---

*Director, Project on Criminal Justice, Cato Institute

[1] See United States v. Booker, 125 S. Ct. 738 (2005). On August 2, 2004, the Supreme Court consolidated the appeal in *United States v. Booker* (No. 04–104) with *United States v. Fanfan* (No. 04–105).

[2] See *id.* at 753 (Stevens, J., delivering the opinion of the Court in part) (hereinafter "substantive majority").

[3] See *id.* at 803–04 (Breyer, J., joined by Rehnquist, C.J., and O'Connor and Kennedy, JJ., dissenting in part). See also Blakely v. Washington, 124 S. Ct. 2531, 2557–59 (2004) (Breyer, J., dissenting).

[4] 125 S. Ct. 738 (2005).

an impact on hundreds of cases pending in the American criminal justice system.

This article will begin with a brief examination of the federal sentencing guidelines and an overview of the relevant caselaw. The article will summarize the opposing arguments that were advanced before the Supreme Court in *Booker*. The article then examines the chasm that exists between the two opposing factions on the Court and concludes that that chasm, though very real, is not as deep as the rhetoric on both sides would suggest. That is unfortunate because it means that the Supreme Court is not nearly ready to untangle the knots that presently encumber the constitutional right to trial by jury.[5] The article will conclude by anticipating further changes in federal sentencing law that are looming on the horizon.

II. Background

To appreciate how the *Booker* ruling fits within the Supreme Court's recent caselaw, it will be useful to begin with a brief review of sentencing law. Over the course of American history, the federal and state governments have tried several different sentencing models. During the eighteenth century, sentencing was based upon a system of fixed sentences.[6] That is, there was a prescribed sentence, established by the legislature, for each particular offense. For example, any person convicted of perjury would receive the same punishment—say, five years imprisonment.

The fixed sentence model did not endure because it was considered to be far too rigid and thus incapable of recognizing a variety of circumstances that ought to bear upon the punishment of offenders. Fixed sentencing gave way to schemes that permitted judges to select a sentence within a range defined by the legislature.[7] Because sentencing judges were closest to the action, saw the conflicting testimony in person, and so forth, appellate courts were extremely reluctant to overrule their sentences. As a result, the decisions of sentencing judges were well-nigh conclusive. From a holistic perspective, the advent of trial court discretion was widely considered

---

[5] See *infra* note 82 and accompanying text.

[6] See *United States v. Pinto*, 875 F.2d 143, 145 (7th Cir. 1989). William Blackstone said fixed sentences were "one of the glories of our English law" because punishment "is not left in the breast of any judge." See *id.* (citation omitted).

[7] See *United States v. Grayson*, 438 U.S. 41, 45–46 (1978).

to be an improvement over the fixed-sentence model. However, from the perspective of an individual defendant who was unfortunate enough to draw an eccentric, biased, or corrupt trial judge, there seemed to be no remedy for an abusive, arbitrary sentence.[8]

The next important development related to federal sentencing was the establishment of a complicated system of probation and parole.[9] Congress broadened the scope of judicial discretion by empowering judges to "suspend" sentences. That meant that even if the statutory penalty for, say, manslaughter, was a term of one to five years, the judge could suspend the sentence and release the offender for a prescribed term of probation. With parole, Congress delegated discretionary power to the executive branch to decide when offenders should be released from prison. That meant that even if a defendant received a thirty-year prison sentence for a violent offense, he could conceivably be released on parole after serving only a tiny fraction of his prison sentence. This "three-way sharing" of sentencing responsibility between legislators, judges, and parole boards persisted for many years.[10]

Over time, dissatisfaction began to grow over the discretionary sentencing regime. The fundamental defect, whether it was real or perceived, was that discretion had led to widespread "disparities" among offenders. Some scholars maintained that there were too many disparities based upon race and socioeconomic status.[11] Other scholars said there was just no rhyme or reason to sentencing. "Tough" judges threw the book at too many while the "soft" judges let too many off easy.[12] The upshot was that even though there was no consensus on the diagnosis, a consensus did emerge on the prescription: Mandatory sentencing rules would improve the justice system by bringing greater uniformity and rationality to federal

---

[8]See Erik Luna, Misguided Guidelines: A Critique of Federal Sentencing, 458 Cato Institute Policy Analysis 2–3 (November 1, 2002).

[9]In 1910, Congress established a system of federal parole. And in 1925, Congress enacted the National Probation Act, which authorized judges to suspend sentences "upon such terms and conditions as they may deem best." Kate Stith & José A. Cabranes, Fear of Judging 18–19 (1998).

[10]See Mistretta v. United States, 488 U.S. 361, 364–65 (1989).

[11]See Luna, *supra* note 8, at 4.

[12]*Id.*

sentencing.[13] The basic idea was that similarly situated offenders should be treated alike.

Congress enacted the Sentencing Reform Act[14] in 1984. That law created the United States Sentencing Commission, which, in turn, promulgated the federal sentencing guidelines, which went into effect in November 1987. The Sentencing Reform Act sought to curb discretion in the system by abolishing parole and by making the Sentencing Commission's guidelines binding upon the courts.[15] Although trial judges have some discretion to depart upward or downward from the guidelines' sentencing range, the trial judge must state his reasons on the record and his departure is subject to appellate review. The term "guidelines" has always been something of a misnomer since any judge that disregards the guidelines will be overruled by a higher court on appeal.[16] Thus, the so-called "guidelines" really had the force and effect of legally binding rules. Still, it must be remembered that the Sentencing Reform Act did not restore the fixed sentence model. The guidelines allow for some judicial discretion because they establish a *range* of punishment and the trial judge may choose a sentence within that range.

Like the federal government, state governments also experimented with sentencing guideline systems. The impact of these elaborate guideline sentencing schemes upon the constitutional right to trial by jury was not immediately apparent. But that issue eventually came to the fore in *Apprendi v. New Jersey*.[17] Charles Apprendi was arrested and prosecuted for firing several gunshots into the home of his African-American neighbors, who had recently moved into the neighborhood. Apprendi entered into a plea bargain with the government, pleading guilty to illegal possession of a firearm for an unlawful purpose. That crime carried a potential prison sentence of five to ten years. After the plea was entered, however, the prosecutor urged the trial court to enhance Apprendi's sentence pursuant to New Jersey's hate crime law. The trial judge held an evidentiary

---

[13] *Id.* at 4–5.

[14] Comprehensive Crime Control Act of 1984, title II, Pub. L. No. 98–473, 98 Stat. 1976 (1984).

[15] See Mistretta, 488 U.S. at 367–68.

[16] *Id.* at 413 (Scalia, J., dissenting).

[17] 530 U.S. 466 (2000)

hearing and thereafter concluded, by a preponderance of the evidence, that Apprendi's crime had been racially motivated. As a result of that finding, Apprendi was sentenced to a twelve-year prison term.[18] A constitutional challenge to that sentence ultimately reached the Supreme Court for a resolution.

By a five to four vote, the Supreme Court declared the New Jersey sentencing procedure to be unconstitutional.[19] Justice John Paul Stevens's majority opinion began its analysis by examining the history and purpose of the constitutional safeguard of trial by jury and the requirement of proof beyond a reasonable doubt.[20] Finding a historic link between the jury's verdict and the judgment of the court, Justice Stevens declared that a legislative scheme that removed "the jury from the determination of a fact that, if found, exposes the criminal defendant to a penalty exceeding the maximum he would receive if punished according to the facts reflected in the jury's verdict alone"[21] was constitutionally impermissible. *Apprendi* stands for the proposition that any fact that increases the penalty for a crime beyond the prescribed statutory maximum (other than the fact of a prior conviction) must be submitted to a jury and proved beyond a reasonable doubt. Four dissenting justices described the ruling as a "watershed change in constitutional law."[22] With this new principle in place, the dissenters said the constitutionality of "sentencing systems employed by the Federal Government and [the] States" was now in "serious doubt."[23]

After *Apprendi*, the Supreme Court continued to examine the extent to which the legislature could manipulate the interplay between the trial judge, the prosecutor, and the jury. In *Harris v. United States*,[24] the Court confronted whether *Apprendi*'s rationale would apply to facts that trigger a mandatory minimum sentence. William Joseph Harris was a pawnshop owner who sold some marijuana to undercover police officers. As was his practice, Harris had

[18]*Id.* at 468–71 (summarizing facts).

[19]*Id.* at 489.

[20]*Id.* at 476–83.

[21]*Id.* at 482–83.

[22]*Id.* at 524 (O'Connor, J., joined by Rehnquist, C.J., and Kennedy and Breyer, JJ., dissenting).

[23]*Id.*

[24]536 U.S. 545 (2002).

been wearing a firearm in a holster while working in his store. Harris was charged with, and convicted of, a drug offense and using a firearm during the drug sale. For those offenses, Harris faced a minimum prison term of five years.[25] After trial, he was brought in for sentencing. The trial judge announced that because Harris had "brandished" his firearm during the drug sale, the mandatory minimum sentence would be seven years, not five.[26] Harris challenged that sentence because the judge had made a critical factual finding that the government had not alleged or proved to a jury, namely, that a firearm had been brandished. A divided Supreme Court rejected Harris's challenge, ruling that judicial fact-finding in that particular context was constitutionally permissible.[27]

On the same day that *Harris* was decided, the Supreme Court issued a related ruling in *Ring v. Arizona*.[28] Timothy Ring was convicted by a jury of first degree murder, but under Arizona law a defendant could only face the death penalty if the trial judge found certain aggravating factors.[29] In Ring's case, the judge found such factors to be present and, accordingly, imposed the death sentence.[30] On appeal, Ring argued that Arizona's sentencing scheme ran afoul of the *Apprendi* precedent. The Supreme Court, though once again divided, agreed with Ring's argument and set aside his death sentence. Arizona could initiate another sentencing proceeding against Ring, but any factual determination that would authorize the imposition of the death penalty would have to be either admitted by Ring or found by a jury.[31]

The next of *Apprendi*'s progeny was *Blakely v. Washington*.[32] Ralph Howard Blakely was arrested for the kidnapping of his estranged wife. Blakely was initially charged with first degree kidnapping, but a plea agreement was reached whereby Blakely would plead guilty

---

[25] *Id.* at 550–51 (summarizing facts).

[26] *Id.* at 551.

[27] For a critique of that ruling, see generally Stephen P. Halbrook, Redefining a "Crime" as a Sentencing Factor to Circumvent the Right to Jury Trial: Harris v. United States, 2001–2002 Cato Sup. Ct. Rev. 187 (2002).

[28] 536 U.S. 584 (2002).

[29] *Id.* at 589–93 (summarizing facts).

[30] *Id.* at 594–95.

[31] *Id.* at 609.

[32] 124 S. Ct. 2531 (2004).

to second-degree kidnapping involving domestic violence and the use of a firearm.[33] Under Washington's Sentencing Reform Act, Blakely's conviction carried a sentencing range of forty-nine to fifty-three months. At the sentencing hearing the judge heard the details of the crime from Blakely's wife and was so disturbed by those details that he rejected the prosecutor's sentencing recommendation and imposed an "exceptional sentence" of ninety months—thirty-seven months beyond the "standard" maximum.[34] Under Washington law, the trial court could impose an "exceptional" sentence so long as his justification for doing so was grounded in the law and put on the record.[35] In this instance, the judge found that the crime was committed with "deliberate cruelty," which was a statutorily enumerated ground for an exceptional upward departure.[36] Blakely challenged the legality of the extra three years of imprisonment that the trial court had imposed, and the case wended its way to the Supreme Court.

By another five to four vote, the Supreme Court overturned Blakely's sentence because it violated his federal constitutional right to have a jury determine beyond a reasonable doubt all facts legally essential to his sentence. Writing for the majority, Justice Antonin Scalia returned to the idea that the *Apprendi* rule is a reflection of "two longstanding tenets of common law jurisprudence."[37] The first tenet was that a jury should affirm the truth of every accusation.[38] The second tenet was that any accusation that failed to allege the existence of a fact essential to the imposition of punishment—for example, failure to allege intent in an accusation of first-degree murder—is not proper.[39] Justice Scalia concluded his opinion by observing that the "Framers would not have thought it too much to demand that, before depriving a man of three more years of his

---

[33] *Id.* at 2534 (summarizing facts).
[34] *Id.* at 2535.
[35] *Id.*
[36] *Id.*
[37] *Id.* at 2536.
[38] *Id.*
[39] *Id.*

liberty, the State should suffer the modest inconvenience of submitting its accusation to 'the unanimous suffrage of twelve of his equals and neighbours,' rather than a lone employee of the State."[40]

Justice Sandra Day O'Connor filed the principal dissenting opinion in *Blakely*, as she had in *Apprendi*. In the view of the dissenters, Washington's sentencing regime did not run afoul of the Constitution: "[T]he guidelines served due process by providing notice to petitioner of the consequences of his acts; they vindicated his jury trial right by informing him of the stakes of risking trial; they served equal protection by ensuring petitioner that invidious characteristics such as race would not impact his sentence."[41] Justice O'Connor said the consequences of the *Blakely* ruling would produce havoc for the lower courts and put tens of thousands of criminal judgments in jeopardy.[42]

The federal criminal justice system did experience some minor shockwaves in the immediate aftermath of *Blakely*. The Supreme Court issued the *Blakely* decision in the final days of its term and then adjourned for summer recess. Because the federal sentencing guidelines operated similarly to the guidelines in Washington State, there was some confusion concerning what adjustments, if any, needed to be made in charging documents, plea agreements, and sentencing procedures. The Department of Justice adopted the view that since the Supreme Court addressed only Washington's system, the federal guidelines should continue to operate as before.[43] However, out of an abundance of caution for the anticipated legal challenges coming in the wake of the *Blakely* case, indictments were rewritten to include any facts that might bear upon upward departures under the federal guidelines.[44]

As the weeks passed, some federal courts declared the federal guidelines to be unconstitutional while others proceeded in the same

[40] *Id.* at 2543 (quoting 4 W. Blackstone, Commentaries of the Law of England 343 (1769)).

[41] *Id.* at 2547 (O'Connor, J., dissenting).

[42] *Id.* at 2550.

[43] See Memorandum to All Federal Prosecutors from James Comey, Deputy Attorney General, Regarding Departmental Legal Positions and Policies in Light of Blakely v. Washington (July 2, 2004), available at http://www.usdoj.gov/dag/readingroom/blakely.htm.

[44] *Id.*

manner as before. A growing chorus of voices, including a resolution from the United States Senate,[45] decried the inconsistent rulings in the federal circuits and called upon the Court to bring clarity and order to the federal criminal system.[46] The Supreme Court responded to the criticism. Less than six weeks after deciding *Blakely*, the Court announced that it would settle the uncertainty regarding the future of the federal sentencing guidelines. The Court agreed to hear *United States v. Booker* on an expedited schedule.[47] *Booker* was set for argument on the very first day of the Court's upcoming fall term.

III. The Supreme Court Returns to the Fray: *United States v. Booker*

Freddie Booker was charged with dealing crack cocaine. In federal drug cases, the amount of drugs at issue is typically the key factor in determining the jail sentence under the federal sentencing guidelines. The larger the amount of drugs, the longer the prison term.[48] A jury convicted Booker after hearing evidence that he had 92.5 grams of crack in his duffel bag.[49] Under the sentencing guidelines, Booker faced a prison term between 210 and 262 months.[50] However, the trial court, in a post-trial sentencing proceeding, concluded by a preponderance of the evidence that Booker possessed another 566 grams and that he had also obstructed justice.[51] With those findings, Booker could have faced between 360 months to life imprisonment.[52] The trial judge ultimately imposed a thirty-year sentence.[53]

---

[45] Expeditious Supreme Court Action in Blakely v. Washington, S. Con. Res. 130, 108th Cong., 2d Sess. (as passed by the Senate on July 21, 2004).

[46] One newspaper, for example, rebuked the Supreme Court for the "unfathomable" legal confusion it created. The editorial urged the Court to interrupt its "summer vacation" to clarify federal sentencing law. See Clean Up This Mess, Wash. Post, July 26, 2004, at A10.

[47] See Lyle Denniston, Justices Agree to Consider Sentencing, N.Y. Times, August 3, 2004, at A14.

[48] USSG § 2D1.1 assigns base offense levels according to a Drug Quantity Table.

[49] United States v. Booker, 125 S. Ct. 738, 746 (2005).

[50] *Id.*

[51] *Id.*

[52] *Id.*

[53] *Id.*

Booker appealed his sentence, arguing that the trial judge had violated his right to trial by jury by making factual findings and then adding extra prison time to his sentence. The Department of Justice advanced two arguments to support Booker's sentence. First, the government tried to distinguish the federal guidelines from the *Apprendi* rule.[54] The government seized upon language in *Apprendi* that barred judges from finding facts that raise a sentence above the otherwise applicable "*statutory* maximum sentence."[55] *Apprendi* did not apply to the federal guidelines because the guidelines do not create statutory maximums. Since the federal guidelines are promulgated by a Sentencing Commission, and since the Commission is "not a legislature," the *Apprendi* rule is not applicable.[56] The government's second argument essentially urged the Court to reconsider and reject the *Blakely* holding.[57]

Very few observers expected the Supreme Court to backtrack from the *Blakely* holding, and it seemed a foregone conclusion that the rationale set forth in *Blakely* would also apply to the operation of the federal sentencing guidelines. The real debate in *Booker* was not so much whether the Court would find a Sixth Amendment violation, but rather what ought to be the proper *remedy* for such a violation.

Several remedy options were bandied about. First, the Court could scrap guideline sentencing per se. Second, if guideline sentencing were retained, the Court could insist on jury involvement in the sentencing phase. Though criticized as unworkable, Justice Scalia had pointed to Kansas' statutory framework in his *Blakely* opinion.[58] After the Kansas Supreme Court found *Apprendi* infirmities in that state's determinate sentencing regime, the state legislature responded by having juries make the necessary factual findings for upward departures in sentences.[59] The third remedy, and the one proposed by the Department of Justice, would have the Court hold that "the

---

[54] Brief for the United States at 12, United States v. Booker, 125 S. Ct. 738 (2005) (No. 04–104).

[55] *Id.* (emphasis in original).

[56] *Id.*

[57] *Id.*

[58] Blakely v. Washington, 124 S. Ct. 2531, 2541–42 (2004).

[59] *Id.* (citing Act of May 29, 2002, ch. 170, 2002 Kan. Sess. Laws 1018–23 (codified at Kan. Stat. Ann. § 21–4718 (Cum. Supp.))).

Guidelines as a whole are inapplicable in cases in which the Constitution would override the Guidelines' requirement that the district court find a sentencing-enhancing fact."[60] Thus, the courts "would then exercise sentencing discretion within the congressional minimum and maximum terms, with the Guidelines providing advisory guidance."[61] Any one of these remedies would significantly alter the system of federal sentencing that had been in place for seventeen years.

The outcome in *Booker* took everyone by surprise. The factions that had been clashing with one another in *Apprendi, Harris, Ring,* and *Blakely* clashed again, but neither faction was able to fully prevail in the case. The "working majority" that had come together to produce *Apprendi, Ring,* and *Blakely* came together again, finding that Booker's Sixth Amendment right to trial by jury had been violated by the trial court's actions. But that majority could not hold with respect to the question of the proper remedy. The bizarre result was that the faction that reached the conclusion that there was a substantive violation of law found itself in dissent with respect to the proper remedy for that violation. And the faction that discerned no constitutional violation in the first instance declared the appropriate remedy for that violation. Here is the summary of the disposition from the syllabus:

> Stevens, J., delivered the opinion of the Court in part, in which Scalia, Souter, Thomas, and Ginsburg, JJ., joined. Breyer, J., delivered the opinion of the Court in part, in which Rehnquist, C.J., and O'Connor, Kennedy, and Ginsburg, JJ., joined. Stevens, J., filed an opinion dissenting in part, in which Souter, J., joined, and in which Scalia., J., joined except for Part III and footnote 17. Scalia, J., and Thomas, J., filed opinions dissenting in part. Breyer, J., filed an opinion dissenting in part, in which Rehnquist, C.J., and O'Connor and Kennedy, JJ., joined.[62]

The ultimate disposition of the case dissatisfied everyone except Justice Ruth Bader Ginsburg. That is because Justice Ginsburg was

[60] Brief for Petitioner at 13, United States v. Booker, 125 S. Ct. 738 (2005) (No. 04–104).
[61] *Id.*
[62] United States v. Booker, 125 S. Ct. 738, 745 (2005). See Roger Pilon, Can Law This Uncertain Be Called Law?, 2003–2004 Cato Sup. Ct. Rev. vii (2004) (discussing the complexity of judicial opinions that are driven by policy concerns, not principles).

the only justice to agree to both the substantive holding and to the holding on the remedy.

Justice Stevens wrote the opinion for the Court on the substantive question—whether Booker's right to trial by jury was violated. After reviewing the *Apprendi* progeny, Stevens had little trouble evaluating Booker's complaint. Booker's sentence was almost ten years longer than the guidelines range supported by the jury verdict alone.[63] To justify the additional ten years, the judge found facts (possession of more crack cocaine) beyond those found by the jury.[64] And those "sentencing facts" were found by a preponderance of evidence standard.[65] Since the judge's actions were precisely the type of unconstitutional conduct condemned in *Blakely*, Booker's sentence had to be overturned.

The dissenters reiterated their previous observation that judges have always found facts when making sentencing determinations and that it is peculiar and misguided for the Court to declare judicial fact-finding unconstitutional.[66] Justice Stevens rejoined that the dissent had failed to grasp the nettle. Judges have broad discretion to sentence within a statutory range—"[f]or when a trial judge exercises his discretion to select a specific sentence within a defined range, the defendant has no right to a jury determination of the facts that the judge deems relevant."[67] If the debate were strictly a matter of "good policy," reasonable jurists could disagree on whether it would be more desirable for a judge or jury to make certain findings. The key point, however, is that the defendant's right to a jury trial has constitutional significance. Justice Scalia made this point plain in *Blakely*:

> Of course indeterminate schemes involve judicial factfinding, in that a judge (like a parole board) may implicitly rule on those facts he deems important to the exercise of his sentencing discretion. But the facts do not pertain to whether the

[63] 125 S. Ct. at 746 (substantive majority).

[64] *Id.*

[65] *Id.*

[66] *Id.* at 803–04 (Breyer, J., joined by Rehnquist, C.J., and O'Connor and Kennedy, JJ., dissenting in part).

[67] *Id.* at 750. Compare Elizabeth T. Lear, Is Conviction Irrelevant?, 40 UCLA L. Rev. 1179 (1993) (challenging judicial power to punish unconvicted criminal conduct at sentencing).

defendant has a legal *right* to a lesser sentence—and that makes all the difference insofar as judicial impingement upon the traditional role of the jury is concerned. In a system that says the judge may punish burglary with 10 to 40 years, every burglar knows he is risking 40 years in jail. In a system that punishes burglary with a 10-year sentence, with another 30 added for use of a gun, the burglar who enters a home unarmed is *entitled* to no more than a 10-year sentence—and by reason of the Sixth Amendment the facts bearing upon that entitlement must be found by a jury.[68]

When pressed to address this principle, the dissenters would admit that the Constitution does limit the government's power to reclassify elements as sentencing factors, but they would not elaborate—except to say that the government could not go "too far."[69]

As noted above, the Court was equally divided, by a five to four vote, on the question of how the government's constitutional violation ought to be remedied. Justice Ginsburg joined the faction that had dissented on the substantive violation. Since four of those justices were of the view that there was no jury trial violation, they basically sought to minimize any change to the operation of the federal sentencing guidelines and, in particular, to any broadening of the role of juries. The "remedial majority" announced that it was invalidating two provisions of the Sentencing Reform Act that were "incompatible" with the substantive constitutional holding.[70] The invalidation of those two provisions had the effect of disabling the mandatory nature of the federal guidelines. The guidelines would now be "advisory" only.[71]

Justice Stephen Breyer authored the opinion of the remedial majority. Breyer's analysis was driven by what Congress would have likely preferred had it known that the Court would step in and prevent "the sentencing court from increasing a sentence on the

---

[68] Blakely v. Washington, 124 S. Ct. 2531, 2540 (2004) (emphasis in original).

[69] See Booker, 125 S. Ct. at 705 (Breyer, J., joined by Rehnquist, C.J., O'Connor, and Kennedy, JJ., dissenting in part); compare Blakely, 124 S. Ct. at 2537 n.6 (the dissent "does not even provide a coherent alternative meaning for the jury-trial guarantee, unless one considers 'whatever the legislature chooses to leave to the jury, so long as it does not go too far' coherent.").

[70] See Booker, 125 S. Ct. at 759–64 (Breyer, J., delivering the opinion of the Court in part) (hereinafter "remedial majority").

[71] *Id.* at 756–57.

basis of a fact that the jury did not find (or that the offender did not admit)."[72] The answer, according to Justice Breyer, was that the Congress would have preferred that the guidelines system be made advisory—so that the federal system would maintain "a strong connection between the sentence imposed and the offender's real conduct—a connection important to the increased uniformity of sentencing that Congress intended its Guidelines system to achieve."[73] Turning to the question of how appellate courts should handle sentencing appeals from guidelines that were now advisory, Justice Breyer declared that the new standard of review would be one of "reasonableness."[74] Justice Breyer acknowledged the difficulty of trying to discern the legislature's preference and noted that the Congress was still free to choose another set of revisions in reaction to the Court's Sixth Amendment jury trial requirement.[75]

Four justices—Stevens, Scalia, Souter, and Thomas—dissented from the Court's remedy. Justice Stevens, who authored the principal dissent, described the remedial majority's approach to the matter as "an exercise of legislative, rather than judicial, power."[76] How, the dissenters wondered, could the Court excise two statutory provisions from the federal code book while acknowledging that those provisions were "unquestionably constitutional" and could thus be reenacted by the Congress immediately?[77] The dissenters accused their colleagues of preempting the legislative debate with their own "policy choice."[78]

IV. Lofty Rhetoric, Limited Impact

Although the *Apprendi* progeny has been marked by lofty rhetoric regarding the importance of the constitutional guarantee of trial by jury and of constitutionalism generally, a close inspection of the

[72] *Id.* at 757.

[73] *Id.*

[74] See *id.* at 765–68. Justice Breyer rejected criticism that he was simply inventing a new legal standard by noting that the Sentencing Reform Act specified that very standard in certain circumstances. *Id.*

[75] *Id.* at 768 ("Ours, of course, is not the last word: The ball now lies in Congress's court.").

[76] *Id.* at 772 (Stevens, J., joined by Souter and Scalia, JJ., dissenting in part).

[77] *Id.*

[78] *Id.* at 771.

American criminal justice system will show that there is a notable disconnect between the high praise that many of the justices have heaped upon the jury and their satisfaction with the shabby state of that once hallowed institution.[79]

There is, to be sure, a philosophical split among the members of the Court regarding the criminal justice system that is envisioned by the Constitution. One faction has played down the significance of the common law tradition of adversarial justice to modern constitutional controversies.[80] The fatal weakness of that approach was identified by Justice Scalia when he observed that *Apprendi*'s dissenters are

> unable to say what the right to trial by jury does guarantee if, as they assert, it does not guarantee—what it has been assumed to guarantee throughout our history—the right to have a jury determine those facts that determine the maximum sentence the law allows. They provide no coherent alternative.[81]

It is lamentable, however, that even though Justice Scalia (and the *Apprendi* majority) has a better answer than Justice Breyer (and the other *Apprendi* dissenters), it is only a partial answer—and one that is still a far cry from what the Constitution actually requires.[82]

At first, the high praise for the Sixth Amendment guarantee of trial by jury and the common law tradition of adversarial justice rings true, but there is a fatal misstep. The jury trial guarantee, we are told, was "the least controversial provision of the Bill of Rights."[83]

---

[79] Albert W. Alschuler & Andrew G. Deiss, A Brief History of the Criminal Jury in the United States, 61 U. Chi. L. Rev. 867, 922 (1994) ("Our system of criminal dispute resolution differs enormously from the one that the Sixth Amendment was designed to preserve.").

[80] Apprendi v. New Jersey, 530 U.S. 466, 555 (2000) (Breyer, J., dissenting).

[81] *Id.* at 498–99 (Scalia, J., concurring).

[82] For a discussion of what the Constitution actually requires, see generally Rachel E. Barkow, Recharging the Jury: The Criminal Jury's Constitutional Role in an Era of Mandatory Sentencing, 152 U. Pa. L. Rev. 33 (2003); Glenn Harlan Reynolds, Review Essay: Of Dissent and Discretion, 9 Cornell J.L. & Pub. Pol'y 685 (2000); Hon. Nancy Gertner, Circumventing Juries, Undermining Justice: Lessons from Criminal Trials and Sentencing, 32 Suffolk U. L. Rev. 419 (1999); Timothy Lynch, Rethinking the Petty Offense Doctrine, 4 Kan. J.L. & Pub. Pol'y 7 (1994); Ann Hopkins, Mens Rea and the Right to Trial by Jury, 76 Calif. L. Rev. 391 (1988).

[83] Apprendi, 530 U.S. at 498.

True. It was not controversial because the Framers made a conscious decision to let laypersons, not employees of the state, administer criminal justice.[84] True. "Our Constitution and the common law traditions it entrenches . . . do not admit the contention that facts are better discovered by judicial inquisition than by adversarial testing before a jury."[85] True. Jury trials may not be the most expedient and efficient method of administering justice, but they stand as "the great bulwark of [our] civil and political liberties."[86] True. Though inefficient and inexpedient, the right to a jury trial "has always been free[ly] [available]."[87] Untrue. Indeed, demonstrably false.

Jury trials are a rarity in the American criminal justice system.[88] The vast majority of cases are not adjudicated at all—they are instead plea bargained. No one can deny the fact that we have essentially adopted a system of charge and sentence bargaining. Still, one can argue that the rarity of jury trials does not necessarily prove that exercise of the right to a jury trial is not "free." True enough, but why would thousands and thousands of criminal defendants enter a guilty plea and forgo their right against self-incrimination and their right to a jury trial? The answer cannot be a matter of sheer happenstance. Fully 95% of federal criminal cases do not go to trial— and that high percentage has been the pattern for many years.[89] The truth is that government officials have deliberately engineered the system to "assure that the jury trial system established by the Constitution is seldom utilized."[90] The Supreme Court has facilitated the decline of jury adjudication by permitting prosecutors to retaliate against individuals who wish to exercise their Sixth Amendment right to trial by jury.[91] As the chief judge of the District Court of Massachusetts, William Young, has observed:

[84] *Id.*

[85] Blakely v. Washington, 124 S. Ct. 2531, 2543 (2005) (Scalia, J.).

[86] Apprendi, 530 U.S. at 477 (quoting 2 J. Story, Commentaries on the Constitution of the United States 540–41 (4th ed. 1873)) (alteration in original).

[87] *Id.* at 498 (Scalia, J., concurring).

[88] See generally George Fisher, Plea Bargaining's Triumph: A History of Plea Bargaining in America (2004).

[89] See United States Booker, 125 S. Ct. 738, 772 (2005) (Stevens, J., dissenting).

[90] See Note, The Unconstitutionality of Plea Bargaining, 83 Harv. L. Rev. 1387, 1389 (1970).

[91] See Bordenkircher v. Hayes, 434 U.S. 357, 365 (1978) (holding that offering a defendant a forced choice between forgoing trial in exchange for a lenient sentence and going to trial based on an escalated charge does not violate the Due Process

Evidence of sentencing disparity visited on those who exercise their Sixth Amendment right to trial by jury is today stark, brutal, and incontrovertible. . . . Today, under the Sentencing Guidelines regime with its vast shift of power to the Executive, that disparity has widened to an incredible 500%. As a practical matter this means, as between two similarly situated defendants, that if the one who pleads and cooperates gets a four-year sentence, then the guideline sentence for the one who exercises his right to trial by jury and is convicted will be twenty years. Not surprisingly, such a disparity imposes an extraordinary burden on the free exercise of the right to an adjudication of guilt by one's peers. Criminal trial rates in the United States and in this District are plummeting due to the simple fact that today we punish people—punish them severely—simply for going to trial. It is the sheerest sophistry to pretend otherwise.[92]

Despite the lofty rhetoric about the importance of juries and the common law traditions, the Court is not prepared to grapple with the root of the problem, which is the coercive, retaliatory nature of prosecutorial plea bargaining tactics. Although the constitutionality of plea bargaining was not an issue before the Court in *Booker*, it has been lurking in the background throughout the *Apprendi* progeny, in the thrust and parry between the justices as to how the parameters of the jury trial guarantee would impact the overall criminal justice system. In *Blakely*, for example, Justice Scalia seemed to be allaying concerns that the new Sixth Amendment ruling might impact the percentage of cases that are actually tried before juries when he wrote: "[G]iven the sprawling scope of most criminal codes, and the power to affect sentences by making (even nonbinding) sentencing recommendations, there is already no shortage of *in terrorem* tools at prosecutors' disposal."[93] In other words, "Don't fret about the

Clause). For a critique of that holding, see generally Timothy Lynch, An Eerie Efficiency, 2001–2002 Cato Sup. Ct. Rev. 171, 177–78 (2002).

[92] Berthoff v. United States, 140 F. Supp. 2d 50, 67–69 (D. Mass. 2001). For an incisive critique of federal sentencing law, see the sentencing memoranda authored by Chief Judge Young in *United States v. Green*, 346 F. Supp. 2d 259 (D. Mass. 2004).

[93] Blakely v. Washington, 124 S. Ct. 2531, 2542 (2004). Justice Scalia notes that the "Sixth Amendment was not written for the benefit of those who choose to forgo its protection." *Id.* True enough, but as Professor Lear has observed, "[T]he framers of the Constitution unquestionably assumed that the jury trial would be the primary method by which guilt and conviction were secured." See Lear, *supra* note 67, at 1237 n.271; Alschuler & Deiss, *supra* note 79, at 922. And, as Chief Judge Young notes, persons accused of crimes are no longer free to invoke the Sixth Amendment right

prospect of more-crowded court dockets. The right to seek a jury trial will remain under the thumb of the prosecutor." In the end, the philosophical gulf between the opposing factions of the Supreme Court, though real, is not nearly as wide as the rhetoric on both sides suggests.[94]

V. Prospective Developments in Federal Sentencing

There is no question that *United States v. Booker* is a landmark case in the field of sentencing law. The Supreme Court arrested a pernicious trend in the law that enabled the government to administer punishment by usurping the jury's traditional fact-finding role and by dispensing with the reasonable doubt standard of proof. The federal sentencing guidelines, which had governed federal criminal cases for seventeen years, were unexpectedly declared to be advisory, not mandatory. Appellate courts were instructed to review appealed sentences under a "reasonableness" standard of review. *Booker* has clearly stirred the pot—and, it is safe to say, that still more change is looming on the horizon.

With respect to future Supreme Court action, the question of how to handle a defendant's prior criminal record is very likely to change in the near term. Under *Apprendi*, the Supreme Court barred judges from making factual findings that led to increased sentences.[95] There was only one exception to that rule: findings related to prior offenses.[96] Over the past five years, it has become increasingly clear that that exception is no longer supported by a majority of the Court.[97] The departure of Justice O'Connor, a staunch proponent of

---

to trial by jury. Prosecutorial extortion is rampant and severe. Berthoff, 140 F. Supp. 2d at 67–69. The defenders of the jury trial guarantee on this Court—Stevens, Scalia, Souter, Thomas, Ginsburg—treat these critical points in a nonchalant manner.

[94] Justice O'Connor, for example, greeted the prospect of more jury involvement as "a No. 10 earthquake." David Kravets, O'Connor Likens Decision to Earthquake, Associated Press, July 22, 2004 (quoting O'Connor). On the other side, Justice Stevens said the right to jury trial—"a common law right that defendants enjoyed for centuries and that is now enshrined in the Sixth Amendment—has always outweighed the interest in concluding trials swiftly." Booker, 125 S. Ct. at 756.

[95] Apprendi v. New Jersey, 530 U.S. 466, 490 (2000).

[96] See generally *id.* at 499–523 (Thomas, J., concurring).

[97] See Shepard v. United States, 125 S. Ct. 1254, 1263–64 (2005) (Thomas, J., concurring in part and concurring in the judgment).

limiting *Apprendi* wherever possible, can only hasten this salutary development.[98]

With respect to the lower courts, there are many questions to grapple with in the aftermath of *Booker*—especially for the cases that were pending when the ruling was announced. Many defendants are seeking to be resentenced in light of *Booker*, for example. Courts are sorting those appeals by asking, among other things, whether it should matter whether an objection was registered at the trial to the judicial enhancement of the sentence. Meanwhile, the appellate courts will begin to apply the new "reasonableness" standard of review for sentencing appeals. As trial judges depart from the guidelines that are now merely advisory, will the appellate courts afford broad leeway toward such departures—or adopt a strict posture? The answers to those questions are uncertain. It is simply too early to venture any predictions on how those questions will be resolved.

With respect to future action from Congress, many observers had expected an immediate reaction to *Booker*. That did not happen. However, Attorney General Alberto Gonzales has made it clear that the Bush administration is anxious to curb judicial discretion by establishing a broad array of mandatory minimum sentences and restoring the mandatory nature of the federal sentencing guidelines. According to Gonzales, federal sentencing "works best when judges have some discretion, but discretion that is bounded by mandatory sentencing guidelines created through the legislative process."[99] The Bush administration seems to want a system that will give judges flexibility with respect to meting out harsher sentences, but where their ability to offer lenient sentences is tightly restricted—hence the call to Congress to enact more mandatory minimum sentences. The House of Representatives did pass "anti-gang" legislation that would, among other things, establish more mandatory minimum sentences.[100] Since the Senate is also anxious to be seen as "tackling the gang problem," it is likely to approve a similar bill in the near future.

---

[98] As Justice Thomas has noted, "innumerable criminal defendants have been unconstitutionally sentenced" under the "flawed" precedents. See *id.* at 1264.

[99] Dan Eggen, Minimum Sentences Urged, Wash. Post, June 22, 2005, at A2 (quoting Attorney General Gonzales).

[100] Gang Deterrence and Community Protection Act of 2005, H.R. 1279, 109th Cong., 1st Sess. (2005).

From both a constitutional and policy perspective, the outlook on federal criminal law and sentencing seems rather bleak. The federal criminal code is a sprawling mess.[101] Jury trial rates are plummeting across the country.[102] And Congress is poised to reverse the marginal improvement that *Booker* brought about by transferring more power from impartial judges to partial prosecutors by enacting more mandatory minimum sentences.[103] These trends need to be reversed. Congress needs to roll back the power of prosecutors by pruning the federal criminal code, allowing more judicial discretion in sentencing, and respecting the right to trial by jury.[104]

---

[101] See John S. Baker, Measuring the Explosive Growth of Federal Crime Legislation (Federalist Society 2004), available at http://www.fed-soc.org/ Publications/practicegroupnewsletters/criminallaw/crimreportfinal.pdf. See also N. Richard Janis, Deputizing Company Counsel as Agents of the Federal Government: How Our Adversary System of Justice Is Being Destroyed, Washington Lawyer, March 2005, at 32.

[102] See Berthoff v. United States, 140 F. Supp. 2d 50, 68–69 (D. Mass. 2001).

[103] See note 100, *supra*. For a critique of mandatory minimum sentencing, see Paul G. Cassell, Too Severe? A Defense of the Federal Sentencing Guidelines (and a Critique of Federal Mandatory Minimums), 56 Stan. L. Rev. 1017 (2004).

[104] See Timothy Lynch, Changing the Gavel, Legal Times, January 24, 2005, at 66.

"Nice Questions" Unanswered: *Grokster*, *Sony*'s Staple Article of Commerce Doctrine, and the Deferred Verdict on Internet File Sharing

*David G. Post, Annemarie Bridy, and Timothy Sandefur**

> "From the advent of the player piano, every new means of reproducing sound has struck a dissonant chord with musical copyright owners, often resulting in federal litigation."
>
> *MGM Studios Inc. v. Grokster, Ltd.*,
> 380 F.3d 1154, 1158 (9th Cir. 2004).

> "In *some* cases where an ordinary article of commerce is sold, nice questions may arise as to the point at which the seller becomes an accomplice in a subsequent illegal use by the buyer."
>
> *Kalem Co. v. Harper Brothers*,
> 222 U.S. 55, 62 (1911) (Holmes, J.) (emphasis added).

I. Introduction

When is the developer or distributor of a copying technology legally responsible for the copyright infringements committed by users of that technology? Over the past twenty years or so, development and deployment of digital copying technologies (personal computers, CD and DVD burners, iPods and other portable music devices, the Internet itself, etc.), and tools for Internet file sharing and file distribution, have thrust that question into the center of a

*David G. Post is I. Herman Stern Professor of Law at Temple University Law School; Annemarie Bridy is a law clerk to the Hon. Dolores K. Sloviter of the U.S. Court of Appeals for the Third Circuit; and Timothy Sandefur is the lead attorney in the Economic Liberty Project at the Pacific Legal Foundation.

high-profile public debate. That debate gave rise to the most closely watched copyright case of recent years, *MGM Studios Inc. v. Grokster, Ltd.*[1] The Ninth Circuit Court of Appeals had held that defendants Grokster and StreamCast, the developers and distributors of peer-to-peer file-sharing software, were shielded from copyright liability by the so-called "*Sony* doctrine" derived from the Supreme Court's landmark 1984 case of *Sony Corporation of America v. Universal City Studios, Inc.*[2] (also called the "Betamax" case). The Ninth Circuit interpreted that doctrine to mean that distributors of copying technology that is "capable of commercially significant noninfringing use" are shielded from liability for the infringement committed by users of the technology, unless the distributors had "specific knowledge of infringement" obtained "at a time at which they contributed to the infringement" and had "failed to act upon that information."[3]

The Supreme Court unanimously reversed, holding that because Grokster and StreamCast had distributed their software "with *the object of* promoting its use to infringe copyright," as shown by "clear expression or other affirmative steps taken to foster infringement," *Sony* did not protect them from liability, whether or not their software was "capable of commercially significant noninfringing use."[4]

The unanimous decision in the copyright holders' favor is, obviously, a big loss for Grokster Inc. and StreamCast, Ltd.; its broader implications for Internet file-sharing practices and file-sharing technology, however, are much less clear. To understand what those implications might be, we have to rewind, as the Supreme Court did, to *Sony*.

II. Rewind: The Betamax Case

When Sony introduced its Betamax™ videotape recorder into the U.S. market in 1975,[5] there were, of course, no personal computers, or home photocopiers, or TiVos, or MP3 files, or home networks— and, needless to say, no Internet. The VCR, for the first time, enabled

---

[1]125 S. Ct. 2764 (2005).

[2]464 U.S. 417 (1984).

[3]MGM Studios Inc. v. Grokster, Ltd., 380 F.3d 1154, 1160, 1162 (9th Cir. 2004) (internal quotation marks and alterations omitted).

[4]Grokster, 125 S. Ct. at 2780 (emphasis added).

[5]The history of the VCR is long and complicated. The first home video recorders were reel-to-reel devices sold in the 1960s. The first cassette recorder was marketed by Philips in the 1970s. Debra A. Sitzberger, Copyright Law—Who Gets The Picture?, 57 Wash. L. Rev. 599, 608 n.74 (1982).

television viewers to record, easily and conveniently and for relatively low cost, television broadcasts right off the air and to play them back at a later time.[6]

The entertainment industries, generally speaking, were not pleased. "We are facing," Jack Valenti, then-president of the Motion Picture Association of America, told Congress,

> a very new and a very troubling assault on our fiscal security, on our very economic life and we are facing it from a thing called the video cassette recorder and its necessary companion called the blank tape. And it is like a great tidal wave just off the shore. This video cassette recorder and the blank tape threaten profoundly the life-sustaining protection, I guess you would call it, on which copyright owners depend, on which film people depend, on which television people depend and it is called copyright.[7]

The VCR, he famously continued, "is to the American film producer and the American public as the Boston strangler is to the woman home alone."[8]

In 1976, in response to this new and purportedly deadly threat, Universal Studios and Walt Disney Productions filed suit, in the Central District of California, asserting, among other things, that Sony was liable for copyright infringement.[9] As a remedy, plaintiffs sought (a) an injunction against the continued manufacture and distribution of the VCR, (b) money damages to compensate for past

---

[6] And not a great deal else; in those early (i.e., pre-Blockbuster) days, *pre*-recorded videotapes were largely unavailable (except at adult bookstores), so the purchasers of VTRs (as they were known then) were, presumably, interested primarily in using their new gizmos for off-the-air taping.

[7] Home Recording of Copyrighted Work: Hearings on H.R. 4783, H.R. 4794, H.R. 4808, H.R. 5488, and H.R. 5705 Before the Subcommittee on Courts, Civil Liberties, and the Administration of Justice of the House Committee on the Judiciary, 97th Cong., 2d Sess., Serial No. 97, Part I, 4–8 (1982) (statement of Jack Valenti), available at http://cryptome.org/hrcw-hear.htm (visited July 18, 2005) (hereinafter VCR Hearings).

[8] *Id.* at 8.

[9] Universal City Studios, Inc. v. Sony Corp. of America, 480 F. Supp. 429, 432 (C.D. Cal. 1979). The defendants in the original action were Sony, the manufacturer of the Betamax; four retailers (Carter Hawley Hale Stores, Robinson's, Bullock's, and Henry's Camera Corp.), and a sole consumer (William Griffiths). Later, the advertising agency of Doyle Dane Bernback, Inc. was added to the list of defendants. *Id.* at 432.

infringement(s), and (c) a share (to be determined by the district court) of Sony's profits from the sale of the VCR.[10]

The precise contours of the copyright claim were noteworthy. Ordinarily, to prove that a defendant is infringing its copyright, a plaintiff has to prove three things:

(a) that the work(s) in question (here, the previously broadcast television shows and movies) are protected by copyright;[11]

(b) that he/she owns one (or more) of the exclusive rights that comprise the copyright—e.g., the exclusive right to "reproduce the copyrighted work in copies,"[12] to "distribute copies ... of the copyrighted work to the public,"[13] or to "display the copyrighted work publicly";[14] and

(c) that the defendant, without authorization to do so, took some action that violated one or more of those exclusive rights.[15]

Elements (a) and (b) were straightforward; no one disputed that plaintiffs' television shows and movies were protected by copyright or that plaintiffs owned the relevant copyrights. Element (c) was trickier, however; what had *Sony* done that could constitute a violation of any of plaintiffs' exclusive rights in their copyrighted works? Sony had not, itself, come anywhere near plaintiffs' copyrighted works; it's not as though it had hard-wired the preceding six months of *All in the Family* or *Bonanza* into each Betamax it sold. If anyone were taking action that violated one or more of plaintiffs' exclusive copyright rights, it was, of course, Betamax *users*, not Sony; Sony wasn't "reproducing" or "distributing" or "displaying" movies or

---

[10]Section 504 of the Copyright Act provides that, in an action for infringement, the copyright owner "is entitled to recover the actual damages suffered by him or her as a result of the infringement, *and* any profits of the infringer that are attributable to the infringement and [that] are not taken into account in computing the actual damages." 17 U.S.C. § 504(b) (emphasis added).

[11]Under the Copyright Act, all "works of authorship fixed in any tangible medium of expression" are protected by copyright as of the moment of their creation. 17 U.S.C. § 102(a) (2005).

[12]17 U.S.C. § 106(1).

[13]17 U.S.C. § 106(3).

[14]17 U.S.C. § 106(5).

[15]17 U.S.C. § 501(a) ("Anyone who violates any of the exclusive rights of the copyright owner ... is an infringer of the copyright or right of the author, as the case may be.").

television shows. It was stamping out circuit boards and transistors and switches, putting assembled machines into boxes, and shipping the boxes to retailers.

The studios, therefore, could not (and did not) claim that Sony was a "direct infringer" of their copyrights. Instead, their claim was that, by manufacturing and selling a device that made it so easy for purchasers to infringe their copyrights,[16] Sony had committed a kind of *indirect*, or third-party, infringement.

There was precedent in copyright law for holding third parties liable for the infringements of others, in certain circumstances; in fact, two theories of third-party copyright liability, so-called "vicarious" and "contributory" copyright infringement, had been recognized by courts beginning in the early part of the twentieth century. Each was a relatively straightforward outgrowth of traditional common law tort principles under which liability can be imposed on one person for the tortious acts of another. "Vicarious" copyright liability evolved from the doctrine of respondeat superior, which extends tort liability to persons *in control of the wrongdoer* (typically employees or agents). Under this doctrine, anyone with the "right and ability to control" a copyright infringer, and "a direct financial interest"[17] in the infringer's actions, is jointly and severally liable with the infringer for those infringements.[18] "Contributory" liability, for its part, derives from the equally venerable doctrine of "aiding and abetting" in tort. Just as you can be liable if you induce or encourage someone else to commit acts that you know (or should know) constitute a tort, so, too, can you be liable for encouraging

---

[16]See VCR Hearings, *supra* note 7, at 5 (Valenti claiming the VCR had a "single mission: . . . to copy copyrighted material that belongs to other people"), available at http://cryptome.org/hrcw-hear.htm.

[17]Universal City Studios, Inc. v. Sony Corp. of America, 480 F. Supp. 429, 461 (C.D. Cal. 1979) (quoting Gershwin Publishing Corp. v. Columbia Artists Management, Inc., 443 F.2d 1159, 1162 (2d Cir. 1971)).

[18]MGM Studios Inc. v. Grokster, Ltd., 380 F.3d 1154, 1164 (9th Cir. 2004). The doctrine of vicarious liability in copyright law goes back at least as far as the famous "Dance-Hall Cases" in which the proprietors of dance halls and similar establishments were held to be vicariously liable for the infringements of the dance bands in their employ. See, e.g., Dreamland Ball Room, Inc. v. Shapiro, Bernstein & Co., 36 F.2d 354, 355 (7th Cir. 1929). See also Famous Music Corp. v. Bay State Harness Horse Racing and Breeding Association, Inc., 554 F.2d 1213, 1214–15 (1st Cir. 1977); Gershwin Publishing, 443 F.2d at 1161–62; KECA Music, Inc. v. Dingus McGee's Co., 432 F. Supp. 72, 74–75 (W.D. Mo. 1977).

CATO SUPREME COURT REVIEW

copyright infringement: one who "with *knowledge* of the infringing activity, *induces, causes or materially contributes* to the infringing conduct of another, may be held liable as a 'contributory' infringer."[19]

Liability under one or another of these doctrines had been imposed, for example, on a department store that had leased space in its store to someone selling infringing recordings;[20] on the proprietors of dance halls, and similar establishments, who employed dance bands that performed copyrighted compositions without authorization;[21] on a radio station that ran advertisements for recordings that it knew were not authorized;[22] on an advertising agency for knowingly promoting the sale of those same infringing recordings;[23] and on a concert artists' management agency for organizing infringing performances.[24]

But the studios' claim against Sony was of a different order entirely—"unprecedented," the district court called it.[25] Copyright liability, of either the "vicarious" or "contributory" variety, had never before been imposed on a defendant solely because it manufactured and distributed a device that *others* used to infringe.[26] Holding

[19]Gershwin Publishing, 443 F.2d at 1162 (emphasis added).

[20]See Shapiro, Bernstein & Co. v. H.L. Green Co., 316 F.2d 304, 306, 308–10 (2d Cir. 1963).

[21]Dreamland Ball Room, 36 F.2d at 355.

[22]See Screen Gems-Columbia Music, Inc. v. Mark-Fi Records, Inc., 256 F. Supp. 399, 401–02 (S.D.N.Y. 1966).

[23]*Id*. at 405.

[24]Gershwin Publishing, 443 F.2d at 1161.

[25]Universal City Studios, Inc. v. Sony Corp. of America, 480 F. Supp. 429, 460 (C.D. Cal. 1979).

[26]The closest the Supreme Court had come was in the case of *Kalem Co. v. Harper Brothers*, 222 U.S. 55 (1911), a case on which Universal relied heavily in its arguments to the district court. In *Kalem*, a moviemaker made an unauthorized silent movie version of the copyrighted *Ben Hur*. *Id*. at 60–61. When sued for infringement, the filmmaker argued that because he had not publicly exhibited the film, but only provided it to others (theater owners) for public exhibition, he was not liable for the infringement. *Id*. at 62. The Court, speaking through Justice Holmes, rejected this argument by appealing to familiar common law concepts of third-party liability. Courts had already found liquor sellers liable "if the sale was made with a view to the illegal resale," for example, *id.*, and the "view" here was even clearer: "The defendant not only expected but invoked by advertisement the use of its films for dramatic reproduction of the story. That was the most conspicuous purpose for which they could be used, and the one for which especially they were made. If the defendant did not contribute to the infringement, it is impossible to do so. . . . It is liable on principles . . . recognized in every part of the law." *Id*. at 62–63. See also Elektra

Sony liable for manufacturing the Betamax would be like holding the manufacturer of a printing press liable for the infringements created by the press—or the manufacturer of nylon stockings liable for the wrongful death of the Boston Strangler's victims. Sony hardly had the kind of ongoing supervisory relationship with its customers (of the principal/agent or employer/employee variety) on which a claim for respondeat superior or other "vicarious" liability was ordinarily built, nor would mere "knowledge" that *some* customers may break the law ordinarily have sufficed for the imposition of liability of the "aiding and abetting" variety.[27]

The district court rejected the plaintiffs' claim,[28] because the Betamax was a "staple article of commerce"[29] that could be used "for substantial noninfringing uses"[30]—such as recording uncopyrighted television broadcasts or making recordings privileged under the "fair use" doctrine. Sony was no more liable for the wrongdoing of Betamax purchasers than would the seller of a typewriter or a printing press be liable for the infringing conduct of *its* customers.

The Ninth Circuit reversed,[31] and the Supreme Court then reversed the Ninth Circuit, reinstating the judgment against Universal in a

---

Records Co. v. Gem Electronic Distributors, Inc., 360 F. Supp. 821, 825 (E.D.N.Y. 1973) (providing customers of sound recording duplication facilities with copyrighted tapes, blank tapes, and a duplication machine made party liable for customers' infringements).

[27] See *supra* note 19 and accompanying text.

[28] *Sony*, 480 F. Supp. at 469–70. To read the 1979 district court opinion in this case is to be reminded how far the technology has progressed during the past quarter-century, as the court felt it necessary to describe, for the reader, the way these strange new devices functioned. See, e.g., *id.* at 435–36 ("The pause button allows an operator to stop whatever function [—] record, play, fast-forward, reverse [—] the machine is in. . . . The fast forward makes it possible to avoid watching on playback a segment that has been recorded. While viewing the tape, an individual can fast forward through an undesired segment.").

[29] *Id.* at 459.

[30] *Id.* at 461.

[31] Universal City Studios, Inc. v. Sony Corp. of America, 659 F.2d 963, 975–76 (9th Cir. 1981). The Ninth Circuit held, under the traditional definition of vicarious liability, that liability attaches to anyone "who, with knowledge of the infringing activity, induces, causes or materially contributes to the infringing conduct of another," and thus there could be "no doubt" that Sony met the test. *Id.* at 975. "[I]t cannot be argued," the court remarked, that Sony did not have "knowledge that the Betamax will be used to reproduce copyrighted material," or that the machine was not a material contribution to the offense. *Id.*

five to four decision that took it, most unusually, more than two *years* to hand down.[32] Justice Stevens's opinion for the Court characterized the lawsuit as an "unprecedented attempt" to "impose copyright liability upon the distributors of copying equipment" and to "expand the protections afforded by the copyright without explicit legislative guidance."[33] When a claim of contributory infringement is "predicated entirely on the sale of an article of commerce that is used by the purchaser to infringe," Justice Stevens wrote, the "public interest in access to that article of commerce is necessarily implicated."[34] The Court saw its task as "strik[ing] a balance between a copyright holder's legitimate demand for effective—not merely

---

[32]Sony Corp. of America v. Universal City Studios, Inc., 464 U.S. 417, 456 (1984). We now know something about the circumstances behind this unusual delay, as a result of the release of Justice Marshall's and Justice Blackmun's papers. The Court was initially disposed to rule in the studios' favor; at the justices' initial conference following oral argument in January 1982, five justices (Blackmun, Marshall, Powell, Rehnquist, and O'Connor) voted to affirm the Ninth Circuit's judgment that Sony's distribution of Betamax recorders rendered it liable as a contributory infringer. Justice Blackmun was given the task of writing a majority opinion for the Court. But Justice Stevens, a mere six days after oral argument, circulated a memorandum containing the "basic outline" of the argument that he expected "to emphasize in dissent" (a memorandum that would ultimately become the *majority* opinion). The next several months saw a flurry of memos, circulating drafts, and shifting views, as Justices Powell and O'Connor, who had formed part of the initial majority to affirm, began to waver. Justice O'Connor's vote was to prove decisive; in June, she informed the chief justice that she had now adopted "a 'middle' position on the merits and a movement toward a more restrictive stance on contributory infringement," and she recommended calling for re-argument. Although the Stevens opinion appeared to command a majority of the Court by this point (Burger, Stevens, Brennan, White, and O'Connor, and possibly Powell), the Court ran out of time, and the case was set for re-argument the following term. Re-argument took place on October 3, 1983, and there was little subsequent change in the justices' positions. The decision was announced January 17, 1984, with Stevens, Brennan, White, O'Connor, and Burger in the majority, and Blackmun, Powell, Marshall, and Rehnquist dissenting.

For informative and entertaining accounts of the behind-the-scenes story of the *Sony* decision, see generally Jonathan Band & Andrew J. McLaughlin, The Marshall Papers: A Peek Behind the Scenes at the Making of Sony v. Universal, 17 Colum.-VLA J.L. & Arts 427 (1993); Paul Goldstein, Copyright's Highway: The Law and Lore of Copyright from Gutenberg to the Celestial Jukebox 149–58 (1994); Jessica Litman, The Sony Paradox 11–23 (February 25, 2005), available at http://www.law.wayne.edu/litman/papers/Sonyparadox.pdf (visited July 29, 2005); Jesse M. Feder, Is Betamax Obsolete? Sony Corp. of America v. Universal City Studios, Inc. in the Age of Napster, 37 Creighton L. Rev. 859, 874–75 (2004).

[33]Sony, 464 U.S. at 431.

[34]Id. at 440.

symbolic—protection of the statutory monopoly, and the rights of others freely to engage in substantially unrelated areas of commerce."[35] Drawing, by analogy, from the doctrine of contributory *patent* infringement,[36] which exempts the sale of "staple articles of commerce" from liability, the Court held that "the sale of copying equipment, like the sale of other articles of commerce, *does not constitute contributory infringement if the product is . . . capable of substantial noninfringing uses.*"[37]

The Court went on to hold that the Betamax was indeed "capable of substantial noninfringing uses," of two kinds: authorized time-shifting and unauthorized time-shifting. As to the former: "[M]any important producers of national and local television programs"—the Court here referred specifically to "televised sports events, religious broadcasts, and educational programming such as Mister Rogers' Neighborhood"—"find nothing objectionable about the enlargement in the size of the television audience that results from the practice of time-shifting for private home use."[38] A finding of contributory infringement would "frustrate the interests" of those broadcasters.[39] Because at least *some* copyright holders "welcome the practice" of home time-shifting, "the business of supplying the equipment that makes such copying feasible should not be stifled simply because the equipment is used by *some* individuals to make unauthorized reproductions of [plaintiffs'] works."[40]

And even where the time-shifting recording is not authorized by the copyright holder(s), the Court reasoned, the recording may be noninfringing because it is covered by the "fair use" doctrine. Copying "for a commercial or profit-making purpose" is "presumptively . . . unfair";[41] but private, non-commercial home taping is a different matter. "The record amply supports the District Court's conclusion that home time-shifting is fair use";[42] the studios "failed to carry their burden" of demonstrating that private time-shifting was

---

[35] *Id.* at 442.
[36] *Id.* at 439–41.
[37] *Id.* at 442 (emphasis added).
[38] *Id.* at 446.
[39] *Id.*
[40] *Id.* (emphasis added).
[41] *Id.* at 448.
[42] *Id.* at 454.

"harmful" or "adversely affect[ed] the potential market for the copyrighted work."[43]

III. Pause: *Sony*, Reconsidered

Most interesting, in hindsight, is not that the courts ultimately rejected the plaintiffs' attempt to extend the principles of third-party liability to Sony—it is that they had so much difficulty doing so. The Supreme Court clearly found the case to be one of unusual difficulty, and of the thirteen judges who considered the studios' claim as it made its way up the appellate ladder, seven actually sided with the studios. But today, one must search long and hard to find *anyone*, on either side of the "copyfights," arguing that *Sony* was wrongly decided,[44] that we all would actually have been better off had the holders of copyrights in television shows and movies been able to enjoin the sale and distribution of the VCR, or to force VCR manufacturers to compensate them for each VCR sold.[45]

---

[43] *Id.* at 451.

[44] For instance, in over 55 amicus briefs submitted in the *Grokster* litigation to the Court, not one urges the Court to overrule the *Sony* result. See Electronic Frontier Foundation, MGM Studios Inc. v. Grokster, Ltd. Resources Website, http://www.eff.org/IP/P2P/MGM_v_Grokster (visited July 29, 2005). Even *Sony*'s sharpest detractors (see generally Brief of Professors Menell, Nimmer, Merges, and Hughes in Support of Petitioners, MGM Studios Inc. v. Grokster, Ltd., 125 S. Ct. 2764 (2005) (No. 04-480), and Brief of Amicus Curiae Law Professors, Economics Professors, and Treatise Authors as Amici Curiae in Support of Petitioners, MGM Studios Inc. v. Grokster, Ltd., 125 S. Ct. 2764 (2005) (No. 04-480)) reject such a suggestion. See, e.g., Brief of Menell et al., *supra*, at 10 ("These determinations relieved much of the pressure on delineating the contours of indirect liability. Once that determination was in place, even under the dissent's 'primary use' test, the VCR would not have violated the Copyright Act. Accepting the majority's conclusion that time shifting by users fell within the bounds of the fair use defense, the net balance strongly favored continued marketing of the VCR technology. Thus, the indirect liability standard selected by the majority in *Sony* was not critical to the outcome of the case.").

[45] *Sony* looks even better when contrasted with the counterfactual world in which Justice O'Connor does not switch sides and Sony loses. The law of the land (as pronounced in Justice Blackmun's now-majority opinion) would then be: "off-the-air recording is an infringement of copyright," and unless "a significant portion of [a] product's use is noninfringing," the manufacturers and sellers are contributorily liable "for the product's infringing uses." Compare Sony Corp. of America v. Universal City Studios, Inc., 464 U.S. 417, 490, 491 (1984) (Blackmun, J., dissenting). It is impossible, of course, to know exactly how these principles would have played themselves out over time, but given that the VCR had failed this test, what would the developers of follow-on copying technologies—DVD recorders, for example, or music-processing software, or the iPod, or even the basic "copying" technologies at the heart of the Internet's routers—have done? How much of a copyright royalty

In retrospect, knowing the rest of the VCR story, *Sony* looks like a win for *both* sides; by declining Sony's invitation to limit distribution of the VCR on a theory of third-party infringement, the Court allowed the cultural and economic potential of the VCR to be fully realized—in ways that turned out to be enormously beneficial for copyright holders, component manufacturers, and the public alike. The VCR, in the end, was capable of noninfringing uses that no one (including the plaintiffs and the justices) had foreseen—for example, the playing of pre-recorded movies produced and distributed by the motion picture industry itself. It was not the Boston Strangler after all; on the contrary, it was the blind date that turned out to be Hollywood's Prince Charming. Instead of trying to block the distribution of VCRs, the movie studios probably should have given them away for free.[46]

But while *Sony*'s outcome has proven uncontroversial, its reasoning has become, if anything, more obscure over time. Perhaps because it began life as a dissenting opinion, or perhaps because of the difficulties attendant upon keeping a fragile, fractured coalition together, the Court's opinion was more than a little obscure.[47] Most fundamentally: what exactly *is* the test to be applied to determine whether a device can withstand a charge of contributory infringement? According to the *Sony* majority:

> [T]he sale of copying equipment, like the sale of other articles of commerce, does not constitute contributory infringement if the product is [1] *widely used for legitimate, unobjectionable purposes*. Indeed, it need merely be [2] *capable of substantial noninfringing uses.* . . . The question is thus whether the Betamax is [3] *capable of commercially significant noninfringing*

would they have had to pay, or how much copyright liability insurance would they have needed to secure, in order to distribute their products? And how much of a drag would that have been on the development of those technologies?

[46] In fact, there is reason to think that Internet file-sharing technology may be good for the music industry. See Jesse Walker, Music for Nothing: Why Napster Isn't the End of the World or Even the Music Industry, Reason, October 2000, available at http://reason.com/0010/fe.jw.music.shtml (visited July 29, 2005).

[47] So, too, was its language. See A & M Records, Inc. v. Napster, Inc., 239 F.3d 1004, 1022–23 (9th Cir. 2001) (noting that Supreme Court itself in *Sony* imprecisely used term "vicarious liability"). Stevens's analysis combined, in Jessica Litman's words, "his own solicitude for private noncommercial copying[,] Justice Brennan's distinction between time-shifting and library building, and Justice O'Connor's preference for the staple article of commerce doctrine." Litman, The Sony Paradox, *supra* note 32, at 23.

uses. . . . [W]e need only consider whether on the basis of the facts as found by the district court [4] *a significant number of them would be non-infringing.* . . . [W]e need not give precise content to the question of how much use is commercially significant. . . . The Betamax is . . . [[2], again] capable of *substantial noninfringing uses.*[48]

How is the "substantiality" or "commercial[ ] significan[ce]" of noninfringing use to be measured? What did the Court mean by saying that a device only has to be "merely capable" of such use to benefit from the *Sony* safe harbor?

And second: what is the relationship between the *Sony* safe harbor (however defined) and other doctrines of third-party copyright liability? Is *Sony* an *immunity* from copyright liability? Even if a defendant otherwise meets the requirements for "contributory" or "vicarious" liability? In some circumstances but not others?

After *Sony,* the formula for third party liability looks basically like this:

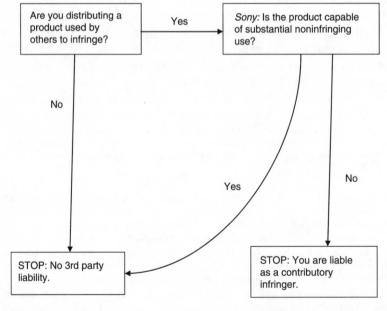

Figure 1. Copyright liabiliy post-*Sony* for distributing devices used by third parties to infringe.

[48]Sony, 464 U.S. at 442, 456 (emphasis added).

IV. Fast Forward: *Napster*

The first high-profile, high stakes legal battle to press the questions left in *Sony*'s wake began, much like the legal battle over home videotaping had begun, with the advent of a new technology that empowered consumers to reproduce and distribute entertainment "content" with unprecedented ease. Napster, an Internet start-up founded in May of 1999 by a college freshman, developed software to facilitate the exchange of files from one Internet user to another. Dubbed "MusicShare," the software was distributed to users for free over the Internet, and it allowed online users to make the MP3 (and other) files stored on their hard drives available in real time to other online users.[49] Napster stored the names of available MP3 files on its servers in a massive collective index that was updated continuously as users logged on and off the system; the files themselves remained stored on users' hard drives. Thus, the file transfers enabled by the MusicShare software were direct from user-to-user, or, in network parlance, peer-to-peer.

---

[49] [The Napster system] works, more or less, as follows. You download the MusicShare software. You run the software on your computer. It scans your hard disk and compiles a directory of the names of the music files it finds there. It then sends that directory—not the files themselves, just the *list* of file names—back to Napster's "home" computer, the Napster server, where it is placed into a database, along with the directories of all of the other Napster users who have gone through the same process (70 million or so at its peak).

The next time you (or any of the 70 million) log onto the Internet, your computer, in addition to doing whatever else it is doing, sends a message to the Napster server: "User John_Doe here—I've just logged on to the Internet, and my 'Internet Protocol address'—the number my Internet Service Provider has assigned to me so that I can send and receive messages over the Internet— is [255.255.4.11]." The Napster server updates the database with this information, so that, in addition to the names of the music files on each Napster user's hard disk, it now contains information about whether each user is, or is not, currently logged on, and the Internet address of all users who are currently online.

So far, so good. If you then find yourself, on some dark and lonely night, desperate to hear, say, Bob Dylan's version of the Stanley Brothers' classic "Rank Stranger," you send a query to the Napster server: "Does your database list any machines that have a copy of this song? If so, can you please provide me with the list of those that are currently logged onto the Internet—with their IP addresses?" . . . When the server sends you back that list, the Napster software conveniently lets you send a message directly to any of those machines—because you have their IP addresses you can easily contact them— requesting the file in question; a copy of the file is then transmitted directly from that remote machine to yours.

David G. Post, His Napster's Voice, in Copy Fights: The Future of Intellectual Property in the Information Age 107, 107–08 (Clyde Wayne Crews & Adam Thierer eds., 2002).

Almost overnight, the Internet start-up that began as the brain-child of a teenager who wanted to share music with his friends grew into a service with fifty-eight million users with access to as many as a billion MP3 files.[50] Napster was a phenomenon; at the time, the fastest-growing software application ever. Like the VCR before it, it quickly drew the attention of the music industry. Within just months of rocketing into the dot-com stratosphere, Napster was sued for contributory and vicarious copyright infringement by a coalition of music industry plaintiffs, including major record companies and music publishers.[51]

The *Napster*[52] plaintiffs filed suit in district court in July 2000 seeking an injunction against Napster's continued operation of its file-sharing service.[53] Napster, not surprisingly, invoked the *Sony* doctrine: like the VCR, it argued, its system was capable of substantial or commercially significant noninfringing uses,[54] and, therefore, like Sony, it could not be held contributorily liable for its users' direct infringements.[55]

---

[50] Adam Cohen, Napster the Revolution: A Crisis of Conduct, CNN/Time, Sept. 25, 2000, available at http://www.cnn.com/ALLPOLITICS/time/2000/10/02/revolution.html (visited July 24, 2005).

[51] Among the plaintiffs, ironically, was Sony, which, in the years between its victory against Universal and the birth of Napster, had transformed itself from an electronics manufacturer ("Sony Corporation of America") into an entertainment giant ("Sony Music Entertainment, Inc."). The proverbial shoe was now on the other foot for the company that had once championed liberal fair use rights for entertainment consumers.

[52] A & M Records, Inc. v. Napster, Inc., 114 F. Supp. 2d 896 (N.D. Cal. 2000).

[53] Continuing in the tradition of droll comparisons begun by the MPAA's Valenti, the Recording Industry Association of America (RIAA) wrote in its brief: "The truth is, the making and distributing of unauthorized copies of copyrighted works by Napster users is not 'sharing,' any more than stealing apples from your neighbor's tree is 'gardening.'" See John Borland, Recording Industry Calls Napster Defense "Baseless," CNET News, July 13, 2000, available at http://news.com.com/Recording+industry+calls+Napster+defense+baseless/2100-10233-243162.html (last visited July 24, 2005).

[54] 114 F. Supp. 2d at 912. Napster pointed to three noninfringing uses of its peer-to-peer music sharing system: sampling (the process whereby users download songs to decide whether they want to buy the CDs containing the songs), space-shifting (the process whereby users copy songs they've already legally purchased onto a portable audio player or other device), and the authorized distribution of new artists' work. *Id.* at 913.

[55] *Id.* at 918.

The district court rejected Napster's proffered noninfringing uses as disingenuous, commercially insignificant, and, in the case of new artist promotion, a mere "afterthought."[56] Unable to find that the Napster system had any "commercially significant noninfringing uses," the district court denied Napster the benefit of the *Sony* safe harbor.[57] The court went on to hold that the plaintiffs were likely to succeed on their contributory infringement claim because they could prove both required elements of the claim, i.e., actual or constructive knowledge of users' illegal conduct, and a "material contribution" to the infringing activity.[58] As far as "knowledge" was concerned, the court found that Napster knew or should have known that its system was being used to infringe: Napster executives had themselves used the software to download infringing files; Napster had promoted its web site with screen shots listing infringing titles; memos between Napster executives acknowledged that users were exchanging "pirated music"; and plaintiffs had provided Napster with actual notice that it was providing access to thousands of infringing files.[59] The plaintiffs' proof of Napster's generalized knowledge of infringing uses was sufficient, the court held, because "[t]he law does not require actual knowledge of specific acts of infringement."[60] And as for "material contribution," the court found adequate evidence of Napster's contribution in the fact that it supplied "support services" for its users in the form of proprietary software; a central database of songs; a means of identifying where the songs were located on the system; a search engine; servers; and

---

[56] *Id.* at 916–18.

[57] *Id.* at 917.

[58] *Id.* at 919.

[59] *Id.* at 918.

[60] *Id.* (citing Gershwin Publishing Corp. v. Columbia Artists Management, Inc., 443 F.2d 1159, 1163 (2d Cir. 1971)).

the means of connecting to other users' computers.[61] Finding that the plaintiffs would likely succeed on the merits of their third-party infringement claims, the district court enjoined Napster "from engaging in, or facilitating others in copying, downloading, uploading, transmitting, or distributing plaintiffs' copyrighted musical compositions and sound recordings, protected by either federal or state law, without express permission of the rights owner."[62] The court charged Napster with the prodigious task of "insur[ing] that no work owned by plaintiffs which neither defendant nor Napster users have permission to use or distribute is uploaded or downloaded on Napster."[63] The day after the injunction, traffic on Napster's website increased seventy-one percent, as users rushed to download MP3s before the music died.[64]

On appeal, the Ninth Circuit affirmed, finding that injunctive relief in favor of the plaintiffs was "not only warranted but required."[65] It found fault, however, with the district court's application of *Sony*. The district court had been incorrect when it held that Napster failed to show any commercially significant noninfringing uses for its system; it had "improperly confined the use analysis to *current uses*, ignoring the system's *capabilities* [and] plac[ing] undue weight

---

[61] *Id.* at 920. The court also held that the plaintiffs were likely to succeed on the merits of their vicarious copyright infringement claim. Napster had both the ability to "police" its users' infringing conduct and a direct financial interest in their infringing activity. *Id.* at 921. The court found that Napster could block, and had in fact already blocked, access to the system by users who had provided others with access to infringing files. *Id.* at 920. The fact that Napster had already blocked infringing users established, in the eyes of the court, that Napster had the means to discern both which users and which files were infringing. *Id.* With respect to Napster's financial interest in its users' conduct, the court found evidence in the record that, although Napster generated no revenue at the time the plaintiffs sought relief, the company planned to derive revenue from increases in the number of Napster users. So long as Napster had "economic incentives for tolerating unlawful behavior," *id.* at 921, the court held, it had a demonstrable direct financial interest in its users' infringing conduct.

[62] *Id.* at 927.

[63] *Id.*

[64] Napster: Stealing or Sharing, CNN Online, available at http://www.cnn.com/SPECIALS/2001/napster/timeline.html (visited July 24, 2005).

[65] A & M Records, Inc. v. Napster, Inc., 239 F.3d 1004, 1027 (9th Cir. 2001).

on the proportion of current infringing use as compared to current *and future* noninfringing use."[66]

But meeting the *Sony* "staple article of commerce" standard, the court continued, did not immunize Napster from liability. *Sony* stood for the proposition that the *knowledge of the infringing acts* required to sustain a claim for contributory infringement would not be *imputed* to a defendant who merely distributed a copying technology that was "capable of substantial noninfringing use."[67] "A computer system operator cannot be liable for contributory infringement merely because the structure of the system allows for the exchange of copyrighted material," absent "specific information which identifies infringing activity."[68] But where the system operator "learns of specific infringing material available on his system and fails to purge such material from the system," the operator "knows of and contributes to direct infringement."[69]

In Napster's case, knowledge of infringing activity did not need to be imputed; the court found that Napster, unlike Sony, had *"actual* knowledge of *specific acts* of infringement,"[70] and, in the face of that knowledge, it had failed to "block access to the system by suppliers of infringing material" or "remove the material."[71] That the Napster software was "capable of commercially significant [lawful] use" was therefore irrelevant; *actual* knowledge that infringements were taking place, plus the ability and refusal to act upon that knowledge to prevent the infringements, eliminated any need to impute knowledge to Napster, and was a sufficient basis for the imposition of liability independent of the (now-narrowed) *Sony* safe harbor.

---

[66] *Id.* at 1021 (emphasis added).

[67] See *id.* at 1020 ("The *Sony* Court declined to impute the requisite level of knowledge where the defendants made and sold equipment capable of both infringing and 'substantial noninfringing uses.'") (citing Sony Corp. of America v. Universal City Studios, Inc., 464 U.S. 417, 422 (1984)).

[68] *Id.* at 1021.

[69] *Id.* (citing Religious Technology Center v. Netcom On-Line Communication Services, Inc., 907 F. Supp. 1361, 1374 (N.D. Cal. 1995)).

[70] *Id.* (emphasis added). The court referred specifically to the notices that the plaintiffs had delivered to Napster, informing it of "more than 12,000 infringing files" listed in Napster's database. See *id.* at 1022 n.6.

[71] *Id.* at 1022.

After *Napster*, the formula for third party liability looks a little more complicated than it had after *Sony*, but it retains the same basic structure:

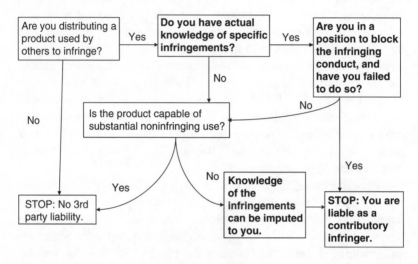

Figure 2. Copyright liability for distributing devices used by third parties to infringe post-*Napster* (new rules in bold).

As a practical matter, the Ninth Circuit's decision brought an end to the Napster phenomenon. The system's users disappeared as quickly as they had arrived, taking all the free music with them. During the pendency of the litigation, Napster's diminishing assets were acquired by Bertelsmann, one of the plaintiffs in the case.[72] Through the magic of the market, the industry's latest antagonist became its hottest new property. The momentum that appeared to be driving the *Napster* case inexorably toward the Supreme Court quickly dissipated, but the legal battle over peer-to-peer file sharing had been joined, and Napster, like Sony before it, would live to fight (for the other side) another day.

[72]See Amy Doan, Napster, Bertelsmann Deal Gives Labels a Fright, Forbes.com, Oct. 31, 2000, http://www.forbes.com/2000/10/31/1031napster.html.

V. Play: *Grokster*

Even before the ink on the *Napster* opinion was dry, new file-sharing technologies were being deployed over the Internet. Grokster and StreamCast were among the developers of a new generation of decentralized, or "distributed," peer-to-peer file-sharing software. Instead of using, as Napster did, a central server to store a master index of all files available on the network, the Grokster/StreamCast systems do their indexing "on the fly," without any need to communicate with a central machine.[73] In a rush to make Napster's loss their gain, Grokster and StreamCast—much to their subsequent detriment, as we will see in a moment—began marketing their systems expressly to former Napster users who had been left high and dry by the latter's demise.

Once again, a coalition of music industry copyright holders sued, seeking an injunction against the continuing distribution of the software on the grounds that it constituted both contributory and vicarious infringement. The defendants argued, in essence, that their software was more like a VCR than it was like the Napster software, at least for the purpose of determining third-party liability for copyright infringement. Because they used no central index database or central server, Grokster and StreamCast claimed that they had no "actual knowledge of specific infringing acts," and, even if they had, could do nothing to prevent users from infringing.[74] Nor could knowledge be imputed to them, they maintained, insofar as their software, like Napster's (and the VCR), was "capable of substantial noninfringing uses."[75]

The district court agreed, granting the defendants' motion for summary judgment on the issue of third-party copyright infringe-

---

[73]Good descriptions of the technical details of the Grokster and StreamCast systems can be found in MGM Studios Inc. v. Grokster, Ltd., 380 F.3d 1154, 1158–60 (9th Cir. 2004), and in MGM Studios Inc. v. Grokster, Ltd., 125 S. Ct. 2764, 2770–74 (2005).

[74]MGM Studios Inc. v. Grokster, Ltd., 259 F. Supp. 2d 1029, 1037 (C.D. Cal. 2003).

[75]*Id.* at 1035.

ment,[76] and the Ninth Circuit affirmed. The court of appeals held that the plaintiffs had not established that defendants had "specific knowledge of infringement at a time at which they contributed to the infringement, and failed to act upon that information."[77] And because the defendants' products were "capable of substantial or commercially significant noninfringing uses,"[78] knowledge of the infringements could not be imputed to them. They could, therefore, avail themselves of the *Sony* safe harbor, and they were absolved of contributory copyright infringement.[79]

The Supreme Court unanimously reversed, adding another threshold requirement to the *Sony* safe harbor: not only must the copying technology in question be capable of substantial noninfringing uses, it cannot have been distributed *"with the object of promoting its use to infringe* copyright, as shown by clear expression or other affirmative steps taken to foster infringement."[80] In other words, regardless of whether the copying technology itself meets the *Sony* "staple article of commerce" test, a distributor who "actively induce[s] infringements"[81] is liable for the resulting acts of infringement by third parties. The focus of this threshold "inducement" inquiry is not on the technology itself at all (or the extent to which

---

[76] In its opinion, the district court noted that "[b]ecause Plaintiffs principally seek prospective injunctive relief, the Court at this time considers only whether the *current versions of Grokster's and StreamCast's products and services* subject either party to liability. This Order does not reach the question whether either Defendant is liable for damages arising from past versions of their software, *or from other past activities." Id.* at 1033 (emphasis added). The precise meaning of this limitation is somewhat obscure.

[77] 380 F.3d at 1162.

[78] *Id.*

[79] The appeals court made the following reference to the somewhat unusual procedural posture in which it found the case (see note 76, *supra*):

Resolution of these issues does not end the case. As the district court clearly stated, its decision was limited to the specific software in use at the time of the district court decision. The Copyright Owners have also sought relief based on previous versions of the software, which contain significant—and perhaps crucial—differences from the software at issue. We express no opinion as to those issues.

Id. at 1166.

[80] MGM Studios Inc. v. Grokster, Ltd., 125 S. Ct. 2764, 2780 (2005) (emphasis added).

[81] *Id.* at 2791 (Breyer, Stevens, and O'Connor, JJ., concurring).

it is capable of noninfringing use) but on the "purposeful, culpable expression and conduct" of the technology's distributors.[82]

The Ninth Circuit read *Sony* to mean that "whenever a product is capable of substantial lawful use, the producers can never be held contributorily liable for third parties' infringing use of it ... unless [they] had 'specific knowledge of infringement at a time at which they contributed to the infringement, and failed to act upon that information.'"[83] In this, the Court said, they erred:

> [*Sony*] dealt with a claim of liability based solely on distributing a product with alternative lawful and unlawful uses, with knowledge that some users would follow the unlawful course [,] [and held] that the product's capability of substantial lawful employment should bar the *imputation of fault* and consequent secondary liability for the unlawful acts of others.[84]

Sony prohibits courts from imputing an intent to cause infringement *"solely* from the design or distribution of a product capable of substantial lawful use,"[85] while it allows courts to so presume if the defendant distributes an article that is "'good for nothing else' *but* infringement."[86] But either way, the Court concluded, *Sony* was "never meant to foreclose rules of fault-based liability derived from the common law,"[87] and if there is "direct evidence of unlawful purpose ... [n]othing in *Sony* requires courts to ignore [it]."[88]

Looking at the record before it, the Court saw ample direct evidence of an unlawful purpose; Grokster and StreamCast had each "clearly voiced the objective that recipients use it to download copyrighted works,"[89] each "took active steps to encourage infringement,"[90] and each, "unlike the manufacturer and distributor in *Sony*,

---

[82] *Id.* at 2870.

[83] *Id.* at 2778 (quoting Grokster, 380 F.3d at 1162).

[84] *Id.* at 2782 (emphasis added).

[85] *Id.* at 2779 (emphasis added).

[86] *Id.* at 2777 (quoting Canda v. Michigan Malleable Iron Co., 124 F. 486, 489 (6th Cir. 1903)) (emphasis added).

[87] *Id.* at 2779.

[88] *Id.*

[89] *Id.* at 2767.

[90] *Id.*

acted with a purpose to cause copyright violations."[91] Among the "words and deeds [that] show [defendants'] purpose to cause and profit from third-party acts of copyright infringement":

- each company showed itself "to be aiming to satisfy a known source of demand for copyright infringement, the market comprising former Napster users,"[92] by "beam[ing] onto the computer screens of users of Napster-compatible programs ads urging the adoption of [defendants'] OpenNap program, which was designed, as its name implied, to invite the custom of patrons of Napster, then under attack in the courts for facilitating massive infringement";[93]
- each of the defendants "communicated a clear message [of encouragement] by responding affirmatively to requests for help in locating and playing copyrighted materials";[94]
- there were "unequivocal indications of unlawful purpose in the internal communications and advertising designs aimed at Napster users."[95]

In the face of such actual *proof* of an unlawful purpose, there was no need for the Court to decide whether the Grokster or StreamCast systems were or were not "staple articles of commerce" under *Sony*:

> We do not revisit *Sony* further, as MGM requests, to add a more quantified description of the point of balance between protection and commerce when liability rests solely on distribution with knowledge that unlawful use will occur. It is enough to note that the Ninth Circuit's judgment rested on an erroneous understanding of *Sony* and to leave further consideration of the *Sony* rule for a day when that may be required.[96]

---

[91] *Id.* at 2781.
[92] *Id.* at 2769.
[93] *Id.* at 2780.
[94] *Id.* at 2781.
[95] *Id.*
[96] *Id.* at 2778–79.

After *Grokster*, then, the model for third-party liability incorporates inducement liability and looks like this:

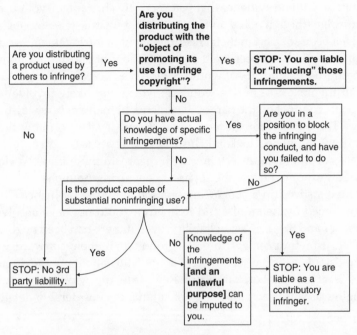

Figure 3. Copyright liability for distributing devices used by third parties to infringe post-*Grokster* (new rules in bold).

VI. Final Words

Precisely how significant the *Grokster* decision will be for the future course of file sharing on the Internet remains to be seen. The next generation of peer-to-peer file-sharing systems is already being widely deployed,[97] and one can confidently predict that distributors and developers will, from now on, be far more circumspect in their

---

[97]See, e.g., the BitTorrent system, described at http://www.bittorrent.com/introduction.html (last checked August 1, 2005). BitTorrent is even more radically decentralized than the Grokster and StreamCast systems; not only is there no central server or master index, but requests for individual files are themselves distributed across the user network, so that each user in possession of the requested file contributes only a small piece of the file to the requestor.

promotional and marketing materials.[98] But what of that? What if you're a software developer and you're just distributing file-sharing software, with no evidence that you "actively encourage" your users to infringe (though many, in fact, do)? What if Grokster/StreamCast had *not* been so overt in their encouragement of infringement; would their systems have been held to be "capable of substantial noninfringing uses" and, if so, would *Sony* have protected them? What about the next case in this sequence, which will likely involve less culpable conduct on the part of the defendant manufacturer/distributor? The opinion for the unanimous Court is silent on how these questions might be and should be resolved. That the *Grokster* opinion leaves considerable uncertainty with regard to these issues is clear from an examination of the separate concurring opinions.

Three justices (in a concurring opinion authored by Justice Ginsburg, joined by Rehnquist and Kennedy) would not have absolved Grokster and StreamCast of liability, even if there had been no direct evidence of inducement, on the ground that their software was *not* a "staple article of commerce" with "substantial non-infringing uses"—at least, not on *this* record. Reviewing the evidence of noninfringing uses presented by the defendants in considerable detail—

---

[98]The following colloquy, which took place at oral argument in the *Grokster* case, reflects some of these questions:

JUSTICE SCALIA: The inducement point doesn't get you very far. Presumably a successor to Grokster, or whatever this outfit is called, could simply come in and not induce anybody but say, you know, "We're setting up the same system," know very well what people are going to use it for, but not induce them. And that would presumably be okay.

MR. CLEMENT [Acting Solicitor General, appearing for the United States in support of the record industry petititoners]: I think that's potentially right . . .

Transcript of Oral Argument at 25, MGM Studios Inc. v. Grokster, Ltd., No. 04-480, available at http://www.supremecourtus.gov/oral_arguments/argument_transcripts/04-480.pdf (last visited July 29, 2005). Subsequently, at the beginning of his rebuttal argument, Donald Verrilli, counsel for MGM and the other record industry petitioners, adverted back to Justice Scalia's question:

MR. VERRILLI: Why is inducement not enough? It's not enough because, as Justice Scalia suggested, these companies already operate in the shadows, and a ruling here . . . that inducement is the only available ground of liability, would just need them to paper over—you know, we do have some paper evidence here, a paper trail here, but . . . they just won't exist next time. And it's just—it's just not enough.

Id. at 51–52.

and finding it a "motley collection of declarations,"[99] "some of them hearsay,"[100] "mostly anecdotal,"[101] and "sometimes obtained second-hand"[102]—they found it insufficient, "in the face of evidence, proffered by MGM, of overwhelming use of Grokster's and StreamCast's software for infringement," to justify permitting the defendants to find refuge in *Sony's* safe harbor:

> [W]hen the record in this case was developed, there was evidence that Grokster's and StreamCast's products were, and had been for some time, overwhelmingly used to infringe, and that this infringement was the overwhelming source of revenue from the products. Fairly appraised, the evidence was insufficient to demonstrate, beyond genuine debate, a reasonable prospect that substantial or commercially significant noninfringing uses were likely to develop over time. On this record, the District Court should not have ruled dispositively on the contributory infringement charge by granting summary judgment to Grokster and StreamCast.[103]

Three other justices (Justice Breyer, joined by Stevens (*Sony's* author) and O'Connor) disagreed. In their view, the evidence "shows that Grokster passes *Sony's* test"; it is "capable of substantial or commercially significant non-infringing uses."[104] The emphasis, for the justices joining in the Breyer concurrence, is on the "capable." Even using data supplied by MGM's experts, Justice Breyer noted, around ten percent of the files shared on the Grokster/StreamCast systems were noninfringing. This is small, in quantitative terms, but

> [i]mportantly, *Sony* also used the word "capable," asking whether the product is *"capable of"* substantial noninfringing uses. Its language and analysis suggest that a figure like 10%, if fixed for all time, might well prove insufficient, but that such a figure serves as an adequate foundation where there is a reasonable prospect of expanded legitimate uses over time. And its language also indicates the appropriateness of

---

[99] Grokster, 125 S. Ct. at 2786 n.3 (Ginsburg, Kennedy, JJ., Rehnquist, C.J., concurring).

[100] *Id.* at 2785.

[101] *Id.*

[102] *Id.*

[103] *Id.* at 2786.

[104] *Id.* at 2788 (Breyer, Stevens, O'Connor, JJ., concurring).

looking to potential future uses of the product to determine its "capability."[105]

Moreover, Justice Breyer found, the record here "reveals a significant future market for noninfringing uses of Grokster-type peer-to-peer software."[106] Noting that file-sharing software "permits the exchange of any sort of digital file—whether that file does, or does not, contain copyrighted material," these three justices thought it likely that, "[a]s more and more uncopyrighted information is stored in swappable form . . . lawful peer-to-peer sharing will become increasingly prevalent" for such tasks as "swapping research information (the initial purpose of many peer-to-peer networks); public domain films . . . ; historical recordings and digital educational materials . . . ; digital photos . . . ; 'shareware' and 'freeware'; secure licensed music and movie files; news broadcasts past and present; user-created audio and video files; and all manner of free 'open content' works collected by Creative Commons."[107] The "foreseeable development of such uses, when taken together with an estimated 10% noninfringing material, is sufficient to meet *Sony*'s standard."[108] We had hoped to learn from the Court's opinion in *Grokster* whether a distributor of a copying technology can be held liable for contributory infringement if the technology is only *theoretically* capable of noninfringing uses, or if it is only *rarely* used for noninfringing purposes. *Sony* left the meaning of "capable" altogether up for grabs. So, too, it left unsettled the meaning of the crucial terms "commercially significant"[109] and "substantial."[110] How commercially significant, how substantial, must the noninfringing uses of a copying technology be for a distributor with "clean hands" to be immune under *Sony*? These questions were engaged by the concurring opinions, but they were left entirely unanswered by the Court's unanimous opinion, an outcome that is somewhat frustrating for those of us who had hoped for a more definitive application of *Sony*. The breakdown of the Court appears to be three-three, with three

---

[105] *Id.* at 2789.
[106] *Id.* at 2790.
[107] *Id.*
[108] *Id.*
[109] Sony Corp. of America v. Universal City Studios, Inc., 464 U.S. 417, 442 (1984).
[110] *Id.*

abstentions, on the "nice question" of whether the Grokster and StreamCast software programs, considered apart from their distributors' culpable acts of inducement, come within the protective limits of *Sony*'s safe harbor. Rather than treating the *Grokster* case as an occasion to define the contours of *Sony* more tangibly in the context of Internet file sharing, the Court, as it turned out, rewound to *Sony*, but it never hit "play."

Granholm v. Heald: A Case of Wine and a Prohibition Hangover

*Stuart Banner**

The national prohibition of what the Constitution calls "intoxicating liquors" ended in 1933 with the ratification of the Twenty-first Amendment. We're still feeling the effects of Prohibition today, however, because the Twenty-first Amendment didn't just repeal the Eighteenth. It also granted power to the states, in an unusual and facially ambiguous way, to regulate interstate shipments of alcohol. This part of the Twenty-first Amendment has generated a steady flow of litigation, the most recent installment of which reached the Supreme Court in the 2004 term in the form of two cases consolidated as *Granholm v. Heald*.[1] These cases raised the same question: May a state permit in-state wineries to ship directly to customers but forbid out-of-state wineries from doing so?

The source of all this litigation is Section 2 of the Twenty-first Amendment, which provides: "The transportation or importation into any State . . . for delivery or use therein of intoxicating liquors, in violation of the laws thereof, is hereby prohibited."[2] This sort of clause is unique in the Constitution. Read literally, it would forbid, as a constitutional matter, whatever acts pertaining to liquor importation the states already forbid, even acts protected by federal statutes or other parts of the Constitution. But Section 2 has never been read literally. As we'll see below, there is a reason Section 2 was written in such a strange way. It was meant to supersede some specific turn-of-the-century Supreme Court cases interpreting the Commerce Clause, not to supersede the entire Constitution. The

*Professor of Law, UCLA School of Law.

[1]125 S. Ct. 1885 (2005). The other case was called *Swedenburg v. Kelly*, and there was also a second certiorari petition in *Granholm* called *Michigan Beer & Wine Wholesalers Association. v. Heald*, but I will refer to both cases and all three petitions as *Granholm*.

[2]U.S. Const. amend. XXI, § 2.

weird language of Section 2, however, is susceptible of a range of interpretations. Because states have been aggressive in regulating the liquor business over the past seventy years, and because lots of money has been at stake, courts, including the Supreme Court, have been wrestling with the Twenty-first Amendment ever since the end of Prohibition.

Granholm posed a classic Twenty-first Amendment question. Everyone agreed that the statutes at issue would have been unconstitutional if the regulated commodity were anything other than alcohol. The Constitution's grant to Congress of the power to regulate interstate commerce has been understood since the mid-nineteenth century to imply that states may not burden interstate commerce in certain ways, and the paradigmatic example of a state law barred by this so-called "dormant Commerce Clause" is a law discriminating against out-of-state products. The question in *Granholm* was whether the Twenty-first Amendment creates an exception allowing states to discriminate where the product involved is liquor. By a five to four vote, the Court concluded that such discrimination is not permitted by the Twenty-first Amendment and, accordingly, held that if a state wants to allow in-state wineries to ship directly to customers it must allow out-of-state wineries to do the same.[3]

I

Since the end of Prohibition, most states have required alcoholic beverages to be sold through a three-tier distribution system: producers must sell to wholesalers, wholesalers must sell to retailers, and only retailers can sell to the consumer. Producers, wholesalers, and retailers are each licensed separately. The traditional justifications for the three-tier system include facilitating the collection of taxes, preventing sales to minors, promoting temperance, and keeping away organized crime. It is not obvious that the three-tier system actually accomplishes these goals any better than one-tier or two-tier distribution, except to the extent that the three-tier system promotes temperance indirectly, by raising prices.

Instead, the three-tier requirement has two primary effects. The first is to raise the price of alcohol to the consumer by placing two intermediaries between the consumer and the producer. One can

[3] 125 S. Ct. at 1907.

imagine circumstances under which a three-tier system would be the most efficient way to sell a product, but then this system would exist without any law requiring it. Where it exists only because of state law, wholesalers and retailers profit at consumers' expense. The second effect of the three-tier requirement is to reduce the consumer's range of choice. Wholesalers and retailers are prevented by cost and space constraints from offering every variety of every beverage produced. They focus on the well-known brands of the largest producers, at the expense of the smaller producers and lesser-known products.

The three-tier requirement has nevertheless persisted for decades, most likely because the wholesalers are a well-organized lobbying force while consumers and small producers are not. In recent years, however, this distribution system has come under pressure from two sources. One has been the phenomenal increase in the quantity and quality of American wine. As of 2001, the United States was the world's fourth largest wine producer (after France, Italy, and Spain) and the world's third largest wine consumer (after France and Italy).[4] The number of wineries in the country has roughly quadrupled in the past twenty-five years, to more than three thousand.[5] The large majority of these wineries produce in quantities so small that their wine is not widely carried by wholesalers.[6] Consumer demand for such wine has increased correspondingly. One measure of this growth is the paid circulation of the magazine *Wine Spectator*, which grew approximately from 150,000 to 375,000 between 1994 and 2003; eight of ten subscribers in the latter year owned a wine collection, the average size of which was 516 bottles.[7] Such consumers are interested in trying a large variety of wines from different

[4] World Wine Production by Country, http://www.wineinstitute.org/communications/statistics/keyfacts_worldwineproduction02.htm; World Wine Consumption in Listed Countries, http://www.wineinstitute.org/communications/statistics/keyfacts_worldwineconsumption2002.htm.

[5] Wine Facts, http://www.americanwineries.org/newsroom/winefacts04.htm.

[6] Alan E. Wiseman & Jerry Ellig, Market and Nonmarket Barriers to Internet Wine Sales: The Case of Virginia (2004), available at http://www.bepress.com/bap/vol6/iss2/art4.

[7] 5 Very Good Reasons to Advertise in Wine Spectator, at 1, http://www.winespectator.com/Wine/Images/Graphics/ads/WS_NAT_EKIT.pdf.

producers. Like the small wineries, they have been increasingly frustrated by the constraints of the three-tier system.

The second source of pressure has been the explosion of commerce over the Internet. Small wineries have been able to sell on-site to tourists for some time under a common exception to the three-tier requirement in the wine-producing states, but before the Internet there was not much of a market for shipping wine directly to consumers in other states. As in other industries, however, from books to collectibles, the Internet has allowed small sellers and small buyers of wine to find one another despite being physically far apart.

States accordingly began allowing wineries to ship directly to customers, but they did so in a few different ways. By 2003 the Federal Trade Commission counted thirty states that permitted direct intrastate shipments, of which twenty-four also allowed some form of direct interstate shipping.[8] Thirteen of these twenty-four were "reciprocity" states, which only allowed customers to receive wine directly from producers in other reciprocity states, while several others placed restrictions on interstate shipments that were not placed on intrastate shipments.[9] Around half the states allowed no direct interstate shipments at all.[10]

Michigan and New York were the two states whose regulatory schemes were challenged in *Granholm*. Michigan allowed in-state wineries to ship directly to in-state customers but required out-of-state wineries to sell to in-state wholesalers.[11] New York in principle permitted wineries located anywhere to ship directly to in-state customers but required them first to establish a factory, office, or storeroom in New York.[12] This requirement was of course a much greater burden on out-of-state wineries than in-state wineries, and too great a burden for the smaller wineries.

The justifications for these differential requirements were the same as those traditionally said to justify the three-tier system as a whole, but here they are even more dubious. Even if a complete ban on direct

---

[8] Federal Trade Comm'n, Possible Anticompetitive Barriers to E-Commerce: Wine (July 2003), at 7, available at http://www.ftc.gov/us/2003/07/winereport2.pdf.

[9] *Id.* at 7–8.

[10] *Id.* at 8.

[11] Granholm v. Heald, 125 S. Ct. 1885, 1893 (2005).

[12] *Id.* at 1894.

shipping could be said to limit underage drinking, for instance—a questionable proposition, as it is no harder for a delivery company to verify the age of a customer than it is for a liquor store—a ban only on *interstate* direct shipping can hardly do so, because the determined underage drinker need only order from an in-state producer. Instead, discrimination against out-of-state wineries is far more likely to be a result of simple protectionism.[13] The states that discriminate do not appear to be trying to protect their own wineries, despite the fact that some have wine industries that face competition for in-state customers from more well-regarded California wineries. Small wineries in New York, for example, have been trying for years to end the state's ban on direct interstate shipping, on the theory that they have more to gain from out-of-state customers than to lose from out-of-state competitors.[14] States instead seem to be primarily protecting their wholesalers and retailers, who stand to lose revenue if out-of-state wineries can bypass them and sell directly to in-state customers. Indeed, one of the most commonly proffered reasons for barring direct interstate shipments is to facilitate "orderly market conditions." As Judge Easterbrook has pointed out, this is nothing but a euphemism for reducing competition.[15]

Reducing competition, as might be expected, raises the price of wine and reduces the variety of wine available to the consumer. The Federal Trade Commission recently examined the wine market in McLean, Virginia (a state that banned interstate direct shipment), and found that 15% of a sample of popular wines available on the Internet were not stocked by any retail wine store within ten miles.[16] If they had been allowed to purchase on the Internet, consumers would have paid 8%–13% less than the store price for wine costing more than $20 per bottle, and 20%–21% less than the store price for wine costing more than $40 per bottle.[17] Had the sample included less popular wines from smaller non-Virginia wineries, the percentage

---

[13] Gina M. Riekhof & Michael E. Sykuta, Regulating Wine by Mail, Regulation, Fall 2004, at 30–36.

[14] Al Baker, Mixed Reaction to Web Wine Plan, N.Y. Times, May 30, 2005, at B3.

[15] Bridenbaugh v. Freeman-Wilson, 227 F.3d 848, 851 (7th Cir. 2000).

[16] Federal Trade Comm'n, *supra* note 8, at 3.

[17] *Id.*

unavailable to consumers in Virginia would no doubt have been much higher.

The plaintiffs in *Granholm* were three small wineries, two located in California and one in Virginia, and several potential customers residing in Michigan and New York. The winery in the Michigan case was Domaine Alfred, in San Luis Obispo, California, which produces only three thousand cases per year.[18] Terry Speizer, the winery's owner and operator, received requests for Domaine Alfred from Michigan customers, but he could not find a Michigan wholesaler willing to list it.[19] Even if he could have found a wholesaler, selling Domaine Alfred through Michigan's three-tier system would most likely not have been profitable, because the markups charged by the wholesaler and the retailer would have made the consumer price too high or the price Speizer charged to the wholesaler too low. Among the plaintiffs in the New York case was Juanita Swedenburg, the owner/operator of a Virginia winery producing only two thousand cases per year.[20] More than 90% of Swedenburg's sales were to tourists visiting the winery, about half of whom lived outside Virginia.[21] When they returned home, some to New York, these out-of-state customers were disappointed to find that there was no way to obtain more of Swedenburg's wine unless they returned to Virginia.

By the time the cases reached the Supreme Court, so many other interested parties had filed amicus briefs that *Granholm* engaged virtually every Washington law firm with a significant appellate practice. On the side of the plaintiffs were a variety of trade organizations representing the wine industry; a handful of the big wine-producing states (including California, Oregon, and Washington); several members of Congress (most representing the wine-producing districts of California and New York); a few ideological organizations interested in free trade; some companies and trade associations involved in Internet commerce (including eBay); the trade association that represents interstate shippers like United Parcel Service and Federal Express; and a group of distinguished economists. On the side of Michigan and New York were thirty-three

---

[18] Granholm, 125 S. Ct. at 1893.

[19] *Id.*

[20] Petitioner's Brief on the Merits at 2, Swedenburg v. Kelly, No. 03-1274 (U.S. Oct. 7, 2004).

[21] *Id.*

other states with similar differential shipment laws; the wine and spirits wholesalers; a collection of groups concerned with temperance and underage drinking; two organizations of state liquor administrators; the National Beer Wholesalers Association; and the trade association representing the country's largest breweries.[22] Temperance organizations and liquor wholesalers would be strange bedfellows in most contexts, but they are not so strange here if one purpose of the three-tier distribution system is to insulate the wholesalers from competition, and if the resulting higher consumer prices reduce liquor consumption.[23] The participation of so many groups in the case suggests the economic importance of the Supreme Court's decision.

II

The outcome of *Granholm* hinged on whether Section 2 of the Twenty-first Amendment allows states to discriminate against out-of-state liquor producers. If Section 2 could be read literally, the case would have been an easy one. The direct shipment of wine from out-of-state wineries to New York or Michigan customers is an obvious instance of the "importation into any State . . . for delivery or use therein of intoxicating liquors, in violation of the laws thereof,"[24] and, under a literal reading, would be exactly what Section 2 prohibits. But the story behind the language of Section 2 is long and complex, beginning several decades before national Prohibition. When Section 2 is placed in its historical context, it is clear that Section 2 was not intended to authorize states to discriminate against out-of-state producers.

Prohibition began, state by state, many years before the Eighteenth Amendment. In dry states, statutes normally prohibited the manufacture and sale of liquor, but not the consumption or simple possession of liquor. Such laws were enforced against manufacturers and shippers, because they could not be enforced against consumers.

States faced no constitutional obstacle to prosecuting in-state producers, particularly after the Supreme Court held in 1887 that a ban

---

[22]See, e.g., Granholm v. Heald, No. 03-1116, http://www.supremecourtus.gov/docket/03-1116.htm.

[23]Cf. Bruce Yandle, Bootleggers and Baptists—The Education of a Regulatory Economist, Regulation, May/June 1983, at 13.

[24]U.S. Const. amend. XXI, § 2.

on the manufacture and sale of liquor did not deprive producers of property without due process.[25] Many of the dry states, however, were adjacent to wet states, where liquor producers were happy to supply a neighboring market lacking manufacturers of its own. To combat the sale of liquor effectively, dry states accordingly needed to restrict the importation of liquor from wet states. That, however, invited constitutional challenge under the dormant Commerce Clause, which was then understood to impose two very different kinds of limits on the regulatory power of a state.

First, state laws discriminating against out-of-state liquor producers were unconstitutional, just like state laws discriminating against out-of-state producers of any commodity. In *Tiernan v. Rinker*,[26] for example, the Supreme Court considered a Texas tax on sellers of beer and wine that exempted beer and wine manufactured in Texas. The Court held that "the statute of Texas is inoperative, in so far as it makes a discrimination against wines and beer imported from other States. . . . A tax cannot be exacted for the sale of beer and wines when of foreign manufacture, if not exacted from their sale when of home manufacture."[27] A few years later, the Court considered a similar Michigan tax on businesses selling liquor imported from other states and reached the same result. "A discriminating tax imposed by a State operating to the disadvantage of the products of other States when introduced into the first mentioned State, is, in effect, a regulation in restraint of commerce among the States," the Court held, "and as such is a usurpation of the power conferred by the Constitution upon the Congress of the United States."[28] This anti-discrimination doctrine was not troubling to prohibitionists. They wanted to restrict the manufacture and sale of both in-state *and* out-of-state liquor.

The second limit imposed on state power by the dormant Commerce Clause, by contrast, was disturbing to prohibitionists. In *Bowman v. Chicago and Northwestern Railway Company*,[29] the Court addressed for the first time the Commerce Clause implications of a

---

[25]Mugler v. Kansas, 123 U.S. 623 (1887).

[26]102 U.S. 123 (1880).

[27]*Id.* at 127.

[28]Walling v. Michigan, 116 U.S. 446, 455 (1886).

[29]125 U.S. 465 (1888).

dry state's efforts to bar liquor imports from wet states. Iowa had recently prohibited the sale of liquor, with certain exceptions, including for medicinal or sacramental purposes. Iowans falling within one of these exceptions were required to obtain a license. In aid of this ban, Iowa prohibited any common carrier from bringing liquor into the state without first having received a certificate stating that the person to whom the liquor was being delivered possessed the required license.[30] This latter rule was the one challenged under the Commerce Clause. The Court observed that the Iowa law was backed by the best of intentions—it was not adopted for the purpose of discriminating against interstate commerce.[31] The Court nevertheless found the law inconsistent with the Commerce Clause, on the ground that the state lacked any regulatory power over imports in transit. "[T]he right to prohibit sales, so far as conceded to the States, arises only after the act of transportation has terminated," the Court reasoned. "The right of importation from abroad, and of transportation from one State to another, includes, by necessary implication, the right of the importer to sell in unbroken packages at the place where the transit terminates."[32] This was, as applied to liquor, the then-current "original package" doctrine—the view that Congress' power over goods shipped between states was exclusive so long as those goods remained in their original packages.

Bowman alarmed prohibitionists, who recognized that dry states would be powerless to enforce their liquor laws if they could not prevent importers from selling liquor to state residents. The leading prohibition organizations reacted by increasing pressure on Congress to enact a national prohibition law. Liquor producers in wet states, meanwhile, began taking advantage of *Bowman*, by opening retail outlets in dry states, where they sold liquor in the original packages.[33]

Prohibitionists became even more alarmed two years later, when *Leisy v. Hardin*[34] spelled out the implications of *Bowman*. The Leisy

---

[30]For a complete recitation of the statutory provisions at issue in *Bowman*, see *id.* at 474-75.

[31]*Id.* at 475–76.

[32]*Id.* at 499.

[33]Richard Hamm, Shaping the Eighteenth Amendment 65–66 (1995).

[34]135 U.S. 100 (1890).

Company was a family-owned brewery in Peoria, Illinois (a wet state), that shipped beer across the Mississippi River to Keokuk, Iowa (a dry state), where John Leisy offered the beer for sale in its original kegs and cases.[35] When Iowa seized the beer, on the ground that Leisy was violating the Iowa statute prohibiting the sale of liquor, Leisy brought suit seeking return of his merchandise. The Court held that the Commerce Clause rendered Iowa powerless to interfere with Leisy's sales. "Under our decision in *Bowman*," the Court explained, "[Leisy] had the right to import this beer into [Iowa], and in the view which we have expressed they had the right to sell it."[36] Only *after* a sale in the original package would the state's regulatory power commence. "Up to that point of time, we hold that in the absence of congressional permission to do so, the State had no power to interfere by seizure, or any other action, in prohibition of importation or sale by the foreign or non-resident importer."[37]

Leisy triggered a crisis. As Richard Hamm, the leading historian of these events, tells it:

> Overnight the *Leisy* ruling created a new liquor business: the original package house. As this trade grew, panic over the control of liquor began to sweep the country. The prohibition states' original package business, which in May was "budding like a bloom," had in June and July spread like a pernicious weed. . . . In Kansas City, Kansas [a dry state], during the summer of 1890 it was impossible to get cool water but "everywhere may be found iced beer." Soon every major town in the prohibition states had its own package house.[38]

Residents of dry states strengthened their call for a federal statute that would override the holdings of *Bowman* and *Leisy* and authorize the states to regulate the sale of liquor in its original package.[39]

Congress responded quickly, with a statute signed by President Harrison less than four months after the decision in *Leisy*. The Wilson

---

[35] *Id.* at 100, 101.

[36] *Id.* at 124.

[37] *Id.* at 124–25.

[38] Hamm, *supra* note 33, at 70–71.

[39] *Id.* at 70–71, 85.

Granholm v. Heald: *A Case of Wine and a Prohibition Hangover*

Act of 1890,[40] named for the prohibitionist Iowa Senator James Falconer Wilson, provided: "All . . . intoxicating liquors or liquids transported into any State . . . shall upon arrival in such State . . . be subject to the operation and effect of the laws of such State . . . to the same extent and in the same manner as though such liquids or liquors had been produced in such State . . . and shall not be exempt therefrom by reason of being introduced therein in original packages."[41] The Wilson Act was a straightforward response to *Bowman* and *Leisy*. Congress, using its affirmative Commerce Clause power to regulate interstate commerce, authorized the states to treat imported liquor exactly as they treated domestic liquor.

The Wilson Act thus did not remove *all* Commerce Clause limits on state authority to regulate interstate liquor shipments. It removed only the limit imposed by the original package doctrine, the limit that had previously forced dry states to tolerate out-of-state liquor. The other Commerce Clause limit, the ban on discrimination against out-of-state producers, remained in force, untouched by the Wilson Act.

The Court removed any possible doubt on this score a few years later, in *Scott v. Donald*.[42] In South Carolina, a state commissioner was statutorily responsible for purchasing all the liquor to be sold in the state. The commissioner furnished the liquor to designated dispensaries, where it could be sold to the public.[43] The statute required the commissioner to purchase from in-state producers so long as their prices were no higher than those of out-of-state producers.[44] The statute also limited the mark-up that could be charged by the dispensaries on the sale of wine to ten percent, but the limit applied only to in-state wine; there was no limit on the price the dispensaries could charge for out-of-state wine.[45] One of South Carolina's theories in defense of the scheme's constitutionality was that the Wilson Act had removed all Commerce Clause limits on a state's

[40] 26 Stat. 313 (1890) (currently codified at 27 U.S.C. § 121).
[41] *Id.*
[42] 165 U.S. 58 (1897).
[43] *Id.* at 92.
[44] *Id.*
[45] *Id.* at 93.

authority to regulate the liquor trade. The Court rejected the argument. The Wilson Act "was not intended to confer upon any State the power to discriminate injuriously against the products of other States," the Court held.[46] Under the Wilson Act, a state could entirely forbid the sale of liquor, or it could regulate domestic and imported liquor identically. "But the state cannot . . . establish a system which, in effect, discriminates between interstate and domestic commerce."[47]

Over the next fifteen years, as dry states tried to stem the flow of liquor from wet states, the Court had several occasions to interpret the Wilson Act. In a few of these cases, the Court construed the Act very narrowly, and found state statutes unconstitutional under the Commerce Clause. These decisions reopened the door Congress had meant to close in the Wilson Act. It was not long before there was once again a flourishing wet-to-dry interstate liquor trade.

The most important of these cases were *Rhodes v. Iowa*[48] and *Vance v. W.A. Vandercook Co.*,[49] decided on the same day in 1898. *Rhodes* asked whether Iowa's liquor transportation statute—the same one at issue in *Bowman*—could be enforced against a common carrier before the liquor had been delivered to its consignee. That is, did the Wilson Act authorize Iowa to intercept the liquor at the state line, or was Iowa required to wait until the liquor had been delivered before seizing it? The Act subjected liquor to state regulatory power "upon arrival in such State."[50] In *Rhodes*, the Court held that "arrival" meant arrival in the hands of the consignee, not arrival within the borders of the state. The state was powerless while the liquor was in transit.[51]

In *Vance*, the Court held that the Wilson Act did not authorize a state to interfere with the ability of a state resident to receive a shipment of out-of-state liquor for his own personal use. The Wilson Act allowed states to forbid the sale of out-of-state liquor in its original package, the Court reasoned, but nothing more. All other

---

[46] *Id.* at 100.
[47] *Id.* at 92–93.
[48] 170 U.S. 412 (1898).
[49] 170 U.S. 438 (1898).
[50] 27 U.S.C. § 121.
[51] Rhodes, 170 U.S. at 421–23.

regulation unconstitutional before the Wilson Act remained unconstitutional after.[52]

Liquor producers in wet states immediately opened up mail-order businesses, shipping directly to consumers in dry states. The dry states fought back with different methods of enforcement, but the Court repeatedly found these state restrictions unauthorized by the Wilson Act. In four cases decided between 1905 and 1912, the Court held that: (1) a state could not interfere with a C.O.D. liquor shipment from out-of-state while the liquor was still in the hands of the delivery company; (2) a state could not interfere with an interstate liquor shipment while the liquor was in the carrier's warehouse awaiting delivery to the consignee; (3) a state could not ban C.O.D. shipments of liquor; and (4) a state could not simply ban the interstate shipment of liquor to dry localities within the state.[53] There was nothing the dry states could do to keep liquor out.

One colorful example of the lively interstate liquor trade during this period can be found in another of the Court's cases, *Kirmeyer v. Kansas*.[54] For many years, Kirmeyer ran an illegal beer-selling business out of a warehouse in Leavenworth, Kansas, a dry state. Leavenworth was on the west bank of the Mississippi River. Just across the river, in wet Missouri, was the village of Stillings, a place with one store, a few residences, and no post office—but with a roundhouse, a freight depot, and eight or ten beer warehouses. In 1907, fearing apprehension by Kansas officials, Kirmeyer moved his office across the river to Stillings. He continued living in Leavenworth, and he continued using the same Leavenworth warehouse to store beer awaiting shipment to his Kansas customers. The only change was that now he received his orders by telephone or mail in Missouri rather than in Kansas.[55] Nevertheless, the Court held, the Commerce Clause protected Kirmeyer's right to ship beer to Kansans, and the Wilson Act did not authorize Kansas to interfere.[56]

---

[52] Vance, 170 U.S. at 451–52.

[53] These were: (1) American Express Co. v. Iowa, 196 U.S. 133, 143–44 (1905); (2) Heyman v. Southern Ry. Co., 203 U.S. 270, 275–76 (1906); (3) Adams Express Co. v. Kentucky, 206 U.S. 129, 136–37 (1907); and (4) Louisville & Nashville R.R. Co. v. F.W. Cook Brewing Co., 223 U.S. 70, 82 (1912).

[54] 236 U.S. 568 (1915).

[55] For a complete recitation of the facts in *Kirmeyer*, see *id.* at 570–71.

[56] *Id.* at 572.

These Wilson Act cases exasperated prohibitionists, who returned to Congress seeking a stronger declaration of dry states' power to keep liquor out. After several years of fruitless lobbying, the leading prohibition organizations gathered in Washington in December 1911 for a bill-drafting conference organized by the Anti-Saloon League. That conference produced a bill introduced in Congress, with the League's assistance, by two prohibitionist members, Representative E. Yates Webb of North Carolina and Senator William Kenyon of Iowa.[57] After some modification, the bill was enacted as the Webb-Kenyon Act of 1913.[58]

The purpose of the Webb-Kenyon Act, contemporaries recognized, was to strengthen the Wilson Act—or more precisely, to authorize dry states to restrict liquor imports in the ways the Court had found unauthorized by the Wilson Act.[59] The Webb-Kenyon Act was accordingly worded more broadly than the Wilson Act. It prohibited the shipment of intoxicating liquor into a state, "to be received, possessed, sold, or in any manner used, either in the original package or otherwise, in violation of the law of such State."[60] Once again, Congress used its Commerce Clause power to allow states to regulate out-of-state liquor just as they regulated in-state liquor. Like the Wilson Act, the Webb-Kenyon Act did not remove *all* Commerce Clause limits on state authority to regulate interstate liquor shipments; it removed only the limit that was troubling to prohibitionists, the one that had prevented dry states from stamping out liquor imports. The other Commerce Clause limit, the ban on discriminating against out-of-state producers, was untouched by the Webb-Kenyon Act, just as it had been untouched by the Wilson Act. The ban on discrimination was a hardship only to those who wished to promote in-state liquor producers at the expense of out-of-state producers, but such people were not the political force behind the Webb-Kenyon Act. As all historians of the subject agree, the supporters of the Webb-Kenyon Act were prohibitionists.[61]

[57] Hamm, *supra* note 33, at 212–13.

[58] 37 Stat. 699 (1913) (currently codified at 27 U.S.C. § 122).

[59] Allen H. Kerr, The Webb Act, 22 Yale L.J. 567, 567 (1913); Winfred T. Denison, States' Rights and the Webb-Kenyon Liquor Law, 14 Colum. L. Rev. 321, 321 (1914).

[60] 27 U.S.C. § 122.

[61] See, e.g., Ann-Marie E. Szymanski, Pathways to Prohibition: Radicals, Moderates, and Social Movement Outcomes 196 (2003); David E. Kyvig, Repealing National Prohibition 7 (2d ed. 2000); Thomas R. Pegram, Battling Demon Rum: The Struggle

Granholm v. Heald: *A Case of Wine and a Prohibition Hangover*

When the Webb-Kenyon Act was enacted, the idea of authorizing states to discriminate against out-of-state liquor producers was the farthest thing from anyone's mind. The point of the Act was exactly the opposite: to end the discrimination *in favor of* out-of-state producers that had existed ever since the Court decided *Bowman* in 1888. During the congressional debate over the Webb-Kenyon Act, the Act's proponents made clear their desire to override the line of cases that began with *Bowman*, but they expressed no interest in overriding *Scott v. Donald*, the case in which the Court held that the Wilson Act did not authorize state discrimination against out-of-state liquor.[62] If the goal of the Webb-Kenyon Act had been to overturn the result of *Scott*, surely someone would have said so.

Because the Eighteenth Amendment was ratified in January 1919, the Webb-Kenyon Act generated only a short period of litigation. (In principle the Webb-Kenyon Act remained in effect throughout national Prohibition, and it still exists today, but it was largely superseded in practice, first by the Eighteenth Amendment and then by the Twenty-first.) During that period there appear to have been only two published lower court opinions addressing whether the Webb-Kenyon Act authorized states to discriminate against out-of-state liquor. Read literally, without any attention to context, the Act did indeed authorize such discrimination: liquor imported into a state, contrary to the state's protectionist legislation, would literally have been imported "in violation of the law of such State."[63] But both courts recognized that such was not the purpose of the Webb-Kenyon Act. The Act "was not intended to confer and did not confer upon any State the power to make injurious discriminations against the products of other States," the South Carolina Supreme Court held in 1916.[64] "Substantially the same thing was said in *Scott v. Donald* of the Wilson Act."[65] A year earlier, a federal district court in Alabama had reached the same conclusion.[66]

for a Dry America, 1800–1933, at 134 (1998); Kenneth D. Rose, American Women and the Repeal of Prohibition 29–30 (1996); James H. Timberlake, Prohibition and the Progressive Movement 1900–1920, at 162 (1966); Joseph R. Gusfield, Symbolic Crusade: Status Politics and the American Temperance Movement 120 (1963).

[62] 49 Cong. Rec. 699–707, 2687–91, 2788–868, 2898–924 (1913).

[63] 28 U.S.C. § 122.

[64] Brennan v. Southern Express Co., 90 S.E. 402, 404 (1916).

[65] *Id.*

[66] Evansville Brewing Ass'n v. Excise Comm'n, 225 F. 204, 209 (N.D. Ala. 1915).

On the eve of Prohibition, then, Congress had created a unique regulatory framework for liquor. States had the power, unimpeded by the dormant Commerce Clause, to restrict out-of-state liquor the same way they restricted in-state liquor. But states could not discriminate against out-of-state liquor. Such discrimination still violated the Commerce Clause.

Prohibition temporarily removed the need to worry about such issues. However, as the end of Prohibition drew near and Congress debated the text of what would become the Twenty-first Amendment, the scope of state power over interstate liquor shipments became an important question once again, as national Prohibition's end promised to restore the state-by-state prohibition of the decades before 1919. The Webb-Kenyon Act was still on the books, but its constitutionality was not entirely assured. Two justices, including Oliver Wendell Holmes, had dissented from the 1917 decision upholding the statute.[67] President Taft had vetoed the Webb-Kenyon bill (Congress overrode his veto) because he and his attorney general, George Wickersham, also thought it unconstitutional.[68] With public sentiment shifting away from Prohibition, meanwhile, there was a possibility that the Webb-Kenyon Act might one day be repealed, and the dry states reopened to liquor shipments from wet states. To protect the dry states, Congress included, as Section 2 of the proposed Twenty-first Amendment, a near-identical copy of the language of the Webb-Kenyon Act, a ban on shipping liquor into a state "in violation of the laws thereof."[69] The Twenty-first Amendment thus in effect constitutionalized the Webb-Kenyon Act.[70] Even after the repeal of national Prohibition, dry states would have the power, enshrined in the Constitution, to keep liquor out.

Nowhere in the debates over the Twenty-first Amendment is there any suggestion that Section 2 was meant to go beyond the Webb-Kenyon Act and allow states to discriminate against out-of-state

---

[67]Clark Distilling Co. v. Western Md. Ry. Co., 242 U.S. 311, 332 (1917) (Holmes, J., dissenting).

[68]Todd Zywicki & Asheesh Agarwal, Wine, Commerce, and the Constitution, NYU J.L. & Liberty, forthcoming, at 19, available at http://www.law.nyu.edu/journals/liberty/Images/Zywicki-FAAP.doc.

[69]See note 2, *supra*, and accompanying text.

[70]Craig v. Boren, 429 U.S. 190, 205–06 (1976).

liquor. States had never possessed that power before national Prohibition, and no one in Congress appears to have suggested that they ought to have it after. In context, the original meaning of Section 2 is clear enough: states can regulate out-of-state liquor just as restrictively as they regulate in-state liquor without worrying about the Commerce Clause. But they cannot regulate out-of-state liquor more restrictively.

III

If the history of the Twenty-first Amendment ended in 1933, *Granholm v. Heald* would have been an easy case. It would have been clear that New York and Michigan lacked the power to discriminate against out-of-state wineries. What made *Granholm* difficult was the rest of the story.

Shortly after the Twenty-first Amendment was ratified, California enacted a statute imposing a license fee of $500 for importing beer into the state. A group of California beer wholesalers challenged the statute on the ground that it violated the Commerce Clause by discriminating against out-of-state beer. The Court rejected the challenge in a short, puzzling opinion by Justice Brandeis.[71] Brandeis began by denying that any discrimination was taking place.[72] It is not entirely clear what he meant, but he may have been taking account of the fact that in-state breweries also had to pay a license fee, one greater than $500; as a result, Brandeis may have assumed the out-of-state breweries and the wholesalers selling their beer were not actually operating at any disadvantage.[73] Brandeis went on, however, to make a broad and incorrect claim about the brand new Twenty-first Amendment that implicitly presumed California *was* discriminating against out-of-state beer. He said that a state need not "let imported liquors compete with the domestic on equal terms."[74] Such a requirement of equality, Brandeis concluded, "would involve not a construction of the Amendment, but a rewriting of it."[75]

---

[71]State Bd. of Equalization v. Young's Market Co., 299 U.S. 59 (1936).
[72]*Id.* at 61.
[73]See, e.g., *id.* at 64.
[74]*Id.* at 62.
[75]*Id.*

Given the long pre-Prohibition history of challenges to state liquor regulation, it is hard to understand why the Court interpreted Section 2 in this way. Brandeis and his colleagues were old enough to remember the legal battles leading up to Prohibition, and they could hardly have avoided knowing about them, because liquor regulation was one of the major domestic political issues of the era. One is tempted to look for clues in Brandeis's personal jurisprudence, particularly his reluctance to find commercial regulation unconstitutional and his general preference for local diversity over national uniformity, but this sort of investigation would not explain the absence of dissenting justices. It is possible (although I do not know of any evidence of it) that during and shortly after Prohibition contemporaries had forgotten the purpose of the Webb-Kenyon Act; and that when the Act's language was constitutionalized in the Twenty-first Amendment, contemporaries believed they were completely freeing the states from Commerce Clause restrictions rather than merely freeing the states from one such restriction while keeping another in place. Whatever the reason, Brandeis repeated the holding in three more cases over the next three years. Under the Twenty-first Amendment, he explained in 1938, "discrimination against imported liquor is permissible."[76] This was so, he twice wrote the following year, because ever since the Twenty-first Amendment, "the right of a state to prohibit or regulate the importation of intoxicating liquor is not limited by the commerce clause."[77] Again, no one dissented. Only a few years after the end of Prohibition, a view of the Twenty-first Amendment had crystallized that was very different from the one that had been intended by the drafters of identical language in the Webb-Kenyon Act.

That new view remained orthodoxy until the 1980s, when the Court once again reversed course, and returned to Section 2's original meaning. The first hint of this return came in 1980, in a case involving a related but different question: whether the Twenty-first Amendment immunized state liquor regulation from the Sherman Antitrust Act. Justice Powell's opinion noted that in interpreting Section 2,

---

[76]Mahoney v. Joseph Triner Corp., 304 U.S. 401, 403 (1938).

[77]Indianapolis Brewing Co. v. Liquor Control Comm'n, 305 U.S. 391, 394 (1939); Joseph S. Finch & Co. v. McKittrick, 305 U.S. 395, 398 (1939) (the quoted language appears in both cases). The Court reached the same conclusion in another case in late 1939, after Brandeis had retired. Ziffrin, Inc. v. Reeves, 308 U.S. 132, 138 (1939).

"the Court has focused primarily on the language of the provision rather than the history behind it," and implied in a footnote that an examination of the history might yield a different view.[78] The break came a few years later. *Bacchus Imports v. Dias*[79] involved a Commerce Clause challenge to a Hawaii liquor excise tax that exempted some locally produced drinks. The tax would have been clearly within Hawaii's power under the view of the Twenty-first Amendment in effect from the mid-1930s onward. For the first time, however, the Court returned to the Amendment's original meaning and held that Section 2 did not authorize a state to favor local interests by erecting trade barriers. "State laws that constitute mere economic protectionism," the Court concluded, are "not entitled to the same deference as laws enacted to combat the perceived evils of an unrestricted traffic in liquor."[80] The three dissenters—Justices Stevens, Rehnquist, and O'Connor, the only members of the *Bacchus* Court who would remain on the bench for *Granholm*—rightly pointed out that this view was impossible to reconcile with the interpretation that had reigned for nearly fifty years.[81] The Court nevertheless stuck to its new (or, rather, the old) anti-protectionist view of the Twenty-first Amendment in two subsequent cases.[82]

Why, after fifty years of literally but inaccurately construing Section 2, did the Court switch back to the non-literal but historically faithful interpretation? In one sense, the switch came at an unlikely time, just as legal interpretive style was shifting in the opposite direction, toward textualism and away from historically contextual methods. In another sense, though, the switch came at the expected time, as originalism was gaining ground at the expense of more instrumentalist modes of interpretation. Textualism and originalism were in conflict when it came to Section 2, and it was a sign that originalism was winning when Justice Scalia, the Court's most thorough textualist, agreed in 1989 that a law's "discriminatory character

---

[78] California Retail Liquor Dealers Ass'n v. Midcal Aluminum, Inc., 445 U.S. 97, 106–07 & n.10 (1980).

[79] 468 U.S. 263 (1984).

[80] *Id.* at 276.

[81] *Id.* at 282–85 (Stevens, J., dissenting).

[82] Brown-Forman Distillers Corp. v. New York State Liquor Auth., 476 U.S. 573 (1986); Healy v. Beer Inst., 491 U.S. 324 (1989).

eliminates the immunity afforded by the Twenty-first Amendment."[83] Maybe, by the 1980s, the self-evident evils of protectionism were beginning to overshadow the dimly remembered evils of drink.

It was this double reverse by the Court that made the outcome of *Granholm* hard to predict. The differential treatment of in-state and out-of-state companies had been a common feature of state liquor control virtually since the end of Prohibition in 1933. That differential treatment was clearly constitutional under the view of the Twenty-first Amendment in effect until 1984, a view unanimously held by the near-contemporaneous members of the Court, a view still favored by three current justices, and a view well supported by a literal reading of Section 2. On the other side of the scale were the more recent Twenty-first Amendment cases and the historical background of Section 2. *Granholm* thus pitted a literal, textualist reading of the Twenty-first Amendment against a contextual, originalist reading, and one group of Supreme Court cases against another.

IV

Justice Kennedy's majority opinion in *Granholm* recites much of the pre-Prohibition history of liquor regulation, in order to demonstrate that the Twenty-first Amendment, like the Wilson and Webb-Kenyon Acts, was intended to level the playing field between in-state and out-of-state liquor, not to authorize states to discriminate against out-of-state liquor producers.[84] Kennedy rejects the Court's late-1930s opinions construing Section 2 for their failure to take this history into account, and relies instead on the newer line of cases beginning with *Bacchus*.[85] There is nothing surprising here: these were precisely the arguments made in the briefs of the wineries and their amici.

The surprising thing about *Granholm* is Justice Thomas's dissenting opinion, which also relies on a history of the Webb-Kenyon Act, but which narrates that history very differently.[86] This revisionist account

---

[83] Healy, 491 U.S. at 344 (Scalia, J., concurring in part and concurring in the judgment).

[84] Granholm v. Heald, 125 S. Ct. 1885, 1898–1902 (2005).

[85] *Id.* at 1902–04.

[86] *Id.* at 1909–19 (Thomas, J., dissenting)

of the pre-Prohibition history seems to have been developed within Thomas's chambers, as it does not appear (except in very sketchy form) in any of the briefs in the case or in any of the secondary literature. Thomas argues that the Webb-Kenyon Act was intended to overrule not just cases like *Bowman* and *Leisy* but *Scott v. Donald*, the case in which the Court had not allowed states to discriminate against out-of-state producers, as well. The evidence Thomas provides for this proposition is, I think, too weak to support it. The only explicit piece of evidence is that a very early and unsuccessful precursor of the Webb-Kenyon Act—a bill that members of Congress considered sixteen years earlier but did not pass—was accompanied by a Senate report that included *Scott* as one of the decisions this bill would have overruled.[87] The rest of the evidence adduced by Thomas consists of legislative documents either repeating or paraphrasing the language of the Webb-Kenyon Act itself.[88] Even after this additional piece of legislative history is taken into account, the conventional view of the Webb-Kenyon Act remains supported by the overwhelming bulk of contextual evidence and therefore is more persuasive.

Thomas was joined by the three *Bacchus* dissenters, who in *Bacchus* had relied primarily on other arguments, and the *Granholm* dissent is on firmer ground when Thomas turns to these arguments.[89] We have two good sources for contemporaries' understanding of the Twenty-first Amendment—the immediate post-Prohibition output of state legislatures and the late-1930s decisions of the Supreme Court—and both suggest that contemporaries believed the Amendment had authorized states to discriminate against out-of-state liquor. We can perhaps discount the relevance of the state liquor regulation of the period, on the ground that it is hardly unknown for state governments to exceed their authority in an attempt to advance the interests of in-state voters at the expense of others. The Court decisions of the late 1930s, however, are not so easily dismissed. The *Granholm* majority cites some contemporary law review commentary critical of these decisions, but the dissent

[87] *Id.* at 1914.
[88] *Id.* at 1916.
[89] *Id.* at 1920–24.

responds with more contemporary commentary that was not criti-cal,[90] so there was clearly some doubt on this score at the time.

But this only restates why *Granholm* was a hard case. In the end, the Court had to choose between the old cases and the new cases, between the literal reading of Section 2 and the historically contex-tual reading. Either choice would have been defensible, and either would have been subject to attack.

After *Granholm*, states can no longer discriminate against out-of-state liquor. Whether they will permit out-of-state wineries to ship directly to customers, however, is another question. The states' only obligation is to treat in-state and out-of-state wineries equally. Some states may allow all wineries to ship directly to customers; others may forbid all wineries from doing so; still others may allow direct shipment but impose restrictions equally on all wineries. How it all sorts out will depend on political battles among winemakers, wine drinkers, and wholesalers, and the relative influence of the three groups differs dramatically from state to state. The most likely over-all outcome, however, will be more direct interstate shipment than we had before.

There is nothing in the Twenty-first Amendment that distin-guishes wine from other "intoxicating liquors," so similar state-by-state political battles may take place with respect to beer and spirits as well. The small wineries have their counterparts in these mar-kets—microbreweries producing beer in quantities too small to be carried by the beer wholesalers, tiny producers of flavored vodka, and so on—who will also have an interest in selling to customers in other states. As with wine, states can still forbid direct shipment of such products to customers, but only at the possible political cost of including in-state producers within that prohibition.

There is likewise nothing in the Twenty-first Amendment that distinguishes one link in the three-tier system from the others. If states lack the power to discriminate against out-of-state liquor *pro-ducers*, they presumably lack the power to discriminate against out-of-state liquor *wholesalers* or *retailers* as well. The majority opinion in *Granholm* is careful to say that the decision does not invalidate the three-tier system as a whole, but, as Justice Thomas points out, the system is normally predicated on forcing alcohol to flow through

[90] *Id.* at 1903, 1923.

in-state wholesalers and in-state retailers, which is another form of protectionism.[91] In *North Dakota v. United States*,[92] the Court (in dicta) called this system "unquestionably legitimate," but that conclusion relied in part on the late-1930s cases repudiated in *Granholm*,[93] and even if *North Dakota* had not relied on them, its logic would require reconsideration now. We should thus in the short run expect to see challenges brought by out-of-state wholesalers seeking to sell to in-state retailers and consumers, by out-of-state retailers seeking to sell to in-state consumers, by in-state retailers seeking to buy directly from out-of-state producers, and from consumers seeking to buy from anyone, anywhere. These cases will embody a clash of logic and experience: the rationale of *Granholm* suggests the challengers should win, but the long history of entrenched practice under the three-tier system suggests they will not. In the long run, if logic prevails, perhaps we will see a restructuring of the entire industry.

Indeed, the first of these challenges was already underway before the Supreme Court decided *Granholm*. The companies with the most to gain from dismantling the three-tier system are the large supermarket chains, which are the biggest retailers. They could save a bundle if they could cut out the wholesalers and buy directly from producers. In February 2004, the supermarket chain Costco brought suit against the Washington State Liquor Control Board, seeking, among other things, to have Washington's three-tier system declared inconsistent with the Commerce Clause.[94] The case was still in the pretrial stage when *Granholm* was decided. The outcome of *Granholm* makes the legal environment more attractive for similar lawsuits in the future.

If these suits do eventually dismantle the three-tier system, that would be good news indeed for consumers, who would almost certainly see lower prices and greater variety. It would be bad news for those wholesalers and retailers who owe their place in the distribution chain to state regulation rather than to their performance of

---

[91] *Id.* at 1905, 1923–24.

[92] 495 U.S. 423, 432 (1990).

[93] *Id.* at 432 (citing *Young's Market Co.*). Compare Granholm, 125 S. Ct. at 1902–03 (discussing *Young's Market* and progeny).

[94] Washington Beer & Wine Wholesalers Association, The Costco Lawsuit: An Attempt to Dismantle Washington's Three-Tier System, http://www.wbwwa.org/legal/legalissues.html.

any useful function. It would not necessarily be a loss for advocates of temperance or those concerned with underage drinking. States would not lose any ability to moderate the effect of alcohol. They would still be free to limit drinking any way they like, so long as the limit is applied evenhandedly to in-state and out-of-state businesses. Drinking might go up as prices go down, but if that is a source of concern, it can easily be addressed by a non-discriminatory alcohol tax.

Granholm is thus unlikely to be the Supreme Court's last Twenty-first Amendment case. In resolving one question it opened up others that may prove to be even more important. The odd wording of Section 2, a hangover of Prohibition and the decades of state liquor regulation that came before, will loom over the liquor industry for some time to come.

International Judicial Decisions, Domestic Courts, and the Foreign Affairs Power

A. Mark Weisburd*

I. Introduction

On December 10, 2004, the United States Supreme Court granted certiorari in *Medillin v. Dretke*.[1] The Court granted certiorari to address two questions: whether American courts were bound by the treaty interpretation in the judgment of the International Court of Justice (ICJ) in the *Case Concerning Avena and Other Mexican Nationals*[2] (*Avena*) and, if not, whether American courts in any event should defer to the ICJ's treaty interpretation as a matter of comity and in the interest of uniformity.[3] On February 28, 2005, however, the president issued a surprise memorandum order directing state courts to give effect to the ICJ's *Avena* judgment. On May 23, 2005, the Court dismissed the *Medellin* writ of certiorari as improvidently granted,[4] explaining that its action was prompted by certain procedural problems with the case unrelated to treaty interpretation.[5] Subsequently, Jose Ernesto Medellin, the petitioner, has pursued a petition for habeas corpus in state court, relying both on the judgment of the ICJ in *Avena* and on President Bush's February memorandum directing state courts to give effect to *Avena*.[6]

---

*Martha M. Brandis Distinguished Professor of Law, University of North Carolina School of Law.

[1] 125 S. Ct. 2088 (2005).

[2] (Mex. v. U.S.), 43 I.L.M. 581 (2004) [hereinafter Avena].

[3] Medellin, 125 S. Ct. at 2089.

[4] *Id.*

[5] *Id.* at 2089–92 (noting the possibility that subsequent proceedings in the matter would resolve the case or, at least, be reviewable in the Supreme Court).

[6] *Id.* at 2090.

Medellin therefore has raised, without resolving, a particularly interesting question: whether the president, acting unilaterally pursuant to his foreign affairs power, can order states to alter their judicial procedures. The issue, while avoided by the justices this time, may well return to the Supreme Court, as the losing party at the state level may be unwilling to acquiesce in its loss.

If the Court has to revisit the case, it will face three related issues. The first is whether the ICJ correctly interpreted the Vienna Convention on Consular Relations[7] (Consular Convention), the treaty at issue, in *Avena* and in the case on which *Avena* principally relied, the *LaGrand Case*[8] (*LaGrand*). The second issue relates to that on which certiorari was granted in *Medellin*: under relevant treaties, what degree of respect is the Supreme Court obliged to accord to the ICJ decisions in *Avena* and *LaGrand*? Finally, and most fundamentally, Medellin's reliance on the president's memorandum in his state court habeas corpus action may give the Court an opportunity to consider whether the president's authority over foreign affairs extends to directing a state to reopen a case in which a final judgment has been rendered when the president believes that such an action would serve American foreign policy interests, even if that action is not clearly required by treaty. This issue is particularly interesting not only because it raises important questions about the president's foreign affairs power and federalism, but because the United States, in its amicus brief in *Medellin*, rightly took the position that the ICJ misinterpreted the Consular Convention and that American courts had, in any event, no obligation to defer to the ICJ's judgment.[9]

This article will first detail the facts in this matter, and then address each of the three key issues in turn.

II. Facts

On June 24, 1993, Jose Ernesto Medellin participated with others in the rapes and murders of two teenage girls in Texas.[10] He was

---

[7] Apr. 24, 1963, 21 U.S.T. 77, 596 U.N.T.S. 261 [hereinafter Consular Convention].

[8] (F.R.G. v. U.S.), 2001 I.C.J. 466 (June 27), 40 I.L.M. 1068 (2001) [hereinafter LaGrand].

[9] Brief for the United States as Amicus Curiae at 18–38, Medellin v. Dretke, 125 S. Ct. 2088 (2005) (No. 04-5928) [hereinafter U.S. Amicus Brief].

[10] *Id.* at 3–4.

arrested for this crime on June 29, 1993. Medellin is a Mexican national and, upon his arrest and shortly thereafter, made statements to local authorities that should have alerted them to that fact. Nonetheless, he was not informed of his right to consult the Mexican consul, despite the obligation of American authorities to so inform him under Article 36(1)(b) of the Consular Convention,[11] to which both the United States and Mexico are parties. In the fall of 1994, he was convicted in Texas state court of the rapes and murders and sentenced to death; he did not raise the violation of his Consular Convention rights at trial and was therefore barred, under Texas law, from relying on any defense based on that violation in any future proceedings—a proscription known as the procedural default rule.[12] Medellin's conviction and sentence were affirmed on appeal in March 1997. In April 1997, Mexican consular authorities first learned of these events. In March 1998, Medellin filed an application for a writ of habeas corpus in state court in Texas, basing his claim for relief on the denial of his rights under the Consular Convention. The application was denied in October 2001.[13]

Meanwhile, the ICJ decided *LaGrand*, which also involved a failure by American authorities timely to inform two foreign nationals (the LaGrands, of German nationality) of their rights under Article 36(1)(b) of the Consular Convention. In that case, the ICJ held that Article 36 created remedial rights for individual foreign arrestees,[14] including a right to review and reconsideration of any conviction and sentence of a person denied his Article 36 rights, even if that person had defaulted on that defense under the procedural rules of the country in which he had been tried.[15] The ICJ's interpretation of the Consular Convention in *LaGrand* implied that Jose Medellin might also have a right to review and reconsideration of his conviction, notwithstanding the Texas procedural default rule.

---

[11] Consular Convention, *supra* note 7, art. 36(1)(b), 21 U.S.T. at 100–01.

[12] U.S. Amicus Brief, *supra* note 9, at 4.

[13] Brief for Petitioner at 5–7, Medellin v. Dretke, 125 S. Ct. 2088 (2005) (No. 04-5928) [hereinafter Petitioner's Brief].

[14] LaGrand, *supra* note 8, at ¶¶ 75–77.

[15] *Id.* at ¶¶ 79–91.

Medellin filed a petition for a writ of habeas corpus in a U.S. district court in Texas in November 2001, and an amended petition in July 2002. He argued that the district court was bound by the *LaGrand* interpretation of the Consular Convention and that he was therefore entitled to an evidentiary hearing, notwithstanding Texas' procedural default rules. The district court denied both relief and a certificate of appealability in June 2003.[16]

Mexico also filed a claim against the United States in the ICJ, asserting that Medellin and fifty-three other Mexicans, convicted and sentenced to death by courts in nine states, had been denied their rights under Article 36(1)(b).[17] The ICJ decided Mexico's claim in *Avena*, holding that Medellin and fifty of the other persons for whom Mexico had sought relief were entitled to (preferably judicial) review and reconsideration of their convictions in light of the Consular Convention violations and without regard to any procedural defaults.[18]

Medellin had sought a certificate of appealability from the U.S. Court of Appeals for the Fifth Circuit in October 2003. In its judgment of May 20, 2004, that court took note of the *Avena* judgment, but nonetheless held that it was inconsistent with circuit and Supreme Court precedent, including *Breard v. Greene*,[19] a 1998 decision in which the Supreme Court rejected another challenge under the Consular Convention to a state procedural default rule in a death penalty case. In light of this contrary precedent, the Fifth Circuit ruled that *Avena* did not control and denied relief.[20] Medellin subsequently sought review in the Supreme Court.[21] While the case was pending, President Bush issued his memorandum directing the courts of the states to provide the persons named in the *Avena* judgment with review and reconsideration of their sentences.[22]

---

[16] Petitioner's Brief, *supra* note 13, at 7–9.
[17] *Avena, supra* note 2, at ¶¶ 1–7, 14, 15.
[18] *Id.* at ¶¶ 128–143.
[19] 523 U.S. 371 (1998).
[20] Petitioner's Brief, *supra* note 13, at 13.
[21] *Id.*
[22] U.S. Amicus Brief, *supra* note 9, at 41–42.

III. The Consular Convention

The first issue this paper analyzes is the proper interpretation of the Consular Convention.[23] Since, as noted above,[24] *Avena* simply repeated *LaGrand*'s conclusions regarding that treaty, the analysis must focus on the reasoning in *LaGrand*.

A. *The* LaGrand *Decision*

The first step in the ICJ's *LaGrand* analysis was determining the entities upon whom Article 36 conferred rights. The Court, rejecting

[23] That treaty provides, in relevant part:

[Preamble]
The States Parties to the present Convention . . .
Realizing that the purpose of [consular] privileges and immunities is not to benefit individuals but to ensure efficient performance of functions by consular posts . . . .

Article 36
Communication and contact with nationals of the sending State
1. With a view to facilitating the exercise of consular functions relating to nationals of the sending State:
(a) consular officers shall be free to communicate with nationals of the sending State and to have access to them. Nationals of the sending State shall have the same freedom with respect to communication with and access to consular officers of the sending State;
(b) if he so requests, the competent authorities of the receiving State shall, without delay, inform the consular post of the sending State if, within its consular district, a national of that State is arrested or committed to prison or to custody pending trial or is detained in any other manner . . . . The said authorities shall inform the person concerned without delay of his rights under this sub-paragraph;
(c) consular officers shall have the right to visit a national of the sending State who is in prison, custody or detention, to converse and correspond with him and to arrange for his legal representation. They shall also have the right to visit any national of the sending State who is in prison, custody or detention in their district in pursuance of a judgment. Nevertheless, consular officers shall refrain from taking action on behalf of a national who is in prison, custody or detention if he expressly opposes such action.
2. The rights referred to in paragraph 1 of this Article shall be exercised in conformity with the laws and regulations of the receiving State, subject to the proviso, however, that the said laws and regulations must enable full effect to be given to the purposes for which the rights accorded under this Article are intended.
Consular Convention, *supra* note 7, Preamble & art. 36, 21 U.S.T. at 79, 100–01.

[24] See discussion *supra* note 8 and accompanying text.

American arguments to the contrary,[25] held that Article 36 conferred rights on individuals, not simply on states. It relied for this conclusion on the Article's statement that "authorities shall inform the person concerned without delay of his rights" to consular assistance and on its prohibition on providing consular assistance to a person who "expressly opposes" receiving such aid.[26] Both statements, reasoned the ICJ, would make little sense unless the Convention conferred a right to a remedy for treaty violations on individuals, and not simply on states who had signed the treaty.

After making this determination, the court addressed whether procedural default rules violated Article 36 in cases where affected persons had not been informed of their Article 36 rights in time to raise a treaty violation as a defense. The court rejected the American argument that procedural default rules were permitted by a fair reading of the Convention, asserting that the American argument "proceed[ed], in part, on the assumption that paragraph 2 of Article 36 applies only to the rights of the sending State and not also to those of the detained individual."[27] The court went on to state:

> The procedural default rule prevented counsel for the LaGrands . . . from attaching any legal significance to the fact . . . that the violation of the rights set forth in Article 36, paragraph 1, prevented Germany, in a timely fashion, from retaining private counsel for them and otherwise assisting in their defence as provided for by the Convention. Under these circumstances, the procedural default rule had the effect of preventing "full effect [from being] given to the purposes for which the rights accorded under this article are intended," and thus violated paragraph 2 of Article 36.[28]

B. The Entities upon Whom the Convention Confers Remedial Rights

To analyze the ICJ's reasoning, we can rely on Articles 31 and 32 of the Vienna Convention on the Law of Treaties[29] (Treaties Convention), which the ICJ, in *LaGrand*[30] and *Avena*,[31] treated as a source of customary rules of treaty interpretation.

[25] LaGrand, *supra* note 8, at ¶ 76.

[26] *Id.* at ¶ 77. See also Consular Convention, *supra* note 7, art. 36(2), 21 U.S.T. at 100–01.

[27] LaGrand, *supra* note 8, at ¶ 89.

[28] *Id.* at ¶ 91.

[29] May 23, 1969, arts. 31, 32, U.N. Doc. A/CONF. 39/27, 8 I.L.M. 679, 691–92 (1969) [hereinafter Treaties Convention].

[30] LaGrand, *supra* note 8, at ¶ 99.

[31] Avena, *supra* note 2, at ¶ 83.

Applying the Vienna Convention standards, it would seem that *LaGrand* is incorrect. Consider first whether the Consular Convention should be seen as creating rights for individuals and not simply for states. Article 31(1) of the Treaties Convention makes clear that the primary focus in any effort at treaty interpretation must be the terms of the treaty.[32] As discussed, the ICJ focused on the appearance of the term "rights" in the last sentence of Article 36(1)(b) of the Consular Convention. Yet, the ICJ ignored other, contrary textual evidence: For example, the chapeau of Article 36(1), with its characterization of that provision as aimed at facilitating the exercise of state consular functions,[33] cuts against the court's reading. Likewise, the statement, in the Consular Convention's preamble, that benefitting individuals is not a purpose of that treaty counts against the Court's conclusion— and Article 31(2) of the Treaties Convention makes clear that the text of a treaty's preamble must be taken into account when interpreting the instrument.[34]

Article 32 of the Treaties Convention permits consideration of the preparatory work of a treaty (the international law analogue to "legislative history") both to confirm conclusions reached through examination of the treaty's text and to determine the treaty's meaning in cases where the text leads either to ambiguities or absurdities.[35] As the United States pointed out to the ICJ in *LaGrand*,[36] the negotiating history of the Consular Convention makes clear that there was deep division among the delegations as to whether Article 36 should be seen as conferring individual, as opposed to state, rights.[37] Indeed, the Article's original wording was changed in response to objections that it gave primacy to the rights of individuals.[38]

---

[32] Treaties Convention, *supra* note 29, art. 31(3), 8 I.L.M. at 691–92.

[33] Consular Convention, *supra* note 7, art. 36(1), 21 U.S.T. at 100.

[34] Treaties Convention, *supra* note 29, art. 31(2), 8 I.L.M. at 692.

[35] *Id.*, art. 32, 8 I.L.M. at 692.

[36] LaGrand (F.R.G v. U.S.), Counter-Memorial of the U.S., ¶ 100, available from the ICJ website, http://www.icj-cij.org/icjwww/idocket/igus/igusframe.htm (last visited Jul. 2, 2005) [hereinafter LaGrand Counter-Memorial].

[37] 1 Official Records, U.N. Conference on Consular Relations 331–36, U.N. Doc. A/CONF.25/16 (1963) [hereinafter Consular Conference Records].

[38] *Id.* at 334–36.

C. Status of Procedural Default Rules

The court's reasoning in support of its conclusion regarding Article 36's creation of individual rights is thus doubtful. More important to its result was the ICJ's conclusion that a state violates the Consular Convention when it applies a procedural default rule to bar untimely assertions of defenses based on violations of the treaty's provisions regarding consular assistance. This second conclusion is even more weakly grounded than the first.

It facilitates understanding of this point to restate the court's reasoning. The chain of logic appears to be: (1) one of the purposes of the Convention was to permit nations the option of providing their nationals, when arrested, with legal assistance; (2) violations of the Convention's notice requirements prevented Germany from providing timely legal assistance to the LaGrands; (3) the procedural default rule, in turn, prevented the LaGrands from raising these treaty violations as a defense to the charges they faced; therefore, (4) the procedural default rule violated the Convention, by failing to give full effect to one of the purposes of the treaty, that is, permitting the "sending nation" (the nation from which foreign nationals on trial hale) to provide its nationals with legal aid.

So stated, there is an obvious problem with the court's reasoning: step three makes sense only if the Convention is understood to regulate the remedies available under domestic law when a host country fails to comply with its treaty obligations. But it does not. Article 36(1), which enumerates the rights to consular assistance afforded by the Convention, says nothing about post-deprivation remedies.[39] To reach its conclusion, the ICJ effectively argues that *any* laws and regulations of the host country that interfere with the general *purposes* underlying the provisions governing consular assistance violate the Convention, whether or not those laws and regulations address the rights to assistance expressly created by paragraph 1 of Article 36. Thus, the ICJ reasons that laws and regulations preventing a foreign national from asserting defenses based on late access to consular legal assistance interfere with one overarching purpose of Article 36(1)(c), that is, affording legal assistance.

To be sure, Article 36(2) states that rights to consular assistance "shall be exercised in conformity with the laws and regulations

[39] See *supra* notes 7 & 23.

of the receiving State," and requires, in turn, that these laws and regulations give "full effect" to the purposes "for which the rights accorded under this Article are intended."[40] But that provision's focus on the "rights accorded *under this Article*" underscores that it offers no support for the *LaGrand* holding. Again, Article 36 creates no right to a post-deprivation remedy. Thus, the better reading of Article 36(2) is that the specific assistance rights created by the treaty must be exercised according to host country law, and, in turn, *only those specific laws and regulations directly affecting the rights* created by the Article (for example, rules restricting the duration of prison visits) are governed by the treaty. By contrast, the ICJ reads the proviso of Article 36(2) as though the "laws and regulations" in question include the entire corpus of host country law, not merely those provisions affecting rights expressly granted.

There is another error in the ICJ's analysis. Article 31(3)(b) of the Treaties Convention provides, "There *shall* be taken into account . . . any subsequent practice in the application of the treaty which establishes the agreement of the parties regarding its interpretation . . . ."[41] This language reflects an obvious point: because treaties are agreements that nations create and to which nations may adhere or not as they choose, a treaty means what the signatory parties think it means. Since the ICJ's interpretation does not derive from the express terms of the treaty, it would seem that the court would have carefully examined the parties' practice to resolve disputes about the meaning of Article 36. Yet it failed to do so.

The United States called actual state practice to the attention of the court,[42] relying on an affidavit by an official of the U.S. Department of State's Bureau of Consular Affairs, which provided:

> States party have not viewed Article 36 as requiring them to provide remedies in their criminal justice systems for failures to provide required consular notification. Roughly 165 States are party to the Vienna Convention. Nevertheless, the United States survey did not identify any State that provides a status quo ante remedy of vacating a criminal conviction or commuting a sentence for failure of consular notification.

---

[40] Consular Convention, *supra* note 7, art. 36(2), 21 U.S.T. at 100–01.

[41] Treaties Convention, *supra* note 29, art. 31(2), 8 I.L.M. at 692 (emphasis added).

[42] LaGrand Counter-Memorial, *supra* note 36, at ¶¶ 92–93.

> . . . Nor have we identified any country that has an established judicial remedy authorizing a foreign government to seek to undo a conviction and sentence through action in domestic courts because of a failure of notification.[43]

The court ignored this evidence; it referred only to a portion of the affidavit discussing Germany's practice in these matters and did so only in the course of rejecting American arguments regarding the inadmissability of Germany's claim,[44] even though the United States had not referenced state practice in its arguments regarding inadmissability.[45]

In addition to its failure properly to apply the interpretive methods prescribed by Article 31 of the Treaties Convention, the court failed to consider the preparatory work of the Consular Convention, as Article 32 of the Treaties Convention requires, notwithstanding the lack of express textual support for the court's reading of Article 36. This is important because, as the United States pointed out in its memorial, the records of the negotiations that produced the Consular Convention undercut any suggestion that it was intended to create a remedy in domestic criminal proceedings for violations of the last sentence of Article 36(1)(b).[46]

In the first place, the commentary accompanying the original draft of Article 36 makes clear that the laws and regulations of the host country addressed in Article 36(2) are those pertaining to such matters as visits to and correspondence with a person in custody.[47] Further, the records of the negotiations demonstrate that the last sentence of Article 36(1)(b)—stating that authorities "shall inform" the person of their rights to consular assistance—was added very late in the negotiating process to address an impasse. A number of delegations believed that a host country should be obliged to inform

---

[43] Declaration of Edward Betancourt, U.S. Dept. of State, LaGrand Counter-Memorial, *supra* note 36, Ex. 8 (copy in possession of author).

[44] LaGrand, *supra* note 8, at ¶¶ 61–63.

[45] See LaGrand Counter-Memorial, *supra* note 36, at ¶¶ 46–66.

[46] *Id.* at ¶¶ 80–81, 88–90.

[47] Report of the International Law Commission to the General Assembly, 16 U.N. GAOR Supp. (No. 9) at 24–25, U.N. Doc. A/4843 (1961), reprinted in [1961] 2 Y.B. Int'l Law Comm'n 112–13, U.N. Doc. A/CN.4/SER.A/1961/Add.1.

a sending country's consulate whenever one of that country's nationals is taken into custody, at least in those cases where the detainee did not expressly oppose the consulate's being informed. Other delegations feared that such an obligation would be too onerous for some nations and favored requiring that a consulate be informed of a detention only at the request of the detainee. This second approach was opposed on the ground that individuals might be unaware of their rights to contact the consul. The United Kingdom proposed adding the last sentence to paragraph 1(b) to ensure that all arrested persons would know of their rights and thus eliminate an objection to the second approach, by addressing the issue in a way that would impose a relatively *limited* administrative burden on host countries.[48] The court's reading of that sentence, however, has the effect of *increasing* the administrative burden on host countries, since it reads into the Article consequences for a host country's criminal justice system never contemplated by the delegates to the Vienna Conference.

From the perspective of an American court, it is also relevant that the Senate consented to ratification of the Consular Convention and Optional Protocol on two bases. First, the Senate relied on a committee report stating that ratification would not change American law.[49] And, second, the Senate relied on a report from the American delegation to the conference that produced the Consular Convention, which stressed (1) that paragraph 2 of Article 36 was intended to emphasize that the Article did not override a host state's law and (2) that the last sentence of that paragraph required full effect be given to the rights *expressly* set out in Article 36(1) (not, as the ICJ had it, to the implicit purposes for establishing the rights).[50]

Taking the parts of this discussion together, it is clear that the ICJ in *LaGrand* misread Article 36. It was probably not intended to create individually enforceable rights, and certainly was not properly interpreted as in effect superseding the procedural requirements of the criminal justice systems of the states party to the treaty. Since *Avena* simply relies on *LaGrand*, its holding, too, seems wrong.

---

[48] See Consular Conference Records, *supra* note 37, at 81–87.

[49] S. Exec. Rep. 91-9, 91st Cong., 1st Sess. 2 (1969).

[50] S. Exec. E., 91st Cong., 1st Sess. 61 (1969).

IV. American Courts and ICJ Judgments

In *Medellin*, the petitioner's argument regarding the effect of the *Avena* judgment was simple: because the United States had, through an Optional Protocol[51] to the Consular Convention, accepted the compulsory jurisdiction of the ICJ, the federal courts were obliged to implement the ICJ's judgment, and the lower courts therefore should have granted Medellin the relief he sought.[52]

It is true that, as a matter of international law, the United States must comply with *Avena*. The ICJ Statute provides that ICJ judgments are final and binding.[53] Article 94 of the United Nations Charter further provides that members of the U.N. undertake to comply with such judgments.[54] Since these instruments are treaties as a matter of international law, the United States has an international legal obligation in this case.

The question remains, however, whether fulfilling that obligation requires American courts to enforce *Avena*. Because treaty obligations are not automatically enforceable in domestic courts,[55] answering that question requires addressing another: do the Optional Protocol and/or Article 94 in and of themselves require the court systems of states party to enforce ICJ judgments?

It should first be noted that the terms of the Optional Protocol make clear that the Protocol is simply an agreement among signatory states that the ICJ will have jurisdiction to hear cases between states party arising from disputes concerning the Consular Convention[56]

---

[51] Optional Protocol to the Vienna Convention on Consular Relations Concerning the Compulsory Settlement of Disputes, Apr. 24, 1963, 21 U.S.T. 325, 596 U.N.T.S. 488 [hereinafter Optional Protocol].

[52] Petitioner's Brief, *supra* note 13, at 18–45.

[53] Statute of the International Court of Justice, June 26, 1945, arts. 59, 60, 59 Stat. 1055, 1062, 1063, 39 A.J.I.L. Supp. 215 (1945) [hereinafter ICJ Statute].

[54] U.N. Charter, art. 94.

[55] See Foster v. Neilson, 27 U.S. (2 Pet.) 253, 314–15 (1829).

[56] Optional Protocol, *supra* note 51, art. I, 21 U.S.T. at 326. The ICJ's jurisdiction over claims by countries against other countries is entirely consensual; nations may agree specially to take a case to the court after a dispute arises, or may agree to do so in advance of any dispute, either by entering into a treaty—such as the Optional Protocol—providing that specific disputes would fall within the ICJ's competence or by a general acceptance of its "compulsory" jurisdiction. See ICJ Statute, *supra* note 53, art. 36, 59 Stat. at 1062.

and has no bearing on questions regarding enforcement of judgments in such cases. This reading is confirmed by its drafting history.[57] The ICJ Statute is also silent with respect to enforcement of its judgments. The only treaty provision addressing enforcement of ICJ judgments is Article 94 of the United Nations Charter, which provides:

1. Each Member of the United Nations undertakes to comply with the decision of the International Court of Justice in any case to which it is a party.
2. If any party to a case fails to perform the obligations incumbent upon it under a judgment rendered by the Court, the other party may have recourse to the Security Council, which may, if it deems necessary, make recommendations or decide upon measures to be taken to give effect to the judgment.[58]

The meaning of this Article is somewhat ambiguous. While the phrase "undertakes to comply" in paragraph 1 can be read to impose an unequivocal obligation on each signatory state, the phrasing normally employed for that purpose would be "shall comply." Further, the discretion accorded the Security Council in paragraph 2 regarding enforcement of judgments fits uneasily with the idea that states are obliged to execute ICJ judgments through their domestic court systems.

Domestic judicial practice seems to clarify this issue, however. There appear to be no cases in which a domestic court has seen itself as obliged to enforce decisions of the ICJ or of its predecessor, the Permanent Court of International Justice (PCIJ). Thus, in *"Socobel" v. Greek State*,[59] a Belgian court refused to permit a private party to execute in Belgium a PCIJ judgment unless the claimant followed the procedures necessary for executing judgments of foreign courts. The court rejected the argument that the PCIJ should simply be treated as a tribunal superior to those of Belgium, with its judgments executable as though they were domestic judgments.[60] It also held

---

[57] Consular Conference Records, *supra* note 37, at 87–92.
[58] U.N. Charter, art. 94.
[59] 18 I.L.R. 3 (Belg., Trib. Civ. de Bruxelles 1951).
[60] *Id.* at 4–5.

that, as a non-party to the judgment, the private party had no standing to seek its execution, even though the judgment required that a payment be made to the private party.[61]

The records of the negotiations of both the Charter and the ICJ Statute reinforce the conclusion that domestic courts are not necessarily obliged to enforce ICJ judgments. At no point in these sets of negotiations was any consideration given to domestic judicial enforcement of ICJ judgments. Rather, the question was whether there was a need to address enforcement of judgments at all. It appears to have been taken for granted that, if the Charter were to address enforcement, such enforcement would be carried out by the Security Council.[62]

Particularly relevant for American courts is the United States Senate's understanding when it consented to ratification of the U.N. Charter and consented to the compulsory jurisdiction of the ICJ. In the ratification hearings, there was clear executive branch testimony that ICJ judgments could only be enforced by the Security Council.[63] Further, in the debate on acceptance of compulsory jurisdiction, Senator Connally offered an amendment providing that American consent to jurisdiction did not apply to matters within the domestic jurisdiction of the United States as determined by the United States.[64] In the ensuing discussion, opponents of the amendment argued that Senator Connally's amendment was unnecessary, since the limitation was inherent in the ICJ's jurisdiction and, if the ICJ exceeded its jurisdiction in any particular case, the judgment could only be

---

[61] *Id.* Similar but distinguishable is *Committee of U.S. Citizens Living in Nicaragua v. Reagan*, 859 F.2d 929 (D.C. Cir. 1988). The court in that case held that Article 94 of the U.N. Charter did not confer rights on individuals having no relationship to an ICJ judgment to enforce that judgment, *id.* at 937–38; by contrast, both *Socobel* and *Medellín* involve claims by, respectively, a corporation and an individual who are the subjects of ICJ judgments.

[62] United Nations Information Organization, 13 Documents of the United Nations Conference on International Organization, San Francisco, 1945, at 297–98; *id.*, vol. 14 at 209, 853.

[63] The Charter of the United Nations: Hearings Before the Senate Comm. on Foreign Relations, 79th Cong., 1st Sess. 286 (1945) (statement of Leo Pasvolsky, Special Assistant to the Secretary of State); Hearings on S. Res. 196 Before a Subcomm. of the Senate Comm. on Foreign Relations, 79th Cong., 2d Sess. 142 (1946) (statement of Charles Fahy, Legal Advisor of the Department of State).

[64] 92 Cong. Rec. 10694–95 (1946).

enforced in the Security Council, where the United States had a veto.[65] Supporters of the amendment agreed with opponents regarding the means of enforcing ICJ judgments, but argued for avoiding a situation in which the United States would be forced to exercise its veto.[66] Had any Senator contemplated that acceptance of the ICJ's jurisdiction obliged American courts to enforce its judgments, the debate would necessarily have taken a different course.

Finally, it is relevant that leading commentators agree that a state's submission to the ICJ's jurisdiction does not necessarily render its judgments binding in that state's domestic legal system. Mosler asserts that, while a state's failure to comply with a judgment of the court engages its international responsibility, its courts and other organs of government "are not directly obliged by virtue of the judgment unless a direct obligation is provided for in the constitutional law of the state concerned."[67] And the American Society of International Law's Panel on the Future of the International Court of Justice recommended, in 1973, that states parties to the statute of the court "make provision in their domestic law for the execution of decisions rendered by the Court,"[68] a suggestion that makes sense only if adherence to the statute of the court did not, by itself, require states to execute ICJ judgments in their domestic court systems.

Moreover, consideration of the general approach to enforcement of the judgments of international tribunals reinforces the conclusion that Article 94 should not be read as, in itself, modifying the domestic law of U.N. members to require execution of ICJ judgments. The General Act on Pacific Settlement of International Disputes[69] required parties to submit disputes either to arbitration or to the PCIJ.[70] Similarly, the Revised General Act for the Pacific Settlement of International Disputes[71] requires parties to either arbitrate disputes or

---

[65] *Id.* at 10694 (statement of Sen. Pepper).

[66] *Id.* at 10695 (statement of Sen. Connally).

[67] Hermann Mosler, Article 94, in The Charter of the United Nations 1003, 1005 (Bruno Simma ed., 1995).

[68] Leo Gross, Chapter 18: Conclusions, in 2 The Future of the International Court of Justice 727, 731–32 (Leo Gross ed., 1976). But cf. 1 Shabtai Rosenne, The Law and Practice of the International Court 1920–1996, at 223–26 (1997).

[69] Sept. 26, 1928, 93 L.N.T.S. 343 [hereinafter General Act].

[70] *Id.*, art. 17, 93 L.N.T.S. at 351.

[71] Apr. 28, 1949, 71 U.N.T.S. 101 [hereinafter Revised General Act].

submit them to the ICJ.[72] Yet both make provision for the possibility that the domestic law of states party could preclude domestic execution of these courts' judgments.[73] Twenty-two countries are parties to one or the other of these treaties,[74] and the Revised General Act was approved by the General Assembly in a vote of 45-6-1,[75] suggesting that a large number of nations agree that a country's acceptance of an international tribunal's jurisdiction does not, without more, render that tribunal's judgments enforceable domestically. Furthermore, a number of dispute settlement treaties, both bilateral and multilateral, provide that an international judgment or arbitral award may include "equitable satisfaction" for a party harmed because a country's domestic law precludes execution of the judgment or arbitral award.[76]

Nor is it assumed that acceptance of the jurisdiction of other international tribunals entails domestic enforcement of the judgments of those tribunals. Though judgments of the European Court of Human Rights are final,[77] they are enforceable in the domestic courts of nations subject to that court's jurisdiction only if those nations' domestic law authorizes enforcement.[78] Similarly, although the instrument establishing the Iran–United States Claims Tribunal[79]

[72] *Id.*, art. 17, 71 U.N.T.S. at 110.

[73] General Act, *supra* note 69, art. 32, 93 L.N.T.S. at 357; Revised General Act, *supra* note 71, art. 32, 71 U.N.T.S. at 118.

[74] For the General Act, see 2 Peter H. Rohn, World Treaty Index 165 (2d ed. 1983); for the Revised General Act, see United Nations, Multilateral Treaties Deposited with the Secretary-General as at 31 Dec. 2003, at 39, U.N. Doc. ST/LEG/SER.E/22, U.N. Sales No. E.04.V2 (2004).

[75] United Nations, Yearbook of the United Nations 1948–49, at 415, U.N. Sales No. 1950.I.II (1950).

[76] Treaty of Friendship Conciliation and Judicial Settlement, Mar. 24, 1950, Turk.-Italy, art. 20, 96 U.N.T.S. 207, 219; Agreement Concerning Conciliation and Judicial Settlement, Nov. 24, 1954, Italy-Brazil, art. 18, 284 U.N.T.S. 325, 334; European Convention for the Peaceful Settlement of Disputes, Apr. 29, 1957, art. 30, 320 U.N.T.S. 243, 256.

[77] European Convention for the Protection of Human Rights and Fundamental Freedoms, Nov. 4, 1950, art. 44, 213 U.N.T.S. 221, E.T.S. 5, as amended by Protocol No. 3, E.T.S. 45; Protocol No. 5, E.T.S 55; Protocol No. 8, E.T.S. 118; and Protocol No. 11, E.T.S. 155.

[78] Rudolf Bernhardt, The Convention in Domestic Law, The European System for the Protection of Human Rights 25, 37–38 (R. St. J. MacDonald et al. eds., 1993).

[79] Declaration of the Government of the Democratic and Popular Republic of Algeria Concerning the Settlement of Claims by the Government of the United States of

provides that "[a]ll decisions and awards of the Tribunal are final and binding,"[80] the tribunal has not read that language to render its awards domestically enforceable. It has stated:

> It is . . . incumbent on each State Party to provide some procedure or mechanism whereby enforcement may be obtained within its national jurisdiction, and to ensure that the successful Party has access thereto. If procedures did not already exist as part of the State's legal system they would have to be established, by means of legislation or other appropriate measures. Such procedures must be available on a basis at least as favorable as that allowed to parties who seek recognition or enforcement of foreign arbitral awards.[81]

That is, the tribunal assumes that the agreement by the United States and Iran that its decisions would be final and binding does not, of its own force, create a domestic legal obligation to enforce those decisions; any international legal obligation requires only that tribunal awards have the same standing as arbitration awards. One American court[82] cited this language in refusing to enforce a tribunal decision for reasons drawn from arbitral practice.[83] Of course, there are international tribunals whose judgments are directly enforceable in the courts of the countries subject to their jurisdiction, but in such cases, the treaty establishing the tribunal expressly provides for such enforcement.[84] Neither the ICJ Statute nor the United Nations Charter contains such language.

In sum, there is no support for the argument that adherence to the United Nations Charter creates a domestic law obligation for American courts to enforce ICJ judgments. The language of Article 94 is at best ambiguous on this point, and the drafting history of

America and the Government of the Islamic Republic of Iran, Dept. of State Bulletin, February 1981, at 3; 20 I.L.M. 230 (1981) [hereinafter Iran Executive Agreement].

[80] *Id.,* art. IV.1, Dept. of State Bulletin, February 1981, at 4; 20 I.L.M. at 232.

[81] Islamic Republic of Iran v. United States of America, Case No. A21, Decision No. Dec. 62-A21-FT, at 13–14 (Iran–United States Claims Tribunal, May 4, 1987), 14 Iran-U.S. Cl. Trib. Rep. 324, 331–32.

[82] Iran Aircraft Industries v. Avco Corp., 980 F.2d 141, 145 (2d Cir. 1992).

[83] *Id.* at 145–46.

[84] Consolidated Version of the Treaty Establishing the European Community, Dec. 24, 2002, O.J. (C 325), Articles 228, 244, 256; American Convention on Human Rights, Nov. 22, 1969, art. 68, 9 I.L.M. 99, 119 (1970), OAS T.S. No. 36.

that Article, the ratification debates in the Senate concerning it, and the views of commentators all argue against the existence of any such obligation. Likewise, international practice with respect to international tribunals generally is inconsistent with the argument.

It should also be noted that there is little support for any argument that ICJ decisions constitute binding precedent for domestic courts. While a court in the French Zone of Morocco in 1952 apparently treated an ICJ judgment as binding precedent,[85] its decision was criticized by a court in the International Zone of Morocco, which not only refused to treat the ICJ judgment as binding but rejected its reasoning as well.[86] Similarly, while Japanese[87] and Italian[88] courts dealing with legal issues addressed by the ICJ in *Anglo-Iranian Oil Co.*[89] reached results consistent with that decision, they cited that judgment as supporting, rather than as controlling, their conclusions. Indeed, such results seem compelled by Article 59 of the ICJ Statute, which provides, "The decision of the Court has no binding force except between the parties and in respect of that particular case."[90]

There remains the question whether American courts, though not bound either to enforce *Avena* or to treat it as binding precedent, should nonetheless consider it and *LaGrand* as persuasive authority. And of course they should—if they are persuaded. American courts have applied that standard in similar situations,[91] and it is consistent with the Court's refusal in *Breard v. Greene*[92] to simply accept the ICJ's interpretation of the Consular Convention in related proceedings.[93] Since, as was demonstrated in the preceding section, the ICJ's *Avena* and *LaGrand* decisions are seriously flawed, their persuasive power

---

[85] Administration des Habous v. Deal, 19 I.L.R. 342 (Morocco, Ct. App. Rabat 1952).

[86] Mackay Radio and Telegraph Co. v. Lal-la Fatma Bent si Mohamed el Khadar et al., 21 I.L.R. 136 (Tangier, Ct. App. Int'l Trib. 1954).

[87] Anglo-Iranian Oil Co. v. Idimitsu Kosan Kabushiki Kaisha, 20 I.L.R. 305 (Japan, High Ct. Tokyo 1953).

[88] Anglo-Iranian Oil Co. v. S.U.P.O.R. Co., 22 I.L.R. 23 (Italy, Civ. Ct. Rome 1954).

[89] (U.K. v. Iran), 1952 I.C.J. 22 (July 22).

[90] ICJ Statute, *supra* note 53, art. 59.

[91] See, e.g., Timken Co. v. United States, 240 F. Supp. 2d 1228, 1239–42 (Ct. Int'l Trade 2002), aff'd, 354 F.3d 1334, 1344 (Fed. Cir. 2004).

[92] 523 U.S. 371 (1998).

[93] *Id.* at 375–76.

ought to be low. Regarding Medellin's argument from uniform treaty interpretation, other states apparently read the Consular Convention as the United States did prior to *LaGrand*.[94] The ICJ's adoption of a doubtful interpretation of the treaty hardly establishes otherwise.

In short, courts in the United States are obliged neither to enforce ICJ judgments nor treat them as binding precedent. If the reasoning in those judgments is persuasive, all things being equal, there is no reason not to take them into account. By the same token, however, there is no reason to defer to the ICJ if its reasoning is not persuasive—which it is not.

V. The President's Directive

Notwithstanding the weakness of the ICJ's interpretation of the Consular Convention, the president has purported, pursuant to his inherent "foreign affairs" power, to unilaterally direct state courts to abide by the *Avena* judgment. The amicus brief of the United States in *Medellin* asserts that, since the president has directed the courts of the states to enforce *Avena* with respect to persons named in that opinion, Medellin can obtain relief in the Texas courts.[95] The key issue raised by this assertion is whether the president has the authority to direct the states as he has purported to do.

The U.S. amicus brief makes two arguments supporting this claim of authority. The first is that Article 94 of the United Nations Charter not only creates an international legal obligation for the United States to comply with the ruling in *Avena*,[96] but also "implicitly" grants the president "the lead role" in determining how,[97] or indeed whether,[98] to comply with an ICJ decision. The second is that, independently of authority derived from Article 94, the president's constitutional authority to control American foreign policy empowers him to issue his memorandum.[99]

The brief supports its first argument by observing that the executive branch is concerned about possible difficulties in providing

---

[94] See discussion *supra* note 43.
[95] U.S. Amicus Brief, *supra* note 9, at 9.
[96] *Id.* at 38–40.
[97] *Id.*
[98] *Id.* at 40–41.
[99] *Id.* at 45.

consular assistance to Americans abroad if American courts refuse compliance with *Avena*[100] and by stating that this concern led the president to issue his directive.[101] The brief justifies the president's decision to act without seeking implementing legislation by reference to the interplay between the Consular Convention and the president's duty of protecting American citizens abroad, and to the "complex calculations" that figure into decisions as to the proper American response to *Avena*.[102]

The amicus brief bases its argument regarding the president's constitutional authority over foreign policy on general language from a number of cases, including *American Insurance Association v. Garamendi*,[103] *Youngstown Sheet & Tube Co. v. Sawyer*,[104] and *United States v. Curtiss-Wright Export Corp.*[105] The brief then cites *Dames & Moore v. Regan*,[106] *Garamendi*,[107] *United States v. Pink*,[108] and *United States v. Belmont*[109] for the propositions that the president has the authority to make executive agreements with other countries to settle claims and, relying on the latter three, that such agreements preempt state law.[110] The amicus brief asserts that the president therefore has the authority to resolve a dispute with a foreign government without entering into a formal agreement, since such governments may acquiesce in arrangements to which they would not affirmatively agree, since a situation may demand action more quickly than would be possible if an agreement had to be negotiated first, and since the requirement of an agreement would permit the foreign government to control the president's exercise of his Article II authority.[111]

---

[100] *Id.* at 41.

[101] *Id.* at 41–42 (quoting Memorandum for the Attorney General from President George W. Bush, Feb. 28, 2005, at 1aa).

[102] *Id.* at 42–43.

[103] 539 U.S. 396, 414 (2003).

[104] 343 U.S. 579, 610–11 (1952).

[105] 299 U.S. 304, 320 (1936).

[106] 453 U.S. 654, 679, 682–83 (1981).

[107] Garamendi, 539 U.S. at 415.

[108] 315 U.S. 203, 223 (1942).

[109] 301 U.S. 324, 330–31 (1937).

[110] U.S. Amicus Brief, *supra* note 9, at 45.

[111] *Id.* at 45–46.

The brief takes the position that state courts, pursuant to the order issued by President Bush, must focus solely on whether the individuals named in *Avena* suffered prejudice because they were denied their rights under Article 36 of the Consular Convention.[112] It also stresses, however, that these limitations apply only to the persons whose rights were adjudicated in *Avena;* courts in other cases would be free to reject *Avena*'s interpretation of the Consular Convention, in light of both the limitations of Article 59 of the ICJ Statute[113] and the rule that non-mutual collateral estoppel may not be asserted against the United States.[114] The amicus brief concludes by explaining that the position taken by the United States is not inconsistent with *Breard,* which held that the procedural default rule is not barred by the Consular Convention.[115] The brief explains that, although the United States unequivocally accepts *Breard*'s interpretation of that treaty, the president has decided that enforcing *Avena* is in the foreign policy interest of the United States nonetheless; it also asserts that *Breard* is no more a barrier to the implementation of the president's directive than it would be to enforcement of a statute providing that *Avena* be enforced.[116]

Analyzing this claim of presidential power requires understanding its sweep. The president is seeking to make procedural rules for state courts (that is, to legislate) and to cause cases that have gone to final judgment to be reopened (that is, to exercise judicial power). Further, the president is at pains to say that the persons who would benefit from his actions would not be entitled under the Constitution, laws, or treaties of the United States to relief but for his decision to grant it. Also, nothing in the amicus brief suggests any principle limiting the president's authority. His position seems to be that he may order the states to alter their law in any way whatever if he concludes that such alterations would further the foreign policy interests of the United States or, at least, help resolve an international dispute.

---

[112] *Id.* at 46.

[113] ICJ Statute, *supra* note 53, art. 59.

[114] U.S. Amicus Brief, *supra* note 9, at 46–47.

[115] Breard v. Greene, 523 U.S. 371, 375–76 (1998).

[116] U.S. Amicus Brief, *supra* note 9, at 48.

The amicus brief's arguments supporting these sweeping assertions of power are, upon examination, quite weak. First, while the
brief is correct in asserting that the United States has an international
legal obligation to comply with *Avena*,[117] as noted above,[118] an obligation binding in international law is not necessarily enforceable in
American courts. Indeed, implementation of such an obligation may
actually be forbidden by American law, as when a federal statute,
enacted after a treaty has become effective, requires actions that
violate the treaty.[119] Thus, establishing that the United States is subject to an international obligation does not establish that the United
States government must implement that obligation domestically, or
even that the government is allowed to do so.

Second, the argument that Article 94 implicitly delegates to the
president the power to issue his directive is unfounded. Nothing in
the language of Article 94 evinces any intent to delegate any authority to the president. Further, such an "implied delegation" is necessarily standardless, providing no intelligible principle to guide the
president's discretion, yet the Supreme Court continues to insist that
delegations of authority contain some such guidance, in order to
avoid serious constitutional difficulties.[120] In any event, as noted
above, the Senate consented to American acceptance of the compulsory jurisdiction of the ICJ on the understanding that the only means
for enforcement of ICJ judgments would be action by the Security
Council.[121] Such an understanding is inconsistent with an intention
to confer upon the president legislative and judicial authority to
enforce such judgments.[122]

There remains the argument that the president's constitutional
authority suffices to support his direction to the states. We may set

---

[117] See discussion *supra* notes 53–54.

[118] See discussion *supra* note 55.

[119] Head Money Cases, 112 U.S. 580, 597–99 (1884); Whitney v. Robertson, 124 U.S.
190, 193-95 (1888); Chinese Exclusion Case, 130 U.S. 581, 598–604 (1889).

[120] See Whitman v. American Trucking Associations, Inc., 531 U.S. 457, 472–76 (2001).

[121] See discussion *supra* notes 63–65 and accompanying text.

[122] Irrelevant here but also puzzling is the assertion that the "delegation" to the
president under Article 94 includes the discretion to refuse to comply with ICJ
judgments, U.S. Amicus Brief, *supra* note 9, at 40–41; it is difficult to understand
how Article 94's undertaking to comply with ICJ judgments amounts to an implied
authorization not to comply with those judgments.

to one side cases asserting the proposition that the president is the prime shaper of American foreign policy. That is true, and not helpful, since the question here is whether authority over foreign policy includes authority to determine whether the judgments of the Texas courts are to be treated as final.[123]

More useful are the four cases dealing with claims settlement, since each involved what could be considered legislative action by the president. We consider them in turn.

The disputes in *Pink* and *Belmont* revolved around an executive agreement made in connection with recognition of the Soviet Union by the United States. That agreement transferred to the United States the Soviet Union's rights to certain property within American territory and permitted the United States to apply that property to claims against the Soviet Union and its nationals.[124] State courts had held that recognizing the rights of the Soviet Union in the property, and therefore the rights of the United States derived from those of the Soviet Union, would both violate state public policy, as expressed by courts, and interfere with the vested rights of non-resident aliens to whom distributions had been ordered.[125] In holding that the president had the authority to make such an agreement and that it superseded state law, both cases placed great weight on the fact that the executive agreement was concluded as part of the recognition process.[126] Both also stressed that the challenged actions taken by the president—involving international claims settlement—were clearly within the authority of the federal government.[127] *Pink*, furthermore, emphasized the acquiescence of Congress in the president's action.[128]

Dames & Moore addressed the domestic legal effects of an executive agreement resolving the Iran Hostage Crisis. Under the agreement, a claims tribunal was established to address claims by Americans

---

[123] While *United States v. Curtiss-Wright Export Corp.*, 299 U.S. 304, 316–18 (1936), characterizes presidential foreign affairs authority as very broad, the arguments in that case are so flawed that its authority seems doubtful, see A. Mark Weisburd, International Courts and American Courts, 21 Mich. J. Int'l L. 877, 913–16 (2000).

[124] United States v. Belmont, 301 U.S. 324, 326–28, 330, 332–33 (1937); United States v. Pink, 315 U.S. 203, 211–14, 222–23, 226–30 (1942).

[125] Belmont, 301 U.S. at 327–330; Pink, 315 U.S. at 226–27.

[126] Belmont, 301 U.S. at 330; Pink, 315 U.S. at 228–32.

[127] Belmont, 301 U.S. at 331–32; Pink, 315 U.S. at 230–31.

[128] Pink, 315 U.S. at 227–28.

against the Iranian government and by the Iranian government against the United States and individual Americans.[129] To implement this agreement, Presidents Carter and Reagan issued executive orders (1) effectively seizing previously blocked Iranian government assets and transferring them to an account to be used for paying the tribunal's awards against Iran, and (2) suspending claims pending in American courts but eligible to be presented to the tribunal.[130] The plaintiff in *Dames & Moore* challenged the presidents' authority to issue those executive orders.[131] The Court held that the presidents had clear statutory authority to deal with Iranian property and refused to hold that the executive branch and Congress together lacked constitutional authority to enact the relevant statutes.[132] The Court held that no statute authorized the suspension of claims[133] but that the suspension was nonetheless valid in light of the presidents' authority to settle claims by American citizens against foreign governments. The Court stressed that presidents had exercised this power since the 1790s and placed special weight on Congress' facilitation of presidential claims settlement by creating machinery to allocate the funds produced by such settlements; the Court also emphasized Congress' failure to object to the executive agreement there in issue.[134] The Court took account as well of the possibility that the establishment of the tribunal might improve the chances that holders of the suspended claims would be able to collect on them, limiting the harm the suspension caused.[135] The Court cautioned, however, that it was not holding that the president had "plenary power to settle claims, even as against foreign governmental entities."[136]

The final basis for the president's claimed authority is *Garamendi*. That case involved a conflict between a California statute aimed at

---

[129] Iran Executive Agreement, *supra* note 79.

[130] Dames & Moore v. Regan, 453 U.S. 654, 662–66 (1981).

[131] *Id.* at 666–67.

[132] *Id.* at 669–74.

[133] *Id.* at 675–78.

[134] *Id.* at 680–82, 687–88.

[135] *Id.* at 686–87.

[136] *Id.* at 688.

pressuring certain European insurance companies to pay Holocaust-related claims, some of the claimants being Californians, and an arrangement embodied in an executive agreement between the United States and Germany under which such claims would be paid by a specially funded foundation.[137] The California law required certain insurance companies to make extensive disclosures, beyond those required under the settlement arrangements memorialized in the executive agreement. That agreement did not purport to preempt state laws dealing with Holocaust claims. However, in response to the desire of the German government to obtain a degree of legal peace for its corporations, it included an undertaking that the United States government would represent in any court hearing that the foreign policy interests of the United States would be served if the foundation was the exclusive forum for the resolution of all claims against German companies and that those interests favored dismissing related cases in American courts.[138]

Insurance companies sued to enjoin enforcement of the California law, alleging that it conflicted with the federal policy expressed in the executive agreement and was therefore unconstitutional.[139] In agreeing with this argument, the Court stressed that intertwined actions of the Nazi government and German insurance companies had given rise to the claims at issue and that the president's clear authority to settle claims against foreign governments by executive agreement therefore extended to these claims, even though they were against private entities.[140] The Court made clear that California's policy was an impediment to the approach taken by the federal government in this matter[141] and noted that the subject of the state statute was so far removed from traditional areas of state competence that the state's interest in its enforcement was not strong.[142] In these circumstances, the Court held, the statute was preempted.[143]

---

[137] American Insurance Association v. Garamendi, 539 U.S. 396, 405–412 (2003).
[138] *Id.* at 406.
[139] *Id.* at 412–14.
[140] *Id.* at 415–16.
[141] *Id.* at 420–25.
[142] *Id.* at 420.
[143] *Id.* at 416–20, 425–27.

Pulling these cases together, we can note three characteristics they share.

First, all four involved problems with foreign governments that could be resolved only through negotiations. Necessarily, the negotiations were carried out by the federal executive. If those negotiations were to succeed, however, the United States had to give as well as take, which meant that the president had to be able to make undertakings on behalf of the entire United States. Thus, resolving disputes and entering into diplomatic relations with the Soviet Union depended in part on the United States offering a means to deal with American claims against the Soviet Union. Resolving the Iranian hostage crisis required dealing with claims against both governments, which in turn required a claims settlement mechanism both governments could accept. The establishment of the special foundation increased the chances that Holocaust survivors would collect on their insurance claims but depended on assuring Germany that its corporations' risks of suit in the United States would be reduced.

Second, the Court, especially in *Dames & Moore* and *Garamendi*, emphasized the long history of congressional acquiescence in, or indeed active facilitation of, the exercise of presidential authority regarding international claims settlements, the issue at the heart of all of these cases.

Finally and most basically, the actions taken by the president—superseding state public policy affecting international claims settlement and vesting authority to decide claims in an international tribunal—were seen by the Court as clearly within the power of the president and the federal government to regulate settlement of international claims. Further, in *Garamendi*, the state's action diverged so far from core state functions as to render it suspect.

The president's action in this case shares none of these characteristics. First, this situation differs from that in the claim settlement cases because the president's action is not a quid pro quo for actions by a foreign state. Even *Curtiss-Wright* justifies its expansive description of presidential foreign affairs power by reference to the president's status as the sole means of *communication* between the United States and other countries,[144] that is, as a function of the bargaining required by diplomatic exchanges. Here, however, the president's

---

[144] United States v. Curtiss-Wright Export Corp., 299 U.S. 304, 319–20 (1936).

action is not part of a bargain with a foreign government, for he takes the position that the United States has never undertaken to enforce ICJ judgments domestically. Therefore, the amicus brief is wrong when it argues that the president's authority is not affected by the absence of an executive agreement here.[145] Since the president's power to supersede state law in foreign affairs matters derives from his authority to bargain with foreign governments, the absence of a bargain eliminates any basis for presidential authority.

Indeed, the president's action is merely a policy determination regarding judicial procedure. As such, there is no reason Congress could not address this matter by statute, *if* the federal government has the authority to address it at all. Even if speed were seen as essential, Congress can act very quickly, as it demonstrated in the Schiavo matter.[146] *Pace* the U.S. amicus brief, it is difficult to see what "complex calculations" would be required to enact such legislation that are not present whenever a legislature must address a question of ordinary legal procedure.

The second difference between this situation and that regarding claims settlements relates to the attitude of Congress. Congress' active acceptance of presidential authority in this area was one crucial reason for the Supreme Court's willingness to uphold that authority.[147] Yet, Congress has emphatically not acquiesced in any power in the president to order states to reopen final judgments of their courts. The Senate consented to the compulsory jurisdiction of the ICJ on the understanding that ICJ judgments could only be executed by the Security Council.[148] The Foreign Relations Committee reported the Optional Protocol favorably in part because it did *not* change American law.[149] The president thus seeks to bring about precisely the result that the Senate thought would not flow from submitting cases, including Consular Convention cases, to the ICJ, a point the amicus brief does not really dispute.[150] This situation

---

[145] U.S. Amicus Brief, *supra* note 9, at 45–46.

[146] See Pub. L. No. 109–3, March 21, 2005, 119 Stat 15.

[147] See United States v. Pink, 315 U.S. 203, 227–28 (1942); Dames & Moore v. Regan, 453 U.S. 654, 680–82 (1981); American Insurance Association v. Garamendi, 539 U.S. 396, 415 (2003).

[148] See discussion *supra* notes 63–65.

[149] See discussion *supra* notes 49–50.

[150] U.S. Amicus Brief, *supra* note 9, at 34–38.

recalls the *Youngstown* "Steel Seizure" cases. Of course, *Youngstown* dealt with a power that Congress had affirmatively denied to the president,[151] while this involves an obligation for the states that the Senate was assured would not be created by Senate action. In both, however, the president claimed authority that legislators clearly intended *not* to authorize. Given the Senate's understanding of the limited obligation of the United States regarding ICJ judgments, then, the president's claimed authority to impose a greater obligation seems particularly suspect.

Finally, and most basically, it is by no means clear that the federal government as a whole, let alone the president acting unilaterally, may constitutionally require a state's courts to enforce *Avena*. To understand this point, consider exactly what such enforcement would entail. At the time the ICJ handed down that judgment, as far as the American courts were concerned, Medellin's case had been resolved. The matter was res judicata. The holding in *Avena*, therefore, amounts to a direction to reopen a judgment that has, under American law, become final.

It was made clear in *Plaut v. Spendthrift Farm*[152] that the political branches of the federal government lack power to reopen the judgments of the federal courts. In that case, the Court held unconstitutional a federal statute purporting to revive cases earlier dismissed on limitations grounds by lower federal courts. In explaining that the statute contravened separation of powers principles, the Court observed:

> The record of history shows that the Framers crafted this charter of the judicial department with an expressed understanding that it gives the Federal Judiciary the power, not merely to rule on cases, but to *decide* them, subject to review only by superior courts in the Article III hierarchy—with an understanding, in short, that "a judgment conclusively resolves the case" because "a 'judicial Power' is one to render dispositive judgments."[153]

The opinion goes on:

> Having achieved finality, however, a judicial decision becomes the last word of the judicial department with regard

---

[151] Youngstown Sheet & Tube Co. v. Sawyer, 343 U.S. 396, 586 (1952).

[152] 514 U.S. 211 (1995).

[153] *Id.* at 218–219 (emphasis in the original) (citation omitted).

to a particular case or controversy, and Congress may not declare by retroactive legislation that the law applicable *to that very case* was something other than what the courts said it was.[154]

Here, however, we deal with state courts. Since Article III of the Constitution does not apply to those courts, analysis of federal power with respect to them turns on different considerations.

On the one hand, there are circumstances in which the federal government clearly has especially broad authority to alter state law, that is, when it concludes treaties with foreign governments. Treaties predating the Constitution established legal rules on matters otherwise subject to state control;[155] at least one imposed duties on state officials.[156] Yet Article VI of the Constitution validated these treaties.[157] Further, Supreme Court decisions dating to the early 1800s applied treaty language to supersede state law regarding subjects that would, at the time the cases were decided, have been thought to be clearly beyond the authority of Congress to regulate by statute, e.g., the right of aliens to inherit real property through intestate succession.[158] Such cases, dealing with matters among those least likely to be seen as subject to federal regulation prior to the New Deal,[159] illustrate the striking breadth of the subjects that the Court

---

[154] *Id.* at 227 (emphasis in the original).

[155] Treaty of Amity and Commerce, Oct. 8, 1782, U.S.-Netherlands., art. IV (liberty of conscience), art. VI (right to testate/intestate disposition of personalty), 8 Stat. 32, 34, 36; Treaty of Amity and Commerce, Apr. 3, 1783, U.S.-Sweden, art. V (freedom of conscience), art. VI (right to testate/intestate disposition of personalty), 8 Stat. 60, 62, 64; Treaty of Amity and Commerce, Sept. 10, 1785, U.S.-Prussia, art. X (right to testate/intestate disposition of personalty, and for heirs to sell realty), art. XI (freedom of conscience), 8 Stat. 84, 88, 90.

[156] Convention, November 14, 1788, U.S.-France, art. IX, 8 Stat. 106, 112. See also Weisburd, *supra* note 123, at 903.

[157] U.S. Const. art. VI, cl. 2.

[158] Chirac v. Chirac's Lessee, 15 U.S. (2 Wheat.) 259, 261, 262, 271–77 (1817). Accord Hauenstein v. Lynham, 100 U.S. 483, 483–87, 488–90 (1880).

[159] See Blythe v. Hinckley, 180 U.S. 333, 340–42 (1901) (questions of inheritance by aliens are matters of state law); Terrace v. Thompson, 263 U.S. 197, 217 (1923) (states' reserved power includes authority to determine whether aliens are permitted to hold land). And for a post New Deal case supporting these conclusions, see United States v. Burnison, 339 U.S. 87, 91–92 (1950).

saw as properly within the scope of the treaty power.[160] Given these decisions and the scope of the treaty power implied by the reach of the pre-Constitution treaties, the statement in *Missouri v. Holland*[161] that "[i]t is obvious that there may be matters of the sharpest exigency for the national well being that an act of Congress could not deal with but that a treaty followed by such an act could ..."[162] seems understandable.[163]

There are, however, cases containing dicta indicating limits on the treaty power's impact on states—including, for example, limits forbidding changes in the "character" of a state government "without its consent."[164] Moreover, there are numerous cases—albeit none dealing with treaties—holding that the Constitution protects the states' rights to structural autonomy and sovereignty, to the extent that powers are not delegated to the federal government. Thus, in holding that Texas did not cease to be a state because of its purported secession,[165] the Supreme Court stressed the indissoluble character of the union created by the Constitution,[166] and observed:

> Not only, therefore, can there be no loss of separate and independent autonomy to the States, through their union under the Constitution, but it may be not unreasonably said that the preservation of the States, and the maintenance of

---

[160] For other examinations of this issue, reaching similar conclusions and collecting cases, see Richard B. Collins, Nineteenth Century Orthodoxy, 70 U. Colo. L. Rev. 1157, 1162–63 (1999); G. Edward White, The Transformation of the Constitutional Regime of Foreign Relations , 85 Va. L. Rev. 1, 24 (1999).

[161] 252 U.S. 416 (1920).

[162] *Id.* at 433.

[163] While it may seem puzzling that the federal treaty power would be broader than the power of Congress, this arrangement seems compelled by the structure of American federalism. With respect to domestic legislation, there can be few subjects that *neither* Congress nor the states could address. The situation with respect to treaties is different. As indicated *supra* notes 156 & 157, treaties may well address subjects that Congress does not, and arguably cannot, regulate. However, states are forbidden to make treaties, U.S. Const. art. I, § 10, cl. 1. Therefore, if the federal government lacks power to make treaties on those subjects, Americans must do without whatever benefits the treaties might confer. Reading the treaty power broadly avoids that result.

[164] DeGeofroy v. Riggs, 133 U.S. 258, 267 (1890); Fort Leavenworth R.R. Co. v. Lowe, 114 U.S. 525, 540–41 (1885).

[165] Texas v. White, 74 U.S. (7 Wall.) 700, 719 (1869).

[166] *Id.* at 725–26.

their governments, are as much within the design and care of the Constitution as the preservation of the Union and the maintenance of the National government. The Constitution, in all its provisions, looks to an indestructible Union, composed of indestructible States.[167]

The Court upheld an Oregon statute requiring payment of state taxes in gold or silver coin, notwithstanding the argument that federal statutes making United States notes legal tender overrode the Oregon statute.[168] The Court held the federal statute was not intended to compel states to accept tax payments in notes,[169] relying on the proposition that "in many articles of the Constitution . . . within their proper spheres, the independent authority of the States, is distinctly recognized"[170] and on the necessity of the taxing power to the states' authority.[171]

The Court also addressed the constitutional limits on federal authority over the states in *Collector v. Day*.[172] The Court there held that federal taxation of the salary of a state judicial officer was unconstitutional, posing too great a risk of subjecting the existence of state judiciaries to the control of the federal government.[173] In its opinion, the Court stated:

> We have said that one of the reserved powers was that to establish a judicial department; it would have been more accurate . . . to have said the power to maintain a judicial department. All of the thirteen States were in the possession of this power, and had exercised it at the adoption of the Constitution; and it is not pretended that any grant of it to the general government is found in that instrument. It is, therefore, one of the sovereign powers vested in the States by their constitutions, which remained unaltered and unimpaired, and in respect to which the State is as independent

---

[167] *Id.* (citation omitted).
[168] Lane County v. Oregon, 74 U.S. (7 Wall.) 71, 72–73 (1869).
[169] *Id.* at 76–78.
[170] *Id.* at 76.
[171] *Id.*
[172] 78 U.S. (11 Wall.) 113 (1870).
[173] *Id.* at 126–28.

of the general government as that government is independent of the States.[174]

While this case was subsequently overruled in *Graves v. New York ex rel. O'Keefe*,[175] *Graves* did not reject *Day*'s analysis of the importance of the states' autonomous control over their judiciaries, holding instead that the tax in question did not threaten that autonomy.[176]

The Supreme Court's recent federalism cases also stress the constitutional importance of state autonomy over structural components of state government. In *Alden v. Maine*,[177] the Court held that Article I of the Constitution conferred on Congress no power to abrogate the sovereign immunity of the states in their own courts.[178] Its opinion stressed in particular that such power would be inconsistent with the structure of the Constitution.[179] Acknowledging that Article III obliges state courts to hear suits involving federal law, the Court stated nonetheless that "[t]he Article in no way suggests ... that state courts may be required to assume jurisdiction that could not be vested in the federal courts and forms no part of the judicial power of the United States."[180] For similar reasons, the Court held that Congress lacked the authority under the Constitution to coerce state legislatures to adopt any particular legislation,[181] or, as held in *Printz v. United States*,[182] to compel state executive officials to execute federal programs.[183]

We thus confront a dilemma. As the treaty cases underscore, the treaty power conveys broad federal authority to override state policy, such as that announced by state political branches. However, dicta in other treaty cases and the reasoning of the cases addressing the basic structure of the Constitution seem inconsistent with a

---

[174] *Id.* at 126.

[175] 306 U.S. 466, 486 (1939).

[176] *Id.* at 483–86.

[177] 527 U.S. 706 (1999).

[178] *Id.* at 754.

[179] *Id.* at 748–54.

[180] *Id.* at 754.

[181] New York v. United States, 505 U.S. 144, 162–63, 175–79, 187, 188 (1992).

[182] 521 U.S. 898 (1997).

[183] *Id.* at 924–34.

federal power broad enough to sustain the president's memorandum. Since the latter cases deal with federal efforts to alter state governmental structure—including the freedom of state officers from federal commandeering—while the treaty cases deal only with state policy, there is a temptation to assume that the former should control. However, the structural cases cannot be mechanically applied in the treaty context; *Printz*, for instance, seems inconsistent with the original understanding of the treaty power.[184] Nonetheless, the cases addressing the fundamental importance of state control over their judiciaries[185] speak in sweeping terms. Further, none of the treaty cases involve treaties altering a state's governmental structure without its consent.

Together these cases suggest the following synthesis: The treaty power permits the president and Senate, acting together, to supersede state policy preferences, as announced by either state political branches or courts, even where the federal action is outside the scope of federal power as enumerated in Article I of the Constitution (subject to the limitation, discussed above, that the treaty power must be used to obtain a reciprocal quid pro quo that benefits the nation as a whole). The president may, through exercise of executive agreements, also supersede the policy preferences of state political branches and courts to get the benefit of such a bargain, especially in cases where Congress has acquiesced in the president's actions and where the state's objection implicates matters peripheral to the state's core powers. But the federal government, in whole or in part, may not act in a fashion that alters the structure of state government—particularly the structure of state judicial decisionmaking, an issue of special structural concern. This synthesis harmonizes evidence about the original understanding of the treaty power with the structural concerns raised in some of the treaty cases and in the Court's recent federalism cases.

It therefore seems reasonable to see the structural cases as more relevant in a case, like this, involving federal efforts to control the finality, and hence the structure of, state judicial proceedings and to conclude that the federal government lacks the authority to interfere with the fundamentally judicial character—the power to decide

[184] See discussion at notes 156–58 *supra*.
[185] See discussion at notes 164–83, *supra*.

cases—of state judicial power. By analogy to *Plaut*,[186] that is exactly what the president's memorandum purports to do. The conclusion is especially compelling where, as here, the president's action implicates concerns—operation of criminal justice systems—at the core of state power.[187] Surely, if the federal government as a whole cannot exercise such power, the president alone cannot.

In short, states are not obliged to comply with the direction in the president's memorandum.

VI. Conclusion

If (when?) the Supreme Court addresses Medellin's case again, it will confront two legal mistakes. The ICJ's tortured treaty interpretation has imposed on the United States an illegitimate obligation. The president's response to the ICJ is also illegitimate. The Court can best address these mistakes by observing that it need not accept the ICJ's treaty interpretations, adhering to its own view of the Consular Convention, and making clear that the president lacks the power he claims.

---

[186] See discussion *supra* notes 152–54.

[187] *Garamendi* implicitly reinforces this conclusion. Unlike the limited state interest there at issue, 539 U.S. 396, 416–20, 425–27 (2003), maintaining judicial integrity is a fundamental state interest, as the cases indicate, see discussion *supra* notes 164–83.

Looking Ahead to the 2005–2006 Term

Jonathan H. Adler*

I. Introduction

The 2005–2006 term may be as notable for what it says about the future direction of the Supreme Court as it is for specific decisions in any particular cases. As always, there are high profile cases of doctrinal or political significance, but no genuine blockbusters—at least not yet. As has been noted before, the Court has a tendency of accepting and deciding some of the most important cases later in the term.[1] *Lawrence v. Texas*,[2] *Kelo v. City of New London*,[3] the Michigan affirmative action cases,[4] and last term's Ten Commandments decisions[5] are but a few recent examples.

This is not to say the 2005–2006 term lacks important cases. Far from it. This coming year the Court will consider the constitutionality of the Solomon Amendment, address the application of the Religious Freedom Restoration Act to religious use of drugs, and determine whether the federal government can effectively preempt Oregon's decision to legalize doctor-assisted suicide. It will revisit contemporary federalism and abortion doctrines, clarify the scope of the Racketeer

---

*Jonathan H. Adler is associate professor of law and associate director of the Center for Business Law & Regulation at the Case Western Reserve University School of Law, where he teaches courses in environmental and constitutional law.

[1]See Thomas C. Goldstein, The Upcoming 2004–2005 Term, 2003–2004 Cato Sup. Ct. Rev. 493 (2004) (noting that "for several years, the most notable cases have coincidentally been selected and argued late in the term"); Michael A. Carvin, Coming Up: October Term 2003, 2002–2003 Cato Sup. Ct. Rev. 280 (2003) ("the most significant cases of a Term often include some in which the Court granted certiorari during the course of the Term").

[2]539 U.S. 558 (2003).

[3]125 S. Ct. 2655 (2005).

[4]Grutter v. Bollinger, 539 U.S. 306 (2003); Gratz v. Bollinger, 539 U.S. 244 (2003).

[5]McCreary County v. ACLU, 125 S. Ct. 2722 (2005); Van Orden v. Perry, 125 S. Ct. 2854 (2005).

Influenced and Corrupt Organizations Act (RICO), and address important questions in antitrust and criminal procedure. Nonetheless, the most striking thing about the upcoming term is that we will see a change in the Court's composition for the first time in over a decade.

Until Justice Sandra Day O'Connor announced her retirement in July, there had been no change in the Court's composition for eleven years. This is the longest period nine justices have sat together as a Court in the nation's history. Indeed, not since the 1820s, when the Court had only seven justices, has the Court gone more than six years without any turnover.[6] This period of continuity has had several important, if somewhat underappreciated, effects. As Thomas Merrill observed, a Court without turnover becomes a "Court in stasis" with remarkably stable institutional norms.[7] After years together, the justices can predict their colleagues' votes, dispositions, and inclinations—and therefore the outcomes of individual cases—with tremendous confidence.

A change in the Court's lineup, even one that does not appear to alter the ideological make-up of the Court, has the potential to disrupt this equilibrium, change institutional norms, and alter the course of existing doctrines.[8] Even the shuffling of seniority can have important doctrinal effects, insofar as it places the responsibility to assign cases in different hands. As a result, it may be more difficult to predict outcomes in once-predictable cases. Even routine applications or clarifications of existing precedent hold the potential to take Court decisions in a new direction. This will make the decisions in upcoming cases that much more worth court-watchers' attention.

II. Cases On the Docket

A. Expressive Association and Conditional Spending

Rumsfeld v. Forum for Academic and Institutional Rights (FAIR)[9] is almost certainly the case of greatest interest to legal academics, in

---

[6] Paul H. Edelman & Jim Chen, The Most Dangerous Justice Rides Again: Revisiting the Power Pageant of the Justices, 86 Minn. L. Rev. 131, 134 n.12 (2001).

[7] Thomas W. Merrill, The Making of the Second Rehnquist Court: A Preliminary Analysis, 47 St. Louis. U. L.J. 569, 573 (2003).

[8] *Id.*

[9] No. 04-1152.

no small part because many are themselves parties to the case. *Rumsfeld v. FAIR* presents a constitutional challenge to a federal requirement that universities receiving federal funds grant the military equal access to campus recruiting opportunities. As such, it presents issues of expressive association and Congress' power to impose conditions on the receipt of federal funds.

The case arose out of the controversy over the U.S. military's "don't ask, don't tell" policy, which excludes open homosexuals from military service.[10] This policy is quite controversial, but has been upheld repeatedly in federal court.[11] Most law schools have non-discrimination policies that protect sexual preference. On this basis, many sought to deny campus access to military recruiters. Congress responded by enacting the "Solomon Amendment," a provision requiring that universities receiving federal funds provide military recruiters with access to campus and students "that is at least equal in quality and scope to the access to campuses and to students that is provided to any other employer."[12] Law professors around the country, as well as several law schools, formed FAIR to challenge the amendment in court.

A divided panel of the U.S. Court of Appeals for the Third Circuit found that the Solomon Amendment violated the plaintiffs' First Amendment rights of expressive association and "compel[led] them to assist in the expressive act of recruiting."[13] There are several reasons to doubt whether this holding will be upheld on appeal. Most importantly, the Third Circuit adopted a significantly more expansive view of the right of association than has been recognized by federal courts to date. In addition, even if the Supreme Court were sympathetic to the expressive association claim at issue, the Solomon Amendment is not more intrusive than other funding conditions previously upheld in federal court.[14] Add the fact that the

[10] 10 U.S.C. § 654 bars homosexuals from military service.

[11] See, e.g., Able v. United States, 155 F.3d 628, 634–36 (2d Cir. 1998); Philips v. Perry, 106 F.3d 1420, 1432 (9th Cir. 1997); Richenberg v. Perry, 97 F.3d 256, 262, 263, 264 (8th Cir. 1996); Thomasson v. Perry, 80 F.3d 915, 934 (4th Cir. 1996) (en banc).

[12] 10 U.S.C. § 983(b)(1). The Solomon Amendment exempts institutions with "a longstanding policy of pacifism based on historical religious affiliation." 10 U.S.C. § 983(c)(2).

[13] FAIR v. Rumsfeld, 390 F.3d 219, 230 (3d Cir. 2004).

[14] See, e.g., Grove City College v. Bell, 465 U.S. 555, 563 (1984) (rejecting First Amendment challenge to conditions imposed on federal funding of educational institutions under Title IX).

Supreme Court does not have a long record of challenging military policy determinations, and that the parent universities themselves are not challenging the funding condition,[15] and it seems *FAIR* is destined to be overturned.

The Supreme Court has never recognized an absolute right to freedom of association. *Boy Scouts of America v. Dale*[16] and *Hurley v. Irish-American Gay, Lesbian, and Bisexual Group of Boston*[17] recognized a right to expressive association, but one that is more limited than FAIR's asserted expressive association claim.[18] *Dale*, for instance, held that governmental action violates the right of expressive association where it "affects in a significant way the group's ability to advocate public or private viewpoints."[19] Forcing the Boy Scouts to accept gay scoutmasters had such an effect because it restricted the Boy Scouts' ability to select their own members and leadership. Here, however, universities are not being told whom to admit or hire, or whose message to endorse. Rather they must allow the military to recruit on campus to the same degree as a multitude of other employers, representing a multitude of interests and perspectives, are so allowed. Moreover, there is no claim that universities or their faculty are in any way prevented or discouraged from criticizing the military's "don't ask, don't tell" policy by the government. The Solomon Amendment focuses solely on whether military recruiters are given "equal access" on campus. The policy does, however, effectively prevent law schools from expressing their institutional values by providing some employers—those that do not discriminate against homosexuals—preferential treatment.

If the Court were to accept FAIR's expressive association claim, its Spending Clause charge may have more force. Assuming that the federal government could not simply require all universities to

[15]See Andrew P. Morriss, The Market for Legal Education & Freedom of Association: Why the "Solomon Amendment" Is Constitutional and Law Schools Aren't Expressive Associations, Case Research Paper Series in Legal Studies No. 05-20 (August 2005), available at http://lawwww.cwru.edu/ssrn/.

[16]530 U.S. 640 (2000).

[17]515 U.S. 557 (1995).

[18]For a libertarian critique of the limited right of expressive association recognized in *Dale*, see Richard A. Epstein, The Constitutional Perils of Moderation: The Case of the Boy Scouts, 74 S. Cal. L. Rev. 119 (2000).

[19]Dale, 530 U.S. at 648.

permit military recruiting on campus,[20] it is not clear why the federal government should be able to leverage its substantial funding of universities, much of it for research, to overcome the First Amendment rights of universities or university faculties to control the educational environment. Conditions placed upon federal funding must "bear some relationship to the purpose of the federal spending."[21] The relationship between, for example, federal funding of particle physics or medical research and military access to law school career service offices is not particularly direct, especially given that the Solomon Amendment applies to non-military funding.

The government's strongest argument here is that the amendment enforces a non-discrimination rule, much like that contained in civil rights laws such as Title VI[22] and Title IX.[23] Such conditions, the government will claim, ensure that federal money is not used to support discriminatory activities. Whereas the civil rights laws prevent racial and gender-based discrimination, the argument goes, the Solomon Amendment bars discrimination against the military in a way that undermines Congress' ability to "raise and support" armies.[24] The Court has upheld the application of such conditions to university admissions, where the expressive association claim is stronger than in *FAIR*.[25] A university's expressive association interest in whom it admits, graduates, and hires is greater than a law faculty's or affiliated law school's interest in whom is allowed to interview students on campus. Moreover, the policy does not impose a significant burden on judicially recognized rights of expressive association because law faculties and law schools are not required to forego criticism of military policies. Thus, even if the Court does reach the conditional spending question, it seems unlikely that *FAIR* will prevail.

---

[20]This assumption has never been tested and may be questioned given the deference often shown to the military by federal courts, and in particular to Congress' power to "raise and support" military forces. See, e.g., Rostker v. Goldberg, 453 U.S. 57, 70 (1981) ("judicial deference . . . is at its apogee when legislative action under the congressional authority to raise and support armies and make rules and regulations for their governance is challenged").

[21]New York v. United States, 505 U.S. 144, 167 (1992).

[22]42 U.S.C. §§ 2000d et seq.

[23]20 U.S.C. §§ 1681 et seq.

[24]U.S. Const. art. I, § 8, cl. 12.

[25]See note 14, *supra*.

B. Drug Use and Religious Freedom

In *Employment Division v. Smith*,[26] the Supreme Court held that the First Amendment's Free Exercise Clause did not prevent the State of Oregon from prohibiting the religious use of peyote.[27] In the process, the Court rejected the application of strict scrutiny to such free exercise claims and held there was no religious exemption to valid and neutral laws of general applicability.[28] Congress responded by enacting the Religious Freedom Restoration Act (RFRA), which provides that the federal government may "substantially burden a person's exercise of religion" only if the state burden serves a "compelling governmental interest" and is the "least restrictive means" of furthering that interest.[29]

In *Gonzales v. O Centro Espirita Beneficiente Uniao*,[30] the Court confronts the question whether RFRA requires the federal government to permit the importation, possession, and use of hoasca, a tea containing the hallucinogen DMT, in religious ceremonies. This question divided the U.S. Court of Appeals for the Tenth Circuit, sitting en banc, which held that members of a religious group were entitled to a preliminary injunction barring federal enforcement of the Controlled Substances Act (CSA) as applied to hoasca in religious ceremonies.[31]

The federal government maintains that it has compelling interests in the uniform enforcement of federal drug laws and in compliance with a United Nations drug control treaty that outweigh the religious freedom claim at issue. All DMT-containing substances are listed as "schedule I"–controlled hallucinogens under the CSA, and Congress asserted that schedule I substances have "a high potential for abuse" and lack any "currently accepted medical use."[32] While Congress,

---

[26] 494 U.S. 872 (1990).

[27] *Id.* at 890.

[28] *Id.* at 879–82 (rejecting religious exemption from valid and neutral laws of general applicability); *id.* at 886–89 (rejecting strict scrutiny).

[29] 42 U.S.C. § 2000bb-1. As enacted by Congress, RFRA applied to all levels of government. RFRA's application to states was, however, struck down in *City of Boerne v. Flores*, 521 U.S. 507, 536 (1997), for exceeding the scope of Section 5 of the Fourteenth Amendment.

[30] No. 04-1084.

[31] O Centro Espirita Beneficiente Uniao v. Ashcroft, 389 F.3d 973, 976 (10th Cir. 2004).

[32] 21 U.S.C. § 812 (b)(1)(A)–(C).

by enacting RFRA, clearly sought to overturn the standard set forth in *Smith*, the government asserts that RFRA was not intended to change the specific result in that case. To the contrary, Congress noted its agreement with pre-*Smith* cases, many of which upheld the application of federal drug laws to religious practices.[33]

In a powerful opinion below, Judge Michael McConnell argued that courts cannot simply defer to government's broad assertion of an interest in enforcing its criminal laws. Rather, he argued, RFRA requires a case-by-case evaluation of the government's interest and whether a given limitation on religious practice advances the government's interest in the least restrictive way possible.[34] Wrote McConnell, courts "are not free to decline to enforce [RFRA], which necessarily puts courts in the position of crafting religious exemptions to federal laws that burden religious exercise without sufficient justification."[35] Congress made no specific findings about the use of hoasca, so courts have less confidence that the blanket prohibition on its importation, possession, and use is the least restrictive means of fulfilling the government's interest in drug prohibition.[36] Given that hoasca is a substance little used outside of specific, uncommon religious ceremonies, it is also questionable whether a ruling against the government here would open the floodgates for claims of religious exemptions to the CSA. As Judge McConnell noted, it may be easier to justify a blanket prohibition on substances that are used more widely.[37] Moreover, a decision against the government here would not preclude Congress from amending either RFRA or the CSA to strengthen federal limitations on the religious use of schedule I drugs.

C. Federalism and Assisted Suicide

The CSA is also front and center in this term's premier federalism case, *Gonzales v. Oregon*,[38] much as it was last term in *Gonzales v.*

---

[33] Brief for the Petitioners at 16–17, Gonzales v. O Centro Espirita Beneficiente Uniao, No. 04-1084 (U.S. filed July 2005).

[34] O Centro Espirita, 389 F.3d at 1018–31 (McConnell, J., concurring).

[35] *Id.* at 1020.

[36] Of course, the government's interest in drug prohibition is itself a question of fierce debate. See, e.g., The Crisis in Drug Prohibition (David Boaz ed., 1990).

[37] O Centro Espirita, 389 F.3d at 1022–23 (McConnell, J., concurring).

[38] No. 04-623.

Raich.[39] Whereas *Raich* focused on California's decision to legalize the medical use and possession of marijuana, *Oregon* concerns the Oregon Death with Dignity Act, a state law twice-approved by Oregon voters that legalizes doctor-assisted suicide.[40] While the issue in *Raich* was the pure constitutional issue of whether federal Commerce Clause authority could reach non-commercial marijuana possession and use for medicinal purposes where authorized by state law, *Oregon* presents a narrower issue of statutory construction.[41] Under current Commerce Clause doctrine, there is little question that Congress *could* prohibit doctors from prescribing drugs to help their patients kill themselves, yet it has never done so in explicit terms.[42] Therefore, the question in *Oregon* is whether an administrative official, in this case the attorney general, can interpret the CSA to achieve the same result absent clear congressional assent.

The CSA erects a comprehensive regulatory scheme covering the manufacture, distribution, and sale of controlled substances. In order to prevent drug trafficking and abuse, it prohibits the dispensing of regulated drugs without a federal registration. Registered doctors are further required to dispense controlled substances only "in the course of professional practice or research."[43] In addition, longstanding federal regulations implementing the CSA require that drug prescriptions "be issued for a legitimate medical purpose."[44] In 2001, then–Attorney General John Ashcroft issued an interpretive rule declaring that assisting suicide is "not a 'legitimate medical purpose,'" even if authorized under state law.[45] In effect, the Ashcroft

---

[39] 125 S. Ct. 2195 (2005) (Commerce Clause challenge to federal regulation of medical marijuana use and possession authorized by state law).

[40] Or. Rev. Stat. §§ 127.800–127.995.

[41] Compare Petition for Certiorari at (I), Gonzales v. Raich, 125 S. Ct. 2195 (2005) (No. 03-1454) (U.S. filed August 2004) (question presented), with Petition for Certiorari at (I), Gonzales v. Oregon, No. 04-623 (U.S. filed May 2005) (question presented).

[42] Of course, current Commerce Clause doctrine has departed from the original meaning of the clause. See, e.g., Randy E. Barnett, New Evidence of the Original Meaning of the Commerce Clause, 55 Ark. L. Rev. 847 (2003); Randy E. Barnett, The Original Meaning of the Commerce Clause, 68 U. Chi. L. Rev. 101 (2001); Richard A. Epstein, The Proper Scope of the Commerce Power, 73 Va. L. Rev. 1387 (1987).

[43] 21 U.S.C. § 802(21).

[44] 21 C.F.R. § 1306.04(a).

[45] 66 Fed. Reg. 56,607 (November 9, 2001).

directive preempted Oregon's decision to authorize doctors to write prescriptions for the purpose of assisting suicides.

Oregon successfully challenged this directive before the U.S. Court of Appeals for the Ninth Circuit, which found that the rule exceeded the scope of federal authority under the CSA.[46] The key legal issue is not the federal government's constitutional authority, but the extent to which the CSA authorizes administrative action that displaces state authority in areas traditionally left under state control, such as the practice of medicine. In 1991, the Supreme Court held that federal statutes should not be interpreted to displace state authority unless Congress' authorization for such action is "unmistakably clear."[47] On this basis, the Court has refused to defer to an agency interpretation of federal law intruding on traditional state authority.[48]

Weighed against these arguments is the federal government's assertion that the CSA creates a comprehensive and *uniform* regulatory scheme that already confines medical authority to prescribe drugs and is administered by the Department of Justice.[49] According to the federal government, allowing Oregon doctors to prescribe federally controlled substances to assist suicides threatens the uniformity of the federal scheme. In addition, there is ample authority to support the Justice Department's claim that assisting suicide has rarely, if ever, been considered a "legitimate medical purpose" by medical authorities.[50] Although Oregon doctors may have more difficulty assisting suicide if they cannot prescribe drugs regulated by the CSA, the federal government further argues it is not preempting state action, as other means of doctor-assisted suicide (however impractical) remain legal under Oregon law.[51]

Although the *Oregon* case turns on the questions of statutory interpretation, it is an important federalism case. As the breadth of the government's asserted regulatory authority under the CSA and

[46] 368 F.3d 1118 (9th Cir. 2004).

[47] Gregory v. Ashcroft, 501 U.S. 452, 460–61 (1991) (internal quotation omitted).

[48] See Solid Waste Agency of Northern Cook County v. U.S. Army Corps of Engineers, 531 U.S. 159 (2001).

[49] See Brief for the Petitioners at 24–37, Gonzales v. Oregon, No. 04-623 (U.S. filed May 2005).

[50] *Id.* at 21–24.

[51] *Id.* at 13–14.

other comprehensive regulatory statutes illustrates, a Court ruling addressing federal agencies' authority to preclude state choices will have significant ramifications. If courts are to give Congress a wide berth in determining the proper exercise of federal power—as the *Raich* decision suggests[52]—clear statement rules are particularly important. If the primary limitation on federal power is to come through the political process, then it is that much more important that Congress be required to go on record when federal law will contravene the policy choices citizens make in their respective states.

D. State Sovereign Immunity

The contours of state sovereign immunity may be clarified by two additional federalism cases this term. In *Central Virginia Community College v. Katz*,[53] the Court will consider whether Congress may abrogate state sovereign immunity pursuant to the Bankruptcy Clause. The U.S. Court of Appeals for the Sixth Circuit held Congress may do so because the Bankruptcy Clause explicitly empowers Congress to enact "uniform Laws on the subject of Bankruptcies throughout the United States."[54] In *Seminole Tribe v. Florida*,[55] *Board of Trustees v. Garrett*,[56] and other cases, however, the Court suggested Congress can never abrogate state sovereign immunity when acting pursuant to the powers enumerated in Article I, Section 8.[57] The Court has accepted certiorari on this question before, only to dispose of the case on jurisdictional grounds.[58] In *Central Virginia*, the Court may finally determine whether states may be subject to suit for money damages under the Bankruptcy Clause, or whether Congress is wholly precluded from abrogating state sovereign immunity other than through the Fourteenth Amendment.

---

[52]See, e.g., Jonathan H. Adler, Federalism Up in Smoke?, National Review Online, June 7, 2005, available at http://www.nationalreview.com/adler/adler200506070921.asp.

[53]No. 04-885.

[54]U.S. Const. art. I, § 8, cl. 4; In re Hood, 319 F.3d 755 (6th Cir. 2003).

[55]517 U.S. 44 (1996).

[56]531 U.S. 356, 364 (2001).

[57]Seminole Tribe, 517 U.S. at 73 ("Article I cannot be used to circumvent the constitutional limits placed upon federal jurisdiction."); Garrett, 531 U.S. at 364 ("Congress may not . . . base its abrogation of the States' Eleventh Amendment immunity upon the powers enumerated in Article I.").

[58]Tennessee Student Assistance Corp. v. Hood, 541 U.S. 440 (2004).

A second sovereign immunity case in which certiorari was granted requires the Court to revisit the precise scope of abrogation under Title II of the Americans with Disabilities Act (ADA).[59] In 2001, the Court held that Congress did not validly abrogate state sovereign immunity under Title I of the ADA.[60] In 2004, however, the Court upheld the abrogation of state sovereign immunity under Title II of the ADA with respect to "the class of cases implicating the accessibility of judicial services" in *Tennessee v. Lane*.[61] The *Lane* holding was limited, however, in that it did not uphold Title II of the ADA "as an undifferentiated whole."[62] Whereas the government sought to uphold the ADA as equal protection legislation, the Court stressed that the case implicated the "fundamental right of access to the courts" and not just discrimination against the disabled.[63] In this way, *Lane* muddied the waters of the Court's sovereign immunity jurisprudence.

In *United States v. Georgia* (consolidated with *Goodman v. Georgia*),[64] the Court may restore some clarity as it considers whether Title II of the ADA abrogates state sovereign immunity in suits by disabled prisoners challenging discrimination by state-operated prisons. The federal government seeks a ruling that Title II abrogates state sovereign immunity across the board.[65] Barring such a broad ruling, the federal government seeks recognition that the poor prison conditions alleged implicate fundamental constitutional rights, such as those protected by the Fifth, Sixth, and Eighth Amendments, that Congress may protect through its Section 5 power, just as the lack of court access allowed for abrogation in *Lane*.[66] Georgia, on the other hand, will argue that the scope of Title II is far broader than necessary to address any constitutional concerns and is therefore not the sort of congruent and proportional remedy authorized by Section 5.

---

[59] 42 U.S.C. §§ 21131 et seq.

[60] Garrett, 531 U.S. at 374.

[61] 541 U.S. 509, 531 (2004).

[62] *Id.* at 530.

[63] *Id.* at 533–34. For more on the *Lane* ruling, see Robert A. Levy, Tennessee v. Lane: How Illegitimate Power Negated Non-Existent Immunity, 2003–2004 Cato Sup. Ct. Rev. 161, 164–68 (2004).

[64] Nos. 04-1203 and 04-1236.

[65] Petition for a Writ of Certiorari at 12 n.6, United States v. Georgia, No. 04-1203 (U.S. filed March 2005).

[66] *Id.* at 14–15.

Moreover, whereas the federal government will seek to frame the issue as one concerning a broad "class of cases,"[67] Georgia will seek to focus on the specific claims at issue in this specific case and argue that prison conditions for the disabled do not implicate constitutional rights protected by the Fourteenth Amendment. As in *Central Virginia*, the outcome may indicate whether the Court intends to stand by its decisions upholding state sovereign immunity.

E. Abortion

The Court wades into the unending controversy over abortion once again in *Ayotte v. Planned Parenthood of Northern New England*.[68] The U.S. Court of Appeals for the First Circuit struck down the New Hampshire Parental Notification Prior to Abortion Act[69] on the grounds that it lacked an explicit health exception and its life exception was drawn too narrowly.[70] While the statute lacks explicit language allowing a doctor to perform an abortion where necessary to protect a minor's health, New Hampshire argued that the statute's judicial bypass provision provides an equivalent safeguard. The First Circuit rejected this argument on the ground that the time required for a minor to avail herself of the judicial bypass, even if only a few days, could place an undue burden on her ability to obtain an abortion and, in a non-trivial number of cases, may increase risks to the minor's health.[71]

Also at issue in *Ayotte* is the proper standard of review in abortion cases. Under *United States v. Salerno*,[72] courts confronted with a facial challenge to a validly enacted statute must uphold the law unless there is "no set of circumstances" under which it could be constitutional.[73] In *Planned Parenthood of Southeastern Pennsylvania v. Casey*,[74]

---

[67] *Id.* at 15 ("[T]he court of appeals here should have assessed Title II's constitutionality as applied to the entire 'class of cases' . . . implicating, in this Court's words, 'the administration of . . . the penal system.'").

[68] No. 04-1144.

[69] N.H. Rev. Stat. Ann. §§ 132:24–28 (2003).

[70] Planned Parenthood of Northern New England v. Heed, 390 F.3d 53, 62 (1st Cir. 2004).

[71] *Id.*

[72] 481 U.S. 739 (1987).

[73] *Id.* at 745. First Amendment challenges to speech restrictions are an obvious exception to this rule.

[74] 505 U.S. 833 (1992).

however, the Court seemed to adopt a different standard for abortion cases, holding that any law that has "the purpose or effect of placing a substantial obstacle in the path of a woman seeking an abortion of a nonviable fetus" imposes an "undue burden" on a woman's right to an abortion, and is therefore unconstitutional.[75] The First Circuit adopted this approach in considering the New Hampshire law, following the approach adopted in most circuits.[76] Of those to consider the question, only the Fifth Circuit has held that the *Salerno* "no set of circumstances" test survives *Casey* in the abortion context.[77]

The Court is also likely to reconsider the constitutional protection of partial-birth abortion. In *Stenberg v. Carhart*,[78] the Court narrowly struck down Nebraska's ban on the dilation and extraction method of abortion, commonly known as "D&X" or "partial-birth abortion."[79] Among other reasons, the Court held the law unconstitutional because it failed to include an exception for cases in which the procedure was necessary to preserve the health of the mother.[80] In response to *Stenberg*, Congress enacted a federal ban on partial-birth abortion.[81] Like the Nebraska law, the federal act contains a life exception, but no health exception.[82] Unlike the Nebraska law, it also includes express congressional findings that partial-birth abortion is "never medically necessary" and that the procedure itself can pose a risk to the mother's health.[83]

---

[75] *Id.* at 877.

[76] See, e.g., Planned Parenthood of Central New Jersey. v. Farmer, 220 F.3d 127, 142–43 (3d Cir. 2000); Planned Parenthood of Southern Arizona v. Lawall, 180 F.3d 1022, 1025–26 (9th Cir. 1999), amended on denial of rehearing, 193 F.3d 1042 (9th Cir. 1999); Women's Medical Professional Corp. v. Voinovich, 130 F.3d 187, 193–96 (6th Cir. 1997); Jane L. v. Bangerter, 102 F.3d 1112, 1116 (10th Cir. 1996); Planned Parenthood, Sioux Falls Clinic v. Miller, 63 F.3d 1452, 1456–58 (8th Cir. 1995).

[77] See Causeway Medical Suite v. Ieyoub, 109 F.3d 1096, 1102–03 (5th Cir. 1997); Barnes v. Moore, 970 F.2d 12, 14 n.2 (5th Cir. 1992). Cf. A Woman's Choice-East Side Women's Clinic v. Newman, 305 F.3d 684 (7th Cir. 2002) (attempting to reconcile the apparent conflict between *Salerno* and *Casey*).

[78] 530 U.S. 914 (2000).

[79] *Id.* at 945–46.

[80] *Id.* at 938.

[81] Pub. L. No. 108-105, 117 Stat. 1201 (2003), codified at 18 U.S.C. § 1531.

[82] 18 U.S.C. § 1531(a).

[83] Pub. L. No. 108-105, § 2, 117 Stat. 1201.

Despite these findings, the U.S. Court of Appeals for the Eighth Circuit struck down the law earlier this year.[84] It held that *Stenberg* established a per se constitutional rule that all abortion restrictions must contain a health exception, even if the legislature believes that a given procedure is never necessary to protect the mother's health. As of this writing, a petition for certiorari is likely, and the Court typically agrees to review lower court decisions striking down federal statutes. As Justice O'Connor provided the fifth vote to strike down the Nebraska statute in *Stenberg*, this is one area in which the impact of her departure from the Court may be seen immediately.

F. Civil RICO

In a 1989 speech at a Cato Institute conference, Judge David Sentelle famously remarked that RICO—the Racketeer Influenced and Corrupt Organizations Act—was "the monster that ate jurisprudence."[85] Although written to combat organized crime, the statute's civil and criminal provisions have become powerful weapons against all manner of targets, expanding the scope and severity of federal criminal law. In the coming term, the Supreme Court may determine whether the beast's size, and appetite, will continue to grow in the civil context.

The 2005–2006 term includes round three of perhaps the most infamous civil RICO case of all time, *Scheidler v. National Organization for Women*. Nearly two decades ago, the National Organization for Women (NOW) and a nationwide class of abortion clinics sued abortion protesters under RICO's civil provisions. NOW and its co-plaintiffs averred that abortion protests including blockades of clinic entrances amounted to a "pattern" of "racketeering activity," including the RICO predicate offense of "extortion" under the federal Hobbs Act,[86] entitling the plaintiffs to substantial monetary relief. In 1994, the Supreme Court held that RICO did not require that the alleged "racketeering activity" have an economic motive, allowing the case to proceed to trial.[87] After an extensive trial, which resulted

---

[84]Carhart v. Gonzales, 413 F.3d 791 (8th Cir. 2005).

[85]David B. Sentelle, RICO: The Monster that Ate Jurisprudence, Remarks at the Cato Institute Conference: RICO, Rights & the Constitution (Oct. 18, 1989) (copy on file with author).

[86]18 U.S.C. § 1951.

[87]National Organization for Women v. Scheidler, 510 U.S. 249 (1994) (Scheidler I).

in a nationwide injunction against abortion clinic blockades and a verdict for the plaintiffs, the Supreme Court overturned the verdict, holding that the abortion protesters' actions did not constitute "extortion" under the Hobbs Act because they had not wrongfully "obtained" any "property."[88]

Now the *Scheidler* case is back again, after the U.S. Court of Appeals for the Seventh Circuit held that a small portion of NOW's original case—that involving four of the 121 alleged predicate acts—survived *Scheidler II* because it was not included in the previous grant of certiorari.[89] Petitioners in *Scheidler III* claim that the Seventh Circuit's order was explicitly precluded by *Scheidler II* and would be happy with a summary reversal. Yet the cert. grant includes two additional questions that may catch the Court's attention: (1) whether the Hobbs Act criminalizes acts or threats of physical violence that are unconnected to either extortion or robbery as the Seventh Circuit suggested (though did not decide) and (2) whether injunctive relief is available in a private civil action under RICO for treble damages.[90]

The first question is interesting insofar as it induces the Court to consider the scope of federal criminal law. If the Hobbs Act were to extend to all acts or threats of violence that obstruct or affect commerce in some way, it would become an incredibly sweeping federal criminal statute. It would also bring all manner of local violent crimes within RICO's reach as potential predicate acts. The Court may avoid this question, however, on the ground that the Seventh Circuit's order did not squarely present the issue. The second question was before the Court in *Scheidler II*, but was never reached because the Court reversed the underlying judgment. As a consequence, this case provides the Court with another opportunity to consider whether RICO allows private litigants to seek equitable relief to enjoin criminal acts.

A second RICO case, *Bank of China v. NBM LLC*,[91] presents the question whether a civil RICO plaintiff alleging mail, wire, or bank

---

[88]Scheidler v. National Organization for Women, 537 U.S. 393 (2003) (Scheidler II).

[89]National Organization for Women v. Scheidler, 91 Fed. Appx. 510 (7th Cir. 2004) (unpublished order), petition for reh'g en banc denied, 396 F.3d 807 (7th Cir. 2005).

[90]See, e.g., Petition for Certiorari at (i), Scheidler v. National Organization for Women, No. 04-1244 (U.S. filed March, 16, 2005) (question presented).

[91]No. 03-1559.

fraud as a predicate act must demonstrate "reasonable reliance." The U.S. Court of Appeals for the Second Circuit held that unless there was reliance upon the alleged fraud, a civil RICO plaintiff cannot show that the alleged fraud was the "proximate cause" of the alleged injury.[92] The petitioners argue that such a showing is not required under the text of the statute, which requires that the alleged fraud be the "reason" for the plaintiff's injury, whereas the respondents argue that fraud cannot be the cause of a given injury unless there was reliance by someone. Although the Justice Department often argues for a more expansive interpretation of the RICO statute,[93] the solicitor general's office sided with the respondent in *Bank of China*, defending the Second Circuit's holding and opposing the grant of certiorari.[94]

Over the summer, the Justice Department petitioned for certiorari in a third civil RICO case that the Court may be likely to grant, *United States v. Philip Morris USA*.[95] In 1999, the federal government filed suit against the tobacco industry alleging the industry engaged in a criminal enterprise to cover up the health risks of smoking. Among other things, the Justice Department sought equitable relief under 18 U.S.C. § 1964(a), which authorizes federal courts to fashion injunctive relief "to prevent and restrain" RICO violations. As part of the requested relief, the Justice Department sought disgorgement of all proceeds obtained through RICO violations, an estimated $280 billion—an amount greater than the tobacco companies' combined net worth.[96]

On an interlocutory appeal, a divided panel of the U.S. Court of Appeals for the D.C. Circuit held that section 1964(a) is limited to "forward-looking remedies" that actually "prevent and restrain" future RICO violations. Because disgorgement is, by its very nature, "a remedy aimed at past violations," the majority held, it "does not so prevent or restrain."[97] The D.C. Circuit rejected both the federal

---

[92] 359 F.3d 171, 176 (2d Cir. 2004).

[93] See *infra* notes 96–98 and accompanying text.

[94] Brief for the United States as Amicus Curiae, Bank of China v. NMB LLC, No. 03-1559 (U.S. filed May 2005).

[95] No. 05-92.

[96] See, e.g., United States v. Philip Morris USA, Inc., 396 F.3d 1190, 1193 (D.C. Cir. 2005).

[97] *Id.* at 1192.

government's aggressive interpretation of the RICO statute, as well as the interpretation of the U.S. Court of Appeals for the Second Circuit, which had previously held that section 1964(a) allows the government to seek disgorgement of those proceeds that "are being used to fund or promote the illegal conduct, or constitute capital available for that purpose."[98] The resulting circuit split increases the likelihood that the Supreme Court will grant certiorari, even though a refusal to hear the case virtually guarantees a settlement between the industry and federal government.

RICO is already an exceedingly broad statute. This case threatens to broaden it even further. The federal government has ample authority under RICO to seek disgorgement or other punitive sanctions through its criminal provisions. Proceeding under those provisions, however, requires the government to abide by costly procedural safeguards that attend to a criminal prosecution, not the least of which is the government's higher burden of proof. By pursuing this case under RICO's civil provisions, however, the government gets to take advantage of a lower burden of proof—"preponderance of evidence" instead of "beyond a reasonable doubt"—even though it seeks what amounts to a criminal remedy. Were the Court to uphold this tactic, it would greatly increase the pressure the federal government could bring in civil RICO cases against all manner of defendants and make RICO an even bigger monster than it already is.

G. Criminal Procedure

If a man's home is his castle, may his wife consent to a police search of the premises over his objection? When the police arrived at the Randolph household on July 6, 2001 in response to a domestic call, they asked Scott Randolph for permission to search the house for drugs. He refused. The police then turned to his wife, Janet Randolph, who had made the initial police call. Not only did Janet consent, she led the police into the home to a room containing drug paraphernalia. A subsequent search of the premises uncovered twenty-five drug-related items.[99]

The trial court denied Scott Randolph's effort to suppress the evidence, on the ground that his wife had "common authority" to

---

[98] United States v. Carson, 52 F.3d 1173, 1182 (2d Cir. 1995).

[99] See Randolph v. State, 590 S.E.2d 834, 835 (Ga. Ct. App. 2004) (summarizing facts).

consent to a police search of the marital home. The Supreme Court of Georgia disagreed.[100] Had Scott not been present, however, the search would have been upheld. Under *United States v. Matlock*,[101] the police may obtain consent to a search from a third party who has "common authority over or other sufficient relationship to the premises or effects sought to be inspected."[102] As generally understood, if a reasonable police officer would believe that the consenting party has authority over the premises, the search is permissible. *Georgia v. Randolph*[103] presents a related question: whether such consent can be given over the present objection of the criminal suspect who himself has common authority over the premises to be searched?

Were the question simply a matter of property law, and who has actual authority to consent to a search of the premises, the police would have a strong case. If, on the other hand, what matters is whether a reasonable police officer would believe there is actual consent—in a sense, whether one occupant is speaking for the household—*Randolph* presents a trickier question. There is no reason for police to assume that one occupant speaks for the other when he is objecting then and there. A homeowner may assume the risk that another occupant may vicariously consent to a search when the owner is away, but that assumption cannot be made when the owner is present and objecting. Georgia claims the defense seeks a rule under which the validity of a search is contingent upon the police's timing, as there would have been no problem if the police had asked Janet Randolph to search the house before Scott came home, or after he left.[104] According to the state, such a rule would focus "arbitrarily on the rights of the objecting occupant, to the detriment of the consenting occupant ... who ha[s] just as much access and control over the home."[105] Perhaps so, but in *Randolph* and similar cases,

---

[100] 604 S.E.2d 835 (Ga. 2004).

[101] 415 U.S. 164 (1974).

[102] *Id.* at 171.

[103] No. 04-1067.

[104] See Petition for a Writ of Certiorari, Georgia v. Randolph, No. 04-1067, 2005 WL 309364 (U.S. filed Feb. 4, 2005).

[105] *Id.*

it is the objecting occupant's Fourth Amendment rights that are at issue.

In *Wilson v. Arkansas*,[106] the Court held the Fourth Amendment requires police to "knock and announce" before entering a home, absent exigent circumstances.[107] *Hudson v. Michigan*[108] presents the question left unanswered in *Wilson*: whether evidence obtained after a "knock and announce" violation is subject to the exclusionary rule, or whether, as the Michigan Supreme Court has held, "suppression of evidence is not the appropriate remedy" for such violations.[109]

Ultimately at issue in *Hudson* is whether "knock and announce" violations are to have any meaningful remedy at all. Whereas evidence obtained after a Fourth Amendment violation is typically excluded from trial, prosecutors may seek to have evidence admitted that would have been "inevitably discovered" had the police complied with relevant constitutional requirements.[110] The doctrine does not excuse the police from obtaining a warrant, however, as such a rule would effectively make warrants irrelevant to evidentiary admissibility. In a sense, the doctrine operates to put the police, and the defendant, in the same position as if the constitutional violation, and accompanying search, had never occurred. If the evidence would have been discovered *independently* of the violation, it gets in; otherwise it's suppressed.

In *Hudson*, the government maintained that evidence uncovered during the search of Hudson's home would have been inevitably discovered because the police had a valid warrant, even if they did not "knock and announce" before they entered the home.[111] If accepted by the Court, this reasoning has the potential to expand

---

[106] 514 U.S. 927 (1995).

[107] *Id.* at 936–37.

[108] No. 04-1360.

[109] See People v. Hudson, No. 246403, 2004 WL 1366947 (Mich. Ct. App. June 17, 2004) (unpublished order) (citing People v. Vasquez, 602 N.W.2d 376 (Mich. 1999), and People v. Stevens, 597 N.W.2d 53 (Mich. 1999)), appeal denied, 692 N.W.2d 385 (Mich. 2005). See also People v. Hudson, No. 230594 (Mich. Ct. App. May 1, 2001) (unpublished order) (same).

[110] See Nix v. Williams, 467 U.S. 431, 448 (1984) ("when, as here, the evidence in question would inevitably have been discovered without reference to the police error or misconduct . . . the evidence is admissible").

[111] See Answer of Respondent, Hudson v. Michigan, No. 04-1360 (U.S. filed April 13, 2005).

the "inevitable discovery" doctrine. Just as applying inevitable discovery to the warrant requirement itself could eliminate the incentive to obtain a valid warrant, civil liberties advocates worry that an inevitable discovery rule could eviscerate the "knock and announce" requirement. It is one thing to allow police to show why "knock and announce" was inappropriate in a given case, perhaps because a suspect would have fled or destroyed evidence. It is quite another to hold, as has the Michigan Supreme Court, that the inevitable discovery doctrine creates an across-the-board exception to the exclusionary rule for "knock and announce" violations.[112]

Turning to the Fifth Amendment, in *Maryland v. Blake*[113] the Court will consider the circumstances under which a court will presume a criminal suspect voluntarily initiated communication with the police after initially invoking his right to counsel. As every American—or at least every American who watches cop shows on television—knows, criminal suspects must be informed of their *Miranda* rights, including the right to refuse to answer police questions without the presence of an attorney, and must also voluntarily waive such rights before the police may interrogate them.[114] Any statement made to the police absent such a waiver is inadmissible in court.

To address concerns that police might badger criminal suspects into waiving their *Miranda* rights before the arrival of counsel, the Court subsequently held that the simple reiteration of the *Miranda* warning provides insufficient evidence that subsequent statements to police made without counsel are voluntary and therefore admissible in court.[115] While a suspect may, of his own volition, re-initiate communication with the police, once the right to counsel is invoked, police must refrain from any conduct that could resemble interrogation. The question in *Blake* is whether curative measures, other than a break in custody or significant lapse in time, can neutralize the harm of improper questioning and render subsequent statements made without the presence of counsel admissible. Rather than a strong presumption that subsequent uncounseled statements were

---

[112]See *supra* note 109.

[113]No. 04-373.

[114]See Dickerson v. United States, 530 U.S. 428 (2000); Miranda v. Arizona, 384 U.S. 436 (1966).

[115]Edwards v Arizona, 451 U.S 477, 487 (1981).

involuntary, Maryland (and the federal government) urge a more flexible inquiry into whether other curative measures sufficiently reduce the risk of badgering or subtle coercion to make a suspect's statements admissible.[116]

H. Freedom of Speech

Two cases this term probe the proper standard for evaluating the constitutionality of alleged government retaliation for protected speech. The first case, *Hartman v. Moore*,[117] pits the constitutional values of separation of powers and the First Amendment against each other. In the decision under review, the U.S. Court of Appeals for the D.C. Circuit broke ranks with several other circuits to hold that law enforcement agents may be liable for retaliatory prosecution in violation of the First Amendment even if the prosecution was supported by probable cause.[118] Once a plaintiff can show that his protected speech—in this case, criticism of the U.S. Postal Service and related political activities—was the motivating factor in the government's decision to press charges, the D.C. Circuit held that the burden shifts to the government officials to demonstrate that they would have pursued the case anyway, reasoning that probable cause "usually represents only one factor among many in the decision to prosecute."[119] While probable cause is all that is necessary to support a prosecution, and courts should not lightly intrude upon prosecutorial discretion, the D.C. Circuit refused to preclude liability "in those rare cases where strong motive evidence combines with weak probable cause," reasoning that such circumstances allow a court to conclude that an individual had been prosecuted in retaliation for exercising constitutionally protected rights.[120] Yet, allowing this ruling to stand, the federal government maintains, could chill legitimate law enforcement actions against politically vocal individuals

---

[116]See Brief for Petitioner at 18–25, Maryland v. Blake, No. 04-373 (U.S. filed Jun. 9, 2005); Brief for the United States as Amicus Curiae Supporting Petitioner at 15–20, Maryland v. Blake, No. 04-373 (U.S. filed Jun. 9, 2005).

[117]No. 04-1495.

[118]Moore v. Hartman, 388 F.3d 871 (D.C. Cir. 2004).

[119]*Id.* at 878.

[120]*Id.* at 881.

and encourage excessive judicial investigation of executive branch decisionmaking at the expense of executive discretion.[121]

In *Garcetti v. Ceballos*,[122] the Court will reconsider the extent to which a public employee's job-related speech is protected by the First Amendment. Under *Pickering v. Board of Education*,[123] a court must balance "the interests of the [employee], as a citizen, in commenting upon matters of public concern and the interest of the State, as an employer, in promoting the efficiency of the public services it performs through its employees."[124] Where a public employee is sanctioned for speech that is not part of her job, such as writing a letter to the editor critical of a government policy, the speech is clearly protected. Yet, where a government employee is speaking as part of her job responsibilities, the extent of First Amendment protection is less clear.

In *Garcetti*, a local prosecutor claims he was subject to adverse employment actions because he authored a memorandum questioning the veracity of a prosecution witness and was subsequently called to testify for the defense. The U.S. Court of Appeals for the Ninth Circuit held that the memorandum was protected speech because it addressed a matter of public concern, outweighing the government's interest as an employer.[125] Therefore the retaliation, if proven, could violate the prosecutor's First Amendment rights. Were this speech not protected, the court held, government employees could be sanctioned for exposing government malfeasance.[126] The government, for its part, maintains that the prosecutor's memo was not protected by the First Amendment, as it was merely one of his job-related duties and did not contain speech made "as a citizen," as opposed to as a government employee. Freedom of expression is a personal right, and "when a public employee speaks in carrying out his job duties, he has no personal interest in the speech."[127]

---

[121] See Petition for a Writ of Certiorari at 19–22, Hartman v. Moore, No. 04-1495 (U.S. filed May 2005).

[122] No. 04-473.

[123] 391 U.S. 563 (1968).

[124] *Id.* at 568.

[125] Ceballos v. Garcetti, 361 F.3d 1168, 1180 (9th Cir. 2004).

[126] *Id.* at 1176.

[127] Brief for the United States as Amicus Curiae Supporting Petitioners at 9, Garcetti v. Ceballos, No. 04-473 (U.S. filed May 2005).

The government's position, in effect, is that any protection for such speech must come from whistleblower protection statutes, and the like, rather than from the Constitution. To paraphrase Justice Oliver Wendell Holmes, a government employee may have right to free speech, but he does not have a right to a job.[128]

I. Antitrust

A trio of antitrust cases this term provides the Court with the opportunity to clarify and modernize the law governing competition. In each case, interestingly enough, the federal government is on the side of the petitioner, urging the Court to overturn outdated precedent, eschew formalist rules that ignore efficiency gains from what might otherwise appear to be anticompetitive conduct, and clarify the scope of antitrust scrutiny. Together, the three cases should continue the trend of rationalizing antitrust law and lessening its potential to impede business innovation and entrepreneurial activity.

Leading the pack is *Illinois Tool Works v. Independent Ink,*[129] a direct challenge to a long-standing, if outmoded, Supreme Court precedent concerning the legality of selling patented or copyrighted products subject to tying arrangements.[130] Illinois Tool Works (ITW) manufactures patented ink jet printheads used for printing barcodes and carton labels. ITW markets the printheads in conjunction with its own unpatented inks. Buyers of ITW printheads are contractually obligated to purchase ITW-supplied ink as well. Independent Ink, an ink manufacturer, alleged ITW committed a Sherman Act violation by tying the printhead and ink sales in this manner. According to Independent, ITW had market power, as a matter of law under existing precedent, due to its printhead patent.[131]

---

[128] McAuliffe v. Mayor of New Bedford, 29 N.E. 517, 517 (Mass. 1892) (Holmes, J.) (a policeman "may have a constitutional right to talk politics, but he has no constitutional right to be a policeman").

[129] No. 04-1329.

[130] "A tying arrangement is an agreement by a party to sell one product but only on the condition that the buyer also purchases a different (or tied) product . . ." Eastman Kodak Co. v. Image Technical Services, 504 U.S. 451, 461 (1992) (internal quotation omitted).

[131] Independent Ink, Inc. v. Illinois Tool Works, Inc., 396 F.3d 1342, 1344–45 (Fed. Cir. 2005) (summarizing facts).

For over four decades, an antitrust defendant who holds a patent or copyright to a product has been presumed to have market power, making the tying arrangement illegal under section 1 of the Sherman Act.[132] In *United States v. Loew's, Inc.*,[133] the Supreme Court adopted a virtual per se rule against tying arrangements involving patented or copyrighted products. Such arrangements are subject to antitrust scrutiny where the seller has "market power"—the power to charge prices above competitive levels or otherwise force purchasers to do something they would not do in a competitive market. In *Loew's* the Court held that "[t]he requisite economic power is presumed when the tying product is patented or copyrighted."[134] The Court's assumption in *Loew's* was that the existence of a patent or copyright was itself evidence of market power, owing to the "uniqueness" or "distinctiveness" necessary to patent or copyright the product in question.[135] Antitrust jurisprudence at the time was highly suspicious of *any* tying arrangements whatsoever, and the law and economics scholarship on the potential efficiency gains from tying was still undeveloped.

The district court disagreed with Independent, observing that the *Loew's* presumption dated from "a time when genuine proof of power in the market for the tying product was not required."[136] Today, however, market power must be proven when alleging that a given tying arrangement is illegal. Not even the antitrust enforcers at the Federal Trade Commission or the Department of Justice presume that patents and copyrights necessarily confer market power.[137] While appreciating the district court's critique of the *Loew's* presumption, the three judge panel of the U.S. Court of Appeals for the Federal Circuit felt bound by existing precedent.[138]

While never overruled, the *Loew's* rationale has been subject to extensive criticism. The academic commentary is nearly unanimous

---

[132] 15 U.S.C. § 1.

[133] 371 U.S. 38 (1962).

[134] *Id.* at 45.

[135] *Id.* at 45, 46.

[136] Independent Ink, Inc. v. Trident, Inc., 210 F. Supp. 2d 1155, 1165 n.10 (C.D. Cal. 2002).

[137] United States Department of Justice and Federal Trade Commission, Antitrust Guidelines for the Licensing of Intellectual Property, §§ 2.2, 5.3 (1995).

[138] 396 F.3d 1342, 1348–49, 1351 (Fed. Cir. 2005).

in its condemnation of the *Loew's* rule. As Judge Richard Posner observed, "most patents confer too little monopoly power to be a proper object of antitrust concern. Some patents confer no monopoly power at all."[139] Several justices have echoed this view, most notably in Justice O'Connor's noted plurality in *Jefferson Parish Hospital District No. 2 v. Hyde*.[140] The American Bar Association, among others, filed briefs supporting Illinois Tool Works' petition for certiorari so that *Loew's* could be overruled.[141] A decision overturning *Loew's* seems likely. The question is whether the existence of a patent will be entitled to any weight at all in a market power determination.

Texaco v. Dagher (consolidated with *Shell Oil Company v. Dagher*)[142] presents the question whether it is per se illegal under section 1 of the Sherman Act for a joint venture to set the prices at which it sells its own products. In 1998, Texaco and Shell Oil formed two wholly-owned joint ventures—one for the eastern United States (Motiva), the other for the West (Equilon)—encompassing the entirety of their respective refining and marketing operations in the United States. Although the joint ventures would continue to sell gasoline under both the Shell and Texaco brands, each in their respective geographic region, neither company would retain a financial stake in the gasoline bearing its name, as profits from the ventures were to be distributed based upon each company's investment. Pursuant to the joint venture agreement, gasoline under each label would sell for the same price.[143]

The case arose with the filing of a class-action lawsuit on behalf of service station owners alleging that the joint venture's common pricing scheme was an illegal "restraint of trade" under the Sherman

---

[139]Richard Posner, Antitrust Law 197–98 (2d ed. 2001).

[140]466 U.S. 2, 37 n.7 (1984) (O'Connor, J., concurring in the judgment) (noting the "common misconception . . . that a patent or copyright . . . suffices to demonstrate market power" and that "a patent holder has no market power in any relevant sense if there are close substitutes for the patented product").

[141]See, e.g., Motion to File Brief Amicus Curiae and Brief of the American Bar Association as Amicus Curiae in Support of Petitioners, Illinois Tool Works, Inc. v. Independent Ink, Inc., No. 04-1329 (U.S. filed May 5, 2005).

[142]Nos. 04-805 and 04-814.

[143]Dagher v. Saudi Refining, Inc., 369 F.3d 1108, 1111–13 (9th Cir. 2004) (summarizing facts).

Act.[144] After the oil companies won a summary judgment in the district court, a divided panel of the U.S. Court of Appeals for the Ninth Circuit held that the decision to set a single gasoline price within the joint venture could be per se illegal price fixing under the Sherman Act if the setting of a single price is not "reasonably necessary to further the legitimate aims of the joint venture."[145]

The solicitor general's office filed an amicus brief in support of Texaco and Shell, arguing that the Ninth Circuit "plainly erred" in concluding that the joint venture's pricing of its own products "could result in a per se violation of Section 1 of the Sherman Act."[146] Antitrust doctrine has long recognized that when "partners set the price of their goods or services they are literally 'price fixing,' but they are not per se in violation of the Sherman Act."[147] Rather, where the setting of prices, or other potentially anti-competitive conduct, is "ancillary" to a legitimate joint venture, it should be subject to rule of reason analysis, if subject to antitrust scrutiny at all.

A joint venture's ability to set the prices for its own products would seem quite integral to the success of the joint venture. Indeed, it is hard to imagine how the Texaco-Shell joint venture could operate at all if it were not able to set the prices for its own products. As a single firm, whether it chose to set the prices for Shell and Texaco gasoline at the same or varying levels is immaterial in terms of its competitive impact. As Judge Ferdinand Fernandez noted in his dissent:

> In this case, nothing more radical is afoot than the fact that an entity, which now owns all of the production, transportation, research, storage, sales and distribution facilities for engaging in the gasoline business, also prices its own products.[148]

The decision to create the joint venture in the first place is subject to antitrust scrutiny under the Sherman Act, but once the joint venture is created, it is hard to see what legitimate purpose is served by subjecting internal pricing decisions to further scrutiny. In the

[144]The only claims at issue in this case concern the western joint venture, Equilon.

[145]369 F.3d at 1121.

[146]Brief for the United States as Amicus Curiae at 8, Texaco, Inc. v. Dagher, Nos. 04-805 and 04-814 (U.S. filed May 2005).

[147]Broadcast Music, Inc. v. Columbia Broadcasting System, Inc., 441 U.S. 1, 9 (1979).

[148]Dagher, 369 F.3d at 1127 (Fernandez, J., concurring in part and dissenting in part).

unlikely event it is upheld, the Ninth Circuit's opinion could have a chilling effect on the creation of joint ventures among potentially competing firms, even though such ventures can have tremendous economic benefits.[149]

The third antitrust case before the Court next term, *Volvo Trucks North America, Inc. v. Reeder-Simco GMC, Inc.*[150] arises under the Robinson-Patman Act (RPA) rather than the Sherman Act. Under the RPA, sellers may not "discriminate in price between different purchasers of commodities of like grade and quality . . . where the effect of such discrimination may be substantially to lessen competition . . ."[151] The RPA is traditionally enforced in the context of sales of fungible goods and was intended to prevent a seller from favoring one purchaser over another. *Volvo Trucks*, however, raises the price discrimination concern in the context of competitive bidding. Specifically, the question is how to apply the RPA's prohibition in the context of special order products that are made for and sold to individual, pre-identified customers after competitive bidding through resellers that are not directly competing against one another.

Volvo argues that the RPA should not apply to its conduct as it is not engaging in price discrimination between dealers competing to sell its products to the same customers. If Volvo provides greater price concessions to some dealers over others, it is not doing so in an anti-competitive fashion. Reeder-Simco GMC, a truck dealership, argued that any practice of giving some dealers greater price concessions than others was illegal price discrimination under the RPA.[152]

Again the solicitor general's office supported the petition for certiorari, counseling a more modest interpretation of federal antitrust law so as to give private firms a wider berth. Specifically, the solicitor general argued that the RPA only bans price discrimination between competing purchasers. Applying the RPA here, the solicitor general's brief argued, "could severely restrict a manufacturer's ability to

---

[149]See, e.g., Copperweld Corp. v. Independence Tube Corp., 467 U.S. 752, 768 (1984) ("combinations, such as mergers, joint ventures, and various vertical agreements, hold the promise of increasing a firm's efficiency and enabling it to compete more effectively").

[150]No. 04-905.

[151]15 U.S.C. § 13(a).

[152]Petition for a Writ of Certiorari at 11–13, Volvo Trucks North America, Inc. v. Reeder-Simco GMC, Inc., No. 04-905 (U.S. filed May 2005) (describing arguments).

compete effectively with other manufacturers. It would sacrifice vibrant interbrand competition, the primary concern of antitrust law, for an illusory gain in intrabrand competition."[153]

III. More to Come

If recent practice is any guide, the Court has filled only half of its docket for the year. In addition to the cases noted above, there are quite a few high-profile issues that could wind up on the Court's plate. For instance, the Court may consider the extent to which the dormant Commerce Clause limits the ability of state governments to encourage in-state economic development through the use of tax credits and other fiscal instruments. In *Cuno v. Daimler Chrsyler*,[154] the U.S. Court of Appeals for the Sixth Circuit held that Ohio's franchise tax credit for additional manufacturing investment made by in-state firms was unconstitutional.[155] The court rejected Daimler's argument that the policy benefited in-state investment instead of penalizing out-of-state investment.[156] A Supreme Court decision in *Cuno* could have a substantial effect on states' use of tax credits and other investment incentives to attract, or maintain, business investment within the state.

On the environmental front, the Court may be asked to consider whether the Clean Air Act requires the Environmental Protection Agency (EPA) to regulate greenhouse gases,[157] as maintained by several states and environmentalist groups, as well as the extent of the EPA's authority to force decades-old coal-fired power plants to adopt newer pollution control equipment in the course of routine maintenance and repairs.[158] The Court may also seek to resolve the brewing circuit split on the scope of the EPA's authority under the Clean Water Act. While most circuits have interpreted the Court's 2001 decision in *Solid Waste Agency of Northern Cook County v. U.S.*

---

[153] Brief for the United States as Amicus Curiae Supporting Petitioner at 10, Volvo Trucks North America, Inc. v. Reeder-Simco GMC, Inc., No. 04-905 (U.S. filed May 2005) (internal citations omitted).

[154] 386 F.3d 738 (6th Cir. 2004), petition for cert. filed, 73 U.S.L.W. 3650 (U.S. April 18, 2005) (No. 04-1407).

[155] *Id.* at 746.

[156] *Id.* at 745.

[157] Massachusetts v. EPA, No. 03-1361, 2005 WL 1653055 (D.C. Cir. July 15, 2005).

[158] See generally United States v. Duke Energy, 411 F.3d 539 (4th Cir. 2005).

Army Corps of Engineers[159] quite broadly, the Fifth Circuit has held the decision places substantial limits on EPA regulatory authority.[160] Therefore, one or more petitions for certiorari on this issue are possible. Much of the above may be overshadowed should the Court, as expected, agree to hear one or more cases relating to the "war on terror" this term. In July, the U.S. Court of Appeals for the D.C. Circuit upheld the executive's decision to try Salim Ahmed Hamdan by military commission.[161] Hamdan was captured in Afghanistan and is reported to have been a bodyguard and personal driver for Osama bin Laden. The D.C. Circuit held that the use of military commissions was authorized by Congress[162] and rejected Hamdan's claims that such a trial would violate the 1949 Geneva Convention governing the treatment of prisoners.[163]

In addition to the *Hamdan* case, the Court could also agree to hear the Guantanamo detainee cases, consolidated and currently pending before the D.C. Circuit.[164] A petition of certiorari is also expected, once again, in the case of Jose Padilla, currently pending before the U.S. Court of Appeals for the Fourth Circuit.[165] While the Supreme Court's decision in *Hamdi v. Rumsfeld* upheld the detention and trial of an "enemy combatant" captured on foreign soil,[166] the *Padilla* case would force the Court to consider whether an American citizen, apprehended on *American* soil, can also be held and tried as an "enemy combatant." Any single one of these cases could have a significant effect on civil liberties and the federal government's anti-terrorism efforts, and there is a reasonable chance the Court could end up hearing all three.

---

[159] 531 U.S. 159 (2001).

[160] See In re Needham, 354 F.3d 340, 344–45 (5th Cir. 2003); see generally Rice v. Harken Exploration Co., 250 F.3d 264 (5th Cir. 2001). Although *Needham* and *Rice* specifically address the scope of federal regulation over "waters of the United States" under the Oil Pollution Act (OPA), both decisions note that federal jurisdiction under the OPA was intended to be coextensive with that under the Clean Water Act. Needham, 354 F.3d at 344; Rice, 250 F.3d at 267.

[161] Hamdan v. Rumsfeld, No. 04-5393, 2005 WL 1653046 (D.C. Cir. July 15, 2005).

[162] *Id.* at *4.

[163] *Id.* at *6.

[164] In re Guantanamo Detainee Cases, Nos. 05-8003 and 05-5064 (D.C. Cir. consolidated on March 10, 2005).

[165] Padilla v. Hanft, No. 05-6396 (4th Cir. oral argument held July 19, 2005).

[166] 542 U.S. 507 (2004).

Contributors

Jonathan H. Adler is associate professor of law and associate director of the Center for Business Law & Regulation at the Case Western Reserve University School of Law, where he teaches courses in environmental and constitutional law. During the Fall 2005 semester, Professor Adler will be visiting associate professor of law at the George Mason University School of Law, where he will teach environmental and administrative law. A contributing editor for National Review Online, his articles have appeared in numerous publications, ranging from *Environmental Law* and the *Supreme Court Economic Review* to the *Wall Street Journal* and *Washington Post*. Prior to joining the faculty at Case, Professor Adler clerked for the Honorable David B. Sentelle on the U.S. Court of Appeals for the D.C. Circuit. From 1991 to 2000, Professor Adler worked at the Competitive Enterprise Institute, a free market research and advocacy group in Washington, D.C., where he directed CEI's environmental studies program. In 1998 he was the Broadbent Research Fellow at the Political Economy Research Center in Bozeman, Montana, and in 1999 he was a visiting lecturer at Catholic University. He currently serves on the board of directors for the America's Future Foundation, the advisory board of the NFIB Legal Foundation, and the editorial board of the *Cato Supreme Court Review*. In 2004, Professor Adler was awarded the Paul M. Bator Award, given annually by the Federalist Society for Law and Policy Studies to an academic under forty for excellence in teaching, scholarship, and commitment to students.

Stuart Banner is professor of law at the UCLA School of Law. He is the author of *How the Indians Lost Their Land: Law and Power on the Frontier* (Harvard University Press 2005), *The Death Penalty: An American History* (Harvard University Press 2002), *Legal Systems in Conflict: Property and Sovereignty in Missouri, 1750–1860* (University of Oklahoma Press 2000), and *Anglo-American Securities Regulation:*

Cultural and Political Roots, 1690–1860 (Cambridge University Press 1998), as well as many articles in law and history journals. After graduating from Stanford Law School in 1988, Professor Banner served as a law clerk to Judge Alex Kozinski of the U.S. Court of Appeals for the Ninth Circuit and Justice Sandra Day O'Connor of the U.S. Supreme Court. He was counsel of record for amici George Akerlof et al., a group of economists, in *Granholm v. Heald.*

Annemarie Bridy is a law clerk to the Honorable Dolores K. Sloviter of the U.S. Court of Appeals for the Third Circuit. She previously worked as a law clerk for the Honorable William H. Yohn Jr., of the U.S. District Court for the Eastern District of Pennsylvania. She holds a B.A., *summa cum laude,* with distinction in English from Boston University, a Ph.D. in English literature from the University of California at Irvine, and a J.D. from the Temple University James E. Beasley School of Law, from which she graduated with high honors in 2004. While attending law school, Ms. Bridy worked full-time on the test development and research staff of the Law School Admission Council in Newtown, Pennsylvania, where she developed questions for the LSAT® and managed the writing portion of the test. She is the recipient of various academic awards, including Temple's John J. Mackiewicz Scholarship for Intellectual Property Law and research fellowships from the University of California and the Andrew W. Mellon Foundation. She has published articles in the *Journal of the Copyright Society of the USA* and the *Journal of Law, Medicine & Ethics.*

James W. Ely Jr. is a professor of law and history at Vanderbilt University, where he holds the Milton R. Underwood Chair in Free Enterprise. He holds an M.A. and a Ph.D. in history from the University of Virginia as well as an LL.B. from Harvard University. As a renowned legal historian and teacher he has published extensively. His works include the books *The Guardian of Every Other Right: A Constitutional History of Property Rights* (Oxford University Press 2d ed. 1998), *The Fuller Court: Justices, Rulings and Legacy* (ABC-Clio 2003), *Railroads and American Law* (University Press of Kansas 2001), *American Legal History: Cases and Materials* (Oxford University Press 3d ed. 2004) (co-authored with K. Hall and P. Finkelman), and *A History of the Tennessee Supreme Court* (University of Tennessee Press

2002) (editor and contributor), for which he received the Tennessee History Book Award. Professor Ely has served as the editor of the *American Journal of Legal History* and has been published in several leading academic journals. He serves on the editorial board of the *Cato Supreme Court Review*.

Richard A. Epstein is the James Parker Hall Distinguished Service Professor of Law at the University of Chicago, where he has taught since 1972. Prior to joining the University of Chicago Law School faculty, he taught law at the University of Southern California from 1968 to 1972. He received a B.A. in philosophy, *summa cum laude*, from Columbia in 1964, a B.A. in law with first class honors from Oxford University in 1966, an LL.B., *cum laude*, from the Yale Law School in 1968, and an LL.D., h.c., from the University of Ghent in 2003. Professor Epstein was elected a fellow of the American Academy of Arts and Sciences in 1985 and has been the Peter and Kirstin Bedford Senior Fellow at Stanford's Hoover Institution since 2000. He served as editor of the *Journal of Legal Studies* from 1981 to 1991, and of the *Journal of Law and Economics* from 1991 to 2001. At present he is a director of the John M. Olin Program in Law and Economics. His books include *Skepticism and Freedom: A Modern Case for Classical Liberalism* (University of Chicago Press 2003), *Cases and Materials on Torts* (Aspen Law & Business 7th ed. 2000), *Principles for a Free Society: Reconciling Individual Liberty with the Common Good* (Perseus Books 1998), *Mortal Peril: Our Inalienable Right to Health Care?* (Addison-Wesley 1997), *Simple Rules for a Complex World* (Harvard University Press 1995), *Bargaining With the State* (Princeton 1993), *Forbidden Grounds: The Case Against Employment Discrimination Laws* (Harvard University Press 1992), and *Takings: Private Property and the Power of Eminent Domain* (Harvard University Press 1985). Professor Epstein serves as an adjunct scholar at the Cato Institute and is a member of the editorial board of the *Cato Supreme Court Review*.

Marci A. Hamilton holds the Paul R. Verkuil Chair in Public Law at the Benjamin N. Cardozo School of Law, Yeshiva University. She has been Visiting Scholar at the Princeton Theological Seminary (1997–98; Spring 2004), Visiting Professor of Law at New York University School of Law (2000–2001), Distinguished Visiting Professor of Law at Emory University School of Law (Fall 1999), and Fellow at the Center of Theological Inquiry (Fall 1997). Professor Hamilton is one of the United States' leading constitutional law scholars specializing in church/state relations, federalism, and representation. She has published extensively and has lectured frequently on constitutional issues in the United States, Europe, and Africa. Her most recent work is *God vs. the Gavel: Religion and the Rule of Law* (Cambridge 2005), which is an Amazon bestseller. She is a columnist on constitutional issues for www.findlaw.com, where her column appears every other Thursday. A frequent advisor to Congress on the constitutionality of pending legislation, Professor Hamilton is the First Amendment advisor for victims in many clergy abuse cases, including the consolidated cases in Northern and Southern California, the Portland Archdiocese federal bankruptcy case, and the Spokane Diocese federal bankruptcy case. She was lead counsel for the City of Boerne, Texas, in *City of Boerne v. Flores* (1997), the Supreme Court's seminal federalism and church/state case holding the Religious Freedom Restoration Act unconstitutional. Professor Hamilton clerked for Associate Justice Sandra Day O'Connor of the U.S. Supreme Court and Judge Edward R. Becker of the U.S. Court of Appeals for the Third Circuit. She received her J.D., *magna cum laude*, from the University of Pennsylvania Law School, where she served as editor-in-chief of the *University of Pennsylvania Law Review*. She also received her M.A. in philosophy and M.A. with high honors in English from Pennsylvania State University, and her B.A., *summa cum laude*, from Vanderbilt University. She is a member of Phi Beta Kappa and Order of the Coif and serves on the editorial board of the *Cato Supreme Court Review*.

John Hasnas is an associate professor of business at the McDonough School of Business at Georgetown University, where he teaches courses in ethics and law. Professor Hasnas has held previous appointments as an associate professor of law at George Mason University School of Law, visiting associate professor of law at the Washington College of Law at American University, and Law and Humanities Fellow at Temple University School of Law. Professor Hasnas has also been a visiting scholar at the Kennedy Institute of Ethics in Washington, D.C., and the Social Philosophy and Policy Center in Bowling Green, Ohio. He received his B.A. in philosophy from Lafayette College, his J.D. and Ph.D. in legal philosophy from

Duke University, and his LL.M in legal education from Temple Law School. Between 1997 and 1999, Professor Hasnas served as assistant general counsel to Koch Industries, Inc., in Wichita, Kansas. His recent publications include: *Ethics and the Problem of White Collar Crime*, 54 *American University Law Review* 579 (2005); *Hayek, Common Law, and Fluid Drive*, 1 *New York University Journal of Law and Liberty* 79 (2004); and *Toward a Theory of Empirical Natural Rights*, 22 *Social Philosophy and Policy* 111 (2005). Professor Hasnas also serves as a senior fellow at the Cato Institute.

Douglas W. Kmiec is the Caruso Family Chair and Professor of Constitutional Law at Pepperdine University. Professor Kmiec served as head of the Office of Legal Counsel (assistant U.S. attorney general) for Presidents Ronald Reagan and George H.W. Bush. Former Dean and St. Thomas More Professor of Law at The Catholic University of America, Professor Kmiec was a member of the law faculty for nearly two decades at the University of Notre Dame. He is the author or co-author of numerous books and articles on the Constitution, including *The American Constitutional Order* (Lexis-Nexis 2d ed. 2004). A constitutional law contributing editor for the American Bar Association, Professor Kmiec writes a syndicated column and is a frequent commentator on national legal developments. He has been privileged to be both a White House Fellow and a Distinguished Fulbright Fellow. He was an inaugural visiting scholar and is an advisor to the National Constitution Center. He also serves as a member of the editorial board of the *Cato Supreme Court Review*.

Timothy Lynch is the director of the Cato Institute's Project on Criminal Justice and the associate director of Cato's Center for Constitutional Studies. Mr. Lynch is an outspoken critic of police misconduct, the drug war, gun control, and the militarization of police tactics. Since September 11, 2001, Mr. Lynch has decried several antiterrorism initiatives for their impact on civil liberties. He has published articles in the *New York Times, Washington Post, Wall Street Journal, Los Angeles Times, ABA Journal,* and the *National Law Journal.* He has appeared on such television programs as the *Lehrer Newshour, NBC Nightly News, ABC World News Tonight,* Fox News Channel's *The O'Reilly Factor,* and C-SPAN's *Washington Journal.* Mr. Lynch has also filed several amicus briefs in the U.S. Supreme Court in cases involving constitutional rights. He is the editor of the book *After Prohibition: An Adult Approach to Drug Policies in the 21st Century* (Cato Institute 2000). Mr. Lynch is a 1990 graduate of the Marquette University School of Law and is a member of the Wisconsin and District of Columbia bars.

Mark K. Moller is a senior fellow in constitutional studies at the Cato Institute and the editor-in-chief of the *Cato Supreme Court Review*. Mr. Moller previously practiced law with the Class Action and Appellate and Constitutional Law Practice Groups at the law firm of Gibson, Dunn & Crutcher LLP. During private practice Mr. Moller engaged in a number of high-profile representations, including as a member of the team that successfully litigated *Bush v. Gore* before the Supreme Court. He also played a key role in the defense of managed care companies and mutual funds against controversial class action and derivative litigation in *In re Managed Care Litigation* and *In re Market Timing Litigation*. His recent article, *The Rule of Law Problem: Unconstitutional Class Actions and Options for Reform*, appeared in: 28 *Harvard Journal of Law and Public Policy* 855 (2005). Mr. Moller's op-eds have appeared in *Legal Times*, Slate.com, Reason.com, and FoxNews.com, among other publications, and he has discussed the Supreme Court on numerous television and radio programs, including Fox News Channel's *Studio B with Shepherd Smith*, *ABC News Now*, Court TV, and the *Sam Donaldson Show*. Mr. Moller earned his B.A. *magna cum laude* from Duke University in 1994, his J.D. with honors from the University of Chicago Law School in 1999, and his LL.M in common law legal history and theory (first class honors) from the University of Cambridge in 2000, where he studied with noted legal historian J. H. Baker.

Roger Pilon is vice president for legal affairs at the Cato Institute. He holds Cato's B. Kenneth Simon Chair in Constitutional Studies and is the founder and director of Cato's Center for Constitutional Studies. Established in 1989 to encourage limited constitutional government at home and abroad, the Center has become an important force in the national debate over constitutional interpretation and judicial philosophy. Mr. Pilon's work has appeared in the *New York Times*, *Washington Post*, *Wall Street Journal*, *Los Angeles Times*, *Legal Times*, *National Law Journal*, *Harvard Journal of Law and Public Policy*,

Notre Dame Law Review, Stanford Law and Policy Review, Texas Review of Law and Politics, and elsewhere. He has appeared, among other places, on ABC's *Nightline*, CBS's *60 Minutes II*, National Public Radio, Fox News Channel, CNN, MSNBC, and CNBC. He lectures and debates at universities and law schools across the country and testifies often before Congress. Before joining Cato, Mr. Pilon held five senior posts in the Reagan administration, including at State and Justice. He has taught philosophy and law and was a national fellow at Stanford's Hoover Institution. At present he is an adjunct professor at Georgetown University through The Fund for American Studies. Mr. Pilon holds a B.A. from Columbia University, an M.A. and a Ph.D. from the University of Chicago, and a J.D. from the George Washington University School of Law. In 1989 the Bicentennial Commission presented him with the Benjamin Franklin Award for excellence in writing on the U.S. Constitution. In 2001 Columbia University's School of General Studies awarded him its Alumni Medal of Distinction.

David G. Post is I. Herman Stern Professor of Law at Temple University Law School. He is an adjunct scholar at the Cato Institute, and the co-founder of ICANN Watch (www.icannwatch.org). He is the author of *Cyberlaw: Problems of Policy and Jurisprudence in the Information Age* (West 2004) (co-authored with Paul Schiff Berman and Patricia Bellia), as well as numerous articles on intellectual property law, Internet law, and the application of complexity theory to the law. (His publications are available at www.davidpost.com.) He holds a Ph.D. in physical anthropology from Yale University and a J.D. from the Georgetown University Law Center, from which he graduated *summa cum laude* in 1986. After clerking with then-Judge Ruth Bader Ginsburg on the U.S. Court of Appeals for the D.C. Circuit, he spent six years at the Washington, D.C., law firm of Wilmer, Cutler & Pickering, after which he clerked again for Justice Ginsburg during her first term at the Supreme Court. He then joined the faculty of Georgetown University (1994–1997) and Temple University (1997–present). He is a sometime contributor to the Volokh Conspiracy blog (www.volokh.com), plays guitar, piano, banjo, and harmonica in the band "Bad Dog" (www.temple.edu/lawschool/dpost/Baddog.html), and has appeared as a guest artist with the band Transistor Rodeo (www.transistorrodeo.com).

Timothy Sandefur is the lead attorney in the Economic Liberty Project at the Pacific Legal Foundation. A graduate of Hillsdale College and Chapman University School of Law, he served as a law clerk at the Institute for Justice and the Claremont Institute Center for Constitutional Jurisprudence. Upon his graduation, he was awarded Chapman University's prestigious Dean's Professionalism Award. He is also a contributing editor for *Liberty* magazine, and has written for a variety of publications, including the *Harvard Journal of Law and Public Policy, Washington Times, The Humanist, The Claremont Review of Books,* and *The American Enterprise.* At the Pacific Legal Foundation his work focuses on restoring constitutional protection for the right to earn a living and on limiting the abuse of eminent domain, as well as on several other issues. He has represented various clients or appeared as amicus curiae in such cases as *Kelo v. City of New London, Johnson v. California,* and, along with David G. Post, in *MGM Studios Inc. v. Grokster, Ltd.* In 2004, he was awarded a Ronald Reagan Medal for his contributions to public interest law by the Claremont Institute. He writes for the weblogs Positive Liberty (www.positiveliberty.com) and Panda's Thumb (www.pandasthumb.org).

Daniel E. Troy is a partner in the Life Sciences Practice and Appellate Litigation Group at Sidley Austin Brown & Wood, LLP, where he practices administrative and constitutional law and litigation, with particular focus on the pharmaceutical, biotechnology, food, medical device, cosmetic, and media industries. Prior to joining the firm, he served as chief counsel of the Food and Drug Administration from 2001 to 2004, playing a pivotal role in raising the FDA's focus on First Amendment concerns. Mr. Troy has testified before the Senate and House Judiciary Committees, the House Committee on Science, and successfully argued before the U.S. Supreme Court in *Vera v. Bush,* a Fourteenth Amendment challenge to race-based admissions. He clerked for Judge Robert H. Bork on the U.S. Court of Appeals for the D.C. Circuit (1983–84), served in the Justice Department's Office of Legal Counsel (1987–90), and was a partner at Wiley Rein & Fielding LLP. In addition, Mr. Troy is the author of the book *Retroactive Legislation* (AEI 2000) and has written numerous law review articles and book chapters, including *Advertising: Not Low Value Speech* in the *Yale Journal of Regulation* and, with Robert H. Bork, *Locating the Boundaries: The Scope of Congress's Power to Regulate*

Commerce in the *Harvard Journal of Law and Public Policy*. He is a contributor to the *Heritage Guide on the Constitution* and has published more than fifty articles in publications such as the *Wall Street Journal*, *Los Angeles Times*, *San Francisco Chronicle*, *Legal Times*, *National Law Journal*, *Weekly Standard*, *Washington Times*, *Commentary*, and *Policy Review*. He received a B.S. from Cornell University and a J.D. from Columbia University.

A. Mark Weisburd is the Martha B. Brandis Professor of Law at the University of North Carolina School of Law. He is a graduate of Princeton and of the University of Michigan Law School and served as a note editor on the *Michigan Law Review*. Between college and law school he served as a foreign service officer in Bangladesh during and after the period of unrest that led to that country's independence. After law school he was an associate at Wilmer, Cutler & Pickering for five years. He joined the faculty at Carolina in 1981 and has taught courses in civil procedure, public international law generally, and the international law of human rights. Professor Weisburd is the author of *Use of Force: The Practice of States Since World War II* (Pennsylvania State University Press 1997) and has also written a number of articles for various law reviews on aspects of public international law and of the relationship between public international law and the law of the United States.

ABOUT THE CATO INSTITUTE

The Cato Institute is a public policy research foundation dedicated to the principles of limited government, individual liberty, free markets, and private property. It takes its name from *Cato's Letters*, popular libertarian pamphlets that helped to lay the philosophical foundation for the American Revolution.

Despite the Founders' libertarian values, today virtually no aspect of life is free from government encroachment. A pervasive intolerance for individual rights is shown by government's arbitrary intrusions into private economic transactions and its disregard for civil liberties.

To counter that trend, the Cato Institute undertakes an extensive publications program that addresses the complete spectrum of policy issues. It holds major conferences throughout the year, from which papers are published thrice yearly in the *Cato Journal*, and also publishes the quarterly magazine *Regulation* and the annual *Cato Supreme Court Review*.

The Cato Institute accepts no government funding. It relies instead on contributions from foundations, corporations, and individuals and revenue generated from the sale of publications. The Institute is a nonprofit, tax-exempt educational foundation under Section 501(c)(3) of the Internal Revenue Code.

ABOUT THE CENTER FOR CONSTITUTIONAL STUDIES

Cato's Center for Constitutional Studies and its scholars take their inspiration from the struggle of America's founding generation to secure liberty through limited government and the rule of law. Under the direction of Roger Pilon, the center was established in 1989 to help revive the idea that the Constitution authorizes a government of delegated, enumerated, and thus limited powers, the exercise of which must be further restrained by our rights, both enumerated and unenumerated. Through books, monographs, conferences, forums, op-eds, speeches, congressional testimony, and TV and radio appearances, the center's scholars address a wide range of constitutional and legal issues—from judicial review to federalism, economic liberty, property rights, civil rights, criminal law and procedure, asset forfeiture, tort law, and term limits, to name just a few. The center is especially concerned to encourage the judiciary to be "the bulwark of our liberties," as James Madison put it, neither making nor ignoring the law but interpreting and applying it through the natural rights tradition we inherited from the founding generation.

CATO INSTITUTE
1000 Massachusetts Ave., N.W.
Washington, D.C. 20001